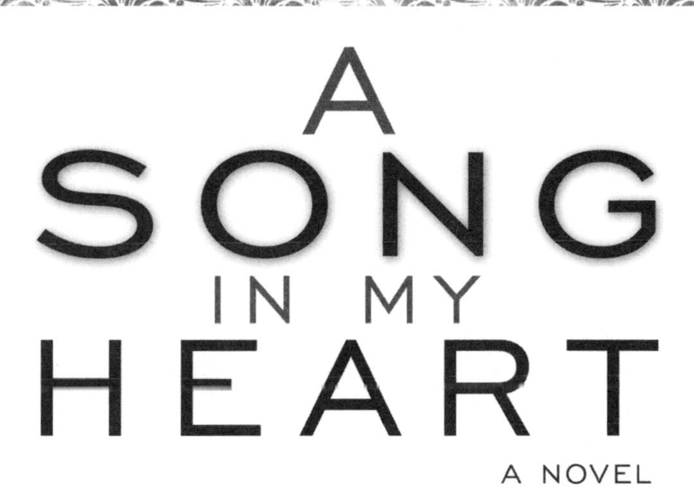

ROMA CALATAYUD-STOCKS

Cover painting by Beatriz Peréz Rubio

ISBN 10: 1-59298-395-2
ISBN 13: 978-1-59298-395-7

Library of Congress Catalog Number: 2011926938

Printed in the United States of America

First Hardcover Edition: 2011

15 14 13 12 11 5 4 3 2 1

Cover and interior design by James Monroe Design, LLC.

Beaver's Pond Press, Inc.
7104 Ohms Lane, Suite 101
Edina, MN 55439–2129
(952) 829-8818

www.BeaversPondPress.com

To order, visit www.BeaversPondBooks.com
or call (800) 901-3480. Reseller discounts available.

Tom, for his ever present love and support.
Beatriz, for her guidance, encouragement, and wisdom.
Anissa and Chris, for impossible dreams that come true.

ACKNOWLEDGMENTS

One often hears the expression “nothing exists in isolation,” and so this is true of writing a book. While the process of writing may be one of the most gratifying solitary experiences, there were many individuals and organizations who provided me with the knowledge, support, and resources that were influential in the completion of this historical novel and musical score.

My gratitude is extended to my parents, Octavio Calatayud Merino and Beatriz Peréz Rubio, who instilled a love for the arts in me at an early age. I am also grateful for my mother, who was the first to read the manuscript; as a writer herself, she gave me guidance which included her vast classical music collection, and one of her paintings is showcased on the cover of the book. Thank you to my great grandparents, Calixto and Delia Merino, who left a legacy of family unity, and after three generations, inspired me to include them in the story. My heartfelt appreciation goes to my husband, Tom, who gave me notable feedback after reading the first draft of the manuscript. I am grateful to Bill and Anne Stocks who shared family stories of German immigrants, and to all for their love and support.

In the development of a musical career, I am very thankful to Chan Poling who has arranged and performed my musical compositions since 1998; I am grateful for his eclectic musical knowledge and enthusiastic performances. Thank you to Chris Osgood for being a wonderful mentor early in my career, and for ongoing encouragement. My appreciation goes out to all the musicians who participated in various stages of the musical production of the *A Song in My Heart* audio, and to all the studio engineers, in particular Matt Zimmerman. Special recognition is due to Ana Luisa Fajer Flores, Consul General of México in St. Paul, and Uri Camarena, who have been supportive, and who are inspirational leaders in the Minneapolis/St. Paul communities.

My deepest appreciation to the following institutions, which have been vital in providing knowledge and invaluable experiences: my alma mater, the University of Minnesota; MacPhail Center for Music; the University of St. Thomas; the Minnesota Orchestra Volunteer Association; Casa de Esperanza; the Minneapolis Institute of Arts and the Walker Art Center Docent Programs; and the Minnesota Historical Society.

Thank you very much to Beaver's Pond Press: Milton Adams, founder; Jordan Wiklund, acquisitions editor; Amy Quale, managing editor; Jenna Zark, editor; and James Monroe, designer.

Finally, I am equally grateful to the rest of my family, friends, and readers who have supported the launching of this book, and most of all to God, who makes everything possible.

AUTHOR'S NOTE

The musical score corresponds to several chapters in the book. Each song or instrumental composition highlights Alejandra's emotional and creative expressions and pivotal moments in her life. The tracks of the audio disc *A Song in My Heart* will be cited throughout the book in order of appearance should the reader wish to play the music.

PART ONE

1 Ode to Minnesota

Minneapolis, 1902

Lidia Stanford, who was in her eighth month of pregnancy, was slowly buttoning her dress in the soft candlelight of her dressing room when she felt slight contractions. She placed her hands on her abdomen and whispered to her unborn child, "It's not time yet." For a moment, she considered canceling her plans for the evening, but knowing her baby wasn't due for another two weeks or more, and with her usual adventurous spirit and desire to accompany her husband to a long-awaited Christmas concert, she proceeded with her plans.

Standing impressively atop St. Anthony Falls, Minnesota's natural waterfall on the Mississippi River, was the Exhibition Building, the birthplace of local musical festivals and concerts. On December 16, Edward and Lidia attended the University's choral Christmas concert, under the direction of German-born Anna Eugénie Schoen-René. With a wave of her baton, Schoen-René led the chorus in a performance of "America," followed by popular Christmas carols. As the program neared its ending, and the choir's harmonious voices sang "Ode to Minnesota," Lidia's labor pains intensified. She held her husband's hand tightly and said, "I believe our first child is ready to be born."

Moments later, Edward rushed his wife to the Minneapolis General hospital amidst a gentle snowfall. He waited anxiously in the hospital's waiting room through the night and into the early morning hours, until he heard a calming voice.

"Congratulations, Mr. Stanford. At 7:18 a.m., two weeks early, your daughter Alejandra Stanford was born. And both your wife and child are in perfect health," the doctor said.

Edward sighed in relief. "Thank you, doctor, it's a most glorious day!" he said.

Paris, 1900

Two years before, Edward Stanford, an architect, met Lidia Merino, an eighteen-year-old portraiture painter, at the World's Fair in Paris, France. Edward, a recent graduate, wanted to see some of the newest structures built for the exposition, including the Orsay railway station, the Grand Palais, and La Ruche. Lidia was set to study painting and art history in the fall at the University of Mexico, the first to be founded in North America in 1551. For her, the opportunity to take the grand tour throughout Europe was beyond any expectations, particularly as she would see in person some of the most renowned art masterpieces.

While her primary interest was Renaissance and baroque art, she had recently become an admirer of the modern style of French Impressionism. On July 20, Lidia and her family visited the Musse de Luxembourg. As she walked through the crowded galleries, she stopped in front of Toulouse-Lautrec's painting of *Marcelle Lender Dancing the Bolero in "Chilperic."* Lidia, a petite brunette with fine facial features and large brown eyes, pulled out her sketchbook from a small briefcase, and her umbrella fell on the floor. Before she could recover it, a twenty-two-year-old man with reddish brown wavy hair, a thin nose, and broad smile picked it up.

"Pardon me, mademoiselle, I believe this is yours," he said as he took off his top hat. She took the umbrella from his hand and graciously said, "Thank you," as she turned toward the painting to continue her sketching.

"Pardon me again, are you a painter or an art aficionado?"

Lidia looked at him, somewhat perplexed by his bluntness, and answered, "Primarily an art aficionado."

"A pleasure to meet you. I'm Edward Stanford from America."

She briefly smiled and replied, "Me too, just south of your border. I'm Lidia Merino Flores."

Edward liked her clever yet graceful response. "Where in Mexico?" he asked.

"Mexico City," she replied.

After a long-distance courtship of eighteen months, Edward and Lidia were married on December 20, 1901, in Cuernavaca, Morelos, Mexico.

MINNEAPOLIS, 1903

The Stanford-Merino family lived in the affluent neighborhood of Lowry Hill within the Lake of the Isles community. The Colonial Revival two-story home, with tall white columns and Corinthian capitals, stood across the west side of Lake of the Isles. Edward, a traditional at heart, designed the home using classical lines and elements. He deeply admired architect Emmanuel Louis Masqueray, who was educated in the Beaux-Arts style of architecture in Paris. Masqueray immigrated to the United States and opened his own educational institution in the late 1800s, Atelier Masqueray in New York, of which Edward was a graduate. He was also interested in the new progressive style coming out of Chicago, later termed Prairie Style, characterized by the modern designs of Frank Lloyd Wright. Later, Edward studied the concepts of comfort outlined by up-and-coming architect William Gray Purcell.

In his own work, Edward sought to combine classical architectural features with open spaces and "built-in" comfort, as he would frequently say. Not an easy task, but one he learned to develop and master over the years, and which he incorporated into his own house. Lidia, who had an eye for interior design, settled on decorating their house in American Art Deco style, with Mexican and Spanish influences. However, the primary focus of the home's décor was her oil on canvas portraiture paintings. As a student of the *Academia de San Carlos* School of Painting in Mexico City before her marriage, Lidia had been influenced by the Spanish painter Pelegrí Clave, and the Mexican painter Juan Cordero. Both painters had left a legacy of using historical themes for their paintings.

It had been several months since Edward and Lidia had their first child, and by spring Lidia was eager to take their four-month-old daughter for walks around the lakes and parks. At times the winter months felt long, and almost intolerable. Lidia missed her family, her homeland, and the warm weather, and often expressed her feelings to her husband. So when spring came, it was literally new life to her. She made plans to visit the newly built park in the city of Minneapolis, Minnehaha Park, and see Minnehaha Falls, which meant waterfall in the Dakota language. It was the abundance of lakes, the river, and the St. Anthony and Minnehaha waterfalls that she loved most about Minnesota's natural resources. But her plans were interrupted in late March when Edward stepped on an icy patch on the second floor of a construction site and landed on his right leg. Fractured in several parts, his leg required surgery, and with a cast up to his knee, he was unable to walk normally for quite some time.

For the next several months Lidia spent most of her days and nights attending to both Edward and Alejandra's needs. In between brief moments of solitude in the early afternoons, while her daughter slept in the nursery and she sat on the white rocking chair, Lidia managed to read the twenty-two cantos that make up the *Song of Hiawatha* by American poet Henry Wadsworth Longfellow, an eloquent tribute to the original peoples and land of Minnesota, the Ojibwayes and the Dakotas, and the great lakes of the Northland. Lidia, who was an avid historian by family tradition, was interested in learning everything about the young state of Minnesota, admitted into the Union in 1858. Enamored with the poetry and epic legend of Hiawatha as described by Longfellow, she painted a portrait of Hiawatha inspired by a vignette of canto nineteen, "The Ghosts."

On Edward's birthday in late August, she surprised him with the oil on canvas portraiture painting, which he later hung above his vintage wooden architect's drafting table in his library. Edward discovered early in their relationship that his new wife had a fascination for painting historical characters and legends, but he never imagined her paintings would fill every wall throughout their house. Perhaps, he thought, their faces might fill the void of being so far away from her family.

The summer months had vanished, Lidia thought as she waited for her husband in the covered porch. With the baby sleeping on a small bassinet next to her and an easel in front of her, she began to sketch the autumn landscape. While scenery was not her forté, she was determined to paint a landscape painting of each of the four seasons as a reminder of the land's beauty. The sunny afternoon brightly illuminated the earthy tones in the changing leaves, as if freshly gold, brown, and green paints had just been splattered on them. As she finished sketching the outline of an oak tree, Lidia saw her husband approach her after he'd returned from seeing the doctor. Despite his difficulty walking with crutches, she smiled when she noticed the cast on his leg was gone. With his usual cheerful good nature, he opened the porch door, placed his crutches on a beige wicker chair, and sat beside her.

"Lidia, how long have you been out here?" he asked.

"Maybe forty minutes."

"You're patient," he said, smiling, but in a whispery voice as he did not want to wake up his baby daughter.

"I want to see you well again," she said.

"It might still take several months before my walking is close to normal," he said as he took out an envelope from his coat pocket.

"Here, my dear, this is only a small gesture of my appreciation for all your dedication in nursing me back to health," he said.

Lidia looked at her husband curiously and opened the envelope. It contained two tickets for the upcoming debut concert of the newly formed Minneapolis Symphony Orchestra.

Her eyes brightened. "Wonderful," she said as she hugged him.

"Indeed," he said. "You'll now have the opportunity to hear your favorite music performed live."

"What a lovely gift," she said.

In the next two months, Edward's walking improved considerably, to the point where crutches were no longer needed. On November fifth, with a smile and a limp, Edward walked down the exterior house steps to the car port and opened the motor car's door for his wife. "Please let me, my dear," he said. She smiled and wrapped her wool scarf around her neck as she stepped into the vehicle.

On their first formal outing in almost a year, and despite the bitter cold, Edward and Lidia drove to the Exposition Building to see and hear this most anticipated premiere of the Minneapolis Symphony Orchestra. With more than two thousand people attending the event, Edward and Lidia never thought they could enjoy, so profoundly, the simple act of walking together arm-in-arm into the concert venue.

When they sat on the wooden chairs, Lidia noticed the immense clusters of white, pink, and red chrysanthemums in front of the stage, and the potted trees located behind the several dozen seated musicians.

The orchestra, under the direction of German-born Emil Oberhoffer, performed a variety of symphonic pieces from Schubert's Symphony in B Minor, to Liszt's symphonic poem "Les Preludes," to other classical pieces by Wagner and Schumann. But to Lidia the most impressive performances of the night were the arias "Fruhlingsstimmen" and one from *La Traviata,* sung by international soprano Madam Sembrich. When they left the concert venue, she said, "I hope we come often."

"We will!" Edward replied. "But first we must make plans for Ale's first birthday," she said with renewed spirits.

On December 17, Edward was in a particularly optimistic mood. Not only was this his daughter's birthday, but as someone deeply interested in the latest technological advances, inventions, and discoveries—which seemed to be happening all the time in the new century—Edward was fascinated by the Wright brothers' successful first human flight on this very day. He pondered the incredible future possibilities this advancement would bring to the world. He shared the groundbreaking news with his wife who was sitting in a rocking chair and nursing their daughter in their bedroom.

Edward, who was ambitious and dynamic, and had high expectations for his daughter, said, "I hope we can impart upon Alejandra's heart and mind that anything is possible. There are no limits to what mankind can accomplish!"

"I'm certain we will," Lidia said as she softly caressed her daughter's face, hoping mostly that she would grow up to be a healthy and happy child more than anything else.

Later in the early evening, the extended Stanford family gathered in the dining room while Alejandra sat in a high chair. As they all surrounded her, Lidia placed a candlelit cake with white frosting on the dining table. The little girl's hazel eyes sparkled as she saw the bright flame on the candle before her and a chorus of voices said, "Happy birthday, Ale."

From that day forward, Lidia began a new tradition. Every Sunday morning she played classical music, beginning with Enrico Caruso's recordings of the music of Giuseppe Verdi, on her daughter's first birthday gift, a Victor-Victrola phonograph.

Ecossaise

Minneapolis, 1910

Alejandra woke up in the middle of a winter night, crying. Whether it was a dream or a memory, she wasn't sure, but it was haunting all the same. Lidia came to her bed and lay next to her. "*Hijita* (little daughter), what's the matter?" she asked.

"Mami, where's Anne?"

"Why do you ask?" Lidia said.

"I see her when I close my eyes," she replied.

It was a recurring dream of herself with another girl named Anne, as they both ice skated on a cold afternoon. Alejandra fell on the frozen lake and started sobbing, and Anne wiped her tears away with her mitten and said, "Ale, Ale, don't cry, I fell, too." Two little boys came and helped them both get up, and one said, "Oh, you better learn to skate or stay home next time."

"I'll learn, I'll learn!" Alejandra replied, feeling upset by his bullish words.

A few weeks after that memory, the image of Anne became less frightening when her mother showed her a new portrait on the easel, located in the art studio, next to the kitchen. The painting depicted Anne, a six-year-old girl, dressed in a pink dress and sitting on a grassy field surrounded by purple and yellow flowers as she threw them up in the air. Her face seemed happy, thought Alejandra as she excitedly said to her mother, "That's Anne."

"Yes, sweetie. Where would you like to hang her portrait?" her mother asked.

She paused for a few moments as she looked around the canvas-filled room.

"In the parlor," Alejandra said.

"Good choice!" Lidia said as she picked up the painting. But before they left the studio, she asked, "Mami, where is Anne?"

"She's not here with us anymore," Lidia said softly. "Anne passed away two years ago."

Alejandra's face saddened, yet the beautiful and impressionistic image of her cousin Anne comforted her until she was no longer frightened by her memory or dreams of her.

She loved the paintings in her house, mostly of artists and composers. Those portraits were her story books, for her mother had painstakingly written the stories of each painting on a leather-bound notebook. There was always a tale behind the faces, a true or an imagined one, she thought; this had fascinated her for as long as she could remember. She developed a skill for observing even the smallest details on paintings. And sometimes, without her mother knowing, she peeked at the portraits in her studio before they were finished.

Late one evening in February, as on most nights, she read from her notebook as she lay in her bed waiting for her mother to read to her. The bedroom, decorated in pastel tones of yellow and blue, had a six-by-eight-foot mural painting across from her bed depicting a maple tree with golden leaves. Her window seat, upholstered in floral patterns, was filled with books, and one solitary doll in the corner stood out in the otherwise toyless room. As the minutes passed by, Alejandra became impatient and began to read silently from the notebook.

> Sor Juana Inés de la Cruz was a poet and writer who was born in 1651 in Mexico City. She learned to read and write at the tender age of three and entered Barefoot Carmelitas convent at the age of fifteen. It was written that Sor Juana preferred the life of a convent, so she could continue with her intellectual studies.

Before she could finish reading the story, Alejandra heard sobbing coming from her parents' bedroom. Then her father knocked on her door.

"Ale, may I come in?" he asked.

"Yes," she replied.

"Your mother isn't feeling well tonight. Perhaps we can read together."

"What's wrong with her?" she asked.

"It's complicated, but she'll be fine in the morning," he said.

Alejandra felt unsettled. "I was already reading about Sor Juana," she said, then continued to read out loud from the notebook.

> Her room in the convent became the place for poets and artists to visit. She assembled a vast library, made scientific experiments, wrote musical compositions, and wrote an extensive work of literature from poetry, to theater, to philosophy.

"What do you think of her?" Edward asked.

"Well, she was beautiful. Sometimes I stare at her face and hands," she said as she turned to see the painting hanging above her floral-painted secretary's desk.

"I mean her story," Edward said.

"I'd like to be like her," she said.

"Good heavens! You want to be a nun?" Edward said humorously.

"No, I don't know," she responded.

"Ale, you will write your own story," he said.

"Father, I like to write stories."

Edward was well acquainted with his daughter's runaway imagination related to the historical portraits in their house, but at the moment he was preoccupied with his own thoughts regarding his wife. "Perhaps it's time to go to sleep, for I need to attend to your mother."

"Yes Papá," she said as he left her bedroom.

She could not fall asleep, for she heard her mother sobbing outside the room, even if faintly. She had never heard or seen her parents argue or be angry with each other, yet she often heard her mother cry, though didn't know the reason behind it.

The next morning, when the young girl walked down the steps to the breakfast room, she found her mother sitting by the table, drinking tea from a blue and white porcelain cup. Her eyes were red and puffy, but she smiled and said, "Good morning, Ale."

"Good morning, Mami. Are you better?" she asked.

"Oh, yes," Lidia replied. "I had Milly prepare your favorite breakfast,

French toast. It's an important day for you as you are reading in class."

"I hope the other children won't laugh when I read the story," she said.

"Did you decide which one to read?" her mother asked.

"Yes, the one about your favorite composer," she said.

"Wonderful choice," Lidia said as she patted her daughter's hand.

"You best hurry, your father is waiting for you. And after school we're going to a new soda fountain shop."

Alejandra smiled broadly and kissed her mother goodbye.

Andrew Sweet Tooth's Ice Cream and Candy Emporium, located on Sixth Street and Hennepin Avenue in Minneapolis, was an ice cream shop unlike any other, Alejandra thought as she walked into the spacious store. Her eyes widened with excitement when she heard beautiful music, Ecossaise in E Flat Major on the player piano rolls, and saw the marble counter filled with jars of colorful candy, bowls filled with fresh fruit, and trays with homemade fudge. But it was the selection of malts, shakes, frappés, parfaits, freezes, and fizzy sodas that brought in a huge crowd. With not a chair to spare, the Stanfords stood in line for nearly fifteen minutes until a table finally became available. With the excitement of a second grader, she ordered a fancy maraschino pineapple sundae and chocolate bon-bons.

As they waited for their order, her cousin Steven, his parents, and a friend walked inside the emporium. After the adults exchanged pleasantries, the two boys sat with her at the table. But Alejandra's happy mood soon faded when her cousin's friend laughed to see her upper lip smudged with chocolate, giving the appearance of a moustache. Embarrassed by his playful laughter, which felt more like mockery, she wiped her mouth with a napkin, but said nothing. Steven, her cousin, turned to her and said, "Oh, Ale, don't pay attention to him—he's a clown."

For the rest of the time at the ice cream shop, she remained silent until her father bought her a bag of bon-bons to take home. When she and her family finally left the shop, Alejandra waved goodbye to her cousin, hoping she would never see his nasty friend again.

Hennepin Avenue was lined with the latest automobile fad—the boogies—and the sidewalks were packed with people and street vendors. What she noticed as they drove by were all the young boys, almost her own age, who sold newspapers, yelled out the latest news, and advertised a variety of products from cure bottles and home-related gadgets to hats.

"Almost every week a new shop opens up," Edward remarked.

As they continued their drive down Hennepin Avenue, they passed a brick mansion when Lidia turned to her daughter and asked, "Ale, how would you like to see an art gallery in that house?"

"Today?"

"No, but soon," her mother said.

"It's a museum?"

"Not exactly, something similar."

"When can we go?" she asked.

"Soon, I promise," Edward added.

A few months later, in the summer, Alejandra's first venture to an art gallery finally happened when she and her parents visited the private residence of Mr. Thomas B. Walker. They entered the impressive mansion at 803 Hennepin Avenue in Minneapolis, and walked through several rooms.

"Mr. Walker is unique in sharing his art collection, for nowhere in the Midwest is there anything like this open to the public," Edward commented. "And free of charge."

The stately residence housed several galleries, fourteen rooms in all. The collection consisted of fine art, Indian portraits, Chinese jades, sculptures, and decorative arts. Mr. Walker's original catalogue, published in 1907, described 191 paintings, which now filled the walls and were assembled in the Paris salon style.

"There have been several art critics coming from as far as New York to review this collection. I can recall such a review published a few years ago in the newspapers," Edward said.

"What did he write?" Lidia asked.

"Something about how this collection spans over five hundred years."

While they were in one of the galleries, Alejandra pulled out her art notebook and penciled in the names of her favorite paintings, mostly those with animals in them, as well as those chosen by her parents. Lidia found the portraits of Thomas Walker, Lucrezia Borgia, Napoleon Bonaparte, and a Van Dyck painting titled *Portrait of a Jewish Rabbi* the most interesting, while Edward preferred the American and European landscapes of Minnesota, Holland, Italy, and one from the near east by Schreyer titled *Evening in Arabia*. But Edward and his daughter's favorite piece of art was the five-hundred-pound "Jade Mountain." The enormous sculpture placed on a table depicted intricate carvings of a manicured landscape and calligraphy.

"Ale, this is the only one of its kind outside China," Edward said.

"Mr. Walker must have an exceptional eye to select all these works, a true connoisseurship. My father would certainly appreciate it," Lidia added.

She thought about how much she missed her family, for she had not seen them in a few years. She looked at her husband and then said, "I received a letter from my sister."

"And?" Edward asked.

"She wants me to be her son's godmother, and would like us to be there in September," Lidia added.

Edward considered her request, and said, rather seriously, "We can discuss it some other time!"

They entered an arched doorway into the last gallery, and the room was filled with several glass cases that included dozens of small framed portraits.

"Who are all these people?" Alejandra asked.

"Not sure," Lidia replied, but the room left a ghostly impression on her young daughter.

"I guess we're not the only ones to have paintings of historical figures hanging on our walls," Edward said playfully as he turned to his wife, in an attempt to diffuse the momentary tension between them. She smiled, and soon after they left the mansion holding hands.

Later that evening, during dinner, Lidia brought up the trip to Mexico once again. There was a long silence between them until she added with firmness in her voice, "It has been too long since I've seen my family."

"I want to go, too," her daughter said excitedly.

Edward acknowledged to himself that his wife was right, and that he had postponed the trip too often.

"I suppose it's time for us to go," he said, turning to her in a pleasing manner.

"When, Papi, when?" Alejandra asked.

"At the end of August," Lidia said.

"And school?" Edward asked.

"We can hire private tutors for the time we're there."

"It seems you already had everything planned," Edward said.

ALEJANDRA

It was a warm afternoon in the small town of San Angelín, outside of Mexico City. With its cobblestone and tree-lined streets, the ancient neighborhood was surrounded by haciendas and colonial-style stucco houses. Two horse-drawn carriages were stationed in front of the Merino residence, and a motor-powered vehicle was parked inside the gated entrance. Calixto and Delia, or as they were affectionately called, *abuelitos* (grandparents), were waiting in their home's parlor when the Stanford family arrived.

For Alejandra, it was like the first time she had met her grandparents, for she was an infant when they last visited Minnesota. They were as her mother had described them. She saw her abuelito Calixto dressed in a navy blue suit and a gray tie, and her first impression of him was very pleasant when he embraced her. She curiously touched his scratchy beard and noticed his gentle smile. Her grandmother Delia was wearing a white dress with a lace-collar neckline. Her auburn hair parted on the side highlighted her delicate facial features and blue eyes. She kissed her and said, "Preciosa Alejandrita, hasta que te veo de nuevo." (Precious little Ale, until I see you again.)

The next day it was Sunday, and the family attended mass at the cathedral in the heart of Mexico City. Located in the *zócalo,* the enormous paved square plaza and once the ceremonial center for the Aztec Empire, was now the *Catedral Metropolitana.* The Spaniard Hernán Cortés placed the first stone of the cathedral's foundation in 1524. The stones, which had once been part of the Templo Mayor of the Great Tenochtitlán, the city of the Aztecs, were now the foundation of the church. Edward was particularly intrigued with its history, which was also said to be the history of Mexico. As the families stood outside the historical church, Edward turned to his young daughter.

"The cathedral was built over three centuries, and its architectural styles include elements of Renaissance, baroque, and Neoclassical architecture." She was used to listening to big words and architectural terms, even though she didn't always understand them. But that morning, she wasn't sure what impressed her most—the intricately decorated interior of the cathedral, the strong smell of incense, the sound of the organ music, or the baptism of her cousin Juvencio Sol Valles, when he started giggling after his forehead was briefly immersed in the large water basin. His laughter lingered in her ear for the rest of the mass. At that moment, Alejandra could have never imagined what profound sorrow he would leave upon her heart and her family.

On September 15, 1910, the Merino and Stanford families participated in the centennial of the Mexican independence celebration, El Grito de la Independencia (Cry of Independence). At 11:00 p.m., Mexican president Porfirio Díaz stood on the illuminated balcony of the National Palace in the zócalo, ringing the same bell Miguel Hidalgo y Costilla did one hundred years before while shouting, "Long live the heroes of the nation! Long live the republic!" Thousands of voices cheered.

To commemorate the centennial celebration, the *Angel of Independence* monument was unveiled the next day. It was this sculpture she would remember the most, a golden angel, maybe two hundred or more feet high, sitting above a stone column and pedestal as if reaching toward the heavens. Alejandra was mesmerized by the sheer size of the monument, the large crowds of people surrounding it, the parades, and the reenactment of the meeting between the Aztec emperor, Moctezuma, and the Spaniard Hernán Cortés.

The following day, the two families traveled to the city of Cuernavaca. After a half day's ride through a mountainous and lush trail fifty miles south of Mexico City, they arrived at the capital city of the state of Morelos. From the windows of their vehicle, the Merinos waved cordially to the people as they drove through the streets, for they were well known in the small town. The Merino family owned a sugar mill, and their fifteenth-century hacienda, named San Antonio del Milagro (Saint Anthony of the Miracle), was one of dozens in the state. The hacienda had been passed on from generation to generation.

As they approached the entrance of the Spanish-style building, a fifteen-foot-tall, carved wooden double door opened. The scent of burned sugar immediately welcomed them—a tempting smell that increased Alejandra's appetite. A small cocker spaniel barked in excitement as both *Abuelita* Delia and her granddaughter petted the squirming dog on his head.

The first thing the young girl noticed was a huge three-tier white fountain at the center of the courtyard. It was bathed in a patina by the age of time and surrounded by a circular path lined with colorful flowers. Every walkway in the hacienda was landscaped with Mexican wild orchids and tabachin red-flowered trees. To the left of the courtyard there was a ten-foot-tall stone statue of Saint Anthony and a corridor lined with half a dozen stucco arches that led to the living quarters. To the right of the garden an arched entrance led to a music salon.

Alejandra ran to the room where she spotted a black grand piano. She looked above it and saw an enormous round wrought-iron chandelier hanging from a dark wood beam. *El salón de música*, with high ceilings and red tiled floors, had several portraiture paintings on the white-washed walls. Three rows of wooden armless chairs with spindle backs from the eighteenth century lined both sides of the music room facing the piano.

She quickly sat on the black piano bench and lifted the piano cover. She had never seen a grand piano, but its large size felt more like a comfortable blanket surrounding her than an imposing furniture piece. With excitement she touched the white and black keys. Her small fingers ran through the keyboard as she heard the varying sounds in awe; they were magical to her. There was something enticing about touching one key, and then another, and another, each with a different tonal quality; two and three keys touched together would bring other sounds, a harmonious or dissonant sound. After that day, she played piano every day, improvising, until one day her Abuelito Calixto announced he would hire a pianist to teach her how to play properly.

The months of October and November quickly passed and as December neared, Alejandra found herself restless and impatient to begin piano lessons. On her birthday, the Merino family hosted their yearly

Christmas concert. When the sixty-plus guests arrived in the evening, they found el salón de música decorated with gladiola flowers and large floor-length wrought-iron candelabras in the front of the room. The dozen or so candles brightly illuminated the grand piano. When the concert attendees were seated, Abuelita Delia, dressed in a fashionable mauve-colored tunic gown, walked into the room and sat in front of the piano. Accompanied by a violinist, Manuel Ramos, and a cellist, Javier Reyes, she performed the music of one of Mexico's most beloved composers, Juventino Rosas. Among the waltzes, danzas, polkas, and mazurkas that they played was his famous waltz, "Carmen," dedicated to the first lady of Mexico.

From her front seat, the young girl listened closely to the music, with a particular interest to her favorite waltz, "*Sobre las Olas*" (Over the Waves), a melody so beautiful that it could indeed summon images of flowing water. What captured her attention most, however, was her grandmother Delia. With her graceful posture, long fingers, and elegant demeanor, she played the piano with such pleasure and emotion. With a certain realization and clear awareness of the inspirational moment and her surroundings, Alejandra knew what she wanted to be—a pianist like her Abuelita Delia.

The following morning, when she joined her family for breakfast in the large dining room, she found that her grandmother had already finished eating and was busy putting out the final touches of the holiday decorations. In seven days it would be Christmas, and everyone in the family was expected to help in some way. Several dozen red flowered plants were being distributed throughout the hacienda, as each member of the Merino family placed poinsettia plants along the corridors and in the various gathering rooms.

As she gently touched the large red leaves of the plant, her grandmother said, "This unique plant, originally a shrub, was used by the Aztecs as a medicinal plant; but after the conquest, Franciscan priests used it for their Nativity processions. Later, it was named poinsettia after it was introduced in your country by the first ambassador to Mexico, Joel Roberts Poinsettia. Now please take this one to the chapel."

With her small hands, Alejandra took the potted plant and walked across the courtyard into the chapel of the hacienda. When she entered the sanctuary she was struck by its large size and ancient interior, for the chapel had been built in the early 1500s. But it was the stunning decorations that instantly captivated her. While it lacked the usual gilded ornamentations seen in churches, the chapel, with arched vaulted ceilings and stone walls, was gorgeously decorated with vases filled with purple orchids. Above a standing silver cross was a glassless window through which a beam of light captured the simplicity of the stone altar and the wooden nativity scene. In the rear part of the chapel, the balcony's wrought-iron railing was draped in wreaths of flowers and green foliage. She took the poinsettia plant and placed it in front of the Nativity figures.

After that day, she visited the chapel daily, following the movements of the birds and several doves that flew in and out of the large arched openings as if waiting to join a choir. From the chapel, she could see another ancient stone fountain, palm trees, and a large courtyard that led to the stables. Every night until December 24 there was a *posada,* and she, her mother, and other neighbors gathered at the hacienda and walked in a procession through the pathways, holding lit candles and singing *villancicos* (Mexican Christmas carols) until they reached the chapel and sang a prayer.

On Christmas Eve day, the Stanford and Merino families gathered for *la comida de Navidad* in the courtyard alongside the chapel. With several tables next to each other, the Merino and Stanford families sat at one, while the hacienda's workers and their families sat at the others, almost ninety people in all.

While it was an unusual tradition to have supper with workers, it was one Calixto and Delia had started at the beginning of their marriage. Before the meal, the Merinos expressed their appreciation for the workers and for a prosperous year, and *Doña* Delia, a devout Roman Catholic, said grace. When everyone finished their supper, Don Calixto threw silver coins up in the air for all the workers' children, a tradition called *aguinaldo.* Lidia turned to her daughter and whispered in her ear, "And tomorrow you'll find your gift by the Nativity scene."

With the excitement of a young child, Alejandra ran to the chapel to find her present early on Christmas day. Next to the red flowered plant was a small box wrapped in white paper and a green ribbon. She read her name and quickly opened it. To her surprise, she found an antique iron key. She paused for a few seconds, not sure what to make of the gift. Then she ran back through the courtyard and into her parents' bedroom, where her mother was waiting eagerly, sitting at the end of a wooden canopy bed.

"Mami, what's the key for?" she asked.

"Your Christmas gift," her mother said, smiling.

"Yes, but it's a key," she said.

"Come with me," Lidia said as she took her daughter by the hand and walked through a natural-light-filled corridor to her father's library. When they opened the tall eight-panel mesquite door, her mother pointed to a wooden chest meticulously carved in high relief with a black wrought-iron keyhole. The chest was placed in the left-hand corner of the room underneath a portrait of a young man.

She noticed the painting and asked, "Who is he?"

"Diego Rivera, a Mexican painter. That is his self-portrait."

The young girl kneeled before the long chest and placed the key in the keyhole, but was unable to lift the very heavy top. Her mother kneeled beside her, and together they opened it to uncover scattered wrapped *dulces*, handmade candies and green and red ceramic decorations in the shape of musical notes. Underneath them was a large stack of printed sheet music and scores. She looked at her mother somewhat baffled, and raised her eyebrows.

"Music for you to learn on the piano," Lidia said.

The first page read, "Alejandra," Waltz by Enrique Mora.

"Your father proposed to me while this waltz was playing," Lidia said cheerfully. "And we decided to name you after this beautiful melody. I love waltzes. They've been very popular with many composers in Mexico, springing up everywhere."

As Alejandra sifted through the sheet music, she recognized some of the composers names. But when she saw the title "Moonlight Sonata" and the name Ludwig Van Beethoven, she suddenly remembered her mother's special devotion to, perhaps even obsession with, the composer. She had read a brief biography about him in her notebook, and she recalled that he was considered one of the best composers of his time, if not the best of all time.

"Beethoven!" she exclaimed.

Lidia laughed playfully and said, "With exceeding practice in the years to come you shall be able to play and perhaps even master his music. I'm sure." She gently caressed her daughter's wavy reddish brown hair.

Lidia's profound admiration for the composer had led her to paint two portraits of him, one for the music room of the hacienda, and another painting that hung on the bedroom wall in their Minneapolis home. With a brimming smile Alejandra asked, "When will I begin piano lessons?"

"In the new year," Lidia said as she softly closed the wooden chest.

Two weeks later on January 8, 1911, it was a usual sunny day in Cuernavaca, also known as the city of eternal spring, when Luis Orozco Vegas arrived at eleven o'clock on Wednesday morning at the hacienda to give piano lessons to Alejandra. A handsome eighteen-year-old with large, expressive dark brown eyes and olive-toned skin, Luis was an excellent pianist and the son of Don Calixto's partner. He had taken time off from his studies at the University of Mexico to help his ailing father with business affairs at the sugar mill.

Initially, Luis did not have the greatest disposition for the task before him, as he did not wish to spend two hours a week with an eight-year-old. He had never taught piano before, and was here as a favor to his godfather Calixto. But knowing it was for only a few months, he agreed to teach Alejandra some fundamentals of music and piano basics. After he met her that morning, he found her delightful, playful, and very eager to learn.

When the lessons first began, her natural curiosity and constant questioning made Luis impatient. But later, his impatience turned to appreciation when she showed a great inclination for music. He began by teaching her scales and arpeggios, how to read notes, and basic music theory. After several lessons, Luis discovered that letting her choose the music she wanted to learn from various selections he played facilitated the more tedious aspects of the piano lessons.

There in the music room, Alejandra felt the happiest amidst the music, the constant stimulation and movement of her fingers as she learned new melodies, and the staring eyes of whimsical faces from the portraiture paintings. Even her walks along the riverbank had decreased, for she preferred to practice at the piano for hours each day.

Later in March, Luis met Don Calixto, one afternoon, in his library to discuss business matters; and he also inquired about Alejandra's musical abilities.

"Bit by bit, part lesson, part fun, and much, much practice, your granddaughter is making an excellent start in her piano studies."

"She seems to love it, I often walk by the salon and listen to her. She is progressing quite well and if she keeps this up, perhaps, some day, she could be a concert pianist," Calixto said proudly.

"Indeed," Luis added.

As spring approached, Edward had decided it was time to return to Minnesota. He was anxious to begin another active season of home building in the rapidly expanding cities of Minneapolis and St. Paul. However, Lidia was reluctant to leave her mother, who had recently become ill from a heart condition. Displeased with Lidia's request, Edward finally accepted his wife's decision to stay with their daughter in Cuernavaca until December. When he said goodbye, Alejandra wanted to go with him. He kissed her gently on the forehead. With tears in her eyes she said, "Papi, don't go. Stay with us."

"I can't, my darling, but I'll return as soon as I can," he said convincingly.

"Promise," his daughter said. She feared she might never see her father again, and continued to whimper softly.

"Yes, I promise," Edward said as he turned to Lidia and lovingly embraced her.

"I shall miss you both terribly! I'm not happy to leave without you, but I understand your predicament. I Love you," Edward said.

"We love you, too," Lidia replied sadly as she watched her husband step into the motor car on the stone driveway. He waved to his family, but could have never predicted what soon would happen.

Alejandra missed her life in Minneapolis, although her piano lessons kept her extremely occupied. She soon discovered that life in Cuernavaca offered new experiences and traditions that she learned to love. On Sunday mornings, the Merino family attended mass at the sixteenth century cathedral in Cuernavaca, followed by a short walk to the main town. And on one of those Sundays, the family was sitting on two benches in the central plaza, listening to Don Calixto as he talked about the grand palace in the foreground.

"Palacio Cortés was the summer place of Hernán Cortés back in the sixteenth century, and later it was the retreat home in the mid-1800s of Austrian-born Ferdinand Maximilian Von Habsburg and his wife Carlota. Maximiliano, as he was commonly known, was a member of the Imperial House of Habsburg-Lorraine. He was briefly emperor of Mexico in 1864; although three years later, Benito Juaréz, Mexico's most admired president, recaptured the presidency," Don Calixto said.

"I don't understand," his granddaughter said.

"The mid-1800s was a difficult period in our country when there was a lot of civil strife, recurrent foreign intervention, and wars," Don Calixto replied.

Before he could explain further, Alejandra became distracted when she noticed her grandfather's workers across the street, unloading dozens of sacks filled with sugar, flour, grains, beans, and other staples.

"Abuelito, what are they doing?" she asked.

"It's something we do every week. Jacinto and Francisco place sacks of dry goods into the storage facility in the building, and later the priests will distribute them to the local people," he said.

Calixto Merino's generous reputation as a Mexican-Spanish landowner in Cuernavaca would later save him from being killed during the Mexican Revolution.

Late in October when the Merino family sat down for dinner in the antique-filled dining room, Lidia, who had heard rumors of the brewing civil war and was worried about its potential devastating effects, faced her father.

"Padre, should we be worried?"

"Well, yes, Porfirio Díaz was president of Mexico for more than three decades, and he resigned last May. The Revolution has gained momentum and violence recently erupted in some parts of our country."

"Why?" Lidia asked.

"The concern is for the basic livelihood of the people and land ownership. And this is at the crux of the conflict," Don Calixto replied. "I've always thought something like this would eventually happen, for it is not possible that so much land is in the hands of only a few people, even if I'm one of them."

"Your father and I share that sentiment, and we only hope there won't be much bloodshed," Delia said as she looked at her daughter with concern.

"I sense a bit of remorse," Lidia said to her father.

"Perhaps it is the Mexican in me, or simply a matter of fairness. I do find it significant that the Revolution is happening one hundred years after the Mexican Independence from Spain," he said. "It's unfortunate that Benito Juárez was unable to finish what he started when he was president, due to his death."

"What do you mean?" Lidia asked.

"Many historians say that Benito Juárez was the Abraham Lincoln of Mexico. They were contemporaries, and shared many values and personal qualities. There is also a well-documented note from Lincoln to Juárez," he said.

"Yes, Benito Juárez was an extraordinary and intelligent, yet quiet, man who excelled in his studies, once even as an experimental physics professor," Lidia said.

"And as you may recall from your studies, it was law and politics that captivated him. He practically wrote the Mexican constitution. Juárez abolished slavery and decreed freedom of religion. As a Zopotec Indian from Oáxaca, he was of the people and for the people. And now you may say that the Revolution is of the people striving for identity and recognition," Don Calixto said.

"The United States also went through independence followed by civil war, with Abraham Lincoln as their hero," Lidia said.

"Many Mexican people, still today, are great admirers of Mr. Lincoln for his support of Mexico in two decisive periods in our history. If given the choice, all people share the values of equality, justice, democracy, and freedom," Don Calixto concluded.

Alejandra, who had been listening attentively, asked, "Abuelito, what did the note from Mister Lincoln say?"

"The note was written in January of 1861. If I may paraphrase his kind words, it said that President Lincoln wished, most sincerely, happiness, prosperity, and liberty to President Juárez, his government, and its people," Don Calixto replied.

While the Merino family hoped they might be untouched by the civil war, they never thought tragedy would strike so soon. Two months later in early December, their youngest daughter, Carolina, arrived with her son Sol at the hacienda in a most distressed state. Her husband, Juvencio Sol Valles, had been shot dead in a cross fire between factions of the Revolution in Mexico City. But nothing could be done, not even a proper funeral, for his body was never returned to her. The Merino family learned, not surprisingly, that Juvencio had been a secret sympathizer of Francisco Madero, a reformer, a member of a wealthy hacienda family, and one of the leaders in bringing forth the revolutionary movement.

This was indeed a complicated matter. They understood and accepted the right of the people to choose its leaders, but feared further consequences. Because the Revolution had already claimed one of their own family members, they knew it was only a matter of time before they incurred additional losses.

From then on everything changed. The Merinos, their two daughters, and their families rarely left their 4,000-acre hacienda, a typical one of the era. It contained dozens of bedrooms and living rooms, sprawling gardens and patios, carpentry and blacksmith workshops, stables, orchards, and personal staff such as the administrator, cooks, cleaning staff, a physician, and a priest, in addition to the laborers involved with farming and the production of sugar cane. Sugar production in the state of Morelos was the third largest in the world at the time. Lidia, along with the administrator, was responsible for the day-to-day management of the hacienda.

It became necessary to turn the chapel into a one-room temporary school and Carolina channeled her grief by taking charge. She developed a curriculum and school hours according to the children's ages and recruited several well-known teachers from Cuernavaca, including one of the family's closest friends, Mr. Thomas Anderson, an English professor from the state of Virginia. Five days a week, for several hours, the hacienda became Escuela San Antonio, a lively place filled with nearly ninety children. The hacienda offered an almost surreal refuge from the chaos that was spreading throughout Mexico, if only for an abbreviated period.

Don Calixto and Doña Delia, whose only son had died in his infancy, had brought up their two daughters Lidia and Carolina to be highly educated and independent, traits that came in quite handily during that precarious time. Because of the Revolution, Don Calixto prohibited all travel in or out of Mexico until the violence had subsided. Edward was unable to return to Mexico that year, and Lidia and her daughter stayed in Cuernavaca, Morelos, indefinitely.

As an only child, Alejandra at times had longed for a brother or a sister. With her cousin Sol, who was becoming like a brother to her, and dozens of children attending the school, she felt her wish was suddenly realized. Still, at times she yearned for silence, which she easily found in her Abuelito Calixto's extensive library, which offered her much more than solitude, as it was a place of learning. For in addition to her regular school hours, she also had private studies in rhetoric, geography, literature, and Mexican and American history. In the floor-to-ceiling bookcases she found first edition books, including *La Conquista de la Nueva España* by Bernal Díaz del Castillo written in 1493, *En voz Baja* by Mexican poet

Amado Nervo, and a Spanish edition of the biography of one of America's founders, Benjamin Franklin, based on original documents and printed in Madrid in 1798.

She would later realize that the most intriguing aspects of these books were the contrasting contents of the former, the truthful account of the Spanish conquest of Mexico as told by a military officer who lived through it, and the latter—the founding of the United States and its Constitution.

In February of 1912, Alejandra came into the library and found her grandfather on his wooden scroll-legged desk, writing one of his usual commentary essays on the state of current politics and social justice. They greeted each other, but he was preoccupied and turned to his task. She walked about the room looking through the bookshelves, and noticed the ancient artifacts from the nearby archeological site Xochicalco, *lugar de la casa de las flores* (place of the home of the flowers), dating back to 600 to 900 A.D.

"Abuelito, you are the second person I know who has an art collection in his house," she remarked.

Don Calixto smiled. "There are many art collectors these days, a result of the industrial revolution," he said. "Also called the Gilded Age."

"I don't understand," she said.

"Well, the enormous progress in new industries has brought about tremendous wealth not only here in Mexico, but much more in the United States. As a result many persons of great means have taken to the popular endeavor of art collecting," he said.

"Why?" she asked.

"Some collectors do so to show their wealth, invest in fine art, or for the pure love of art, or for all three. But for me, art collecting is a matter of history, primarily," he said as he folded the letter and placed it in an envelope. She stood silently in front of a bronze of the Mayan calendar that hung on the south wall of the library.

"Abuelito, I'm writing new stories in my notebook. Can you tell me more about some of the things in your collection?" she asked.

"First, let me tell you about the Mayan calendar. It's a timeline, perhaps beginning in the fifth century B.C., and it goes into the future two thousand years," he said.

"Wow!" Alejandra said, amazed.

"These objects are all testaments to people's lives, traditions, and accomplishments. They are *historia viviente* (living history), for each artifact has preserved a moment in time," he added.

He continued to express his admiration for the ancient civilizations of Mexico and the Americas, including the Olmecs, Toltecs, Mixtecs, Zapotecs, Aztecs, the Mayans, and dozens of others, and their accomplishments in monumental architecture, mathematics, the concept of zero, astronomy, and the ball games.

"When Hernán Cortés arrived in the city of the Aztecs, before modern-day Mexico, to his great astonishment, he found roads, canals, irrigation, temples, schools, markets, art, music, and books," Don Calixto said. "My mother was a descendent of the Mayan people. So, you see, we are very much the product of both the natives of this land and the *conquistadores*," Don Calixto said with mixed emotions of pride and regret. "Most of history is recorded through the arts. And it is worthy of collecting it, preserving it, and ultimately sharing it for the sake of knowledge, beauty, and understanding."

Alejandra remained silent as she thought about everything her grandfather said.

"And what do you plan to do with all the stories?" he asked her.

"Sometimes I go back and read them again and imagine other stories," she replied.

"Everything you learn will be useful at some point in the future," he said.

"What is this?" she asked as she pointed to a cylindrical drum with intricate carvings of figures.

"It's a *huehuetl*, a venerated musical instrument of the Aztecs," he said.

She sat in front of a small desk opposite her grandfather's desk and began to write in her notebook. After a few minutes, she walked toward several framed drawings.

"And these?" she asked as she pointed to a set of three plates hanging behind his desk, and a sketch of a man next to them. They were one of his most precious possessions.

"Well, let me tell you about the man in the sketch. He was the famous Spanish tenor Manuel Garcia, and the head of the Garcia Opera Company. When my mother Beatriz was a young girl, she attended the very first performance of opera in Mexico City in 1827. In fact, Don Manuel Garcia and his company are also credited with being the first to bring Italian opera to the United States in New York in 1826, which was very successful with famous operas like *The Barber of Seville* by Rossini, and *Don Juan* by Mozart. My mother was so inspired by Garcia's extraordinary singing abilities and poise that when she returned home that night, she sketched his face from memory. Ever since, she became a huge opera fan. I might add that your mother inherited the talent of drawing from her."

"Oh! And why she likes to play opera for us every Sunday," Alejandra added as she rolled her eyes playfully.

Don Calixto smiled.

"And the other sketches?" she asked.

"These sketches are part of a series called *Los Caprichos*," he said. "Each etching with its own title—*El Amor y La Muerte (Love and Death), Que Sacrificio (What a Sacrifice)*, and *Todos Caeran (Everyone will Fall)*—are part of a series of eighty, created by the Spanish artist Francisco Goya to condemn human flaws, superstition, and the Inquisition," he said.

"Inquisi . . . what?" she questioned.

Don Calixto closed his eyes momentarily and stood up from his chair. He patted his granddaughter on her head.

"That's a very serious topic for my *nietecita* (little granddaughter)," Don Calixto said playfully. "Besides, I think I've given you enough history to last you for a while."

"One more question, Abuelito," Alejandra said.

"Sure!" he said, amused by her interest.

"And which print do you like best?" she asked.

"*El Amor y La Muerte*, because we all hope to love and wait to die," Calixto said with a little humor. Alejandra remained quiet, even with certain fear at his words. It would take her some time to understand it all, even though his words would turn out to be prophetic.

The Merino family had lived up to early 1912 somewhat protected from the consequences and chaos of the Revolution, but their life changed once more in April of the same year. General Azúnsolo, accompanied by 500 men, took over the hacienda as he prepared to give the keys of the city of Cuernavaca to General Emiliano Zapata, another leader of the Revolution and a native of the state of Morelos. He was perhaps one of the most admired revolutionaries, for he did not seek nor want any wealth for himself. His main focus was the distribution of lands among the Mexican farmers and people throughout the country, including those of Cuernavaca.

As expected, the Merinos' vast land of 4,000 acres was stripped away. But in a great gesture, in fact in an unprecedented show of good will toward Don Calixto's compassionate and generous reputation, he was allowed to rent the hacienda and four acres of land, since it was being used as a school. The sugar mill, as all the others in the region, closed, and the majority of the workers left, not entirely by choice.

Considering the turn of events, Don Calixto was grateful to have escaped the worse fate of the Revolution, and in his heart, he knew justice had prevailed for the Mexican people. By no means, however, was the Revolution over. In fact at least another three years would pass before some semblance of peace began to take root once again in Mexico.

4 Vals del Sol

Cuernavaca, Mexico, 1915

As Sol grew up, he became Alejandra's brother of the heart, and a shadow on her path, as she frequently reminded him teasingly. He followed her everywhere. As a five-year-old, he was curious, playful, and mischievous, but always affectionate. Carolina said he was her sun, everyone's sun, because he always smiled and made everyone laugh. In fact, that is why he was called by his middle name. Sol's brown hair and almond-shaped brown eyes were those of his mother, but his gentle smile was that of his grandfather, Calixto.

There was nobility in his spirit, for once he found a dead bird by one of the trees and cried intensely, asking that it be buried properly. He often shared his last candies with the other children, even if he was left with none of it. One day in May, as Alejandra saw him disappear with his favorite canine companion Prado while playing hide and seek, she looked for him until his giggles gave him away, as always. She found Sol and the dog in a little cove on a passage to the kitchen that had been a rustic pantry to store sugar and she called it his *rinconsito de dulce*, little sweet corner, because he loved to eat sweets.

Moments later, when he had tired from running all over the hacienda, the two cousins walked toward the fountain and sat underneath a palm tree. Alejandra began to tell him stories from her art notebook, but he wanted to hear the story from *Tales of the Alhambra* by Washington Irving, a gift from Edward to Don Calixto. The little boy was enchanted by the description of the Moorish-style palaces filled with colorful mosaics, and how Alejandra placed him in the story walking about the streets of the picturesque city of Granada, Spain.

"Ale, will you take me there someday?"

"Well, certainly," she replied.

"For real," he said.

"Yes," she said with some hesitation, as she felt an unexplainable shiver down her back and closed the book.

"You know it's time to go with Abuelita," she added.

"Yes, yes, but first let me get her flowers," he said as he went around the garden and put together a bouquet of fresh flowers.

Moments later when they entered the large bedroom, Abuelita Delia was sitting in her favorite chair with an afghan covering her legs. While she had improved slightly from her illness, she limited extraneous activity. Sol ran up to her and gave her the flower bouquet. "Abuelita, estas flores son para ti." (These flowers are for you.)

"Muchas gracias mi Solesito, son las mas bonitas que he visto," (Thank you very much, my little Sol, they are the most beautiful I've seen,) Abuelita Delia said as she brought them up to her nose and smelled their sweet fragrance. She took her handmade ceramic vase, painted with motifs of lilac flowers, and placed them inside, filling it with water from the water pitcher on her side table. Sol climbed on her lap and waited for her to tell him another story of his mother when she was a child, as she had often done in the last year. However, he always got distracted by her cross collection across from the chair. Looking at almost thirty Christian and Latin crosses in all sizes, made of copper, wood, silver, and ceramic, Sol pointed to his favorite.

"Why do you have so many of them?" he asked.

Abuelita Delia laughed and replied, "Because they are gifts. I began to collect them when my mother gave me the first one on my wedding day. I've been very blessed, and since then family and friends give them to me on special days."

"Can I have one?" Sol asked.

"Claro que si, mi Solesito, tu escoge la que te guste," she said. (Yes, of course my Solesito, you choose the one you like). Sol smiled, kissed his grandmother, and walked across the room as his cousin took down a wood and silver cross with a carved image of a little boy and gave it to Sol.

"Gracias, Ale," Sol said as he ran out of the room to show his mother his new cross.

Alejandra stayed behind to converse with her grandmother.

"Abuelita, I miss you playing the piano," she said.

"Yes, but I enjoy listening to you play more. Soon you'll return home and I'll have those memories," Delia said.

"Why do you think we'll be going back soon?" she asked.

"Because it's time you and your mother return home to your father. A man must not be alone for so long," Abuelita Delia said. "Besides, your grandfather says the Revolution seems to be coming to an end. I'm sure your father will return in no time now."

"Oh! I do hope so, I miss him so much," Alejandra said. "Abuelita, can I ask you something else?"

"Sure, anything," she replied.

"Did you ever want to be a concert pianist?" she asked.

The question was unexpected. "No, I never considered it, and I don't like to travel," Abuelita Delia said. "Why do you ask?"

"Just wondering, something Abuelito mentioned once," Alejandra said with a puzzled look on her face.

"Would you like to?" Abuelita Delia asked her.

"Yes, yes, I'd love to see the world and play in concert halls here and everywhere," she said.

"Well, you are going to have to work very hard," her grandmother added.

"I will! I'm going to look for mother; perhaps she has some news from father," Alejandra said as she kissed her grandmother goodnight. She walked across the courtyard to the parlor room, but her mother wasn't there, or in the library, or the kitchen, or her bedroom—nowhere, in fact. She became a little concerned, and then she thought of the chapel. She ran, and found her mother kneeling on the cement floor, praying and softly crying. Alejandra quietly joined her. "What's wrong, Mamá?" she whispered.

"I miss your father so much. It has been four years since we saw him. The days have turned into months, and now months into years," she said. Lidia and Edward had corresponded frequently, although the letters usually took months to arrive.

"When will he return?" Alejandra asked.

"I don't know. The Revolution seems to be dissipating, but there's still several factions fighting with one another."

"What factions?" Alejandra asked.

"Los Villistas, Los Zapatistas, and Los Carrancistas; however, your grandfather recently told me that Carranza had defeated the other two groups and as such, has obtained the support of the majority of the Mexican people. The United States is on the verge of recognizing the new government of Venustiano Carranza. So, I am hoping and praying it will be a matter of months, if not weeks."

A few months later, in September, Lidia received a letter from Edward:

June 23, 1915

Dearest Lidia and Alejandra,

Your absence has become intolerable. Too many years have passed without you, and I am no longer willing to wait or much consider any potential danger to myself in traveling to see you. We must be resolute in God's will. The loneliness I have felt is at times blinding and deafening, and only thinking and seeing you again will calm my spirit. I understand how difficult it will be for you, my beloved Lidia, to leave once again your loving family, the comfort and beauty of your surroundings, and your traditions.

My deepest respect for Don Calixto and Doña Delia encourages my decision to return for you. I know it will be painful for them to see you both go, but I am also convinced they will understand your place is here with me. Please do not worry for me; my sources have informed me the precarious situation in Mexico has diminished. My plans are to be with you this December. I will count the days until I will see you both again.

Much has happened here since your departure. My parents are well, and so are my sister and her family. Steven often asks for Alejandra. But the changes in the city are remarkable, as Minneapolis and St. Paul continue to expand at an ever faster rate. Thousands of new immigrants arrive, almost monthly, from Europe.

On a most pleasurable note, which you will no doubt appreciate, are the additions of cultural institutions. After extensive efforts and vision from the Minneapolis Society of Fine Arts and one of its founders, Mr. Washburn, and the generosity of distinguished members of our community, the Minneapolis Institute of Arts opened its doors to a most enthusiastic public last January 7th.

This grand building standing two hundred feet tall in the Beaux-Arts architectural style was built on land generously donated by Mr. Clinton Morrison. The celebration and dedication exercises were held at the Minneapolis Auditorium. The Minneapolis Symphony Orchestra performed "Festival Prelude" by Richard Strauss and "Hymn to Liberty" by Hugo Kaun. The inaugural exhibition provided some of the most interesting and important works of art from around the world, including an extensive cast collection of Greek and French sculptures, Flemish tapestries, Rembrandt drawings, and paintings by Degas, Delacroix, Renoir, and Homer.

Walking through the galleries of this new fine museum brought me back to remarkable memories of you in Paris and the museums we visited last in 1900. The architects also envisioned a concert hall to be housed in future additions of the museum. Imagine, one day we will see some of the finest works of art, and on another day listen to some of the finest music ever composed, all under one roof. I am certain you will find Minneapolis a most enriched city in the arts. You and Ale will indeed enjoy this splendid cultural addition in Minnesota. I've also made a few changes in the house, which I hope you'll find to your satisfaction.

Most lovingly, Edward.

On December 17, three months later, Edward Stanford arrived in Cuernavaca, Mexico. It was early in the morning when he found his wife still sleeping. As she opened her eyes, she gently caressed his face. He most lovingly embraced his wife as she whispered, "Gracias a Dios," (Thanks be to God). An hour later he walked through the poinsettia-filled corridor toward his daughter's bedroom and quietly opened the door. He sat on a chair across from her bed as he waited for her to wake up. When she did, she was incredulous and rubbed her eyes. She could not believe her father was there. His face had aged slightly and he had a moustache, but his eyes expressed a profound joy. Barefoot and in her blue ruffled nightgown, she got up from the bed and hugged him. "Papi, Papi, I've missed you so much."

At that moment, Lidia, dressed in a garnet colored dress with a face radiating happiness, joined them. With teary eyes and a blissful smile, she held her husband's hand.

The New Year began with much gusto, particularly for Edward who was overjoyed to be with his family once again. And to his delight, his daughter had made remarkable progress with her piano lessons. Playing a musical instrument was not only a virtue expected of young ladies, but also customary as a preparation for future courtship, he thought as he listened to her play the piano one afternoon in early February.

After five years of lessons, she had mastered all of the music that Luis had put before her. Furthermore, she had become very dedicated to her musical studies, sometimes practicing for up to three hours a day. As he admired his daughter's musical abilities, he observed she had developed physically and mentally into a lovely and highly inquisitive young girl, quite reserved in manners, yet graceful in her demeanor.

Edward also noticed her deep affection and admiration toward Luis which had become quite noticeable, as she always dressed in her best apparel whenever she had piano lessons. Luis, who was sitting next to Edward, also noticed her subtle flirtatious smiles, but he acknowledged to himself he had gone as far as he could with her musical training, and he decided to end the lessons. Luis was twenty-three years old, ten years her senior, and he was ready to return to Mexico City to continue with his own more advanced musical studies now that many of the academic institutions had re-opened. That afternoon, when Alejandra finished playing, she turned to Luis, looking for his approval. "What would you like me to learn next?" she asked.

"Well, Ale, I don't think there will be any more lessons," he said.

She was taken by surprise, and her face turned rather sullen. "I don't understand," she added.

Edward noticed his daughter's disappointment.

"Ale, we will be returning to Minnesota soon, you know," he said.

"Yes, indeed, and you already know everything I could possibly teach you and more," Luis replied.

After what seemed to Alejandra a brief and sudden goodbye, Luis gracefully but seriously excused himself from the music salon. Alejandra was left heartbroken and confused, but this would be but a diminutive moment of sadness compared to what lay ahead for her and the family. Edward stood up from his chair and walked toward his daughter who was standing by the piano, speechless. He softly lifted her chin, and said, "Ale, now, now, don't be sad. I'm sure you'll see him again."

"Yes, father."

The following month, on the morning of March 22, Alejandra, Carolina, and Sol ventured across town, as they had frequently done in the past year, when it had become safer to do so. Alejandra mounted her Paso Fino stallion, named El Rubio for his golden markings, while Carolina and Sol also mounted a Paso Fino brown stallion, named El Noble for his pleasing nature and enjoyment of human companionship.

What was supposed to be a routine expedition turned into a tragic event when Carolina's horse got spooked at the sound of firing shots from a distant scuffle. Her horse bolted and threw her and Sol to the ground. Sol landed on his head, and Carolina, conscious but unable to move, yelled, "Solesito, Solesito, despierta, despierta (awake)." She attempted several times to wake up her son as she stretched her arm to touch his body, but there was no movement from him. Alejandra quickly got off her horse to see Sol, who was still not responding. "Ale, Ale, go and get your grandfather, hurry!" Carolina said desperately.

In a flush of anguish, Alejandra whipped her horse, galloping as fast as she could, and headed for the hacienda. Minutes later, she found her grandfather at the stables talking to the foreman. She yelled in panic as soon as she saw him.

"Abuelito, Abuelito, come quickly, Carolina and Sol fell from their horse."

Soon after, Don Calixto, Doctor Medina, and others returned to the scene to find Carolina unconscious. The doctor kneeled by the little boy as he felt for a pulse on his neck. He looked up at Don Calixto, and solemnly shook his head. "Solesito is dead."

Four days later, the day of the funeral was an unusually cloudy day. Carolina was dressed in a black dress, and her whole body and face expressed grief. One of her arms was in a sling, but it was her eyes, red and absent, that looked into the distance as if she was not in this world. Calixto and Delia stood by their daughter in complete silence, and the sadness on their faces was not only visible but almost palpable, as though one could touch a bouquet of dead roses. Alejandra stared into the small coffin as it was placed in the barren hole when Carolina exclaimed, "My baby, my baby." Her father placed his hand on her shoulder. "My dear, we are all here with you."

There was a communal cry among the family members, as each sobbed for their loss. All of their extended family and friends came to offer their condolences, but nothing could console Carolina. In two tragic consecutive events within a span of less than five years, she had lost both her husband and her son.

"What injustice!" she cried out at the funeral as she gently placed a bunch of white gladiolas on her son's coffin. The grave diggers lowered the coffin and then began to fill the pit with soil. That strong image and profound sorrow left an indelible impression in Alejandra's heart. One she would never forget.

The next day, there was a chilling silence in the hacienda. In the evening after dusk, the skies were almost black, and Alejandra walked toward the music salon holding an oil lantern to guide her path. The heavy clouds made the night so grim and obscure, as if the moon itself had disappeared. She entered the cold and dark salon, and as the chandelier was not lit, she placed the lantern on the piano and sat in front it. Music had been entertainment to her in the past, but now, she hoped the music would appease her, temporarily silence her cries. She remembered how a week ago Sol had been sitting next to her as she played Beethoven's "Para Elisa" and he played back the first phrase.

A cold breeze swept through the room and she felt it on her shoulders. Her hands were trembling and her tears fell onto the piano keys. She wiped her eyes and started moving her fingers through the keyboard, but continued to cry, now profusely, to the point where her vision became very blurry. Once again, she wiped her tears with her cotton shawl, but the sadness she felt moved her to continue playing.

She wanted to play something soothing, as she thought of her cousin's essence and all the happiness he had brought to everyone who knew him. She had improvised short musical phrases many times before, yet this time, she slowly began to play a new melody, and then she realized she had put all her feelings into the music. She closed her eyes and whispered, "For you, Sol." She then stopped playing and covered her face with her hands as she let all her emotions out. A few moments later, she placed, once more, her fingers on the piano, and note by note, phrase by phrase, a new waltz emerged, "*Vals del Sol.*"

This was her first complete composition, a serenade inspired by her cousin. Music for her had taken on a profound emotional meaning.

A few months later in June, the Stanford family departed for the United States.

TRACK ONE

PART TWO

Dance of Nymphs & Satyrs

After being away for almost five years, a mixture of sadness, fear, and excitement overcame Alejandra as she and her family approached their old neighborhood in the city of Minneapolis in 1916. This was as different a life as anyone could imagine, she thought as Edward parked the vehicle in front of the Colonial-style house.

Moments later, Milly opened the door and happily greeted them, and then, bag in hand, Alejandra got out of the car and walked to the front of the house and stopped. Before she entered her home, she turned back and looked at her father and mother from afar, and noticed how happy they both seemed. Her father's usual optimism was evident when he carried the luggage and said with his broad smile, "Welcome home." If at that point she had felt some insecurity in returning, his attitude gave her reassurance, for this was indeed where she belonged.

When she entered the open single mahogany door with stained glass sidelights, she placed her small travel bag on the parquet floor in the parlor. The brightly colored walls, painted in washed pastel yellows and filled with several small square mirrors, was a familiar sight. She saw the staircase on her right, and a small seating area on the left with the painting of Anne on the wall. She proceeded into the arched entrance that led to a spacious rectangular area. The dining room was on the right, directly across was her father's library, and on the left there was a large drawing room. Alejandra walked into the latter, and it was like she remembered it. Those familiar portraits were welcoming her back—Mozart, Rosas, and Sor Juana, which her father must have brought down from her bedroom.

She sat on the golden-toned velvet divan looking toward the bay window, and discovered the sugar maple tree she had planted with her father when she was five years old. It had grown to almost twenty feet tall. This marvelous tree, which might seem common in the streets and woods of Minneapolis, was significant to her, for it reminded her very simply of her roots.

She glanced through the room and noticed an oval mahogany coffee table in the Chippendale style. On the table there was a leaded-glass vase filled with yellow tulips, and next to it two stacks of magazine-like pamphlets. One had Lidia's name on it, and the other had her name on it. She first looked through the pile with her mother's name, and discovered a collection of bulletins from the Minneapolis Institute of Arts. The other pile included dozens of program notes from the Minneapolis Symphony Orchestra. As she began to browse through them she was interrupted by her father who briefly came into the room. "This Sunday afternoon your grandparents and the rest of our family will be joining us for dinner." She nodded, as she was immersed in her reading.

What a treasure of information, she thought, and then grabbed a few of the program notes to bring up to her bedroom. Before she left the room, she noticed above the grayish stone mantle fireplace a wedding photograph of her parents, another of her as an infant, and other photographs of the Stanford family. Above the fireplace there was a Belgian tapestry with an illustration of the Grand Canal in Venice. This was indeed a most pleasant arrival, she acknowledged.

It was a hot summer Sunday when the Stanford extended family arrived. The terraced garden was in full bloom with irises, cardinal flowers, and Minnesota's own lady slipper flowers. The smell of jasmine flowers was in the air. As she put together a fresh-cut flower bouquet in her basket, she saw her grandmother Clara approach. She was cheerful and humming a tune that Alejandra didn't recognize. Meticulously dressed in a light green dress and a large embroidered hat with violet-colored flowers, she was holding her ever-present knitting bag.

"Ale, you left a child, and you've returned as a young lady," Clara said as she hugged and kissed her granddaughter.

"Grandma Clara, it's wonderful to see you again," she said affectionately.

"Come, child, let's go inside. It's too hot out here," Clara said.

Her grandfather George, with a cigar in his mouth, entered the house behind them. After he placed his hat on the coat rack and his smelly cigar on a nearby ashtray in the parlor, he warmly embraced Lidia and Alejandra. Then Steven came, carrying a large box containing her grandmother's famous canned vegetable goods.

"Ale, you've changed," he said.

"So have you," she replied as she opened the door for him. Aunt Margaret and her husband James followed closed behind.

"Please, come in, I'm so glad to see you all," Lidia said. Clara turned to her and jokingly said, "My dear, I thought we might never see you again."

"Things got very complicated, but we are so thankful to be back here," Lidia replied with her usual charm as she and the others went into the drawing room.

"I think that is why Edward took so long to take you back home in the first place, for he knew you might want to stay in Mexico's warmer climate," Clara said laughingly.

George, who was always interested in current national and international politics, quickly changed the subject. "What can you tell us about the Revolution?"

"Some say it's not quite over, and I'm sorry to say, we suffered many losses."

"Yes, our condolences for your nephew," George said.

"And your land?" Margaret asked.

"The land was indeed a great loss, but expected. However, the loss of my brother-in-law, and later Sol, was devastating," Lidia said in a quiet voice, as she briefly closed her eyes. "Thankfully, my parents were able to lease the hacienda, at least temporarily, with the hope that my father can buy it back someday once everything has settled. That is some measure of comfort for all of us," she added.

"No more of this solemn talk, today is a happy day," Edward said while Lidia excused herself to check on dinner. George and Edward engaged in an intense conversation about the Great War, and whether the United States should remain neutral. Before the conversation became a source of tension due to their differing opinions—for Edward's mother was the daughter of German immigrants and still had relatives in that country—Lidia politely said, "Dinner is served." Edward looked at his wife and whispered to her, "Perfect timing, my dear."

Moments later the family sat down at the wooden dining room table, covered with a fine white linen tablecloth with yellow embroidery in fleur-de-lis motifs and fine white china with floral patterns. After Edward said grace, Lidia and Milly began to serve an authentic Mexican meal. For the first course, they served a cream of corn soup, followed by a baked dish of tomatoes, whole pinto beans, garlic, and onions, and for the main entree they served *pollo con mole rojo* and rice (chicken with mole sauce and rice). On the side there was a serving of fresh salsa and freshly made soft corn tortillas. Lidia had brought some of the ingredients with her from Mexico.

"Lidia, what's the parsley-like ingredient?" asked Clara.

"Cilantro," she replied.

"I suppose, Ale, you helped your mother select the menu," Clara said.

"No, she has not shown much interest in anything related to the kitchen," Lidia said jokingly.

Edward cleared his throat and proudly said, "Perhaps she may develop that interest later. For now she seems to have a talent for music."

Alejandra smiled at her father in appreciation for coming to her defense.

"I told your father to get you a piano years ago," Clara said. "For now, you must come and practice at our house."

"Yes, that will do just fine," Edward added.

"And what do you like to play?" George asked.

"Everything," she replied.

"She expanded her mother's art notebook into a musical journal," Edward added.

"Musical journal?" questioned Clara.

"Yes, it's like a diary, but with musical ideas," she added.

"What sort of musical ideas?" George asked.

"Stories about the music, musical phrases, and lyrics," she said.

"You've given this a lot of thought," Edward added.

"Steven likes to sing. Maybe you and he can put together a duet," Aunt Margaret said to her niece.

"Yes, Ale, you and I can start the Stanford duet," Steven said laughingly.

"Sure," she said as her mother poured Mexican hot chocolate into porcelain cups.

"Grandma Clara, I can tell you an interesting story about the origins of chocolate."

"Oh, then you must," she replied.

"My grandmother Delia told me once that the ancient peoples of Mexico and Central America mixed ground cacao seeds with various seasonings to make a spicy, frothy drink. At one point the cacao beans were even used as currency. Later, the conquistadores brought cacao seeds and beans back to Spain to create other recipes. And eventually, hot chocolate spread to the rest of Europe and the world."

"And it was quite an expensive commodity, I might add," George said.

"Who would have ever known that?" Clara said with a smile as she drank the last of her hot chocolate.

At the end of the meal, Lidia and Alejandra gave the Stanford family small ceramic bowls made by artisans in Cuernavaca, containing pure tablets of dark chocolate along with Lidia's recipe. When the visitors left that evening, Lidia, who had been apprehensive about the family reunion, was quite relieved to find the years she spent in Mexico did not affect her relationship with her husband's family. Edward turned to her as she turned off the lights in the dining room before they retired to the bedroom. "You see, my dear, nothing to worry about," he said. "They love you as much as they did when they first met you."

"It was wonderful to see everyone again," she added as they ascended the steps and then reached the top floor.

Later that week, Alejandra was invited by her cousin Steven for a stroll around Lake Harriet. As she waited for him to arrive, she felt a little anxious about leaving the safety of her home. After all, she had been quite sheltered for many years with limited contact to the outside world. Fortunately, Steven, who was two years her senior, was as kind with her as she remembered him. He walked into the parlor and greeted her, and she noticed his blondish hair was more curly than ever, but his big smile was the same. Moments later they both left, and waiting outside her house was her cousin's friend, Richard Morrison. When she met him, the first thing he said was, "So! You're the missing cousin."

"No! I was never missing, only away," she replied with a firm voice.

She thought he was utterly unpleasant yet familiar as they walked away from the house. Richard continued to lead the conversation with his constant bragging regarding his athletic prowess and unrivaled skills in tennis. She found him quite unattractive, with blemishes on his face and languid brown hair. But what she found the most unfavorable the more she heard him speak was his pretentious personality, as he referred often to his family's wealth and famous connections. They stopped at a bench by Lake of the Isles when she paused momentarily. Steven noticed her discomfort as she turned away briefly, and he changed the topic.

"Ale, what school are you attending?" he asked.

"West High School," she said.

"Wonderful, we will all be schoolmates. A freshman?" Richard asked.

"No, a sophomore, the youngest one in the class, according to my father. I'm a little nervous about it," she said.

"You mustn't be, I'm sure you'll do fine," Steven said. "Will you continue to study piano, and our duet?

"I certainly hope so, although at this time we don't have a piano."

"You can always come to my house. Ours sits mostly unplayed," Richard added.

"Thank you, but I'll be practicing at my grandparents' house."

Steven commented that a new museum had recently opened and it was the talk of the town.

"Would you like to go there next week?" Steven asked her.

"Yes, I've been told there's a mummy. Imagine that!" she replied.

Richard laughed sarcastically. "That would be the most boring thing to do, unless you could talk to it."

She felt bothered by his comment, even if it was a little amusing. She was tempted to argue with him over his unreasonable viewpoint about visiting the museum, but she did not. Moreover, she made sure he knew she was unaffected by his silly remark. Her cousin laughingly said, "Oh Rich, I'm afraid you are leaving a terrible impression on Ale."

She discreetly turned to Steven and said, "I'm not sure I'll be able to go with you to Lake Harriet."

"Oh, why?" Richard asked.

She took a few seconds to respond, thinking, "because of you," but instead replied, "Pardon me for not going this time. I remember there is something I must do."

"Certainly, Ale, we will return at once," Steven said.

"It was nice to see you again, Steven," she added.

"I hope you can come to my tennis match on Sunday," Richard told her.

"I don't know what plans we have," she replied, but to herself she thought, not a chance.

"Let us walk you back," Steven said.

She hesitated.

"We insist," Steven and Richard said together.

"All right," she replied, and started to walk as fast as she could.

Early September brought the first day of classes at West High School, and for Alejandra the day held a mix of surprises, embarrassment, and excitement. As the new girl at school, she garnered much unwanted attention. Some of the students wanted to know about the strange name of Cuernavaca, and many had all sorts of questions and were interested in learning more about Mexico. So when it was time for lunch, she was relieved to take a break from the hectic morning. But as she placed her tray on the table, she accidentally spilled grape juice on her white pleated linen skirt. She was mortified at the insinuation this could provoke. For the rest of lunch, she refused to stand up from the table. She waited until everyone had left the dining hall. On her way to the washroom, she walked through the almost-empty hallway when she heard a familiar male voice calling from behind.

"Alejandra, you'll be late for class," he said.

Not wanting to turn to him, she continued toward the washroom until he caught up to her. She quickly covered the skirt with her books and turned to him.

"Richard!" she exclaimed.

"Shouldn't you be in class?" he said.

"Yes, of course, and so should you. Please excuse me," she said in a dismissive tone while entering the ladies washroom. He was about to say something, but she shut the door before he could.

She approached the sink and wet a piece of a paper towel to try to wash off the juice stain on her skirt. After several unsuccessful attempts, a friendly student turned to her.

"Hi, would you like to use my scarf?" she asked.

"Yes, thank you very much," Alejandra said as the girl pulled the scarf off her neck and extended it. She placed the scarf over her stained skirt. It looked a little weird when she looked in the mirror, but better than the stain, she thought. The girl's name was Olga, a petite girl with green eyes, long reddish hair, and rosy cheeks. Alejandra knew then that Olga would be her closest friend.

By the end of the school day she felt a bit tired, and with only English class left, she walked into the crowded classroom and noticed that almost all the seats were taken except for a few desks in the back of the room. She picked the one on the end and placed her books on the scratched-up flat wooden surface. A minute before the bell rang, a very handsome boy with blondish hair and the most inquisitive blue eyes she had ever seen sat next to her. His hair, combed backward, highlighted his charming smile and cleft chin. He promptly introduced himself as Franz Wensing. She smiled back as the teacher made a screeching sound while he wrote on the blackboard.

"This is English literature, and prepare your-selves for a very demanding class," he said in a stern voice.

After school, Alejandra had agreed to meet Olga in the library. As she waited at one of the tables, she saw her new friend approach her, and to her most pleasant surprise, she was accompanied by her fraternal-twin brother Franz, the boy Alejandra had just met in English class. From then on they would be inseparable.

Olga and Franz were interested in learning more about Mexico and its culture. Alejandra wanted to learn more about them, as they had moved from Germany the previous year. She felt an instant connection with them because they were German like her own paternal grandmother. While Olga and Franz were a year older, they had much in common. They had lived in another country and experienced another culture, yet for them, living in Minnesota was as much like back home as they could have imagined, for since the late 1800s, thousands of immigrants had come to Minnesota from Northern Europe, though Germans were the largest ethnic group in Minnesota. Both of their families had German relatives who lived in Melrose, Minnesota. Furthermore, the German language was spoken throughout the state in schools and churches, and many newspapers were published in the German language.

"At home we speak only German," Olga said.

"Some of the family at the farm don't even speak English," Franz added.

"Yes, I know, my grandmother Clara told me similar stories of her family growing up on a farm. She also talked often about how much work she and her siblings had from dawn til dusk. But what she liked best, growing up, were the Saturday gatherings when her father played the fiddle and all the kids danced," Alejandra continued. "I'd love to learn German."

"And I wouldn't mind learning Spanish, either. Can you teach me?" Franz asked.

"I'm certain my mother could," she said pleasantly. She looked up at the clock on the wall. "Oh! My cousin is waiting to take me home. See you tomorrow."

Steven was standing by his car outside the school parking lot when she reached him. He suggested they stop first at an ice cream shop. She was more than happy to go with her cousin, yet to her great disappointment, waiting at St. Francis Ice Cream Parlor was no other than Richard Morrison. She immediately realized he was the same boy she had met at another ice cream parlor when she was in second grade. He looked so different but was as unpleasant as before, she thought. She ordered a cherry ice cream soda, and both her cousin and Richard ordered the parlor's specialty, a "Berrylicious Sundae."

As they talked about their classes and new teachers, she noticed the most unusual type of piano she had ever seen. She was tempted to get up and play it, but with Richard there, she held back. The two boys conversed mostly, except for when he reminded her that she had not attended his tennis match nor had she and Steven been to his house.

"Play for us!" he requested.

"No!" Alejandra replied.

"Why not?" he asked.

"I don't think I can. It looks mechanical and besides, I have to leave soon," she added.

Steven then turned to the unusual looking instrument.

"It's a violano, combination piano and violin," he said. Then Richard turned to her once more. "So, where do you need to go?" he asked.

"I help with catechism classes," she said.

"You must come with Steven to my house," Richard insisted.

My goodness this boy is so forward, she thought.

"So have you been to the museum yet, cousin?" Steven asked.

"Not yet," she said.

"Let me know when you go," Steven said as they left the ice cream parlor.

"I will," she said.

Later in the month when Alejandra arrived home from school and stopped at the mailbox, as she usually did, she found something unexpected in the mail. As she eagerly looked for a letter from her grandparents in Mexico among letters mostly addressed to her father, she saw the museum's bulletin cover, which depicted the image of an Egyptian mummy named Lady Teshat.

She placed the mail in her large bag and walked up the pathway, which was covered with fallen leaves. She hated the crunching sound of the dried leaves as she stepped on them because it reminded her the fall season would soon be over and a cold winter would follow. She opened the front door and moments later she found her mother in the dining room, polishing the silver. She placed her belongings on the table.

"Ale, how was your day?" she asked.

"Good, very good," she answered.

"Want something to eat?" her mother asked.

"No, thanks, but something to drink," she replied.

Lidia wiped her hands on her apron and then poured her daughter a glass of hibiscus water from the pitcher on the nearby buffet console. Alejandra took the glass and sat by the table, drinking the tasty fruit water in its entirety. Then she took the bulletin from the table, read the front page, and turned to her mother.

"Do you think it's odd that I like museums? One of Steven's friends laughed in my face a few weeks ago when I mentioned it," she said in bewilderment.

"No, not at all. When I was your age, and I suspect still today, people travel abroad for the opportunity to learn about other cultures. The museum offers that without having to leave the city. Although, I suppose some young people might not know how interesting it is, and all the beautiful things they'll see there. Don't worry about what others think, as long as you like it," her mother said.

"Steven wants to come with us," she said.

"Wonderful, maybe you can also invite your new friends," Lidia added.

"I'll tell them tomorrow," she replied.

A week later, the Stanford family, Steven, and the Wensing twins attended the Minneapolis Institute of Arts. Situated in front of Washburn Fair Oaks Park, the building stood out like a Greek temple, and as they ascended some forty steps to the entrance doors, Alejandra thought it was like stepping back into ancient Greece. As they entered the classical-style building, she noticed the grand three-story foyer with marble floors and walls, and a dome covered in decorative plaster. Beneath the dome, there was a large fountain imported from Italy surrounded by flowers in autumn colors. Edward walked to the information desk and asked for a map. He looked for the Egyptian collection, which was housed in Gallery B-7. "Let's go there first," he said to his family.

"There is so much to see," Lidia added.

The four adolescents rushed to the gallery and discovered, to their amazement, that the Egyptian collection included hundreds of objects from sculptures, to furniture, to jewelry and daily-life utensils that offered a glimpse into the ancient culture that lived along the Nile River four thousand years before. But naturally the object that drew most of the attention among people there was the Egyptian mummy. Alejandra was fascinated when she saw Lady Teshat, for she felt a certain reverence at the sight of her coffin and cartonnage, a shell-like encasement of linen, richly decorated with colorful hieroglyphs, as explained on the object's label. "It's haunting!" she said.

"Just in time for All Saints Day," Steven said playfully.

They spent almost thirty minutes looking through the collection. Olga was drawn to the jewelry in particular, made of lapis lazuli, turquoise, copper, malachite, onyx, quartz, and amethyst crystals. The necklaces were intricately crafted.

"I'd love to wear any of these necklaces," she remarked as she pointed to one in a case.

"Not me, but I can imagine how they must have looked on the necks of the pharaohs," Steven added.

"Come, there are other things I want to show you," Edward said as they all went to a different gallery on the second floor, which housed the permanent collection. Among them there were some of the museum's first acquisitions, paintings by French artists including *Vacationers on the Beach at Trouville* by Eugéne-Louis Boudin and *Deer in the Forest* by Gustave Courbet.

"The latter was donated by James J. Hill, a Canadian immigrant who is also a collector of fine arts," Edward said to his daughter as she admired *Ray of Sunlight* by American painter John W. Alexander that showed a young female musician playing the cello as a ray of sunlight illuminated her hands. Meanwhile, Steven had discovered a bronze statue of Buddha and joining his hands, he bowed to it in a playful manner.

"So funny," Olga told him.

With seriousness, Franz added, "I wish there were more Buddhas in the world."

"Yes," Steven responded.

"We'll have to return here often," Alejandra said.

Lidia, who had join them, added, "Perhaps next time when there's a tour."

Later, as the visitors walked down several dozen marble steps onto the main floor, Edward said to Lidia, "You know they have an art school here, too."

"Yes, I know. I'll be studying there next month. But first I have to finish a painting for Thanksgiving," she replied.

"Who are you painting this time?" he asked.

"It's a what," she replied with a smile. You'll have to wait until it's finished."

"Do I have a choice?" he asked.

"No!" she replied as they all left the museum late in the afternoon.

For Thanksgiving, Lidia finished an oil on canvas still life painting that illustrated several very personal items chosen and arranged on the marble top buffet console by both her and her daughter. For weeks, Lidia worked on the painting while Edward was at work, and in the afternoons it remained covered behind a white cloth on the wooden easel next to the window in the dining room. When she finally unveiled it a day before the holiday, the painting depicted a ceramic vase with sunflowers, a crystal-blue bowl with purple squash, green apples, grapes, and plums, and a blue wool *rebozo* draped under a wooden and silver cross. When Edward came home that evening, he found the painting hanging above the console and immediately recognized all the items except for the cross, which he later found out had belonged to little Sol. He paused for a few seconds and then said with a pleased expression, "So this is what you've been doing for the past month."

"I wanted to commemorate our return," Lidia replied.

"Perhaps you should do one of me, so you'll never forget me and leave me behind," Edward said smiling.

Lidia shook her head and laughed, too. "One of these days."

It was four o'clock in the afternoon on the next day when the Wensing family arrived at the Stanford's Colonial house for Thanksgiving dinner. Ralph, a tall, corpulent man, extended his hand to Edward as he entered the house, followed by his wife, Ana, a plump, petite woman with red hair.

Olga and Franz mostly resembled their mother in both facial features and stature, Edward thought, as he invited them to the drawing room. Alejandra placed a tray of beverages on the cocktail table and they walked into the harvest-themed room. The two families greeted each other and sat down to converse, but at first there was some awkwardness between them. Lidia's outgoing personality soon broke the silence when she spoke a few welcoming words in German.

"Herzlich willkommen in unser Haus (Welcome to our home). Please have a cup of hot apple cider."

"We're pleased you've come to share this most authentic American holiday," Edward said.

"Likewise, we've heard so much about all of you from Franz and Olga. This is our second Thanksgiving here in America," Ralph said with a thick accent.

"We understand you have family here," Edward said.

"Yes, my uncle came here as soon as he heard America was offering farm land for very reasonable prices, particularly in Minnesota. And with its dense woods that was a great advantage, for it provided inexpensive fuel and building materials that were quite tempting for newcomers," Ralph said.

"Show them the advertisement you carry in your wallet," Ana said. "He carries it as if it was his legal paper."

"Advertisement?" Edward asked.

"My uncle Wilhelm gave it to his mother when he left Germany, and she gave it to me when I left," Ralph said as he pulled out from his wallet a stained, wrinkled, and folded flyer. He carefully unfolded it, and began to read and translate the written words from German:

> The whole surface of the state is literally saturated with innumerable lakes. Their picturesque beauty and loveliness, with their pebbly bottoms, transparent waters, wooded shores, and sylvan associations must be seen to be fully appreciated. There is no western state better supplied with forests . . .

"And so forth," Ralph said.

"Oh yes, I recall my father telling me that the St. Paul and Pacific Railroad had flyers written and printed in several languages. His representatives distributed them throughout many of the European cities and Canadian and American ports," Edward said. "Thanks to the wave of new immigrants, my father met my mother who is second-generation German."

"When my uncle first arrived, he and his family were given immediate shelter in transitional housing for those acquiring land. They were called reception houses," Ralph said.

"Yes, indeed, Stearns County is mostly farms owned by Germans," Edward added.

"Beautiful indeed, but did you imagine it would be so cold?" Lidia asked.

"No, but Germany can get plenty cold, too, and the landscape is quite similar, actually," Ana added.

"I hope someday we can visit there," Alejandra said.

"You'd like it very much. Our grandparents still live in Berlin. I too hope we can return some day," Franz said.

"Please, let's walk across to the dining room, for Milly tells me dinner is served," Lidia suggested.

When the two families sat for dinner, Edward tapped the crystal and then raised his wine-filled glass. "Here is to you, your family, and all who come from close and faraway lands to this blessed state," he said.

As tradition would dictate, Edward asked each of the guests to share what they were thankful for, and after his parents spoke, it was Franz's turn to speak. He turned to Alejandra and stared intensely into her eyes. "I'm thankful for my family, for the opportunity to come to America, and especially for having the acquaintance of Ale and her family."

She blushed, hoping nobody noticed, but for the rest of the evening she avoided him and his penetrating gaze, which made her uncomfortable. Thanksgiving was her favorite holiday, although that night she was thankful when the celebration had ended.

The next day, the Stanfords stayed home to witness the first big snow storm of the season. It was remarkable to see how quickly the weather changed in Minnesota, thought Alejandra as she looked through the window in the drawing room. She had learned to appreciate nature in her daily wonderings at the hacienda, and she wished she could do the same here. She felt a nostalgia for Cuernavaca's warm weather, but the beauty of the falling snow, the snow-covered trees, the glow of the fireplace, and the happiness she saw once again in her mother's facial expression and attitude gave her much comfort.

Yet she missed her music and piano, and felt as though something significant had been ripped away from her. She wondered if and when she might write a new composition.

Sometimes she had the strong urge to sit at the piano. She practiced her music several times a week at her grandparents', but that was barely a taste compared to what she used to do. She had asked her mother when they would get a piano and all her mother said was soon, soon. She recalled her father saying that she already played as well as she needed to. But she wasn't satisfied with playing very well—she wanted to excel. Her thoughts were interrupted when she heard her mother's voice in the room.

"Ale, I need your help in getting down the Christmas decorations from the attic. We have much work to do," she said.

"Yes, Mother," she replied and left the room with her.

On Christmas day morning, with the excitement of a still-young girl, Alejandra walked down the steps and into the drawing room. Underneath the Christmas tree she found an envelope with her name on it that she quickly opened. She found three concert tickets to hear the Symphony Orchestra, with a special performance by a piano soloist Miss Theodora Troendle. At a time when there was little entertainment available, particularly in the winter months, and when musical concerts took center age in the city, Alejandra was thrilled with her gift. She walked across the vestibule and joined her parents in the breakfast room.

"Thank you," she said as she sat and placed the tickets on the table.

"I think you'll find it most stimulating," Edward said. "This will be your first time seeing the Symphony Orchestra."

"Yes, I can't wait to go," she said. "Do you know anything about the pianist?"

"No, but the program notes will tell us," Lidia replied.

"Ladies, it's almost nine o'clock. We'll need to hurry if we want to be on time," Edward said as he looked at the pocket watch he pulled from his coat pocket.

Later that morning, the Stanford family attended mass at St. Anthony de Padua Catholic Church. For Alejandra it was quite a welcoming sight when she recognized many of the children who she knew from catechism classes singing in the choir. One of the most beautiful Christmas carols she heard was "Silent Night, Holy Night" (*"Stille Nacht! Heilige Nacht"),* with music by Austrian composer Franz Gruber and lyrics by Josef Mohr.

If she had heard it before she did not recall, and that morning she didn't even hear much of the sermon, for she focused her attention on the musical instruments and the music performed at mass. The random pitch of the bells was singular compared to the pipe organ's majestic sound, she thought. And for the rest of the religious service all she could think of was the upcoming concert at the Minneapolis Auditorium.

After mass, Edward, Lidia, and Alejandra left the church and drove to the home of George and Clara Stanford, Edward's parents. The Victorian-style house in the Whittier neighborhood of Minneapolis was decorated for Christmas with one large wreath above the entrance door. The smell of fresh pine needles was in the air. Edward rang the doorbell and Mr. Minty, the butler, who was dressed in a dark uniform, opened the door with his usual serious face and very low voice.

"Merry Christmas, sir, madam, Miss Ale," he said.

"Merry Christmas to you," they all replied.

The small parlor led to a large hallway and dual staircases with wooden carved banisters, and behind the landing there were large stained-glass windows with floral designs. As they walked through the wide corridor and into the drawing room, a twelve-foot Christmas tree next to the fireplace was decorated with blown glass ornaments, Christmas cards, and colorful lights. A carved wooden mantle displayed two bronze reindeer. In the corner of the room was an upright piano with the Boston trademark. Clara decorated her house in the Victorian style, but it was visually uncluttered with a few carefully selected landscape paintings. For while George and Clara Stanford were of quite reasonable means, they did not like to indulge in conspicuous consumption, as George would frequently say. They preferred simplicity over ostentatious décor.

Both Edward and Lidia commented frequently on how their two families were similar in their values and beliefs, with some minor differences. But the qualities the families shared and strongly imparted to their children were education, a strong work ethic, and a sense of humility in their spirits. While both the Stanford and Merino families were quite distinguished, they always imparted appreciation for their service staff in public, and treated them with a familial closeness and appreciation that was rare during this period.

Lidia would often comment that the life of the help wasn't easy, for many spend long hours attending to their employers' every need from making soap from scratch to laundering, cooking, and keeping the rooms warm while making little money. It was a time when the economic differences between the classes were as marked in the United States as they were in Mexico. So as not to take anything for granted, Lidia and Edward always made sure their daughter took on added responsibility with house chores.

When the grandfather clock chimed at three, dinner was served in the spacious dining room. Twelve guests sat around the mahogany table. George, who was at the head of the table, raised his glass and said, "I'd like to make a toast to the safe return of Edward, Lidia, and Ale. I'm most gratified to have all our family together once again." They all raised their glasses filled with fine red wine in agreement.

With the help of Lena, the cook, and their butler, Mr. Minty, Clara passed platters of Christmas delicacies, served on china dishes passed on to her from Edward's mother who was of English descent. Clara served a traditional Christmas meal, including tomato soup, roast Vermont turkey, cranberry sauce, celery dressing, mashed potatoes, and plum pudding for dessert. But the best news of the night came toward the end of the evening, when Edward made a surprise announcement. "By the miracle of God, Lidia and I are expecting a new child," Edward said, brimming with happiness and his familiar broad smile.

"That is indeed your reward for your return, Lidia," Clara said poignantly.

"Oh mother, the reward is all ours," Edward replied.

"Perhaps this time you'll have a boy," George said. "But another girl like Ale would be as wonderful."

Alejandra smiled at the news, for as long as she could remember she had wanted a sibling, although Sol had been like a brother to her. Perhaps after all these years, it was like her father said—a miracle.

"When, mother?" she asked.

"In the spring," Lidia replied.

Later that night, when she and her family returned home, Alejandra ran up the steps into her bedroom. There on her nightstand by a Tiffany lamp was the envelope. She picked it up and opened it once again to read:

> Eleventh popular concert of the
> Minneapolis Symphony Orchestra.
> December 31, 1916—3:30 p.m.
> Price: 50 cents

As she changed into her nightgown, she thought of how she would have to wait a whole week to go to the concert. With great anticipation in her heart, she turned off the lights.

On New Year's Eve day, the Stanford family drove to the Minneapolis Auditorium. Alejandra had been waiting feverishly for this day, and when she and her parents arrived at the concert venue, beautifully adorned in holiday décor, they took their seats in the middle of the fifth row of the crowded hall. From there she had a perfect view of the stage, which had an enormous mural of the North Woods as the backdrop for the eighty-five-piece orchestra that waited patiently for its conductor.

Moments later, Emil Oberhoffer stepped onto the stage as the public applauded enthusiastically. He took his position in front of the podium and seconds later waved his baton. The orchestra began to play Dvorak's *New World Symphony* followed by Wagner's overture "Tannhauser." Then the piano soloist Miss Theodora Troendle walked onto the stage wearing a rose-colored lace dress. Her striking smile captured the audience, but when she sat at the bench and began to play the grand piano, her fingers moved through the piano keys with great lightness, as if a bird was flying across the blue skies.

Alejandra was impressed by her virtuosity and the emotion she expressed through the music. During intermission, she read the program notes and learned the concert pianist started playing piano at the age of five. As she waited for her parents to return, she glanced at the stage and stared at the musical instruments that lay neatly arranged on the empty chairs. A few minutes later, everyone returned to their seats.

Once all the musicians came together to complete the program as they performed Georg Schumann's "Dance of Nymphs & Satyrs" from *Cupid and Psyche,* opus 3, Alejandra came to a full realization. She listened attentively to every phrase the musicians played on flutes, oboes, clarinets, bassoons, trumpets, and the strings, but it was the conductor who caught her attention. What would it be like and feel like to stand there as a conductor? To direct the wind, string, and horn sections? To interpret the music of Bach, Strauss, and Beethoven? What a privilege! Alejandra's heart swelled with joy and wonder. It was all something to dream about, to be a concert pianist, or perhaps even a conductor. She smiled at herself for having such grand ambitions.

This was the first time she thought about music, not as entertainment or enjoyment, or even as comfort and creativity as she had in the past. That night, amid the huge crowd, applauses, and symphonic music, she thought of music as a profession. Didn't her father tell her countless times, anything was possible with hard work and determination? As she escaped into her daydreaming and imagined herself at the podium conducting the orchestra, she heard the thunderous applause once more, and her attention returned to the festive scene before her as Miss Troendle stood up and bowed her head. She remembered her Grandmother Delia and the first time she saw her play the piano all those years before. The two ladies are both graceful, both filled with pride, and both inspiring, she thought as she joined the rest of the audience in a standing ovation.

6 Nostalgia Mexicana

On New Year's Day 1917, not even the winter freeze could keep Alejandra indoors, nor could it stop hundreds of other spectators who attended the pre-winter carnival pageant at the Town and Country Club in Minneapolis. Bundled up in a sweater and her winter-white coat, hat, and gloves, she accompanied her parents to witness the most entertaining celebration she had seen yet, as thousands of costumed marchers passed before them holding up colorful posters in lime green, blue, and red, a notable contrast to the white- and gray-colored mountains of snow piles on the street corners and sidewalks.

"Since 1886, Minnesota's St. Paul Winter Carnival has been a tradition and was the first one in the United States. It was imported from Montreal and Russian traditions dating back to Peter the Great, although Germans would also claim a tradition of Carneval of Fasching, a pre-Lenten celebration in the 1800s," Edward said to her loudly and with pride as the marchers passed by.

"Father, how do you know all this?" his daughter asked.

"I was one of the many volunteers who worked tirelessly back in my teens," he said. "We Minnesotans don't let a little cold keep us indoors."

"But I might prefer to stay indoors, father," she said in rebuttal, smiling.

When the date of the outdoor carnival finally arrived on January 27, Alejandra, Steven, Richard, and Olga attended the festival on the first day. It was a chilly day as the group gathered in St. Paul Park on Kellogg Avenue, and joined a celebration that eclipsed the previous years', at least according to Richard. Thousands upon thousands of marchers wearing costumes lined the streets. There were skiing, skating, and curling teams, grand processions and parades, and to complete the outstanding event, huge blocks of ice were cut to create a massive Ice Palace on Rice Park. Alejandra and Olga couldn't contain their excitement as they giggled like two little girls. "It's an icy extravaganza," Olga added.

The parades were followed by tournaments, and Richard was eager to show off his skills as he was a member of the Wacouta Toboggan Club. Steven and Olga seemed to have developed a liking for each other, and soon they were a few steps behind Richard and Alejandra, as the group walked toward the sports recreation area.

"How are you liking the winter?" Richard asked her.

"The snow is beautiful, but not the freezing cold," she answered.

"It's only a matter of time before you get used to it. Steven tells me you spend every waking hour at the museum," he said jokingly.

"A bit of an exaggeration, don't you think?" she said.

"Of course, what could you possibly find there so amusing? I suppose seeing the mummy was quite to your liking," he said.

"Show some respect! Even you must find it incredible that we can know so much about someone after three thousand years. And for someone who claims to like science you should be at the very least intrigued by the whole process of mummification," she said, as she resisted bursting into laughter at his comments, which she found distasteful, but funny nevertheless. Richard blinked and said, "Oh my, I think I like this side of you."

"What side?" she asked.

"Sassy," he said. Alejandra ignored the remark, and turned around to walk toward Olga, when she noticed her speaking to a third person. It was Franz, who eagerly waved at her.

She placed her hands on her face momentarily.

"Is something wrong?" Richard asked.

"No, I'm just terribly cold, "she said.

"Here, take my jacket," he said.

"No, thanks, with a little more walking I'll be fine," she said.

Franz, Olga, and Steven caught up to them.

"Hello, Ale, I've not had the fortune to talk to you since Thanksgiving," Franz said.

"I've been busy with my studies," she replied. "It's nice to see you, too."

"You spent Thanksgiving together?" Richard asked.

"Yes, Olga and her family joined us for dinner," she replied.

She tried to change the conversation by pointing to an ice sculpture, but Richard insisted. "I wasn't aware you were such good acquaintances," he said.

"Most certainly, we've been the closest of friends since we met on the first day of school," Olga said boastfully.

"Olga, would you like something to drink?" Steven asked.

"Yes, thank you, a cup of hot chocolate."

"Would you like one, too, cousin?" he asked.

"Yes, thank you."

Steven and Olga walked to the drink stand while Franz, Richard, and Alejandra stayed behind, the two boys on either side of her. For the next ten minutes, what seemed an eternity to her, she was bombarded with questions from the two young men, as if they were competing in a tennis match.

"How is school? How do you like your teachers? What subjects do you like? Have you been to the winter carnival before?"

Unable to extricate herself from the situation verbally, she walked faster toward Olga and Steven who were still waiting in line to purchase their drinks. "Olga, can you please come with me to the ladies room?" she asked.

"Yes," she replied.

Unknown to Olga, she found her brother very attractive and charming, but too intense since Thanksgiving.

Upon their return, the boys suggested they all go skating. Alejandra had not skated since she was a little girl. Fortunately, Steven knew this, so he instead suggested they all go toboggan sliding. "Alejandra, you must come down with me," Richard said.

"No, thank you, I've not had much practice with winter sports, or any sports for that matter. I'd rather see you from down here."

"I'll stay with you," Franz said.

"See you later," Steven said as he left with Olga and Richard.

Thirty minutes later, the group of friends finally took their last slide down the hill. Steven, who was always hungry, noticed it was time for dinner and invited everyone to a Minneapolis restaurant known for its generous meals and reasonable prices.

Schiek's Café was a cozy place and a welcome contrast to the outside freezing temperatures, thought Alejandra as they entered the dark tavern, decorated in splendid Victorian décor. The restaurant's specialty was German food, potato pancakes and hearty sauerbraten. However, they all thought the best part of the night was the German music, and while they waited for dinner, they danced a few polka numbers. Soon after, as the five students ate their suppers, the conversation turned tense when the three boys discussed the possibility of the States entering the Great War.

"If we go in, I'll immediately enlist in the navy," Richard said.

"Likewise," Steven added.

Franz remained silent, and even refused to discuss the subject further. It was quite a delicate matter for him and his family, as some of his close relatives still lived in Germany; therefore, he was completely against the States entering the war. As they finished their last cup of hot apple cider, Franz got up from the table and angrily said, "Olga, it's time for us to go home."

"Now?" she asked.

"Yes, now!" he added, but then softened his voice when he turned to Alejandra. "When will I see you again?"

"In school," she replied.

Franz took his coat and left the café with Olga.

Steven and Richard continued to discuss the topic, but Alejandra stopped them and said, "You know it's not easy for them. Let it go. Besides, don't forget we too have German ancestry," she said to Steven.

"You're right, Ale," Steven said. "Let's go home." He paid the check, and then Richard took the opportunity to put on her coat. She thanked him for his gallantry, and the three left the restaurant.

After weeks of snow flakes and below-freezing temperatures, Alejandra became nostalgic about sunny Cuernavaca once again. In late February after helping at her church for several hours, she had an irresistible desire to play piano.

All weekend she had been thinking how much her life had changed, and mostly it was all pleasant, but the gray skies made her feel melancholic. She longed for the walks around flower-lined pathways, the smell of fragrant flowers, the commotion of the children's coming and going, the warm evening breezes, the books in her grandfather's library, and their piano. Most of all, she missed her abuelitos. This had been her life for more than five years. In fact, the feeling of nostalgia seeped through her pores.

In the candlelit hallway of St. Anthony de Padua, she sat on the piano bench, placed her fingers on the keyboard of the piano, and began to improvise. As before, she started to play a few notes with her right hand, then the harmony with her left hand. And as if in a trance, an hour later the few notes had evolved into a full new composition that, not surprisingly, she named "Nostalgia Mexicana."

TRACK TWO

Over the Waves

The snow melted and the white ground faded, spring came to life, and sunny days prevailed; but not without a dark cloud on the horizon. For on April 6, 1917, the United States officially entered the Great War. Four days later, a new commission was created and the Minnesota Commission of Public Safety was signed into law by the Governor.

> The commission's mission to define and enforce loyalty for America, and to create: One Country, One Flag, One People, and One Speech.
>
> With sweeping powers, the commission began a survey, especially in the schools, to determine the content and the language that was spoken in the instruction of students, as the German language was the most widespread non-English language commonly used in Minnesota during this period.

This event had long-lasting changes for anyone with a certain European heritage. Franz and Olga Wensing became profoundly concerned with the anti-German sentiment around them when they learned that simple words such as sauerkraut and hamburger were renamed liberty cabbage and liberty sausage, respectively. Although they took it with some humor, they became more careful in speaking German publicly, and Alejandra interrupted her German lessons.

Looking for a pleasant distraction after a tense spring, the Stanford family turned to the museum. Lidia was very enthusiastic to see the newest exhibition, a collection of forty-three paintings by Spanish artist Ignacio Zuloaga considered breathtaking by reviewers. In June, the Stanfords attended the acclaimed exhibition.

As they slowly walked through the galleries on the first floor, Alejandra had the distinct sensation of being elsewhere, in a place most similar to Mexico. Whether it was the images, colors, or familiar scenery of Spanish landscapes in the paintings, she felt an instant appreciation for the artist and a connection to the museum, which frequently showcased art collections from various cultures. Zuloaga's painting *My Uncle Daniel and his Family* was particularly memorable, for it illustrated five members of a family, some smiling, but mostly all dressed in black, with gray clouds hovering over them. Still fresh in her mind was her cousin Sol's funeral from the previous year. To be sure, this was a painting of the artist's family in 1910.

When they left the museum, Lidia, who was inspired by the colorful images created by the Spanish painter, made her own resolution as she went into the nursery room of her home. She sat on the window bench and, gazing around it, realized the décor lacked color and imagination. Moments later, Alejandra joined her mother in the future baby's room.

"Mother, are you all right?" she asked her.

"Oh, yes, a little tired," she replied. "Ale, I need your help."

"Yes?"

"With only six weeks left in my pregnancy, I don't have a lot of time," she said.

"For what?"

"To paint a mural in this room," Lidia remarked.

"A mural?"

"Yes, I want something that will inspire him. It seems rather sterile in here, don't you think?"

"What do you want to paint?" she asked her mother.

"I have several ideas, but what do you think I should paint in your brother's room?"

"How do you know it will be a boy?" she asked.

"Intuition," Lidia replied.

"Well, father seems to have a penchant for inventions, and perhaps an image of an airplane similar to that of the Wright brothers might be fun?" she suggested.

"What a marvelous idea, Ale! Can you get a book from the library that may have photographs of that event?" Lidia asked.

"Yes mother, I will, tomorrow after school."

"Perhaps your brother will have the opportunity to travel by plane someday," she said.

"What about us?"

"I suppose we might, too," Lidia replied. "Your father says it will happen sooner than we think."

For the next six weeks, Lidia painted the portraits of Orville and Wilbur Wright on one side of a blue, red, and white airplane and on the other side a portrait of Leonardo Da Vinci and a sketch similar to one of his flying machine drawings. The ten-by-twelve-foot mural was the highlight of the room. When she was almost finished, Lidia stood in front of the mural. My son will see it from his crib, she thought, as she painted the final touches on Da Vinci's face.

Lidia looked like the painter she was, as her apron was spattered with blue and red paints. Her once-neat bun was almost unraveled, and her oval face was smudged with white paint on the side of her right cheek.

"Ale, go and get your father, he's anxious to see it," Lidia said as she wiped off as best she could the paint on her hands. She sat on the window bench as she felt a slight kick on her abdomen. She placed her hand on it, and softly said to the unborn child, "If you are a girl, we will love you the same."

Moments later, Edward came into the room and stood in complete admiration, an expression of love. He joined his wife and gently wiped the paint from her cheek with the rag she was holding in her hand.

"Lidia, this is why I fell in love with you," he said. "Your enthusiasm, your creativity, and your ability to surprise me every time."

Alejandra looked at her parents from the door. This was the most loving moment she had ever witnessed between them, she thought. "Mother, you still need to sign it."

"Let us all sign it, for we each had something to do with it," Lidia said as she took the smallest paint brush and dipped it into white paint, and then signed her name on the right-hand corner of the impressive mural.

On July 29, after a difficult and long delivery, Lidia gave birth to a healthy boy, Edward George Stanford. A week later at around lunch time, they were welcomed at their home by a lively extended family. Alejandra placed blue balloons around the exterior columns of their house while Grandma Clara and Milly prepared a dinner with summer treats. Waiting in the dining room was George, who in a boisterous voice said, "We have great pleasure in congratulating our dearest Edward and Lidia on the birth of our second grandson. May his mother's spirit and his father's wit be Edward George's guiding will!"

Alejandra started the month of August by helping her mother with baby Edward, for she didn't sleep very much during the night. After Lidia fed her baby, in the morning she usually went back to sleep while her daughter took her brother to his room and stayed with him until lunch. When the baby slept, she read the biographies of classical music composers. By the end of the first week, she had read about Mozart and Bach. She hoped that when she finished her readings, she could discover something in common between them. However, what she found most remarkable was the musical genius of Mozart at such a young age.

Midmorning on Monday of the second week in August, baby Edward woke up hungry and wet. Alejandra didn't call Milly to help her change his diapers. She'd become an expert—it was disgusting but natural, she said to herself as she changed his soiled diapers on the bed. The strangest but funniest thought occurred to her: Was Mozart still wearing diapers at age three when he started selecting tunes to play on the piano? "What are you going to be doing at three?" she asked her little brother lovingly as she gently touched his tiny little nose with her index finger. She laughed for having such thoughts about the musical genius who grew up to be the greatest composer of his day, and who excelled in every form of music: opera, symphony, chamber, and choral, and was the finest conductor. He was one of her favorite composers of the classical music period.

By the end of the week of taking care of her brother, Alejandra had the routine down, and she especially enjoyed rocking him until he went to sleep. On Friday she was going swimming at Lake Calhoun with Steven and her friends, so she was anxious to finish her shift. At exactly noon, Steven picked her up. With the temperature at almost 80 degrees, she wore a sleeveless floral dress with blue blossoms that looked like something out of a palette of one of Monet's paintings.

"Ale, you look beautiful," her cousin said.

"Thank you," she replied as she picked up a large bag containing her swimming clothes. Waiting in the car were Franz and Olga, and when the four friends arrived, the park was completely crowded. The boys carried folding lounge chairs and a large umbrella, and they wandered for a few minutes until Steven spotted Richard, who was saving a place by the beach. They greeted each other, and then Alejandra and Olga left to change into their long swimming pants. When they returned, Steven commented on their apparel. Alejandra became a little embarrassed to show so much skin, as she felt Richard staring at her bosom. Olga, on the other hand, coquettishly pulled down her sleeves farther, so her shoulders were almost completely bare.

"Ale, we are not living in the 1890s anymore. Don't be so prudish," Olga admonished her.

"Oh, I know," she replied as she instinctively pulled up her swim top and covered her chest.

"Stop with the fashion and let's go swimming," Steven said as he grabbed Olga's hand, and together they ran to the water.

"Aren't you going to swim, too?" Franz asked.

"Yes, but someone needs to stay with all our belongings," she replied.

"Don't worry about them," Richard said.

"Perhaps she's right. You go on Richard, I'll stay with her," Franz said as he sat on the sandy beach next to Alejandra.

"How is your family doing?" she asked.

"They are fine, a little worried. My father is even thinking of changing our name to something that sounds more American," Franz said.

"Oh, I do hope this will pass soon," she added.

"Yes, if things continue like this, my mother thinks we should return to Germany," he said.

"Isn't that a little extreme?"

"Yes, I suppose so," he said.

"Maybe the results of the survey will bring some closure to the matter, and everything can be back to normal," Alejandra said as their friends returned sometime later, dripping wet.

"It's our turn now," Franz said. "Come, Ale."

She ran to the beach with great excitement, for the lake was always one of her top favorite places to be. She immersed herself slowly until she was completely under water. When she surfaced, Franz splashed her on her arms, as they both swam as far as was allowed. She let herself float on the water for a few seconds and closed her eyes as she took in the full sun on her face. It was delightful, she thought. Franz tapped her shoulders.

"You'll get your face all sunburned," he said.

"I want to soak up the sun as much as possible," she said as Franz stared at her and took her hand, which she quickly withdrew.

"I think we better get back," she said as she swam back to the beach. She momentarily lost sight of where Steven and Olga were, but then suddenly saw Richard waving his hand.

"I don't know why Richard is always around," Franz said. She agreed, but said nothing. When they reached the rest of the group, they dried themselves and she placed a towel around her shoulders. For the next two hours the group ate lunch, conversed, played ball, and swam some more. Steven looked at his pocket watch.

"Gosh, it's almost four o'clock."

"Oh, yes, I'd forgotten all about Chase's party," Richard said.

"Do you girls want to come?" Steven asked.

"Yes, yes," Olga said.

"Not me," Alejandra replied.

"Why not?" Steven asked.

"We're going to my grandparents' for dinner, and I want to practice a new song on the piano," she said.

"I don't understand you. How can you prefer that over going to a social gathering?" Richard said to her, annoyed.

"You don't have to understand me! It's what I love to do, and that is that," she replied confidently and left to change her clothes.

"You could never understand," Franz said defiantly to Richard.

"And you do?" Richard asked.

"Yes, of course," he said.

"Now, you two, let it be," Steven said as he folded the lounge chairs. "Let us take her home, and then we'll go to your house to change," he said to Franz and Olga.

"See you next week in school," Richard said to Alejandra.

"Sure," she replied.

It was the beginning of the school year. She looked forward to resuming classes, for she had been asked to attend a meeting from the music club. When she approached her school building with its arched windows, she noticed the large oak trees that had begun to change color. She took a deep breath and walked through the main entrance. She had a sense of optimism, and with schedule in hand, she proceeded to her first class, biology, which was not one of her favorites. She was relieved when Franz walked into the room. At least they could study together, she thought as he sat next to her. For the rest of the day, all she could think about was the music club. At the end of the day, she rushed to the music room, and bumped into a boy who rudely said, "Watch where you're going."

"Sorry! I was distracted," she replied. "No need to get angry."

When she arrived at the designated room, she saw her cousin and sat next to him. With fifteen other students present, Steven was about to start the meeting when a short and stockily built boy with thinning hair and a broad nose arrogantly said, "Hi, my name is Randall Cunningham, and I am in charge."

Alejandra sighed in disapproval, for this was the boy she had bumped into in the hallway. Calm down, it will be fine, she said to herself. Each student introduced him or herself, and declared the instrument they each played. With a variety of instruments represented including piano, violin, guitar, trumpet, drums, and several vocalists, Randall asked, "What are we going to do with this many musicians?"

"We could form two groups, and compete with one another, or form one band, and take turns performing," Steven suggested.

"Who will direct us?" Desirée, one of the vocalists, asked.

"Mr. Fischer will," Randall replied. "I'm his assistant."

"I propose one group," Alejandra said.

"That will be difficult, since there are several keyboard players," Randall said.

"We can always take turns," she replied.

"We'll see about that," he said.

The group of fifteen students agreed to meet the following week to form a band. This was more than she could have hoped for, and perhaps the beginning of something new, Alejandra thought when she left school that day.

For the rest of the week, she imagined all the possibilities. They would practice together, maybe even perform publicly for special events. It would certainly provide her with the experience of performing with other people. She had all sorts of expectations, which unfortunately were unrealized.

For when the group gathered the following week in the music room, Randall declared, "We have news! Some of us met during the week, and we decided to select the members of the band."

"Shouldn't you have waited until we all met?" Steven commented.

"No, I'm sorry to say, we can't all be in the band," Randall said smugly.

"Why not?" Desirée said.

"Because it's going to be an all-boys band, due to practice hours and other things. We came to the conclusion it wouldn't be suitable to have ladies in the band," Randall added.

"Says who?" Steven asked.

"I say," Randall replied as he looked at the other musicians.

Alejandra felt disappointed, but she saw no point in disputing the decision, for she could sense her objections would go nowhere.

"And the singers?" Desirée asked.

"No female singers, either," Randall said.

"So, what was the point of inviting us to begin with?" Alejandra finally said with some defiance.

"We didn't think any of you would show up," Randall said disdainfully. "When was the last time you saw a girl in a band?"

This was true, she thought, and felt such impotence. She knew women couldn't even vote, but to be left out, in a school of all places, was upsetting. And then completely out of character, she summoned all her courage, for she knew she was taking on a powerful student, no other than the head of the student council and a senior.

"Well, I guess there will be two bands after all," she said.

"What do you mean?" Desirée asked her.

"Well, it's very simple—those who are not in Randall's band can join me in another band," she replied. His face turned red with anger at her gutsy response.

"You're quite humorous, little lady. I'll enjoy seeing you and your band," Randall said sarcastically.

"It's not my band, it's our band!" she said as she looked at some of the students.

"We will meet here tomorrow at the same time to discuss all the particulars," she said and left the room.

That night, she lay in her bed wondering if anyone would even show up. She must have been crazy to have done what she did with no experience, she thought. What will my cousin do? It must have been close to one o'clock in the morning when she finally fell asleep. The next morning she woke up with a stomach ache, and with such anxiety she thought she would not survive the day. When she went downstairs for breakfast, her mother took one look at her and said, "Ale, what's the matter, are you sick?"

"No, mother. I couldn't sleep very well last night."

"Why not?"

"I think I've done something quite daring," she said as she related the story to her mother.

"Well, it's not crazy, but it will be a challenge."

"I don't know if I can do it, but I will try my best," she said as she ate a bowl of fresh fruit.

"That is all we can do, our best," Lidia said to her daughter, patting her on the shoulder when she left for the kitchen.

Alejandra stayed there quietly, thinking about what she had done. Then she thought, if I can't stand up to one boy, how in the world will I stand in front of a room full of male musicians if I ever want to be a conductor? Somehow that thought gave her the strength she needed to go forward with her plan. She drank her glass of milk and left the house with her father, who was already waiting in the car for her.

During school, at lunch time, Franz and Olga sat with her. She could feel all eyes on her.

"We heard what happened yesterday. Are you going through with it?" Olga asked.

"I'm not sure, but I said so, and now I have to do it," she replied.

"That is very courageous on your part," Franz said.

"Thanks, but perhaps it's more foolish than courageous. We shall see," she said.

"Good luck," Olga said.

"Thank you, I'll need it," she replied.

As the end of the day approached while Alejandra was in math class, her hands were sweaty and her heart pounded as if it was about to explode. Maybe no one will show up. I will be humiliated but that will be the end of it, she thought as her teacher gave instructions for an upcoming quiz. When the class ended, she gathered all her books and slowly walked to the music room. She was five minutes early at 3:25 p.m. She sat on one of the chairs and looked up at the clock, and it was so quiet she could hear it ticking away: tick-tock, tick-tock... At 3:29 p.m., Desirée walked in. Alejandra sighed with relief; they could have a duet. Then two other students walked in; now they would have a quartet. By 3:35 p.m., six students sat around the table, except for Steven.

"Thank you all for coming," Alejandra said cheerfully.

"So now what?" Paul, the drummer, asked.

"Well, let's talk about it," she said as she wrote down their names and instruments.

"We have a violinist, a drummer, a bassist, a pianist, and two female vocalists," she said as she heard, "And one male vocalist." It was Steven. "Sorry I'm late," he said.

She felt like hugging her cousin, but she didn't.

"I was thinking about the ensemble last night. What type of music do you all want to play and sing? When do you want to practice? And so on," she asked the group. For the next twenty minutes the band discussed their preferences.

"And who will direct us?" Steven asked.

"Perhaps the choir director, Mrs. Sullivan," she said.

"Next week, bring your favorite sheet music, and together we will decide which pieces to practice first."

After all the students left, only Alejandra and Steven remained.

"I thought for a moment you weren't coming," she said.

"Do you think I'd abandon you? Remember, we were supposed to form a duet, except now it will be a complete ensemble," Steven said pleasantly.

She hugged her cousin. "Now don't get all sentimental on me," Steven said.

"Just this once, let me say you are more like a brother than a cousin," she said.

"I know, I feel the same way," he said. "Let's go home."

For the next two months the students met weekly for music practice. And as their recital was approaching, Randall Cunningham managed to secretly coerce the rest of the male students to join him in the band, and the boys could not refuse him. While greatly discouraged when she was informed of their decision, she thanked them for their participation and took the temporary setback with much grace, wanting to end on a good note. The opportunity to play with her fellow musicians was a very gratifying experience, she thought as they all said goodbye to each other before the last day of Christmas break. Fortunately, that day also brought welcome news when the principal published the findings and a resolution by the Minnesota Commission of Public Safety:

> From the 221 high schools surveyed, 198 of them used the German language as content and as instruction by the teachers. The Commission urges schools, boards, principals, and teachers as their patriotic duty, to require the use of the English language as the exclusive medium of instruction in all schools of Minnesota, and the prohibition of the use of all foreign languages, except as a language for religious instruction.

While this was no surprise for many teachers, it was a positive outcome, as everyone could return to some type of normalcy, even if it required major changes. After months of distress experienced by Olga, Franz, and their family, the hysteria over the German language had finally subsided and the Wensing twins were once again open to invitations.

On December 16, the Stanford family and their guests attended an afternoon concert at the Minneapolis Auditorium. The Symphony Orchestra opened its concert with the composition "America," as they always did, followed by "Don Juan's Serenade" by Tchaikovsky. Before the last performance, the orchestra played Grieg's "In the Hall of the Mountain King" from *Peer Gynt*, which turned out to be Franz' favorite piece.

Later, in the lobby of the concert venue while the three friends and Lidia waited for Edward to return with their coats, Franz said, "Thank you for inviting us tonight."

"It was our pleasure, and a most enjoyable evening." Lidia said.

"Yes indeed," Edward added as he joined them moments later, and gave them their coats. "We are very happy you came with us," he said. "It should be noted that some of the greatest contributions from German immigrants have been the development and enrichment of fine music in Minnesota since the last century—from the Danz orchestra to the University of Minnesota choirs to St. Paul's Schubert Club to the Minneapolis Symphony Orchestra."

"And don't forget Anna Schoen-René," Alejandra added.

"Yes, of course, how could we," Lidia said. "Perhaps you can join us next time we come."

"Yes, we would like that," Olga said as she wrapped her arm around Alejandra's arm, and together the group walked outside to the chilling cold.

After they dropped off Franz and Olga at their home, Lidia turned to her daughter and said, "I'm convinced that your natural talent and creativity are best expressed through music. I have finally found you a piano teacher who can provide additional training."

Her face lit up and she smiled. "Who is he, who is he?" she asked excitedly. "When do I start? You have no idea how much I've missed having lessons. I was wondering if you were ever going to take me seriously."

"What do you mean?" Edward asked as he continued to drive toward their house.

"I might want to be a concert pianist, or even . . . " Alejandra said without finishing.

"Even what?" her father asked.

She took a deep breath. "A conductor. There, I said it," she said, smiling.

While progressive in some areas, Edward was conservative in his views regarding the role of women, so he didn't consider that possibility. Lidia, however, had an independent spirit, more like her own father, which at times was a source of conflict between her and Edward.

"A little difficult, but it would be wonderful, Ale," her mother said.

Edward paused for a few moments and then said, "I suppose there is no harm in studying further, so long as you understand that certain roles are primarily for men."

"Forgive me, father, what about your philosophy, anything is possible?" his daughter questioned him.

"This is not the place nor time to discuss it."

"Yes, father," she replied, but his words and refusal to even discuss the matter made her momentarily question herself. Perhaps he was right, yet in her mind it was not impossible. She felt conflicted by his words, but at the moment it didn't matter, for he had agreed she could continue with her studies.

It was six o'clock in the morning when she woke up to the smell of cinnamon and freshly baked pastry. She got up and walked toward her window. The lights on the evergreen tree outside their residence were still on, and the tree sparkled like a star against the snow-covered ground. She turned on the light by her bedside and noticed a small box wrapped in green paper on the nightstand. Inside the small box she found a key, as she did when she was a child. As she put on her white feathered slippers to go downstairs, her mother knocked on the door and came in with a tray.

Lidia placed a cup of hot chocolate and a plate with apricot-filled scones by her bedside.

"Feliz cumpleaños, hijita (Happy birthday, daughter)," Lidia said as she embraced her daughter. Before she left the room, Alejandra playfully asked, "Mother, a key, what's it for?"

"To unlock the doors of the drawing room," Lidia said as she walked out of her room.

For a moment she stayed there, filled with curiosity. She put on her white woolen robe and then went downstairs into her father's library. Edward, who was always up before six in the morning, was sitting in his brown leather chair reading the newspaper. He seemed to be in a very good mood.

"Good Morning, Father."

With a mischievous smile, he said, "Happy birthday, Ale."

"Thank you, Papá." With the key in her hand, she kissed him on the cheek and asked, "Are you going to tell me what it is?"

"No! It's probably your piano teacher stored in a chest," he replied with a laugh.

Alejandra stepped out of the library and walked toward the locked double doors of the drawing room. She slowly unlocked and then opened them. There, in the center of the room in front of the arched bay windows she saw her gift, a black Steinway grand piano. She felt a tremendous thrill, as if a rush of energy had passed through her spinal cord—in fact, her whole body. She walked to the piano and gently caressed the keys as if they were made of velvet. And her usual serene composure dissolved when she saw her Abuelita Delia's sheet music scattered on the piano's wooden cover. A letter addressed to her lay among the scores of music. She quickly opened it and began to read:

> Dear Ale:
>
> Since you left the salón de música is quiet most days. We miss you, and hope this music will bring you as much happiness as you gave us playing it while you were here. When you play the music, think of us, your family in Mexico that deeply loves you, and wishes you a happiest fifteenth birthday. Among the sheet music you will find an original signed copy of the manuscript of the composition "Sobre Las Olas" by my favorite Mexican composer

Juventino Rosas. Enjoy the music, enjoy your *Quinceañera* (fifteenth birthday celebration).

Most lovingly, Your abuelitos, and Tia Carolina

Alejandra was so deeply moved, she kissed her grandparents' letter as if she were kissing them. A flood of tears came down her face as she sat down to play the piano. She took Juventino Rosas' sheet music, published by A. Wagner and Levien who were two businessmen from Hamburg, Germany, and who established their business in Mexico in the 1800s. "Sobre Las Olas" (Over the Waves) had been one of their most successful international publications. She remembered it from her conversations with her grandmother Delia, many years before, and she knew the manuscript was a family heirloom. At that moment her parents walked into the drawing room to hear her play the famous waltz.

In the evening, she and her family attended the traditional fifteenth birthday celebration similar to a debutante ball at her grandparents' home. When all the women arrived dressed in their beautiful gowns, they first went to the parlor on the second floor to fluff up their skirts and powder their cheeks. After twenty minutes had passed, the string quartet began to play the waltz "Alejandra" by Enrique Mora, and the ladies walked down the stairway, as if floating on air. The gentlemen waited at the foot of the steps.

Alejandra's white dress glittered, and her eyes sparkled as they did on her first birthday so many winters before. It was her father who took her by the hand to start the first dance. The rest of the evening she danced with members of her family and friends. Toward the end of the evening as she danced with Richard, he said, "Alejandra, we're having a New Year's celebration. Would you like to come?"

"Thank you Richard, we already have plans," she replied.

"You do! May I ask what plans?" he said.

"The museum is hosting quite an event," she said.

Richard's disappointment was shown by his peculiar tendency to burst into a derisive laughter. Then he said, irritated, "What nonsense! Perhaps you'll change your mind and come to our New Year's celebration."

Alejandra, still not favoring his company, attention, or manners, replied, "The museum is planning a night with costumed dancers, music, and Japanese fencing. Doesn't that sound like a most enchanting evening?" She smiled.

"Are Olga and Franz going, too?" he asked.

"Yes, and their family," she replied. And at the end of the dance, she quickly excused herself.

When the festivities ended a little before midnight and the guests said their farewells, still in the drawing room, Franz turned to her. "Ale, see you in a couple of weeks."

"Perhaps we'll all be there," Richard said to him.

Two weeks later on New Year's Eve, the Stanford and Wensing families attended the gala celebration at the Institute of Arts. With a crowd of several thousand people, many of whom were dressed in period costumes of English and Italian couture, they thought it was a most entertaining evening. When the clock struck midnight, Lidia said with a luminous face, "Feliz Año Nuevo (Happy New Year). May this new year bring our families together once again."

"What do you mean, Mother?"

"Your abuelitos and aunt are coming for your brother's baptism in the spring."

"What wonderful news," Alejandra said.

"Happy New Year to the two loveliest ladies in my life," Edward said.

8 America the Beautiful

The usual season of snow storms and freezing cold turned into a season of new beginnings, musical preludes, and warm winter nights. For in early January, Alejandra enrolled at MacPhail School of Music and Dramatic Arts. In her first lesson she met her new teacher, Robert Parker, a twenty-eight-year-old pianist from Chicago. The classroom on the second floor of the four-story building was small, yet engagingly appointed with walls covered in concert posters and photographs. The black upright piano had been recently purchased, so its ebony keys shined brightly in the otherwise dark room. The piano teacher, who was a slender, tall African-American man, was playing the piano when she entered the room. She quickly noticed his long fingers, which stretched to almost an octave and a half on the keyboard.

When he finished the piece, he pulled a chair next to him and asked her to sit down. He was affable and had a magnificent baritone voice, which she heard while listening to him sing before entering the room. He soon shared his biographical and musical background. Originally from New Orleans, he moved to Chicago when he was fifteen years old, and six years later he moved to Minnesota. He introduced her to the music of Jelly Roll Morton, Benjamin R. Harney, and Scott Joplin, and the unique sound of ragtime. Robert, an incredibly skilled pianist himself, played "Maple Leaf Rag" during the first lesson. Versed in early New Orleans music, African roots, and music history, he told her about the origins of ragtime.

"It has been said that ragtime initially derived from Cuban-African compositions such as *danza*, *seguidilla*, and the *habanera*. Even some of

Joplin's rags contained rhythms specific to the habanera. Sometime in the late 1890s, an orchestra composed of Mexican musicians named Orquesta Típica came to New Orleans to perform their own habaneras," he said.

"How interesting. I don't know much about popular music," she commented.

"Now, I should like to hear you play."

She played a variety of classical pieces, and while she wanted to expand her classical music repertoire, the highly syncopated style of ragtime captivated her. She liked the upbeat rhythm, and as before, Alejandra showed a streak of independence and curiosity, and expressed interest in learning how to master this unique musical style. She also desired to learn more popular music, including the danceable rhythms of fox trot and tango.

The new year had started with quite a blast, for besides her music lessons, a month later among the freshly fallen snow, she found a long, silver-colored box on her doorstep that she opened carefully. Inside, she found two roses, one white and one red, and an anonymous note that read: "Your eyes are full of beauty and wonder."

This Valentine's Day, shrouded in mystery, sparked a new light in Alejandra. For the rest of the day she pondered who might be the person who sent the roses. She then recalled that she and Steven had invited several of their friends for dinner that very night. Throughout the day while in school, she looked for clues from everyone she knew, but nothing emerged. When the evening came, she was anxious to receive them all. Among the guests who came were former band members, Olga, Franz, and Steven.

Later that night, after they all ate Milly's specialty gooseberry pudding for dessert, Steven suggested the former music ensemble perform "Kiss Me Again" by V. Herbert, to which they all enthusiastically agreed. The group of seven musicians had brought their instruments at Steven's request and they gathered around the piano, and Desirée and Steven sang a fantastic vocal duet that made Olga very jealous, and even more flirtatious than usual with the other student musicians as she flaunted her low-cut dress. Steven did not take it well, yet kept his composure, as he and the ensemble performed the last song. When they all said goodbye to each other at the end of the night, she was still left with the mystery of the roses, but decided not to ask her cousin if he knew anything when she saw him sitting sullenly on the sofa after everyone left.

"What's wrong?" she asked as she patted him on his arm.

"Ale, do you think you can talk to Olga about her behavior tonight? Does she like me or not?" he asked her.

"Steven, she likes you, although she thinks you like Desirée, too," she said.

"I like them both."

"Well, you better make up your mind," she told him.

"I really don't like her lack of modesty. She's going to give someone the wrong signals," he said.

"What do you mean?" she asked.

"Oh! Never mind," he replied.

"Thank you for inviting all the band members tonight," she said.

"It was a good ending for our band," Steven said. "I know how heartbroken you were after the group was dismantled."

"Maybe a little. We'll try again in the fall. I'm not giving up," Alejandra said as she hugged her cousin.

"We can still have our duet," he said playfully.

"Yes, of course," she replied.

"But for now, don't be upset. We have much to look forward to with my brother's baptism," she said. "My grandparents are coming from Mexico, and we need to start addressing invitations. We can also use your help when planting flowers."

"Yes, I'm happy to do it. Let me know when," he said.

"We will," she said.

"See you on Monday," he replied as he said goodbye and left the room.

She stayed there a few more moments, wondering if she would ever know the identity of the person who sent her the roses.

It was mid-May when Edward unloaded dozens of flower pots and planters from his car and placed them in the front yard. Gardening was his and his daughter's annual tradition, which he started when she was five years old. Since then, every year he planted dozens of hearty winter plants such as lilacs, dogwoods, and hostas, but that morning Edward was more enthusiastic than usual, for in a few days his family and friends would come together to celebrate his son's baptism. He had waited for years to have a son, and now as he approached midlife, he was the father of a nine-month-old boy, and happy as ever.

He went to the back shed and retrieved all the necessary tools for the work ahead. As he compiled heavy boots, gloves, sun hats, shovels, black dirt, and large containers, Alejandra and Steven joined him. They first cleaned the dead branches of perennial plants from the previous year. They then planted beds of geraniums, variegated brunnera, lavender and Casablanca lilies, daffodils, Persian blue alliums, and clusters of impatiens, pansies, and petunias, and a maple tree in the front yard dedicated to the new member of the family. Edward had created his own version of an English garden with rose bushes and hydrangea shrubs. For Alejandra, seeing the blooms of annual and perennial plants every year was all worthwhile, even if at times it seemed like lots of work. Her favorite were the fragrant hyacinths and lemon verbenas, which exuded the most powerful scent.

A few days later, the Merino family arrived in Minnesota and witnessed a colorful and magnificent landscape on the grounds of the Stanford residence. When the day of the baptism finally arrived on the third Saturday of the month, the garden was a rainbow of red and purple blossoms, as were the dresses of the ladies attending this most anticipated family gathering. Alejandra and her mother wore almost matching soft blue laced gowns, while Delia and Clara wore pale purple gowns with floral prints and embroidered hats. However, it was Carolina who looked the most stunning as the godmother to be with her yellow chiffon dress. And for the first time in more than two years, she had stopped wearing black.

Early in the morning, the two extended families drove their vehicles in a procession to the Cathedral of St. Paul and joined friends for the baptism of Edward George Stanford. As they walked into the splendid religious structure, a magnificent example of classical Renaissance-style architecture recently constructed, Edward felt a certain jubilation knowing that his former teacher, Emmanuel Louis Masqueray, had designed and overseen the construction of the cathedral after he moved from New York to Minnesota. The 186-foot-high dome and central interior space, while immense, were inviting and inspiring, Alejandra thought when she first walked into the enormous nave of the cathedral.

Edward and Lidia chose the Chapel of the Blessed Virgin Mary as the site of the religious ritual. As the family surrounded baby Edward before the small altar, the Merino family was visibly affected by the moment when Carolina held her nephew in her arms and gently kissed him on the forehead. Her countenance was peaceful and loving when Father Flannery spattered water upon Edward's curly hair and pronounced his name as he bestowed baptismal rights. Little Edward smiled happily.

Alejandra looked up at the stained glass as the eastern light pierced through one of the three windows, illuminating the image of the Annunciation. And she couldn't help but remember her cousin Sol all those years ago. Now her family was together once again under very pleasant circumstances. Edward's life was indeed a miracle of God, and the presence of the Stanford and Merino families witnessing this moment had an ephemeral quality to it. After the ceremony ended, and before the families left to return to the Stanfords' residence, Alejandra took her abuelitos through the ambulatory section of the cathedral to the Shrines of the Nations. As the Merino family stopped at each of the shrines and admired the sculptures, their granddaughter read from the cathedral's brochure.

> The Shrines commemorate six of the cultural groups that first settled in Minnesota; the Italians represented by Saint Anthony, the French by Saint John the Baptist, the Irish by Saint Patrick, the Germans by St. Boniface, the Slavs by Saints Cyril and Methodius, and the patron of missionaries, Saint Therese of Lisieux.

Later, on a sunny afternoon with the scent of flowers and spring in the air, Edward and Lidia hosted the baptismal celebration. A large group of family and friends came together, including a most unexpected guest. While she was talking to her maternal grandparents, she saw him approach her.

"Alejandra, glad to see you again," he said as he entered the front porch.

"Thank you, Richard. These are my grandparents, Calixto and Delia Merino from Mexico," she said as she sat next to them on the wicker bench.

"It's a pleasure to meet you both," he said as he took off his hat respectfully. "I hope you don't mind I came here today. Steven suggested it."

"No, everyone is welcome," she replied.

In that instant, Richard, who was still standing by the door, noticed several little boys playing ball in the front yard when a very small child began to run toward the street to catch the ball, which was rolling away. Richard ran off the porch and stopped the boy seconds before a fast-moving Overland model 54 vehicle could have run him over. He picked up the boy and brought him back to his mother who was yelling, "Stop, Billy, stop!"

"Young man, thank you so much. You've prevented a terrible accident," the boy's mother said as she took her son from Richard's arms. "Thank goodness my little Billy is all right."

When Alejandra was about to leave the porch to join Richard in the front yard, Franz arrived at the scene and said, "Pardon me, Ale, your mother needs you in the parlor."

For the rest of the morning, Richard attempted to talk to her, and while she noticed his intense gaze upon her and their eyes met briefly, Franz was always with her. Finally, Richard approached her.

"I must leave now," he said as he bid goodbye to her and the rest of the family.

"Yes, thank you for coming. You did something extraordinary today," she remarked.

His fast action and concern certainly saved what could have been a disaster, and his attitude seemed much more pleasant than it had in the past, Alejandra thought as she saw him walk away.

Soon after, Carolina announced the buffet lunch was being served in the dining room.

Two hours later when the guests were in the drawing room enjoying a variety of pastries, including Lidia's famous apple *empanadas* and coffee, Delia Merino, who had made a remarkable recovery from her illness, performed several selections on the piano, including Manuel Ponce's "Strellita" and Brahms' "Lullaby."

It was almost four o'clock in the afternoon when all the guests had left and only the immediate family stayed behind in the drawing room. "I have something for you, Edward," Lidia said as she brought out a large wrapped package and gave it to him. He looked her in the eyes, surprised. "What do we have here?" he asked.

"Something you asked me for a long time ago!" Lidia replied.

As he tore open the wrapping paper, he unveiled a new painting with a gilded frame. He was speechless at the sight of his own image sitting on a wooden chair and surrounded by a rose garden similar to the one in their own house. Lidia, who was an admirer of the Dutch style of portraiture painting, applied a similar technique to all her paintings. And it was always the eyes that were the focus of her work, as she applied lights and darks to enhance their expression. While the painting was not of a dramatic nature, it conveyed emotion. Edward's gray-blue eyes expressed infinite kindness as he stared into the distance. She had worked on his portrait for almost five months in secrecy. Edward put the painting aside, walked toward his wife who was standing by the window, and kissed her hand. The rest of the family looked at the portrait.

"Lidia, this is, perhaps, your best painting yet," Delia said.

"I think all her paintings are gorgeous and demonstrate richness and a style of her own. Furthermore, she should exhibit them publicly."

"Thank you, my dear, but not now. Perhaps in the future," she said. "However, we will have the opportunity to show one of the paintings in our collection," she said with a mischievous smile. "The Society of Fine Arts has requested its members submit a list of their art possessions, including sculptures, tapestries, old furniture, fine jewelry, rugs, you name it."

"For what purpose?" Delia asked.

"I suppose they would like to catalogue important artworks owned in Minneapolis," Lidia replied.

"Will there be an exhibition?" Calixto asked.

"Yes, in June," Lidia replied.

"Which pieces are you considering loaning?" Edward asked.

"Certainly, *El Paseo de los Melancólicos* by Diego Rivera," she replied.

"Abuelito, how did you come into possession of this painting?" Alejandra asked.

"I attended his first exhibition in Mexico City in 1904, when he was a young boy, maybe seventeen years old. I thought at the time he was an artist with great talent and charisma, so I purchased two of his paintings, this one in the drawing room and the self portrait in the hacienda's library," he said.

"Yes, indeed, Diego Rivera is already gaining international recognition, for just last December, one of his portraits was showcased at the Museum of Modern Art in New York," Edward said.

"What portrait was that?" Lidia asked.

"That of his Russian companion, Angeline Beloff," Edward replied.

Lidia loved Rivera's landscape painting, and was hesitant to part with it, if only for a short time, but she decided to submit it for the upcoming loaned exhibition. She knew well it was best when private collections were shared with the general public. She also submitted two other valuable art objects for consideration, an original bronze bust of Beethoven—a gift from Edward to Lidia on their first wedding anniversary—and a seventeenth-century Belgium tapestry with an illustration of the Venetian Grand Canal, a wedding gift from Calixto and Delia.

In June, the Merino and Stanford families attended the exhibition at the museum. It had become a tradition to visit there the last Saturday of every month. Lidia in particular appreciated the knowledgeable staff and the tour guides who showed profound respect for the art and all the cultures represented, not to mention the opportunity to keep up-to-date with the world of fine art.

On this occasion there was also an exhibition by American painters. Don Calixto was impressed with the portrait of President Wilson by John Singer Sargent. Delia loved his painting titled *Madame Ramon Subercaseaux*, which depicted the portrait of a young brunette woman sitting by the piano wearing a white flamenco-style dress. Lidia commented that during their monthly visits, each family member chose a favorite work of art from the museum's permanent or loaned collections, which Alejandra methodically recorded in her notebooks. She later researched the stories behind the paintings or wrote down a brief summary of the museum's label. Don Calixto was very pleased to see that he had successfully transmitted his love of history to his young granddaughter.

Later in the month, Edward and Lidia took the Merino family to various important sights in Minnesota, including St. Anthony and Minnehaha falls. A new bronze sculpture of Hiawatha had recently been erected in the park, funded by school children. The next day they boarded the train to Northfield, Minnesota, to see the nationally recognized Goodsell Observatory located at Carleton College. Edward commented that it was considered one of the leading time stations in the United States and possessed various astronomical instruments, a telescope, and other innovations that accurately measured the positions of the planets and the stars. The observatory also provided the most precise time to all the railroads operating in Minnesota. The family then visited the Two Harbors Light Station, and the famous Gothic-style house of Paul Watkins in Winona, Minnesota.

Several days later, to complete the tour, Edward took Calixto to the grounds of Peavey Grain Company in St. Louis Park, Minnesota. As a former businessman in the production of sugar, he was interested in the latest technology on grain storage as a possible future business venture. When they arrived at the main site of the grain company, Don Calixto saw a massive concrete elevator, which was the first of its kind, designed by Mr. Frank H. Peavey and erected by him and architect Charles F. Haglin. "Some may not consider it interesting," Edward remarked. "But this elevator's design revolutionized the way grain was stored throughout the world."

"Isn't Peavey where your father works?" Calixto asked.

"Yes."

"I would like to talk more about this with him," Calixto added.

"Next week he and my mother will host a Fourth of July celebration," Edward said. "However, I can also arrange a lunch meeting with him."

"Thanks, that won't be necessary," Calixto said.

Before their departure back to Mexico, the Merino family attended their first American independence celebration at the residence of George and Clara Stanford. As they sat down for dinner in the elegant dining room, George said grace and then made his usual eloquent toast. It had become a type of competition between him and his son, as to who could come up with the most clever phrase.

"Welcome to the Merino family, and as I may borrow from the words of Dickens or Twain, 'I wish thee health, I wish thee wealth, I wish thee gold in store, I wish thee heaven upon earth, what could I wish thee more?'" he said.

To which Edward replied with an anonymous quote, "He only is generous whose gift, by willing hand proffered, is swift."

All the guests laughed and called it a tie. Moments later, Mr. Minty and Lena brought out several platters containing an assortment of traditional summer dishes, including grilled steak, chicken, hamburgers, cold slaw, baked beans, corn soufflé, and for dessert, Clara's famous walnut brownies. While she and Delia could not communicate directly due to a language barrier, George and Calixto, who were sitting next to each other, found many topics in common.

"I hope you and your family have enjoyed summer in Minnesota," George said to Calixto.

"Yes, having all our family together has been delightful. Edward and Lidia have taken us to see a variety of interesting attractions, including your company's headquarters. I understand the grain business is very important in Minnesota," Calixto said. "I'd like to know more about it."

"Well, since you're a history buff, let's start from the beginning. Frank H. Peavey founded Peavey Grain Company. His avid business acumen brought him to Minnesota to establish Peavey Grain Company in Minneapolis," George said.

Steven interrupted. "So it is Peavey Grain Company and your hard work, Grandpa, that we should thank for such good fortune?"

"Most certainly, it's a great company to work for. Moreover, Minnesota as a whole has immensely prospered from this industry and dozens of flour mills. Minnesota is known as the "flour milling capital of the world, as coined by the London *Times*. Some would say the flour mills were one of Minnesota's first and utmost important industries," George added.

"Grandfather, where is Mr. Peavey now?" Alejandra asked.

"He passed away years ago. Coincidently, his son George was one of the financial backers or supporters of the Minneapolis Symphony Orchestra, and his daughter Mary Drew Peavey Wells donated four paintings to the Society of Fine Arts in his memory," George said.

"Do you know who the artists were?" Lidia asked.

"No, the only one I remember is Charles Daubigny. It was a painting of a river scene and I once saw it at an exhibition. And Mr. Peavey was also well known for his philanthropy and strong work ethic. He believed in helping those who could help themselves. According to an obituary article, he made an interesting proposition to the Minneapolis newsboys," George said.

"What proposition?" Steven asked.

"'For every dollar they deposited in the Northwestern Bank, he deposited an equal amount. It is said he took personal interest in each one of them, and wanted to impress upon the young men the wisdom of saving at an early age,'" George said.

"There's a beautiful Peavey memorial fountain in the intersection of Lake of the Isles and Kenwood boulevards," Edward said.

As George and Don Calixto continued to converse for another hour about the grain business in Minnesota, Edward suggested everyone else step into the drawing room for a chess game competition.

When all the family reunited later in the evening, the much-talked-about Stanford duet finally made its appearance. Alejandra performed on the piano "America the Beautiful," and Steven sang, "O, beautiful, for spacious skies, for amber waves of grain..."

The family, many of whom had never heard him sing, was astounded by Steven's clear and powerful tenor voice. And George, who was very patriotic, was extremely proud of his two grandchildren and their heart-felt performance. When the cousins finished with their musical program, Edward reminded everyone that they would need to leave soon to find a good spot by the lake to see the fireworks.

"Which lake?" Steven asked.

"Calhoun," he said.

"But be sure to wear long sleeves, for the mosquitoes are ruthless," Steven added.

"Happy Fourth of July," Edward said with his usual laughter.

Two days later, the Merino family departed for Mexico. Lidia, however, convinced her sister to stay through the holiday season. Carolina, who was still very much in mourning, reluctantly agreed.

Pack up Your Troubles in Your Old Kit Bag

Grow to my lip, thou sacred kiss, On which my soul's beloved swore, that there should come a time of bliss, when she would mock my hopes no more, and fancy shall thy glow renew . . .

—by Thomas Moore

Alejandra received this poem, scribbled on parchment paper, on the morning of her first day of school. Since last June, she and Franz had seen each other often throughout the summer. They had frequently walked together around the various Minneapolis lakes, and sometimes conversed until dusk. Franz was her kindred spirit and shared her love for the arts, but it was their mutual desire to discover the world that brought them closer as friends. She played all her cherished music for him and showed him her favorite paintings, and he shared with her the poems of Robert Frost, William Yeats, and others. They possessed a youthful idealism, and talked endlessly about the philosophies of Enlightenment, and the writings of Rousseau, Voltaire, Hume, and others.

But on that morning what she had on her mind, once again, was the music club. The experience of performing with other students had been exciting and challenging the previous year, and she thought perhaps she and other students could form another music ensemble. Randall Cunningham had left the school after his graduation and therefore she did not see any obstacles. That afternoon, after school, a total of twenty student musicians attended the music club's meeting and decided to form an ensemble composed of pianists, guitarists, a string quartet, wind-instrument players, a drummer, and several singers.

As in the previous years, Mr. Fischer and Mrs. Sullivan agreed to serve as co-directors of the ensemble. After a successful start, and having met six times, the group shared the camaraderie that comes from making music together. Unfortunately, their exhilarating experience was cut short once again, when on October 13, 1918, all the Minneapolis schools, churches, and theaters were closed immediately due to the flu pandemic that was sweeping all of America and the world. All public gatherings were prohibited. The influenza was a horrendous disaster as thousands of Minnesotans became ill.

For the next few days, Alejandra and her classmates stayed home. When the school finally re-opened, she learned Desirée, one of the vocalists of the ensemble, had become infected with the virus. As a result all the parents prohibited their children from getting together for band practice. After two weeks, fortunately, her friend recovered, but since the epidemic was just taking hold everywhere, teachers and students alike agreed to dismantle the band, at least until the devastating illness subsided.

The only hopeful event that fall was the end of the Great War on November 11. Early in the morning of November 12, Steven loudly knocked on the door of the Stanfords' residence. After Milly their housekeeper opened it, he asked to see his cousin. As he waited in the small parlor, she came down in her pajamas and slippers.

"Ale, Ale, hurry and get dressed, come with me. There's something incredible happening in downtown Minneapolis," Steven said.

"What?" she asked.

"Hundreds of people are pouring into the streets to celebrate the end of the war," he said.

"What about the influenza?" she asked.

"It seems everyone has forgotten about it, for today, anyway," he replied.

"Let's go, we'll be fine."

Alejandra went upstairs to ask for her father's permission to leave the house, and he reluctantly agreed. Steven waited for a few minutes until she came down dressed in winter clothing, wearing a brown woolen hat that covered nearly all her forehead and a beige scarf wrapped around her neck.

"Steven, don't stay out too long, and please be careful," Edward said as he came down the steps behind his daughter.

"I can't believe my father let me go," she said as she and Steven drove away.

"Ale, we need to pick up Richard," he said.

She frowned, and said, "Is he coming, too?"

"Yes, of course, he was the one who suggested I come to get you," Steven said laughingly. She rolled her eyes in disapproval.

"Oh! Steven, you should have told me. I would have stayed home."

"Ale, it will be all right," he said.

When they stopped at Richard's house on Mount Curve Avenue, also in the Lowry Hill neighborhood, Steven asked, "Ale, you want to come in?"

"No thanks, I'll wait in the car," she said.

As she waited, she looked at the stately Mediterranean mansion that looked to be twice the size of her own residence. She was not impressed by the size, or even the apparent luxury of it, but instead admired the architecture. The Renaissance-style home, mostly constructed of stone quarry, was gorgeous, like a house in an Italian city. The façade included a balustrade on the front porch, pediments over the arched windows, and Doric columns.

The classical-looking structure was elegant and very appealing visually, thought Alejandra. She had seen many different architectural styles in the books in her father's library, although this architectural style was perhaps her favorite. She looked toward the equally impressive landscape and a large hedge by the entrance door as Steven and Richard walked out of the house. When Richard stepped into the automobile he said, "Alejandra, good morning. I'm so pleased you agreed to come."

"Good morning, Richard. I didn't know you were coming," she said playfully.

The three students drove past Hennepin Avenue, and Steven parked the car in an alley. Together they walked toward the center of town, and slowly but steadily thousands of men, women, and children flocked the streets in the rarest of spectacles in Minneapolis. For one day, there was no sign of the dreaded pandemic. It was a carnival of sorts, with people singing, laughing, and weeping. Some passersby blew their horns and rang bells. Even rainbows of confetti fell from the sky like snow in a winter storm. The chattering was loud, as many yelled out, "The war is over, the war is over." It was as though people were breathing a huge sigh of relief, and finally expressing themselves freely.

The happiness was contagious, and Steven and Richard ran into many of their friends, some of whom came accompanied by their families. As she took in the gaiety around her, Alejandra noticed the bare trees. And while it was cold, she felt the full warmth of the sun hovering over the large crowds of people. It was a magical scene she would remember for years to come as she, her friends, and dozens of other students hugged each other and begin to happily and loudly sing, "Pack up your troubles in your old kit bag . . . "

After spending most of the day on and about the streets of downtown, only Steven's voracious appetite took them away, and as they walked down the street, Alejandra was gratified. After all, she was there with her cousin and his friend to share with each other and the rest of Minnesotans this magnificent celebration of peace in the world.

Unfortunately that euphoric feeling vanished a few weeks later, as the flu epidemic raged on. Clara Stanford became infected with the influenza. George ordered relatives to stay away from their home, but early in December, in another tragic turn of fate, Clara Stanford succumbed to the viral illness. As the news spread, the family gathered at Edward and Lidia's house to comfort one another. The sadness pervaded their home as if water had flooded every inch of it, and while Lidia tried to offer some consolation through prayer, Edward was devastated. He excused himself to his office to cry. As the sibling closest to his mother and the oldest of the family, he made all the funerary arrangements despite his wrenching pain.

On December 10, the Stanford family and a small of group of friends attended the funeral service of Clara Rose Stanford at St. Anthony de Padua Catholic Church. It was once again another unexpected event in their lives, and as Edward stood in front of the podium to give the eulogy, his eyes welled up with tears and the look on his face was profoundly sorrowful. Several times he paused before he could even utter the first words.

"My mother was a gift to all of us, not only because of her love, cleverness, and beauty, or even her delicious cuisine which we all thoroughly enjoyed, but mostly she was a gift because she let those around her be themselves . . . "

That was the first time Alejandra saw her father cry as he spoke in a broken voice, barely containing his emotions.

"May the good Lord keep her in his care," he added as he sullenly looked at his father George, who didn't speak a word. But her father's words gave Alejandra and the rest of the family some measure of acceptance, and his final words lingered in her ear. "She let those around her be themselves." What did he mean by that, she asked herself. As the priest read from Clara's favorite biblical passages, Edward and the others tried their best to contain their pain, until George let out a gripping moan that allowed the family to fully express their grief, and soon everyone began to cry. Lidia held her husband's hand as he continued to weep until almost the end of the service.

By the middle of December, the schools were closed once again, and there was general apprehension everywhere. The holiday season felt heavy and grim. Edward, Lidia, Alejandra, Carolina, and baby Edward had a quiet Christmas dinner. It was the most solemn of days. The only bright light was in the giggles of little Edward when he saw his Christmas gift in the drawing room, an electric train with real "choo-choo" sounds.

What a wonderful thing it is to be a child, Alejandra thought as she heard her brother's innocent laughter while he threw himself on the floor and watched the train go around in circles. Perhaps that's what her father meant when he spoke at her grandmother's funeral. It is comforting to be able to express ourselves freely, unfettered by prejudice and rigid norms. On that note, the year ended.

Minneapolis, 1919

The death of Clara had left an immense void in their family. George became a recluse, and his once happy disposition evolved into downright depression. Edward and his family visited him twice weekly, but even his grandson could not lift his spirits. Margaret and Lidia had the painful task of putting away Clara's belongings and storing them in the attic, for George did not want them given away. He insisted that they each divide up her jewelry, something that Lidia strongly resisted. She thought it distasteful, but Edward encouraged it and also insisted that his mother's favorite cameo ring be given to her only granddaughter.

While the situation was indeed sad for the family, it became even more precarious when Alejandra herself became ill with influenza. The family feared the outcome might also be fatal. After she spent almost two weeks in the hospital, her fever begin to subside, but only a little, and when they returned home, they placed her in quarantine for another week for good measure. Daily visits and extra caution from the doctor reassured them everything possible was being done.

On the first night she returned from the hospital, and against the doctor's orders, Lidia lay asleep next to her daughter, who at times still had a high fever. She couldn't conceive her child would be taken away, as her sister's child had. She lay there, praying for hours and gripping her rosary. Lidia hadn't always been obsessively religious, but in times of anguish and pain, as people do, she turned to her faith. She stared at her daughter, gently touching her strands of hair while she slept, praying and hoping she would see the next day.

Oddly, a few days later on February 14, a package was left at the Stanford's doorstep. Milly brought it upstairs and placed it outside Alejandra's bedroom. As she picked up a tray with dirty dishes she knocked on the door. "Miss Ale, there is a package here for you," she said.

"Thank you, Milly," Alejandra said faintly from her bedroom.

At that time she was alone, and once she heard Milly's steps on the staircase, she opened the door and took the silver-colored box. Shivering, she sat on her bed and removed the cover of the box, finding red and white roses. Alejandra read the anonymous note, as if for the first time: "Your eyes are filled with beauty and wonder." She thought about the last word, wonder, and couldn't help but wonder herself if she would ever know who the roses were from, or even if she would ever see her family and friends again.

The situation seemed surreal, and just then she brought the roses to her cracked lips, kissing them and smelling their sweet fragrance. She then cut off the stem with her fingers and accidently pricked herself with the sharp thorns of the rose. A drop of blood, as if in slow motion, fell on her white nightgown. She took a deep breath, as if gasping for one last breath of fresh air. She walked toward her dresser and looked at her sickly complexion in the mirror. Her sunken eyes, with dark circles underneath them, stared back at her.

Not entirely immune to vanity, she placed the red rose behind her ear, still shivering, and combed through her tangled auburn hair which fell loosely on her shoulders. Then she dropped the hair brush on the floor and, tired and weak, she walked a few steps to the window and kneeled by the bench, as she prayed for her family and their health. She got up and lay on the bed as she reached out her hand, gently grabbing the white rose from the box and placing it next to her as she rested her head on the plush pillow. She closed her eyes until she fell asleep in the warm winter morning sunlight.

The Blue Danube

One weekday morning, Lidia and Carolina attended their daily morning mass at the Cathedral of Saint Paul. When the mass ended, they met Lidia's friend Marianne Miller. The three ladies conversed for a short time, as they stood in one of the side entrances. Marianne, who was very much involved with settlement houses since 1912, informed Lidia of a new one in West St. Paul. It had opened the previous year under the direction of Canadian-born Constance Currie.

The settlement house served a variety of immigrants from Europe, most recently from Mexico. During World War I, many had come to Minnesota to work on the meat-packing plants in St. Paul and as farmers, growing sugar beets. Lidia was very interested in helping in some way, but at the time she had her hands full. Carolina noted that her plans to return to Mexico in December had been thwarted by the horrendous epidemic. "I have plenty of time. Do you think I could meet with Miss Currie? Perhaps I can help in some way," Carolina said to Marianne.

"Yes, I think that would be great. There's much need and work to be done, and I'm sure Miss Currie will appreciate any assistance," Marianne said.

When Lidia and Carolina returned home they met Franz at the door.

"Good morning, Mrs. Stanford and Mrs. Merino," Franz said.

"Good morning, Franz. I'm afraid there is no change in her condition, although we are praying every day she'll make a full recovery," Lidia said.

"Yes indeed, Mrs. Stanford, I will visit again tomorrow," he said. "Please tell her I was here."

"We certainly will," Lidia said.

Later in the morning, Milly, quite amused, informed Lidia that several days before Franz and Richard showed up at their house at the same time. When Milly opened the door, she saw two very disgruntled faces when they encountered each other. After that incident, Franz came in the morning, while Richard came in the afternoon.

"Milly, you must tell Ale, when she's well again. I know our good Lord will grant me my pleas," Lidia said with a hopeful smile.

As spring came, Carolina Merino was doing volunteer work eight to ten hours a day at the settlement house. She had found Miss Currie to be one of the kindest persons she had ever met, particularly with the Mexican immigrants. Carolina had organized a clothing drive, prepared and served meals, translated documents from English to Spanish, and even started a class to teach English to all the newcomers. She seemed to have found a new calling and a new purpose in her life.

In early May, a new wing of the settlement house was being finished. A blond, tall, and slender twenty-nine-year-old carpenter was working on a window trim when he spotted Carolina from across the room. She was standing by her desk in one of the offices, preparing for class.

Anthony, the carpenter, felt an immediate attraction toward the mysterious brunette woman who kept to herself. "Do you know who the lady is over there?" the man asked his coworker.

"I don't," he replied.

For the next few days, Anthony came to work early, hoping for the chance to see her. That opportunity arrived when Carolina, distracted by her own thoughts, did not see a piece of molding lying carelessly across the entrance door of the settlement house. She tripped, but did not fall.

"Oh my goodness," she said, as she picked up the trim piece and walked toward the carpenter crew in the new room.

In an angry tone she said to the men, "I believe you'll need this!"

"Forgive me, miss, I don't know what I was thinking by leaving it on the floor. Are you all right?" one of the men asked. When she saw his face, blushing with genuine embarrassment, she said, "Oh, yes, I'm fine. Fortunately nothing happened, and I was distracted, too."

He wiped his dusty hands on a rag hanging from his belt and bowed his head. "I'm Anthony Solberg. Pleased to meet you," he said. Carolina paused for a second when she heard his name.

"Solberg?" she asked.

"Yes, Solberg, it's a Swedish name," he said.

Carolina stood there in silence for a moment. "Does it have a meaning?" she asked.

"It means sunny hill," Anthony replied.

"Oh, that is a lovely name," she said with sadness in her voice, as she walked out of the room.

"Miss, miss, what's your name?"

"Carolina Merino."

Since that day, Carolina Merino and Anthony Solberg became friends. He was exactly the kind of man she needed to bring out her once gregarious personality. Anthony, who was relaxed but shy, allowed her to speak her mind and express herself openly. Perhaps being away from her home and all her tragic past gave her the freedom she needed, and learned to embrace. Yet her heart still belonged to her homeland.

On their third date, Carolina waited in the parlor of her sister's home for Anthony to arrive. She was reading a book, a gift from her friend, Marianne Miller, about the suffrage movement. A few minutes later she heard a knock on the door, and then proceeded to open it, for Milly was gone for the day. There, dressed in his Sunday best, she found Anthony holding a bouquet of red carnations.

"Good afternoon, Carolina, these are for you," he said.

"Hello, Anthony, thank you. Please wait here, let me put them in water."

A few minutes later, she returned.

"It's a beautiful spring day for a tour," he said with a smile. "I have much to show you. Shall we?"

After they walked down to the street, Anthony opened the door of a horse-drawn carriage. He then checked the straps on the horse, and stepped up onto the center of the carriage. He took the reins and steered the old horse straight down the street. After almost two hours of riding past the lakes and on busy Hennepin Avenue, Anthony brought Carolina to his carpentry shop along the Mississippi River as they crossed the Stone Arch Bridge.

Anthony, who had not had an advanced education, was a hard worker and proud of his skills in the construction of wood furniture. His father still worked for one of the sawmills on the east side of the river, and lumber work was all Anthony had known since he was a boy. When they arrived at his workshop on the west side of the river, he helped her out of the carriage. As a lover of horses, Carolina carefully approached the old-looking horse with white markings, and petted him on the shoulder.

"He's as gentle as he seems," Anthony said to her.

"What breed?" She asked.

"Appaloosa," he said.

"And his name?"

"Wild One," Anthony said, laughing as he noticed her expression, for the name didn't go with the horse's temperament.

"He was a wild one in his younger days, but became mild with age."

Before they proceeded to his workshop, she noticed a worn-down stable in the distance.

"I'd like to go there," she said.

"Yes, but first there is something I'd like to show you in my workshop," Anthony said.

When they walked in, Carolina saw a very cluttered but clean space with chairs and tables stacked one on top of the other. The furniture seemed to be made of a variety of wood species, including maple, pine, and American white oak. The smell of freshly cut wood was a reminder of the carpentry shops back in her parents' hacienda in Cuernavaca.

"So here it is! Doesn't look like much, but between my work as a trimmer and furniture maker, it's enough for a decent living for me, and sometimes, even enough to help my family," he said proudly.

"Yes, you're a very good craftsman," Carolina said as she observed his work, and passed her fingers through one of the unique carvings on the dusty chair. "The carving on the furniture is impressive," she said.

"Thank you," he said.

They left the carpentry workshop and walked toward the stable, and Carolina imagined herself riding her horse El Noble across the fields of her native land.

"Oh how I miss home and my horse," she said.

"Perhaps next time we can ride to St. Paul," he said.

"Yes, I'd like that very much," she said as they reached the stable. She entered it, and the smell of hay transported her once again to Cuernavaca, but this time, it was the memory of when she and her son entered the stable on the fatal day he died. Sol had grabbed a bunch of hay in his hand, and then playfully threw it up in the air, minutes before his accident. From that sorrowful memory which she had suppressed deep in her unconscious, she began to cry profusely, as if she had been restraining her emotions for years. Anthony, who had no knowledge of her grievous past, was overtaken with compassion, for she seemed ever so fragile and vulnerable.

"Carolina, I don't understand. What's the matter?" he asked as he surrounded her with his arms, and then together they walked to a bench outside the stable and sat down. She recounted her story, and the deaths of both her husband and son.

"You are so brave," he said as he looked into her eyes.

"How am I brave?" she asked in disbelief.

"To have come here, and to work the way you do with all those families, volunteering up to fifty hours a week, when you could be back home," he said.

"The work here has been a blessing. It has helped me to deal with my feelings," she said.

Anthony now understood Carolina's sometimes aloof and sad demeanor. There was always something mysterious about her, which was alluring. For her part, Carolina felt comforted by his words and his gentle manners. A new feeling she had not felt since her husband's death emerged. When they returned to the Stanford's residence, Anthony kissed her while still in the carriage, and she reciprocated.

Sometime later in the month, Carolina, Lidia, and Alejandra, who thankfully survived the influenza, attended a conference sponsored by the Minnesota Woman's Suffrage Association, which was founded in 1881. Their friend Marianne Miller, who was one of the keynote speakers, eloquently spoke about the work of Clara Hampson Ueland and dozens of other supporters of the movement.

"Since its inception, the MWSA has organized marches, rallies, speeches, and appeals to legislators. The campaign for women's right to vote in the United States is on the verge of fulfilling its mission. We ask for your continued support in this most just cause," she said as she went on to talk about the history of the organization and the progress they had made.

When she finished, Lidia elatedly said to her daughter, "We are living in extraordinary times. The beginning of this century has brought us tremendous advances in industry and technology, as your father frequently says, but we are also seeing advances in moral causes. Imagine that if Congress is indeed able to ratify an amendment to the Constitution, it will give us the right to vote. You'll be able to vote when you turn 18 years of age."

"It's a universal movement, for I recently read that New Zealand was the first country to give women the same rights as men, and so have other European countries," Carolina added.

"We are overdue," Lidia said.

"When will we be able to vote?" Alejandra asked.

"Maybe this year or next year. I think some states already can," Lidia said as Marianne greeted them.

"Thank you so much for inviting us to this event. The energy and optimism among all these women is inspirational," Lidia said.

"It has been a long road, but we are almost to the finish line," Marianne said as someone called her name from across the hall.

"Pardon me, I'll see you tomorrow," she said.

"Yes, lovely to see you again," Carolina replied.

"Aunt Carolina, perhaps I can go with you tomorrow to the settlement house. It's Saturday," she said.

"You could read stories to the children, or even play the piano for them. We have an old one, but it still sounds pretty good," she said.

"Yes, I have dozens of stories in my notebooks," Alejandra said eagerly. "I can come with you every Saturday. Is that all right, mother?"

"Yes, that's a great idea, and now that you've stopped helping with catechism classes, you have more time. So long as you don't neglect your musical studies," Lidia said playfully.

"Of course not!" Alejandra replied. "I wouldn't think of it!"

The following morning she accompanied her Aunt Carolina to the west side of St. Paul. The area was bordered on three sides by the Mississippi River. Many newly arrived immigrants settled in this area, called the Flats. Its first inhabitants were Germans and Irish in the 1870s, and then later Jewish Americans from Mount Zion Temple who founded the Neighborhood House in 1897. After World War I, Mexican Americans settled in the area. Carolina quoted her boss, saying, "Constance Curry envisioned the Neighborhood House to be a gathering place for resources and help, and a strong sense of community." When Alejandra met Miss Curry, a tall woman with a strong presence, she was impressed by her kind and disciplined manners and how she often said, "Being at the Neighborhood House is a privilege."

Alejandra was assigned to read to all the children in the reception area, ranging in ages from two to eleven. Reading stories from her musical journal turned out to be more difficult then she envisioned, for the little ones would not stay still and were easily distracted. But those who were interested in the stories sat around her on the floor, and the others were allowed to play freely.

She read the stories first, summarizing biographies of Johann Strauss II and Juventino Rosas, and then played on the nearby piano short versions of their respective waltz compositions, "The Blue Danube" and "Over the Waves." One boy in particular, dressed in ripped clothes held together by safety pins, caught her attention because he seemed to be swaying his body to the music. When she finished playing the waltzes, he asked, "Can you teach me how to play?"

"Certainly," Alejandra replied, but then all the children said, "Me too, me too."

"How about if you each take turns," she said.

But soon, most of the kids became engrossed in other things, except for the six-year-old boy. His face was dirty, and his shoes were completely worn out, but his eyes sparkled when listening to the beautiful melodies. He sat next to her on the piano bench and played every note she played. After a few minutes, he recalled the complete first musical phrase of the waltz.

"What's your name?" she asked.

"John."

"John what?"

"Whitman," he replied.

"Well, John Whitman, if you like, I can teach you a little bit of the music every week," she said.

"Yes, yes!" he said as he shook his head up and down excitedly.

"Is your mother here?" she asked.

"Yes, that's her over there," he said.

Alejandra held the little boy's hand, and together they walked to his mother who was so skinny her bones stuck out of her body, as if the hand of death had pulled them out.

Her face was gaunt and afflicted, but it was her droopy eyelids that made the biggest impression on Alejandra. She felt such compassion for this strange woman standing in front of her.

"Pardon me, madam, your son likes to play the piano. Would it be possible for you to bring him every Saturday, about this time?" she asked.

"Will try!" she said with a stern voice.

"Thank you, and may I ask what your name is?"

"Estaire Whitman," she said.

"Pleasure to meet you, Mrs. Whitman," Alejandra said as she extended her hand to the lady, who first wiped her hand on her apron.

She felt the woman's hand, rough and dry, but beneath the cold appearance, she could see the love she had for her son in her eyes, as if he alone was keeping her from giving up on life. From that moment on, Alejandra was determined to do whatever she could to help Estaire and her son.

When she returned home, she couldn't stop thinking about the little boy John, who was only a few years older than her brother Eddy—but what a difference in their circumstances, by no fault of their own. Her mother Lidia would often tell her people make so much of coming from a high-ranking family, but it was all pure luck. Alejandra always remembered her mother saying that "a person may be judged by their character, honesty, and their accomplishments, but nothing more."

In fact, many of the grand classical music composers whom she had read about throughout the years had come from humble beginnings. Perhaps she and her family could do more for John Whitman, and he too, through his talent, could rise to where he wished or deserved to be. At the very least she would see him every week, or so she hoped, and teach him how to play the piano. Her conviction to faithfully teach the boy would be her mission until she graduated from high school. With these thoughts in her mind, Alejandra ran up to her bedroom, pulled out her musical notebook, and wrote, "John Whitman—The Blue Danube."

I'm Always Chasing Rainbows

A week before the end of school on Saturday afternoon, when she returned from volunteering at the settlement house, she found a letter on her desk with no return address. She opened it.

May 20, 1919
Dear Alejandra,

I am very pleased to hear of your full recovery. Unfortunately, I did not have the opportunity to visit or converse with you on the telephone. I have attempted to call you several times. As you know, Steven and I will be graduating very soon from high school. The Class of 1919 will have a special celebration, and it would be wonderful if you would agree to accompany me to the graduation dance.

Sincerely, Richard Morrison

She was astounded by his invitation. What should she do? What would Franz say? He was only her friend, and while she sensed he might have other feelings for her, they had never talked about them, much less expressed them. She had never cared much for Richard in the past, but since her brother's baptism, something seemed different about him. He had been more pleasant, but it was also his demeanor toward her that was sincere.

A few days later at school, during lunch, Olga told her, "Ale, I have the happiest news to tell you."

"What?" she asked.

"Your cousin asked me to accompany him to the graduation dance!"

"How delightful! I also have news of my own," she said. "I received a letter from Richard, and he wants me to go to the dance with him."

Olga looked at her friend with skepticism. "I thought you didn't like him."

"I don't, I didn't, I don't know, it's confusing," Alejandra said.

"And Franz?" Olga asked.

"We're friends, but I should tell him," she replied.

After school the same day, she was studying in the library when Franz coarsely sat next to her. In a most accusatory tone he said, "Olga just told me Richard invited you to the dance? I'm sure you said no!" His tone of voice caught her by surprise and made her feel intensely uncomfortable.

"I haven't replied yet," she said.

"Then you must tell him no immediately!" Franz said, in a demanding voice.

She greatly disliked his rude demeanor, but rather than confront him, she said, "Franz, I don't care to discuss this anymore. I will be late for piano class, and must leave at once." She then gathered all her books and walked away from the table, leaving Franz in a stupor.

When she returned home, she could not help thinking about Franz and Richard. It seemed to her that things were upside down. She was planning on saying no to Richard's invitation, but the way Franz talked to her made her feel uneasy, and even angry. She went to look for her mother who was reading to her son in the nursery. Alejandra sat on the edge of the bed, and related the situation to her mother. Lidia took the toddler and placed him on his crib.

"Ale, it's quite a dilemma, but I know you will do what is right for you," she said.

"Mother, how do you know the difference between liking and loving someone?"

Lidia paused for a few moments, trying to decide how to explain such a complicated question to her daughter.

"Loving someone is an intense feeling that can come suddenly, from a first look or an action, or it can develop after a courtship. Liking someone is simply feeling comfortable with that person. You'll know the difference when it happens."

"Thank you, Mother," Alejandra said, leaving her brother's room and walking across the hallway into her own bedroom. She was confused about her feelings. For certain, she did not appreciate Franz's tone of voice, attitude, or his imposition upon her. She had always been encouraged and allowed to make her own decisions. Once in her room, she sat on the chair by her desk and pulled out a sheet of paper from the drawer and a black-ink pen, and wrote:

Dear Richard,

I accept your invitation to the graduation dance.
You will need to ask my parents for their permission.

Alejandra Stanford

She folded the note, placed it in the envelope, and then sealed it. The next morning she asked Steven to give it to his friend.

When the school year ended, she had not spoken to Franz, and as the graduation dance approached, she felt she might have acted in haste in her decision to go to the dance. However, she told herself she would be pleasant with Richard; after all, it was his graduation. And, as she was told later by her cousin, it was the first one permitted since the influenza epidemic.

On a warm evening in June, Steven and Richard came to the Stanford residence, dressed in their fashionable striped suits, and Steven knocked on the door. Milly, who opened it, greeted them and directed them to the drawing room. Edward, who was sitting in his favorite leather wing chair, put down his book on the cocktail table when he heard footsteps.

"Please join me, the girls will be down soon," he said.

"Thank you, Mr. Stanford, good to see you," Richard said.

"Uncle, good afternoon," Steven said as he and his friend sat down across from him in two blue damask chairs.

"Congratulations on your graduation," he said.

"It's nice to be done," Steven said.

"What are your plans for the future?" Edward asked. He noticed Richard was surprised by his direct question. "Very blunt, I know," Edward added. "No sense beating around the bush."

Steven responded first. "Electrical engineering at the University, they have a good program in that field. And as you know I also enjoy singing, and their glee clubs are exceptional," he said as they heard steps coming down the stairway in the parlor.

"You two go on," Edward said.

"Thank you, sir," Richard said as he left with Steven.

The graduates excused themselves and walked toward the foot of the staircase. Alejandra's hair was parted on the side, and her sleeveless pink and blue chiffon dress with a white collar delineated her slim figure perfectly, thought Richard. Olga's bright peach cotton dress was daring, if not provocative, with a low-cut neckline that enhanced her large bosom compared to the rest of her petite body, Steven noticed. His eyes fixed on her chest and he smiled.

"I'm pleased you agreed to accompany me to the dance," Richard said to Alejandra.

"I hope I'll be pleased by the end of the night," she said with a mischievous smile.

"Shall we go?" Steven said.

"It will be a terrific night," Olga added.

Once they arrived at school, the great hall was modestly decorated, and one of the walls was filled with photographs—a memorial, in fact, to honor the dozens of students who perished in the Great War.

"If the war would have gone for another year, it could have been any of us on that wall," Richard said somberly. "It is truly regretful we lost so many classmates, including one of my friends since second grade."

"But at least the war has ended," Steven said as they walked into the makeshift theater.

With about seventy-five couples attending and most seats taken, the four friends sat in the last row. Richard turned to Alejandra and whispered, "Thank you for being here with me." She smiled back at him.

Then Mr. Watkins, the principal of the school, spoke for a few minutes as he congratulated the graduates, honored the fallen students, and thanked his staff for dealing so masterfully with what had been, perhaps, the most exacting year in the history of the school. A few minutes later the lights were turned off, and the play *Mary Jane's Pa* began.

After an entertaining theatrical production, the students returned to the dance hall, and lined up by the refreshment table when the song "I'm Always Chasing Rainbows" began to play. Before Alejandra could finish her glass of punch, Richard looked directly into her eyes. "Dance with me!" he said. "Please."

"Sure," she said and placed her half-full glass on the table. While dancing, she was struck by the melancholic words of the song.

"You're so quiet," he said.

"Just listening, and hoping nobody's dreams are denied," she said in a whispery but playful tone as she reacted to the words of the song.

"Some fellows look and find the sunshine, but I'm one of those who believe in happy endings," he said as he gently pulled her toward him, saying his own version of the lyrics.

"That is a good thing, then," she replied. Once more, she was stunned by his forwardness.

When the music ended, she suggested they return to the table, and moments later they sat at an empty table, as the rest of the students continued dancing.

"Do you have any plans after high school?" Richard asked.

"It's still a year away, but I must confess I do," she replied. "What about you?"

Richard paused for a moment, "Science," he replied.

"Is that something you always wanted to do?" she asked.

"No, not at first, but for now those are the plans, and perhaps later with an eye toward medicine."

"I would have never thought of you going into that field."

"Why not?"

"You didn't seem the caring type," she said playfully.

"What's the caring type?" he asked her.

She wanted to say he seemed so brazen, but instead said in a pleasant manner, "More sensitive to others."

Richard thought about her comment, but remained silent.

Later, and after dinner, they danced several more times, until Steven noticed it was almost 9:00 in the evening.

"Good gracious, I promised your father to be back by now," he said.

Soon after, the two couples left the school building. As they drove back to Alejandra's house, Richard, who was in the back seat with her, asked, "Are you pleased you came tonight?" And as if he had read her mind, she had to agree it had been a pleasant evening, although she wasn't ready to tell him so.

"Yes, it wasn't as unpleasant as I thought it might be," she said smiling.

For the rest of the drive home she thought about how comfortable it felt to be with him. Once at her house, he opened the car door for her and walked her to the front door.

"I like being with you," he said.

"Thank you. See you sometime in the summer," she said.

When she entered her house, she walked toward the window of the parlor, saw him walk away, and waited until the car was out of sight. Then, she noticed the lights on in her father's library. She walked into the room to say goodnight to him. Her father was sitting by the architect's table.

"How was the dance?" he asked.

"Very nice, better than expected," she said as she kissed her father on the cheek and left the room.

Moments later, when she entered her bedroom, she turned on the light, closed the heavy drapes, and slowly undressed, but kept on her white cotton camisole as she hung her dress in the closet. She went to her desk, took out a letter from one of the small drawers, brought it with her to bed, and began to read it once more:

June 4, 1919

Dear Ale, It has been the most miserable two weeks since I last saw you. Please accept my heartfelt apology for my distasteful behavior two weeks ago in the library. The thought of you liking or loving someone else struck me like an arrow through my heart. Being apart from you has confirmed that what I feel for you is more than our sweet friendship, which I indeed cherish. I have written you this poem, and it's not Moore or Yates, but it's what I feel, and I hope you like it. Franz.

To say I love you, no words are necessary.
Seeing you play the piano, I hear your waltz,
Your singing hands speak to me.
The melody fills my heart with love.
Perhaps my eyes reveal it, or my quivering voice,
Go on, go on, playing, your sweet Vals del Sol.

As she read his poem, an affectionate feeling overcame her. This was the Franz who had been her confidant, her ever-present companion. Perhaps she had secretly suspected she was the object of his affections; yet still quite young and innocent in these affairs, she had convinced herself they were only the best of friends. She wished her relationship remained as it had been, but she knew it could not. Could she feel the same kind of love as he did? She did not know, and only time would tell, she thought as she turned off the light from her bedside lamp and went to sleep.

On a lovely summer day full of promise at the end of July, the Civic Players of Minneapolis produced their second annual pageant, *Swords and Plowshares* by L.L. Schwartz, at the steps of the Minneapolis Institute of Arts. The play auspiciously described in historical terms, words, and allegory the profound story of the progress of mankind and the reasons for waging wars since the beginning of time. Franz summarized the reasons for war in one brief line as he read from the museum's bulletin to Alejandra as they arrived at the unfolding theatrical scene.

"War for sustenance, for conquest, for religion, for dynastic ambition, for national liberty, and finally for world democracy."

"What a clever and perfect title for the play, if only war could be so brief and painless," she said.

The Wensing twins, dressed in costumes, joined over two thousand performers who scattered around Twenty-fourth Street and Fair Oaks Park. Olga, who was a naturally gifted performer, danced with dozens of young maidens who wore flowing white gowns and sandals from the eras of Socrates and Aristotle.

Meanwhile, Alejandra and Steven assembled with thousands and thousands of spectators who saw and heard the most eloquent story of art imitating life. Except the reality of war was no entertaining matter, Alejandra told Steven, as she herself had seen and experienced some of the consequences of wars. The play went on for almost ninety minutes, and as she thought about the topic, she heard Franz speak his one line, "Go thou to the right, and go thou to the left. There is land and sustenance for all."

Toward the end of the performance, Richard joined Alejandra and Steven, to their utmost surprise. When the play ended, he turned to her and said, "That was quite a spectacle."

"There is a sense of much good will among the people," Steven said as he observed the optimism conveyed in all the opinions he overheard around him.

"I must admit it was an impressive play." Richard said.

Alejandra turned to Richard with a teasing expression, and said, "I thought I'd never see you anywhere near a museum." Then she laughed.

"Near you will, but inside you shall never!" he said laughingly, too.

"We shall see about that," she replied in a confident tone of voice.

There With You

On a Saturday morning in the month of August, the Stanford family, along with other guests including George, Carolina, Steven, Franz, and Olga, left for a week's vacation to the legendary Lake Minnetonka district, known for its picturesque towns around the lake. Edward was very pleased to return to his childhood vacation place. In its heyday since the late 1800s, Lake Minnetonka had more than thirty hotels and resorts, but that week they would be staying at Hotel del Otero (hotel on the hill), one of the few remaining resorts on the lake. The drive through the winding road, one hour west of Minneapolis, brought back many memories for Lidia and Edward, which they shared with their daughter and her friends while the rest of the family drove in a separate vehicle.

"By way of the Great Northern Railway, my parents, my sister, and I traveled to the city of Wayzata and to our final destination, the Lafayette Hotel. The train stopped right in front of it, and it was considered the finest hotel west of New York City with over five acres of land," Edward said. "I can recall enjoying breakfast and dinners from the balcony of our room and watching spectacular sunsets over Crystal Bay. Vacationers from all over the United States came to visit these shores, including diplomats, dignitaries, and even one former U.S. president, Ulysses S. Grant," he added.

"That must have been marvelous," Alejandra said.

"Did they have rowing regattas then?" Franz asked.

"Yes, they certainly did. One of my father's friends competed every year," Edward replied. "However, my most memorable memory was aboard the *Belle of Minnetonka*, a boat large enough to transport 2,500 passengers. On one occasion, we were aboard the boat, and it was my first time ever on a boat. While it was quite full I ran up and down like a puppy, free to roam in a grassy field, until the captain stopped me. 'Hey you, little lad, how would you like to maneuver the ship's wheel?' he asked. It was a sensational experience, to say the least," Edward continued.

"Father, is that hotel still there?" asked Alejandra.

"No, unfortunately it was completely destroyed in a fire in the late 1890s," Edward said.

Alejandra's face showed a bit of disappointment.

"I have my own sweet memories of another very special place on this lake, and you were there. Do you remember I once told you that in the summer of 1902, when I was pregnant with you, your father and I traveled to the township of Tonka Bay?" Lidia asked.

"No, I don't recall, mother," Alejandra replied.

"We stayed at the Lake Park Hotel, only a short walk from the train depot in Excelsior," Lidia said.

"Mother, tell me more," her daughter requested.

"It was a three-story hotel with an expansive lakeshore, and an observation tower with breathtaking views of Gideon's Bay. The hotel was more like an enormous amusement compound. We attended plays, listened to opera, and from our veranda we enjoyed refreshing breezes and moonlight sonatas. It was like another honeymoon," Lidia said.

"You sound so poetic," Edward added.

"Oh mother, do you have any photographs?" she asked.

"I'm afraid not, but this time we must make sure we do," Lidia replied. "I still have the box camera your father gave me a few years ago."

"That old thing," he said.

"Still works, not to mention that this was the type of camera that many Impressionist painters used at the turn of the century," Lidia added. "So, if it was good for them, it is certainly good for me."

An hour later when everyone arrived at Hotel del Otero, the four adolescents got out of the car and ran to the lakeshore with carefree innocence and delight, as if they were small children. They took their shoes and socks off and splashed at each other until almost completely soaking wet.

"We best stop this reckless behavior, and help my uncle and grandpa unload the luggage," Steven said to his friends.

The Stanford family, Grandpa George, Carolina, and Olga stayed at one of the individual three-bedroom cottages by the lakeshore, while Steven and Franz stayed in the hotel rooms.

The next day, the group of teenagers set out to discover the historic area of connected yet secluded bays and towns. They went aboard a steamboat, leaving from the public dock in Wayzata, and toured part of the enormous lake. While Steven, Olga, and Franz sat on the upper deck, Alejandra excused herself, walked toward the railing, and stood there admiring the calming waters of the lake. The gentle breeze was soothing as she felt the hot sun on her face. She heard Olga say, "Ale, come join us."

"I will in a moment," she replied.

"Let her be, she sometimes likes being alone," Steven said. "Even when we were young kids, she occupied herself walking around the garden of her house."

Later they drove back to the hotel, passing through forests, wetlands, sun-bathed lakeshores, and apple and plum orchards. "This is the most charming place I've ever seen," Alejandra commented.

"It certainly is," Franz replied.

"Perhaps Uncle Edward can bring us here every summer," Steven said when they parked in front of their hotel. They walked into the hotel restaurant, and to their dismay, the Stanford family was not alone. Four unexpected guests were also waiting for them: Richard, his sister Vivian, and two other acquaintances, noted high school pranksters Philip Barnes and Chase Sullivan. They all stood up when they saw each other.

"What are you doing here?" Steven asked as he patted Richard on the shoulder.

"We came to join the fun!" Richard replied with laughter.

Steven was very pleased, though Franz was not; but Alejandra and Olga were happy to see Vivian, who was their classmate.

"Well, it looks like you all will have much to do here," Edward noted. "But we should all eat dinner first."

"Indeed," Steven said.

For the next week, the adolescents participated in a variety of lively activities from picnics with races and contests to swimming and dancing. Richard won most of the games, and while Franz did his best to compete, he was no match for Richard's athletic build and fine sportsmanship. Mr. Smith, the owner of the hotel, offered prizes for winners in every conceivable category: hundred yard dash, biggest fish caught, potato bag race winners, and even best lady dancer, which Olga proudly won when she and Chase danced a fox trot one night in the lakeshore dancing pavilion.

Two nights before the end of the week, the visitors entered the crowded dance venue. Even Lidia and Edward managed to escape for a few dances, when Carolina and Grandpa George offered to stay with little Edward George back in the cottage. Vivian and Philip tried their best while dancing "Liberty Bell," while Alejandra danced with Franz and her cousin Steven all night. Richard looked on in great disappointment, and toward the end of the evening, he asked, "Ale, may I have the last dance?"

Visibly annoyed, Franz tightened his lips but stopped short of saying, "Absolutely not."

"Richard, thank you, but I'm exhausted, and my feet won't allow it," she replied as Franz gleefully added, "It's been a most agreeable night, don't you think Richard?"

"For you, yes!" he replied.

"Tomorrow it will be our last day. What are we doing?" Olga asked.

"Us boys will spend the morning on the lake fishing," Steven said.

"What about us girls?" Vivian asked.

"You can always sunbathe," Steven said as he took Olga by the hand. "Maybe at night we'll have a bonfire by the lake."

"That would be fun," Alejandra said.

"With lots of marshmallows," Vivian added.

"Great, it's a date," Richard replied.

After sunrise the following day, Steven, Franz, Philip, and Chase met on the dock, sporting their fishing gear and old dusty hats. Philip was holding a basket with fruits and water canteens as the others stepped into the medium-size wooden boat.

"Where's Richard?" Franz asked.

"He woke up indisposed. He will meet us later for lunch at the dock in Wayzata, I'm sure," Chase lied, for he knew that Richard had no intention of meeting the boys. Moreover, he and Philip planned to take Steven and Franz on a day-long fishing trip, losing themselves in the archipelago of interconnected bays and islands of Lake Minnetonka.

Meanwhile, back in the hotel, Richard met the rest of the visitors for breakfast. As he approached the table in the restaurant, Edward shook his head.

"What are you doing here, and why didn't you go fishing with the boys?" he asked.

Grandpa George smiled, as he had noticed competitiveness and even dislike between Richard and Franz, and suspected the reason behind it.

"Sir, the truth is I had no interest in fishing this morning," Richard said.

Edward knew exactly why he stayed behind.

"Mr. Stanford, may I have your permission to take the girls to Excelsior?" Richard asked.

"That is certainly up to them," Edward replied.

"Please let's go, I'd like to go canoeing and I hear the town has adorable shops," Vivian said.

"I suppose it would be all right, if you promise we will be back early this afternoon before the rest of the boys return from fishing," Alejandra said.

"Of course, we shall," Richard said.

"I'm not too keen on going, but I'll go to be with you," Olga said to her friends.

An hour after breakfast, Richard drove the young ladies to the small, quaint town. He parked the car a block from the dock, and they walked for a while along Main Street, stopping at many of the local shops. To Alejandra it was like retracing her parents' visit there seventeen years earlier. It seemed quite different from how her mother described it, yet it was still very pleasant to see the town.

When they reached the lakeshore, Richard went to rent the water vessel. Minutes later, he was aboard a four-person yellow-painted row boat and waved to the girls. Vivian ran to it, while Olga and Alejandra walked slowly. The girls took off their sandals and walked on the sandy beach then they climbed into the canoe. Alejandra and Olga sat next to each other with Richard and Vivian across from them. The weight of four people proved to be quite a rowing effort for Richard. Fortunately he was in great physical condition, and his desire to be with Alejandra was a strong motivation.

During the ride, she could not help noticing his muscular and chiseled body, as he was wearing a short-sleeve shirt and looked very masculine. Sweat was dripping off his forehead, and his face, once covered in blemishes, was clear. He was quite handsome, Alejandra admitted to herself. She turned toward the sun-drenched scenery when Richard's vibrant, earthy green eyes gazed directly upon her, and their eyes met. She thought of how different he was from Franz physically, and in personality.

After a forty-minute ride, she suggested they return to shore.

"I agree, it's getting quite hot here, and I'm sure we are all thirsty," Richard said.

"Besides, we still have some shopping to do," Vivian added.

"But first let's eat lunch," Olga said. "I'm starving."

Upon their return to dry land, they walked several blocks to eat at Sampson's House Corner Cafe on the lake. Vivian and Olga rushed ahead of Alejandra and Richard, which is what he had hoped for when hatching his plan the night before.

"Alejandra, are you enjoying yourself?" he asked her.

"Yes, it's wonderful. I'm especially pleased that my grandfather came along. He is spending a lot of time with Eddy. It has done him lots of good, and this area is perhaps my favorite place," she said cheerfully.

"I would have to agree with you, although, on this occasion," he said and paused for a few moments. Then he stopped walking and turned to her. "If truth be told, I came here for the sole purpose of seeing you," he added. Alejandra blushed and remained quiet.

"May I ask you a most indiscreet question? You may not answer if you think it inappropriate," he said.

"You may ask, but I may decline to answer," she said.

"Am I to understand that you and Franz have progressed to the stage of courtship?" he asked.

Alejandra thought about her reply, as she briefly looked him in the eyes. She was familiar with his directness.

"We are friends most certainly, and courtship seems to be his intention," she said.

"And are you in agreement?" he asked.

She sighed. "I'm not sure. Perhaps we should catch up to the girls," she said as she started walking again at a faster pace toward her friends.

"Yes, of course," he said.

In the afternoon, when they returned to Hotel del Otero, there was still no sign of the boys. Alejandra excused herself to go to the cottage when she saw, from afar, her grandfather playing with her brother on the sandy beach. When she reached them, she sat down.

"Grandpa, I'm so glad you came," she said, and began helping her grandfather and brother build a sand castle.

"Yes, it has been marvelous. This place brings back lots of memories of my dearest Clara. I miss her everyday."

"We do, too," she said.

"I miss you! Now that you have your own piano, I don't get to see you as much. Perhaps you can come and play for me once in a while," he said.

"Oh Grandpa, of course, I promise to come more often," she said. Her brother began to get a little fussy.

"Would you like me to take him to mother?"

"Yes, I think he's hungry," he said. "I shall stay here for a while longer."

She picked up her brother and carried him to the cabin that was fifty feet or so from the beach, and found her parents relaxing on the screened porch. Little Eddy reached out to his mother, who immediately took him inside while Alejandra sat next to her father.

"Can we come here every summer? I love this place," she said.

"You can't do better than the view from here. But yes, we will try," he replied. "How was your canoe outing?"

"Interesting," she said.

"How so?" he asked.

"Richard." she said.

"You must be careful not to give him or Franz false hope," he said.

"I know. I like Franz, he understands me, but Richard confuses me," she said.

"You are young, and you don't have to decide now. Get to know them without committing yourself to anything," he suggested.

"Yes, father," she said.

As the evening came, Edward and Lidia became concerned, for it was nearly seven o'clock and there was still no sign of the young men. Finally, just before a late supper, Steven, Franz, Chase, and Philip, sunburned, exhausted, and long faced, returned to the hotel with a bucket full of sunfish, which they dropped off in the hotel's kitchen. Moments later, they met the Stanfords in the dining room hall. The group of twelve visitors ate a tasty meal of grilled fish, fried chicken, and mashed potatoes. As they ate a dessert of apple pie, Edward reminded everyone it was their last night.

"It has been a pleasurable vacation with all of you, but all good things must come to an end. We leave tomorrow at 9:00 a.m.," he said.

"We promised the girls a bonfire," Steven said.

"Do we have your permission, father?" Alejandra asked.

"Sure, why not. There's a great spot by our cabin free of shrubs and trees," he replied.

"We'll have to wait until ten, when it's completely dark. So let's reconvene later at my uncle's cabin," Steven said. "I'm filthy and need to get rid of this fishy smell." They all laughed as he made faces after smelling himself on his shoulder.

"I'll get the marshmallows and skewers," Phillip said.

"We already did," Vivian said.

"Richard, you should get the wood since you left us hanging," Franz said.

"I didn't leave you hanging, but sure, I'll do it," he said.

"See you all in a little while," Steven said as all the girls left the dining area.

Alejandra woke at dawn and walked to the lakeshore as the sun slowly began to emerge. There were still traces of the bonfire, mostly ashes, except for the memories that were still fresh in her mind. She turned her eyes to the lake and walked to the lake barefooted, feeling the cold water on her feet when she saw him from a distance. She waved to him and ran to the cabin before he approached her. Yet, after the night before, under piercing stares in the fiery light, she could sense that soon she would have to make a decision about her feelings. She heard her mother call out to her and returned to the cabin.

When she and her family were back at home, she went to the drawing room to play the piano. She closed her eyes as the images from the trip ran through her mind. Her favorite place on the lake, with its stunning sunrises and sunsets, and the laughter of family and friends still rang sweetly in her ear. Something hidden in this idyllic scene appeared in her mind's eye—two images, two portraits, one of Franz and the other of Richard.

She felt her fingers wander about her magical keyboard, as they had many times before, and, note by note, a new playful melody surfaced, "There With You." She took her pencil and wrote lyrics to go with the musical composition.

When I think of happy days in the spring or summer days,
walking in the park . . . walking, until sunset comes,
unexpectedly I'm thinking of you . . .

TRACK THREE

Prelude in E Minor

September day, oh what a beautiful afternoon it was. Walkways through bright-colored trees of earthy tones of gold, browns, and greens. Among the scent of fire burning and a golden sunset, I felt the kiss of first love.

At last Franz and Alejandra were officially courting. The morning of their first class as high school seniors, Franz, who was sitting next to Alejandra in social studies class, whispered a few words in German asking her to read his latest poem. After taking two years of German lessons, she understood him perfectly. Yet before he could say anything else, the teacher looked in his direction and admonished him. The two students contained their laughter and avoided further reprisals from the strict and serious Mr. Wolfgang—or so they thought until he walked to Alejandra's desk and picked up the poem, which was on top of her book. He looked at it, and sternly said to Franz, "This isn't poetry class." The other students laughed out loud and Franz felt so angry that he almost got up to confront the teacher, but Alejandra placed her hand on his arm to calm him down and pleaded with her eyes for him to remain quiet.

For the rest of the day she didn't see him until later that afternoon when he visited her at home. She was doing homework when he arrived, and finding her in the dining room, he sat across from her. He rested his elbow on the table, and then looked into her eyes intensely and said,

"Your beautiful face, I have known all these years.
Calls to me, in the twilight of my dreams.
And your tender lips, I feel, on my dreaded tears."

Alejandra covered her face momentarily with her hands and then asked, "Franz, two poems in one day, what I am going to do with all of them?"

"Collect them. Maybe someday they'll be worth something," he said with a laugh.

"They are already worth something to me," she replied. "And to Mr. Wolfgang." She laughed. "You're not upset anymore?

"No, he's an old dried-up soul," Franz said.

"That's not a very nice thing to say," she added. "But come now, let us get some fresh air. I want to hear all about the Christmas pageant you're planning."

They walked outside and sat on the swinging bench on the back porch.

"I think you'll enjoy this year's play, it's Shakespeare. I'm seriously considering studying theater and English studies at Oxford University next year," said Franz.

"Really, why England?"

"My Uncle Wilhelm lives there, and I feel it would be a wonderful opportunity and place to be, don't you think?" he asked her.

"Oh Franz, that would certainly put you at the center of Shakespearean history," she said.

"Ale, do you know where you might want to go to continue with your musical studies?" he said.

"Perhaps here at the university, but there's a very good music school in New York, although I'm not sure how my father would feel about letting me go so far from home. Sometimes I don't understand him," she said.

Franz seemed visibly uncomfortable with this possibility, as he stood up and briefly walked away from her. He knew he needed to give her more time before his proposal. His secret plans were to marry her the following fall so they could leave together for England, but he didn't say anything regarding his thoughts on the matter.

"Perhaps it's too early to discuss universities. I certainly would not be in favor of being apart from you for any reason," he said.

"Yes, we still have time to decide," she said as Milly came outside to collect clothes that were hanging from the clothesline.

She stood up and walked toward Milly to help her, as they both placed the dry dresses, shirts, and pants into a large hamper.

"Thank you, Miss Ale," she said.

"It's nothing Milly," she replied. When they finished, she turned to Franz and sat next to him.

"Don't look so sullen. Maybe we'll both stay here."

"You're right, we have all the time in the world," he said. He knew they didn't, but said nothing more.

On a windy early morning in October, Steven unexpectedly visited his cousin. While he waited for her in the drawing room, he seemed serious and disturbed, walking gloomily around the room. Moments later, she came down the steps and met him.

"What brings you here at this hour?" she asked worriedly.

"I have the most awful news to give you. Richard's father suddenly passed away in an automobile accident," he said.

"How, where?"

"While traveling on the East Coast."

"It's terrible. You were quite fond of Mr. Morrison. And Richard?" she asked.

"Shaken," he replied.

She stood there quietly without anything to say, and lowered her eyes as she thought about Richard.

"On Sunday there will be a wake at his house," Steven said. "I know he'll appreciate you being there," he added.

"Yes, we would like to give him and his family our respects."

Two days later, the Stanford family attended the wake at the Morrison family's residence. When Alejandra entered the stately mansion, she greeted some friends in the main entrance as she spotted Richard, surrounded by his family. She was hesitant to interrupt him, but he noticed her from afar, and immediately excused himself and approached her with a sad expression and watery eyes. Before she could say her condolences, Richard embraced her so closely and tightly for a few seconds that she felt his heart beating. She softly pulled away, but stretched her hands out to his and said, "I'm profoundly sorry for your loss."

"Forgive me Ale, I was moved with affection when I saw you. Thank you for your kind words and being here," he said.

At that moment Edward and Lidia joined them, offering words of sympathy. Throughout the service, which took place in the Morrisons' large drawing room, she observed Richard's family as they sat in the front row. His mother's grieving face was covered with a black veil. She and Vivian cried softly as Richard held his mother's arm. This was the third funeral Alejandra had attended, and as the others had, this one reminded her of the fragility of life.

Upon her return home, with a saddened heart, she stayed on the front porch contemplating the cloudy skies, which did not mar the beautiful autumn landscape before her. The falling leaves on the trees were floating amidst a gush of wind when she heard a soft voice from behind.

"You know, Ale, sometimes a descriptive phrase or a chance gesture can give us a glimpse of the true character of a person," her mother said as she sat with her daughter on the wicker bench.

"Mother, it must be devastating to lose a parent. I cannot even imagine. We've had a few deaths in the family, and sometimes, I'm afraid for the future," Alejandra said wearily.

"Oh darling, you mustn't be afraid of what might come. I know perhaps you have grown up too soon, from the experiences you've lived through in your short life. And while life is indeed quite fragile, you must enjoy it to the fullest. Your father always looks forward, remember that," Lidia said as a rush of rain began to fall, and thunder and lightning broke the quiet of the moment.

Before six o'clock on Tuesday of the following week, Richard knocked on the door of the Stanford's residence. Milly, the housekeeper, opened it and said, "May I help you?"

"Yes, thank you, I'm Richard Morrison, and I'd like to see the Stanford family," he said.

"Please come in, let me take your coat. Miss Ale is in the drawing room," she said.

This was the second time he'd ever been inside her house. As he walked through the arched entrance, he heard her playing the piano, and when he reached the French doors he stopped in the passageway. She heard footsteps and immediately stopped playing, turning toward the doors.

"Richard! I wasn't expecting you," she said.

"Please continue playing, it's a very beautiful melody."

"Yes."

"Please, go on, I'd like to hear it."

Alejandra was hesitant, but played the piece until the end. When she finished, he asked, "Whose music is that?"

"Frédéric Chopin, 'Prelude in E Minor,'" she replied.

He walked toward her. As she got up, and before she could speak, he brought her right hand to his lips and kissed it.

"How are you?" she asked, embarrassed by his show of affection. "And what brings you here?"

"Not so good, but I wanted to personally thank you and your family for attending my father's service and your kind attentions," he said.

"Shall I get my mother?" she asked.

"Please, thank you," he replied.

"My father isn't here. We will both return in a moment."

A few minutes later, Lidia and Alejandra came downstairs to the drawing room.

"Good evening Mrs. Stanford, pardon my sudden visit. On behalf of my family and I, we were very appreciative of your courtesies this past week, and the lovely wreath and most gracious note you sent our family," he said.

"You are most welcome; you and your family are in our prayers. Please sit down," Lidia said.

"Thank you, but you must excuse me now, I've taken much of your time," he said.

"Not at all," Lidia said.

"I probably should go," he said.

"Well, then goodbye. Milly has your coat and she'll see you to the door."

"Glad to see you both again," he said as he tipped his hat and left the room as suddenly as he came.

Alejandra walked toward the window and saw his car drive away, but his kiss on her hand left her baffled. She reminded herself she was now with Franz, and that perhaps she should let Richard know somehow that was the case, to avoid any future uncomfortable situations.

It had been a few weeks since she'd seen her cousin, and in early November, Steven came to Alejandra's house for dinner. As Milly served a cream of celery soup, followed by a breast of chicken with gravy sauce and Waldorf salad, Steven, who always had a healthy appetite, commented that he had not eaten homemade food in the last month. His cousin smiled when Steven practically swallowed the whole bowl of soup very quickly.

"Cousin, are they starving you at the university?"

"No, but the food is not always the best," he said. "And today, I skipped lunch because of rehearsals."

"Other than that, how do you like university life?" she asked as she poured him a glass of cider.

"It has been excellent, with lots of interesting experiences."

"How is your friend Richard?" Lidia asked.

"Still not himself, but he has come to terms with his father's passing," he said.

"It takes time to get over something like that," Edward added.

"Yes, indeed," Steven said. "Ale, what plans do you have for tomorrow?"

"It's Saturday, and we're going to see an exhibition of the poet William Blake, who was an engraver and a mystic," she said.

"Would you like to join us?" Lidia asked.

"At what time are you planning on going?" he asked.

"Two o'clock," she replied.

"I may have a previous commitment, but I'll do my best to meet you there," he said.

"Good. Franz and Olga are coming, too," Alejandra added. "And . . . ah . . . you do know that Franz and I are courting."

"Yes, Olga told me weeks ago," he said.

The following afternoon she was playing with her brother when Franz walked into the parlor room. With wooden blocks scattered all over the floor, he almost tripped, and looked annoyed by the messy scene.

"Hello, Ale and Eddy," he said.

"Hello, Franz, is it time already?" she asked.

"Yes, it's almost two o'clock," he replied.

"And Olga?" she asked.

"She has one of her headaches," he said.

"Hope she'll feel better soon," she said as she picked up her brother in her arms and called out to Milly, who was in the kitchen. "I will be back soon."

Franz pushed the wooden blocks to the side of the room with his feet as he waited for her. When she came back, he helped her put on her black-and-white checked fall coat and her familiar black wool clochet hat.

"I think you'll find this exhibition the most interesting yet. Mr. Blake had a unique talent for bringing together text, poetry, and drawing in his work," Franz said.

"Yes, shall we go? Father is outside in the car port" she said as her mother came down the steps.

"Lovely to see you, Mrs. Stanford," Franz said.

"Good to see you, too," Lidia said, and then she reminded Milly it was time for her son's nap.

"Yes, Mrs. Lidia," she answered as she carried Eddy upstairs.

When the Stanford family and Franz arrived at the museum at half past two o'clock, they encountered Steven and his ever-present friend, Richard.

"Good afternoon Mr. and Mrs. Stanford, Alejandra and Franz," Richard said as he took off his hat.

"Good afternoon to you," everyone replied except for Franz, who rudely said, "What are you doing here?"

"Steven invited me," Richard replied.

"Perhaps it was the poet William Blake that inspired him. I've read he was a mystical soul who could converse with the spirits of Dante and Homer," Alejandra said playfully in an attempt to break up the tension.

"No, I must admit it wasn't him, but it was an inspiration just the same," Richard said as he looked her in the eyes.

"Let's all go and see his work in the print gallery, and perhaps we will all leave here inspired," Edward added in a serious tone.

As they walked through the gallery, Alejandra stopped in front of one of the artist's prints, but what caught her attention was his framed quote, next to it:

To see a world in a grain of sand,
And heaven in a wild flower,
Hold infinity in the palm of your hand.

She pulled out her notebook from her purse, and penciled in the words on a blank page when Richard approached her and asked, "Which line would you choose?" She read the three-part poem again, and said, "I don't know, but why did you come to the museum?"

"My father—I thought about all the things he didn't get to see and do.

But of course, if I'm completely honest, I wanted to see you," he replied.

She ignored part of his answer and pleasantly said, "And now you want to see the world in a grain of sand?"

"No! Heaven in a wild flower, the world's greatest mystery," he replied when Franz came and stood next to them.

"Ale, I want to show you something," he said as they walked away. However, Richard's words left her mystified.

A month later, the high school production of *Troilus and Cressida* was presented in the school's theater. Franz and Olga participated in the pageant, and with more than twenty actors in the cast, the Wensing siblings proved to be quite the pair of brilliant performers, and possibly two of the best, Alejandra thought as she and her family watched the story unfold. The long-running Trojan war, made into a dark comedy by William Shakespeare, brought Olga's character Cressida to the fore as the love interest of Troilus, played by Chase Sullivan. Betrayal, jealousy, and the contradictions between a person's words and his actions were central themes of the story. The role of King Priam, played by Franz, was executed perfectly, bringing forth his ease with words and passion for the spoken word. His most admired quote from the play was: "The common curse of mankind—folly and ignorance."

Alejandra always thought Franz was charming and interesting, but this was a new talent she readily admired in him, and she realized then that if given the chance he would become a great actor someday.

As the Wensing twins' eighteenth birthday was approaching, Alejandra and Steven decided to host a celebration at the Stanford residence. On December 6, they invited the cast of *Troilus and Cressida*, their families, musicians from the former band, and Robert Parker, the piano teacher, who kindly agreed to be the entertainer for the night. When Franz and Olga arrived at the scene, they were welcomed with a fanfare of admirers and well wishers. And Mr. Parker, who was quite versatile in playing several types of music, opened the evening with festive polka music. After dinner, several students from the cast, dressed in costumes, performed a short version of the play in the drawing room, giving the twin siblings the opportunity to display their fine acting abilities once more.

Later, Robert played some very popular early New Orleans music including "St. Louis Blues" by W. C. Handy. The tango section of the piece caught Lidia by surprise. When he finished playing the catchy rhythm, she enthusiastically asked him, "Mr. Parker, do you know 'Dame la Lata' by Juan Perez? I have not listened to tango music in years."

"No, Mrs. Stanford, I don't believe I do," Robert said.

"Tango?" Steven asked.

"A style of music very popular in the streets of Argentina, but several years ago it became an international phenomenon when it hit Paris," Lidia added. "I love the passionate nature of the music. Do you know any other tango tunes?"

"No, but let me play, 'Georgie Rainbow,' a fox trot by Leo Gordon. You young lads get ready to dance," Robert said.

Alejandra, who was wearing a satin ultramarine-blue gown, stood up from the gold velvet divan when Franz extended his hand to hers, as they joined the rest of the students in the dancing. But, in the end, as always, it was Olga and Chase who stole the show. After the group of students danced for nearly thirty minutes more, Milly brought out a lemon pudding cake which she placed on the top cover of the piano, moving some of the framed photographs to the side.

When eighteen candles had been lit, Franz and Olga closed their eyes as everyone gathered around the piano and sang, "Happy Birthday." The Wensing parents yelled out to their children "Alles Gute zum Geburtstag!" (Happy birthday!)

Lidia turned off all the lights except for the Christmas lights on the tree as the two siblings made their secret wishes. When they blew out the candles, Steven asked, "So what did you wish for?"

"If it comes true, I'll tell you," Olga replied.

The siblings could not have known that one wish would come true while the other would not.

After most of the guests had left, only Franz remained. He placed a small box wrapped in red wrapping paper in Alejandra's hand. She looked surprised. "It's an early Christmas gift," he said.

"Thank you," she said as she carefully took off the wrapping paper and then opened the box. She found a delicate gold chain with a porcelain heart pendant.

"Franz, it's beautiful. I'm not sure I can accept it," she said.

"It's but a small symbol of my love for you," he said.

"It's so sweet of you, thank you. Can you please put it on me?"

He then gently moved her silky auburn hair to the side and placed the gold chain on her long and sensuous neck. He was about to kiss her there, when Lidia stepped into the room and said, "It has been a most enjoyable evening, has it not, Ale and Franz?"

"Yes, thank you, Mrs. Stanford, for the birthday party," Franz said.

"Well, it was all Ale's doing," she said pleasantly.

He turned to her and held her hand. "It was the best birthday celebration I can remember."

"Glad to hear it, although I'm sure as a child you had very memorable birthdays," she replied graciously.

"I believe it's time for me to leave. Good night," Franz said as he saw himself out.

"Good night, Franz," both Lidia and Alejandra replied.

Piano Concerto No. 1

On January 1, 1920, Alejandra woke up to the sound of Claude Debussy's "Reverie." The music was playing on the family's Victrola down in the drawing room, yet it was loud enough so she could still hear it from her bedroom, even if faintly. That morning she thought of how this most expressive composer, who had died less than two years before, had left a brilliant musical legacy. His music would live forever, she thought. She considered her own musical aspirations, but uncertain about her future plans, she realized she needed guidance.

A few weeks earlier, when visiting her cousin Steven at the University, she met a music professor who was well versed in symphonic music. Perhaps, between his counsel and that of her piano teacher, she would have a better understanding of her possibilities. She excitedly got up from her bed, wearing her long white cotton gown, and opened the velvet drapes. For a minute, she stood there, admiring the majestic scene before her, a snowy field and frozen icicles hanging from bare tree branches. Through the window everything seemed still, as if frozen in time. She gripped Franz's necklace on her neck as she thought about what might happen in the year 1920. A wide smile brightened her face when she heard her little brother walk in the room and say, "Ale, take me sledding."

The following week on a Monday afternoon, Steven arranged for a meeting with Mr. Johann Hausberg, the university's choir director, who kindly agreed to meet Alejandra in his office. When Steven picked her up at her residence, she seemed enthusiastic but highly nervous, asking

Steven, "What is he like? Will he think I am crazy? Should I forget about it? I hope I can make a good impression."

"It is only a meeting," Steven said as he opened the car door for her.

As the two cousins crossed the Mississippi River toward the school's east campus, they drove by a dozen buildings, including Nicholson, Wulling, Burton, and Pillsbury halls, before reaching the building for music education. When they got out of the car, she felt the chilling wind on her face, but the sun felt warm, and the anticipation of meeting the music professor was exhilarating. She looked around and noticed dozens of students going in and out of the brick building. The office of Johann Hausberg was located at the end of a dark corridor on the first floor. Moments later, Steven knocked on his door.

"Please come in," a voice said. "Welcome, Miss Stanford, Steven, please sit down," Mr. Hausberg said as he pointed to two empty wooden chairs.

"Thank you for seeing me," Alejandra said as she took off her white coat and sat down. She looked at the very distinguished person in front of her, who appeared to be in his early thirties; his demeanor was youthful and refined. She then noticed the room, filled with music memorabilia, books, and music scores scattered on the professor's desk.

"I have told her so much about you," Steven said to his professor.

"I'm delighted to be of help. I hear you are an excellent pianist," Mr. Hausberg said.

"My cousin is too kind with his compliments," she said, smiling.

"May I offer you water?" the professor asked.

"No, thank you," she replied.

"Please, tell me what's on your mind," he said.

She took a moment and then said, "I've been thinking for a long time whether to continue with musical training, perhaps as a profession. I've taken piano lessons since I was eight years old, mostly classical training. More recently I've been learning popular music."

"She composes, too," Steven added. Alejandra smiled humbly.

"I'd like to have formal training in compositional theory, musical arrangements, orchestral music, and perhaps even try to be a musical director," she said as she nervously laughed at her far-reaching ambitions.

"Goodness! I see," Mr. Hausberg said.

"Is this a possibility for a woman?" she asked.

"It certainly is!" he said. "Let me tell you a true story, which is often forgotten. In 1898 a woman by the name of Anna Eugénie Schoen-René came to Minnesota from Germany."

"Yes, yes, I've heard about her from my parents since I was a child, but please tell me more," Alejandra said as she straightened her back and focused all her attention on the professor.

"She is today considered to be one of Minnesota's musical pioneers. She became perhaps the first woman to be an orchestra conductor in the United States in the late 1800s. Her training was as comprehensive as other renowned conductors of the day, as she studied at the Berlin Music Conservatory, and under the great Garcia family."

Alejandra suddenly remembered the name Manuel Garcia from her great-grandmother's sketch of him back in the hacienda in Mexico.

"Was the Garcia family related to Manuel Garcia, the head of an opera company?" she asked.

"Oh, yes indeed, Manuel Garcia was the father of Pauline Garcia-Viardot who was Anna's long-time teacher."

"I see, but please continue," she said.

"Anna Schoen-René organized and directed the first men and women's glee clubs at the University of Minnesota. I know this because I was her student. She was brilliant. She knew many of the famous opera singers such as Enrico Caruso and Marcella Sembrich through her teacher Pauline Garcia, who was herself one of the greatest opera singers."

Alejandra's interest in Anna Schoen-René became ever greater. If she could only meet her, she thought.

The professor continued to talk about Schoen-René as someone most admiring of her accomplishments and talents.

"Schoen-René taught music history, voice, and organized musical festivals, including the Great Northern May Music Festival in the spring of 1897 in which she brought some of the best performers of the time. She brought together a twenty-one-man orchestra that provided the music to her various productions, including musical programs for commencement exercises at the university. And if all that wasn't enough, she outlined her ideas for a school curriculum at the University of Minnesota. And thankfully, soon after, the music department at the university was finally launched," Mr. Hausberg said.

"I've not heard of her recently. Is she still here?" Alejandra asked.

"Unfortunately not! She left the United States in 1907. So as this story was possible, it is definitely in the realm of possibilities for you to receive the musical training you desire. Although, be aware you may encounter some resistance, as she did. You must be determined and work very hard," he added. "Are you prepared for that?"

"Yes, absolutely. What kind of training would I need?" she asked.

"First, you would need four to six years of musical study specializing in choral or orchestral conducting," he said.

"Where do you think I should study?" she asked.

"You can start here, but there are several music conservatories in the States, and of course all over Europe, and in New York, there's the Institute of Musical Art," he said.

"I'm quite fond of both classical and popular music, and at times it is difficult for me to decide which to pursue more vigorously as a musical profession," she said.

"You'll need to choose one for purposes of career development. It's more established for symphonic and philharmonic orchestras to perform classical music, although one could say that any popular composition can be arranged for a full orchestra. Popular music may be performed with a smaller music ensemble, and perhaps it's also more accessible to the general public," he added.

"I don't think I can decide at this time," she said.

"You don't have to; perhaps during the course of your musical training after a year or two, you'll know," he said.

"Thank you very much, this is very helpful," she said.

"Now, I'd like to hear you play," Mr. Hausberg said.

"Yes, of course," she said as she stood up from the chair and walked toward an upright piano in the corner of his office. With much excitement, energy, and hope for the future, she said, "If I may, I'd like to play the first piano solo of Mendelssohn's Piano Concerto Number 1," Alejandra said.

When she finished, the encouraging professor said, "Bravo! And perhaps next time we shall hear you play it with an orchestra by your side."

She smiled at his kind words, for she knew that to fully appreciate the lively concerto, a complete orchestra was required. "Thank you, I'm very grateful for your time and guidance. There is much to consider in the next months," she said.

"It was a pleasure to meet you. Please call on me for any other concerns you may have," Mr. Hausberg said.

"Surely," she said as she politely got up and curtsied.

"Goodbye, professor, and thank you again," Steven said as they both left his office.

When she returned home from meeting with the professor, Edward was working in his library. She knocked on the door and then sat on the cracked brown leather armchair in front of his desk.

"Father, I have so much to tell you," she said.

Edward stopped his work and turned to her as he sat on a high stool next to his drawing table.

"What did the music professor say?" he asked.

She recounted the story, and then said, "Father, I would like to study in New York."

"So far," he said.

"The Institute of Musical Art is considered one of the best in the country for musical training," she said.

"True, but couldn't you continue your studies here in Minnesota?" he asked.

"Yes, but I would prefer to go there," she said.

"Ale, I don't think that is a good idea," he said.

"Why not?" she asked with disappointment in her voice.

"There are too many problems with that proposition," he said.

"What problems?" she asked, almost defiantly, but respectfully.

"Housing, a young lady there alone," he said.

"Well, I would be there with other students," she said. "You've always told me anything is possible."

"No! It's not that simple. I don't want to discuss it further," he said as he turned to his drawing.

Alejandra couldn't understand his reaction and left the room. What could she do to convince him to let her go? For the next few weeks, all she could think about was studying in New York, even though going there seemed a bit scary, and maybe her father was right. Nevertheless, her desire to get the best musical training possible overcame any fear or objections in her mind.

The morning of Valentine's Day, she was so preoccupied with her thoughts that she almost stepped on the silver-colored box placed outside the entrance of her house as she left for school. She noticed the stone pots filled with green shrubbery on each side of the door when she took the box inside the house and opened it. As she had for the last two years, Alejandra found a white and a red rose, and a note with the same words she'd seen before, saying, "Your eyes are filled with beauty and wonder."

Franz is the quintessential romantic with a tinge of the mysterious, and certainly tonight he will confess, she thought as she walked to the dining room. She took out a vase from the glass étagère and, placing the roses in a crystal flower vase, she went to the kitchen sink, turned on the faucet, and filled it with water. She took the vase and hurriedly went into the drawing room, placing it on the piano. She kissed the roses, as she remembered seeing them when she lay sick on her bed with influenza the previous year. Then she left the room.

During school, she did not see Franz, but Olga gave her a note from him after school that read:

> Dear Ale: My plans were to see you tonight, but I've been ill with a high fever. Please forgive me. I hope to visit you next Saturday. Happy Valentine's Day.
> Most affectionately, Franz

She sighed, hoping he would feel better soon, and her curiosity remained with her all the next week. The following Saturday, she was in the parlor while reading a novel titled *The Education of Henry Adams* when Franz walked in the room.

"If not playing, reading," he said warmly. She shrugged her shoulders.

"Franz, it's good to see you! How are you feeling today?" she asked.

"Much better," he said. "And thanks for your lovely note."

"Please sit down. Franz, you've been so mysterious since the last time I saw you."

"I have something to tell you," he said as he first handed her a package.

"What is it?" she asked as she opened the box, and discovered two long, white tapered candles trimmed with red ribbons.

"Thank you. Candles?" she questioned.

"A German tradition, candles for the bride and groom on their wedding day," he said with his usual intensity.

She was incredulous. "Franz, what are you saying?"

"Marry me, Ale!" he said as he kneeled before her.

Still completely stunned, she remained there in silence, and then he lifted one of the candles from the box to reveal an engagement ring.

"It's dazzling. It seems rather sudden," she said in a state of disbelief.

He took the ring and said, "We've known each other for over three years, and we've been courting for six months, and soon we'll be graduating from high school. I want us to be together."

"Franz, I don't know what to say."

"Say yes! I asked your parents for their permission yesterday."

She was quiet momentarily, and then said, "You know I want to study music at a conservatory."

"Yes, we can go wherever you want," Franz said.

"Even New York?" she asked.

"Yes, wherever," he said.

"And you know I'm traveling abroad with my parents after graduation."

"Yes, will you say yes now!" Franz said.

While she had some initial reservations, the thought of being with Franz and studying in New York seemed to be the perfect solution.

"Yes, Franz, I will," she said, suddenly excited.

Franz smiled broadly as he placed the ring on her second finger, and then kissed both of her hands lovingly.

"I must leave now, but I'll see you tomorrow," he said as he left with a most cheerful and animated attitude.

She felt butterflies in her stomach, and practically ran to see her father in the next room. She found him writing at his antique desk.

"May I come in?" she asked as she tapped softly on the door.

"Yes, of course," he said, and she walked toward the window for a brief moment before turning to him.

"Father, you know, Franz asked me to marry him."

"Yes, he came to see us yesterday to ask for your hand in marriage." There were a few seconds of silence.

"What did you say?"

"We said yes, if that is what you wanted," he said. "And is this in your heart?"

"I believe so, I'm certain. He loves me, he is good to me, we have love for the same things," she said.

"But do you love him?" he asked.

"Father, surely I must, otherwise I wouldn't have said yes."

"Did you tell him about your musical aspirations?"

"He assured me I could continue with my studies, and we could go wherever I wanted," she said. "Aren't you pleased?"

"Your mother and I have always believed in your ability to discern what is best for you. And despite minor mistakes, you've always managed to choose wisely. However, we feel you are yet too young," he said. "How will he support the two of you?"

"He will look into that in the next several months, we haven't even set a date," she said. "Father, there is some hesitation in your questions and your voice."

"We're still not convinced, although perhaps time will change that. I do hope so, and your mother and I trust you completely," Edward said.

"Thank you for the confidence in me," she said and left the room.

Edward stayed in the library, immersed in his own thoughts. He knew Lidia had been opposed to the marriage, and he himself had some reservations for their future, but he wanted to see his daughter happy. Perhaps this turn of events would also give her what she wanted most—to study music in New York; and if needed, Edward would contribute financially while they both completed their studies. He did not want to influence her decision in any way, for he recalled that Don Calixto had been opposed to his own marriage with Lidia, and their union was a successful one—why couldn't her daughter's be, too? She seemed as happy as ever, he thought as he took a deep breath and resumed his writing.

The last Saturday of April, the Stanfords visited the Minneapolis Institute of Arts, and as Alejandra admiringly observed a new installation titled *Jacobean Room*, she heard a voice from behind her say, "I knew I'd find you here today."

She turned around. "What a surprise, how are you doing?" she asked.

"A little better. You don't forget, but you learn to live with it," Richard replied.

"Good to hear you feel this way," she said with a smile. "Am I to believe you are now most appreciative of the arts?" Alejandra asked playfully.

"Not exactly. I knew you'd be here, and I wanted to see you."

"You must know the news by now," she said.

"Yes, Steven told me. Congratulations on your engagement. Have you set a date for your wedding yet?" he asked.

"No, we have not and probably won't until we return from our trip abroad. My mother traveled to Europe on the grand tour when she was my age, and now she'd like me to have that experience."

"Steven and I are also planning on traveling to England, but we will only stay in London, perhaps visit Wales, too," he said.

"A change of scenery will be most advantageous for you," she added. "Maybe you'll even have the opportunity to be in a room at a manor house such as this one."

"I already have."

"In England?"

"No, at the Alfred Pillsbury mansion. Mr. Pillsbury imported a complete seventeenth or eighteenth century library from somewhere in England," he said. "In fact, he has a secret vault next to it where he stores all his fine art," Richard said.

"How interesting. Perhaps someday you'll tell me more details."

"A large part of his collection is Asian, and I can take you there any time you'd like," he said.

"And Franz, too," she said.

"Certainly, I'll take you both," he said with a resigned smile.

"What will you and Steven do in London?" she asked.

"I'd like to see a few polo matches and horse races."

"Richard, I wish you a most relaxing and enjoyable trip, and I probably should look for my parents," she said.

"Alejandra, it is you who will have the most enjoyable trip visiting all those historic cities, museums, and bohemian cafés."

"It's true, I can't even imagine," she said as she walked away smiling.

A few weeks later, it was time for Carolina Merino to return to Mexico. As she helped her sister Lidia make preparations for her daughter's high school graduation celebration in the afternoon, Anthony Solberg came to visit before all the guests arrived. He was directed to the backyard, as Carolina was setting up tables. It was a beautiful summer day, and the garden was filled with blue, yellow, and red blooms. Carolina was standing by a large maple tree.

"Good morning," Anthony said to her.

"Anthony, I wasn't expecting you here so early," she said.

"Yes, pardon me, but I couldn't wait to see you," he said.

At that moment Alejandra came outside to bring the silverware.

"Congratulations, Ale," he said.

"It's very nice to see her all grown up, and with such a promising future ahead of her," Carolina said.

"Thank you to both, and I wish you were going with us to Europe, Aunt Caro," Alejandra said.

"Maybe next time," Carolina said.

"Nice to see you again," Alejandra said to Anthony as she left the backyard.

Anthony took Carolina's hands and said, "Since you told me of your departure, I feel a hole in my heart. I love you, Carolina, please marry me and stay," he said forcefully.

Carolina reciprocated his feelings. "Anthony I will marry you, but I cannot stay here."

"Why not?" he asked.

"I have lost too much already, and I cannot leave my family. I have seen up close how difficult it was for my parents when Lidia left. These two years living in Minnesota have been purposeful, and most unexpectedly brought you into my life. Yet I also miss my life in Mexico; it's where my baby Sol is buried!" Carolina said with emotion in her voice.

"What shall we do then?" Anthony asked.

"You can come to live in Mexico," Carolina said.

"But how will I support us?" he asked.

"You have special skills and knowledge in the furniture business. I'm sure we can start our own business there."

"If that is what it takes to be with you, then I shall. If my parents left Sweden and their families to come to a new country for opportunities, I can leave this one for love," he said optimistically.

Carolina smiled and hugged him, and for the first time since her son's passing, she felt the touch of happiness spread through her being. "Anthony, you'll like it there, especially the year-round spring-like weather," she said, laughing.

"I shall leave with you tomorrow, and stay for a week or two. I would like to meet the rest of your family, and begin our plans for the future," Anthony said enthusiastically at the prospect of a new life with Carolina.

The next morning, Carolina Merino and Anthony Solberg left for Mexico.

A day before the Stanford family's departure for Europe, Franz arrived at eight o'clock in the morning at their residence. Milly opened the door and he stayed in the parlor looking anxious, placing his hands on his forehead, then standing, then sitting, and shaking his head. Alejandra came down the steps and found him in a nervous fit. His face seemed quite upset and his eyes narrowed as he was about to speak, but she spoke first.

"Franz, what's the matter, is everything all right?"

"No! Something is very wrong," he said in a brash tone.

"What?" she asked.

"Steven came to see Olga last night. He told her that he and Richard are also going to Europe, to my great displeasure," he said. "You must have known this!"

"Yes, I did, but they will be going a few weeks later after we arrive there, and they'll be in London, and we will not," she said.

"Can you assure me you will not meet with Steven in Europe?" Franz demanded.

"I can most certainly assure you we have no plans to meet with Steven. Why is this of such concern to you?" she asked.

"You must have noticed how Richard manages to be around you whenever possible," he said.

"Well yes, but not entirely because of me. He has been Steven's closest friend since childhood. They're like brothers."

Franz was trying, most unsuccessfully, to hide his deep jealousy and anger. Alejandra held his hands lovingly and said, "Franz, please calm down. Remember, I am marrying you!"

"Yes, but we have not even set a date, and I feel that it's of utmost importance that we do so at once," he said firmly.

"Now?" she asked.

"Yes, now! We love each other, and there is no reason to wait. Let's get married when you return from Europe," he said.

"In August? There wouldn't be enough time for proper wedding plans," she added.

"Well then in December, that should give you the time you need," Franz said as he almost desperately kissed her hands.

"When in December?" she whispered.

"Saturday, December 11. I'd like us to be married before Christmas," he said.

"All right, Franz, we shall get married then. Are you happy now?"

"No, I don't want you to go abroad, my sweetness, but knowing that soon we'll be married gives me a great peace of mind."

The following day, the Stanford family departed for New York and then Europe.

ONE STEP

The Stanford family stepped aboard the magnificent ocean liner the *R.M.S. Mauritania*. Once a hospital and troopship during World War I, the ship had been outfitted for passenger travel in the last year. The grand staircase and public rooms were as lavish as could be expected, decorated with more than a dozen types of intricately carved wood species, marble inlays, tapestries, and other European décor. When she and her family were taken to their first-class cabins, which were luxurious beyond anything Alejandra had envisioned, she felt some discomfort at the thought of the differences in accommodations between the various sections of the ship.

"Father, why can't they make it all one class?" she asked.

"It's economics, and if the liners had only one class, it might not be affordable for many passengers to travel," he said.

"And safety?" she asked with concern, recalling the *Titanic* tragedy.

"Not to worry, I'm sure there are now enough life boats for everyone."

"I hope so," she said as she and her mother unpacked their clothes in the elegantly decorated cabin with carved wood furniture, upholstered chairs, fancy draperies, and fine linen.

"Hurry up, ladies, Eddy and I are starving," he said as he picked up his young son in his arms and showed him a view of the ocean through the small window of the cabin. Moments later, the family of four ascended a flight of steps into the dining salon, which was exquisitely decorated in Francis I style.

As they were seated at their table, she noticed a penetrating beam of light from the ravishing dome skylight that centered on a string quartet, as musicians delighted the passengers with waltzes and other popular favorites. But perhaps the most impressive aspect of the ship, as they found out a few days later, was its speed; it was the fastest of all the ocean liners and had received a blue ribbon award for fastest transatlantic crossing. In less than a week, the Stanford family arrived at Southampton, England. After a night's rest in London, the family traveled all the next day. They crossed the English Channel into France aboard a ferry, filled with cheery tourists, but most unpleasant drafts.

Paris, France, June 1920

From the train station, the Stanford family was driven to the Plaza Athenne hotel located between Champs Elysees and the Eiffel Tower. They took the elevator to the fifth floor and entered a spacious room with two full beds. Alejandra immediately went to the French doors and opened them, and she stepped onto the small balcony. A subtle wind caressed her face. She took a deep breath and sighed as she looked at the lush trees and a famous landmark.

"Papá, was the Eiffel Tower here when you last visited?" She asked.

"Yes, it was built, I believe, in the late 1800s for another international exposition to commemorate the centennial anniversary of the French Revolution," Edward said.

"Can we go there today?"

"We have many amazing places to visit. We shall have plenty of opportunities to see it later in the week," he said.

"Papá, Papá, I want to see," the young boy said as his father picked him up and took him onto the balcony.

"I don't know why, but I'm exhausted," Lidia said as she sat on a chair next to the balcony.

"Perhaps we should all rest for a while," Edward said.

"I'm not tired in the least," Alejandra said. "I'll be downstairs in the lobby, may I go?"

"Yes, we know what you're looking for," her father said with a smile, knowing his daughter's desire to find a piano.

The following day, they visited Notre-Dame Cathedral, and while the family stood in the courtyard contemplating its facade, Edward said, "This magnificent structure in Gothic style was built from the mid 1100s to the early 1300s."

"It took a long time to build," Alejandra said, impressed.

"Notre-Dame, Our Lady, was the first cathedral your father and I visited together back in 1900. Do you remember what you said when we went inside?" Lidia asked him.

"Yes, wait, in two minutes the bells will ring to welcome us," Edward said.

"And I said, laughing, naturally, it will be twelve o'clock in the afternoon," Lidia added. "I think it was your father's wit and good sense of humor that won me over."

"Not the good looks?" he asked humorously.

"Only a little," Lidia replied.

After spending part of the morning in Notre-Dame, they returned to the hotel. While Lidia stayed with her son for his afternoon nap, Edward took his daughter through the streets of Montparnasse, the place most visited by artists from around the world. Once they arrived there, they found it a splendid and energetic community. Walking through the streets, she noticed vendors, painters, sculptors, musicians, and writers all crowded together along the narrow sidewalks.

"The inexpensive rents and artists' communes like La Ruche are very attractive to all these artists, and they come here to sell their work for a few francs to buy something to eat. Yet they barely support themselves," Edward said.

"Is that why mother doesn't like to come here?" she asked.

"That is primarily her reason. It's difficult for her to see, sometimes, very exquisite work sold for such little money. She feels that the artists are exploited by tourists and art dealers. Although I think the artists appreciate the talent and creativity around them. Some made excellent connections here, and many artists like Rivera, Picasso, and Beckett, to name a few, have visited and lived in Paris. And France's own Edgar Degas, who died two years ago, is buried in Montmartre Cemetery. In fact, many famous artists have been buried there," Edward added.

"Can we go there?" Alejandra asked.

"If we have time," Edward said.

Several artists offered to paint or draw Alejandra, but every time Edward said no, until he finally agreed when a man in his late sixties offered to do so.

"Why him, father?"

"Because he is quite experienced," he said.

"How do you know that?"

"Look at his work."

She smiled at the gray-haired man whose clothes smelled of tobacco and alcohol, with hands that were wrinkled and rough looking. She posed for about twenty minutes until he revealed the pencil sketch of her, which highlighted her long wavy hair, delicate oval face, and expressive eyes. Edward paid the artist generously.

"Merci," (thank you) she said as she linked arms with her father, while he held the wrapped sketch with his left hand.

Before returning to the hotel, father and daughter stopped by a café where they were making Crêpe Suzettes on the spot, on what looked to be a very hot grill, Edward remarked. The smell of caramelized sugar, Grand Marnier liquor, and orange peel proved irresistible for Alejandra, who loved desserts. They sat on two black wrought-iron chairs with a small table between them, facing the busy street. They each consumed two crepes and two cups of hot chocolate.

Later in the evening, on their walk toward the taxi stand, she stopped to buy her brother a French beret, her mother a fuchsia-colored satin scarf, and a black fedora hat for Franz. Edward purchased the latest stereoscope and stereographs of Paris streets to bring back to his son. As they walked down the street to the taxi stand, he whistled to hail a cab, and by eight o'clock that evening they were back in the hotel, where Lidia and little Eddie were sound asleep.

The next day the family visited the Musée du Luxembourg, where Edward and Lidia had met almost twenty years before. Upon their arrival, they learned that the museum exhibited primarily the modern works of living artists and impressionist-style paintings, of which Manet's *Olympia* was perhaps the most popular. As they approached the painting, Lidia commented that it was one of her favorites.

"Why do you like it so?" her daughter asked.

They stood there silently as they admired the painting.

"It is the innocent expression on Olympia's face, compared to her lack of modesty as she lays naked on the divan. I read somewhere, her image was that of a famous courtesan. It seems there is a lot of symbolism, and

I'd love to know its meaning," Lidia replied. "In fact, I've been told she was the source of inspiration for one of my favorite operas, *La Traviata*."

"It's very interesting. I like the woman with the flowers next to her," Alejandra said. "Can we see, now, the painting where you and father met?"

"The Toulouse-Lautrec?" Lidia asked.

"Yes, what was it called, something ... *Marcelle ... Dancing the Bolero in ...*" she said. "I want to compare it with your sketch." She remembered seeing it above her parents' bed.

"Well, let me ask someone where they may have it on display," Lidia said.

After ten minutes, Lidia returned to inform her daughter that the painting in question was no longer at the museum. "It is probably in a private collection somewhere in America," she said. "Well, perhaps we can find it in one of the art books."

"What did you like about that painting?" Alejandra inquired.

"I liked the image of the French actress Marcelle Lender dancing a bolero, it was familiar. Just as composers have been inspired by poems and paintings to create their works, so have painters been inspired by music. The composition is very colorful, and the feeling and mood are cheerful and Spanish," Lidia said.

"Mother, do you ever regret that you didn't get to study at the Sorbonne because you married father?"

"Heavens, no, a love like I feel for your father only comes once. I paint whenever I like, and with several museums back home, we see some of the best touring exhibitions," Lidia said.

"Wouldn't you have liked to paint professionally?" Alejandra insisted.

"Perhaps, but the life of the painter is not always lucrative or as glamorous as you might think. I might add, not at all, unless he or she dies, or he is lucky to be recognized in his lifetime. Do you know that the great Vincent van Gogh only sold one painting during his lifetime?" Lidia said.

"His work was stunning! It's so sad," Alejandra said.

"No more of this serious conversation. Let's go to another gallery," Lidia said.

As they continued to walk through the art galleries, Alejandra stopped in front of a painting titled *Two Young Girls at the Piano* by Pierre-Auguste Renoir. "I love this one," she said.

"Ale, come and see these two paintings by Winslow Homer, *Summer Night* and *Whistler's Mother*," Lidia said as she heard her son in the gallery.

"Mami, Mami, I want to stay with you."

Lidia picked him up, then proceeded to show him the paintings, but the little boy had no interest. "I'm hungry," he said.

"Yes, we're going very soon," she replied.

Before the Stanford family left the museum, Alejandra stopped by the gift shop and purchased a print of the three muses showing three young ladies surrounded by chestnut trees and a landscape in autumnal colors. It reminded her of the fall day when Franz gave her one of his poems, and told her she was one of the muses who brought him inspiration.

After a day of entertaining their little son in Paris, Edward convinced his wife to leave the boy in the care of the hotel's nanny, Madame Louise, for the evening. Edward was informed by the hotel's concierge that the original Dixieland Jazz Band would be performing at Le Grand Duc Jazz Club in Montmartre. It was the first American band with this style of music to tour Europe, and he wanted his daughter and wife to have the opportunity to see them live.

When the Stanfords arrived at the dark and crowded club, they spotted a small table with two chairs. Lidia and Alejandra sat down, while Edward left to find a third chair. Lidia noticed the audience was mostly French people, and commented that they were big fans of the new musical style. Moments later, Edward came back holding a chair, which he placed next to his wife as the band was introduced on stage. A roaring applause welcomed the musicians, and for the next forty minutes the band performed with great energy.

The incomparable sounds of American jazz were mesmerizing, thought Alejandra. It was like discovering a new color more vibrant than any other, with a rhythm that was incandescently expressionistic. Unable to contain her euphoria in the smoky jazz club, she unleashed her usually restrained personality, and accepted a dance with a Parisian lad by the name of Pierre. Her parents, with surprise and laughter, watched their daughter dance with the bohemian-looking gentleman with the dance moves of a twenty-year-old, though he was in fact fifty-some years old. For the rest of the night, Alejandra and Pierre upstaged all the other dancers, until Pierre brought out his trombone and joined the band to play the first jazz tune ever recorded, the upbeat "One-Step."

With three days left in Paris, Lidia, who was fluent in French, convinced her husband she needed to take their daughter shopping the next day. Edward, who hated shopping, opted to stay behind with his son and the hotel's nanny. As the mother and daughter walked along the wide avenue of Champs-Elysees, a street filled with fine couture shops, they noticed a whole new fashion trend displayed in the storefronts. With the beginning of the 1920s, fashion entered a new era, and it was in full vogue in the Parisian streets. The new style of clothing was modern and light weight. The two ladies stopped by several boutiques until they found the shop La Vie en Rose (Life in Pink), which, according to the concierge, had the best clothing selection.

Lidia insisted her daughter get a complete new wardrobe for her bridal trousseau. Alejandra settled on three day dresses with floral and silk accents, a slightly fitted style, and hemlines nearing the knee. Some people considered the shorter hemlines scandalous, her mother remarked, smiling. Alejandra's favorite outfit was a crepe de chine silver evening dress with loose, side-pleated panels decorated with peach-colored rose brocade, accompanied by a melon-colored wrap in velvet with full arm sleeves and a widened hipline. When she finished trying on a most exquisite cherry red night gown, Lidia said, "Ale, we still have plenty of time to look for lingerie and your wedding dress."

"Mother!" Alejandra paused. "The lingerie can wait. As for the wedding dress, I'd like to wear yours."

"Surely you may. That would be lovely, although perhaps you may also want to have fabric on hand, should you later decide to have your own dress made," her mother added.

"Not today, let's wait until Barcelona for the rest," she said.

After a light lunch at Café Intermezzo, the mother and daughter drank one cup of café espresso as a trio of musicians—an accordionist, a guitarist, and a violinist—played a unique-sounding music that caught Alejandra's ear. The musicians did not speak English, so her mother translated for her and asked them who the composers were. The musicians laughed and replied warmly in French, "This music has been passed on from generation to generation among our people, and everybody around here knows it's Gypsy music," the violinist said.

"Well, then, tell them I absolutely love their music," Alejandra said as they stayed for another twenty minutes in the restaurant.

Not long after, Lidia explained to her daughter she was a little tired from lack of sleep, as fellow hotel guests in the next room had stayed up the night before singing and drinking until the wee hours of the morning. Before they left the café, Lidia asked her, "Is there anything special you would like to do in Paris?"

"Yes! I'd like to visit the music conservatory."

"Well, perhaps on the last day before our cruise on the River Seine. Tomorrow we're going to the Louvre," Lidia said.

In the early morning of the following day, the family of three had breakfast at a small French pastry café. Later they walked through Tuillerie Gardens and took several pictures of the flower-filled park. As they slowly approached what perhaps might be the most famous museum in the world, Edward gave his usual discourse on its architecture. "A former royal palace of various French kings, first built as a military fortress in the late twelfth century. The museum stands as a witness to eight centuries of French history. It became a museum during the French Revolution," he said.

Impressed by its history, Alejandra recalled her grandfather Calixto saying, "Living history is everywhere." As they entered the Louvre museum, composed of four wings and thousands upon thousands of art objects, archeology, architecture, and history exhibits that would take weeks to see, she asked, "Where shall we start, Papá?"

"Well, with only a day, we must choose the highlights," he said.

"Highlights! They are all highlights," Lidia exclaimed, smiling.

They settled on seeing the obligatory and most famous painting of Leonardo Da Vinci, but before that, Alejandra wanted to see a painting she had come across in her art research back in Minnesota. As she walked toward the massive canvas measuring 262 by 390 inches, the colorful painting stood out in the gallery as a body of water might stand out in the middle of a desert. The painting depicted a wedding feast in the city of Cana with a backdrop of classical architectural features—fluted columns, towers, statues, and dozens of people under a blue sky.

Alejandra remembered from her readings that this painting had once graced the wall of the refectory in a Benedictine monastery on the Venetian island of San Giorgio Maggiore for over two hundred years. But what was most significant to her was its story from the New Testament, when Jesus and his disciples attended the wedding celebration, and He commanded the jugs be filled with water, which he then turned into wine. It was written that this was the first of seven miracles He performed.

"One of the most significant accomplishments of religious leaders and their devotees has been the magnificent creations of works of art, including paintings, sculptures, structures, and music, which they commissioned throughout the centuries in the service of religion," Lidia said as they all admired the faces on the massive painting. *The Wedding Feast of Cana* by Paolo Caliari, known as "The Veronese," was created from 1562 to 1563.

Later they visited the Near Eastern, Egyptian, Greek, and Roman antiquities, Islamic art, and decorative arts. At the end of the day, they returned to European paintings from the Renaissance period, and said goodbye to the *Mona Lisa* as she stared and smiled back in her graceful and eternal pose. It was in fact a miracle to have her back after the painting had been stolen from the museum in 1911, commented Lidia.

Edward looked at his pocket watch and noted it was already late in the evening and they had dinner reservations at 6:00 p.m. at Maxim's Restaurant. It was famous for its delicious French cuisine, in particular bouillabaisse, tarte flambeé, and the famous madeleine desserts. The restaurant was well known for its Art Nouveau interior décor, so Lidia did not want to miss it, and the family left the museum at five o'clock.

On their last day, the Stanfords visited Conservatoire de Paris, considered to be one of the best in Europe since the 1700s. When they entered the classical-style building, Alejandra imagined herself studying there, as she saw students as young as twelve walking about the hallways of the music institution. She met with the admissions counselor who informed her it would take up to five years to become an orchestral conductor as she read through the course options: compositional style, harmony, counterpoint, fugue, polyphony, and so on. When they left the conservatory, Alejandra felt more determined than ever to pursue professional musical studies.

Two hours later, the Stanford family took a cruise on the River Seine. Lined with beautiful quays, historic buildings in the background, and sunset-filled waterscapes, the river enchanted Alejandra. She threw a couple of coins up in the air and made a secret wish as the boat crossed underneath the oldest bridge, the Pont-Neuf, built in 1607.

The next morning they left by train for Spain.

Castanets

It was a splendid, sunny day in the month of July, when the family arrived in Barcelona. As they were driven to El Palacio Hotel, Lidia had a most unusual sensation of having been there before. There was an unexpected familiarity to the place.

The truth was she had never visited there before, but Barcelona was the birthplace of her mother's father, Ignacio Flores Valencia, who had immigrated to Mexico in the 1800s. While still in the car, Lidia commented that she would later share some of her grandfather's stories.

Edward, fascinated with the buildings of Barcelona, said, "Ale, in here you'll see some of the most diverse architectural styles, from classical, to Gothic, to Barcelona's own unique designs by architect Antoni Gaudí."

They drove through the Gothic Quarter and Plaza Catalunya and arrived at their hotel. Located on Gran Via de les Corts Catalanes, a wide avenue with leafy trees, the hotel had marvelous views of Paseo de Gracia (Gracia's strolling place).

On Sunday, the family took a leisurely walk to la Sagrada Família. The church, designed by Gaudí, was still being built, though it was started in the late 1800s. The unfinished expressionist Gothic Revival structure with soaring twisting spires was astonishing. From the busy, unpaved walkway, she observed the visual elements of the exterior façade, which were surreal, like nothing she had seen or would ever see again. And she felt inspired by the enormous output of creative energy displayed in the architectural design and the number of people, and the amount of time it would take for its completion, estimated at another eighty years or more into the future.

Affected by the poverty-stricken people asking for alms, a shoeless woman was kneeling and praying on the dirt steps of the church. Alejandra, who was next to her, felt moved by the woman's unwavering faith, despite her apparent grim circumstances. She momentarily closed her eyes, and in that peculiar moment heard in her mind a melody, as if light drops were falling from the sky. But suddenly, she heard the woman's voice say to her, "Vaya en paz a servir a Dios," (Go in peace to serve the Lord). Alejandra smiled at her and the woman walked away.

She thought that indeed this woman, like all people involved in the construction of a church, was compelled to be and do extraordinary things by an inner prodigious force. Alejandra's parents were rather unusual in their beliefs, particularly her mother, who while Christian by birth, had her own conception of God—one of a spiritual nature, rather than a religious one. Both her parents had a sensibility and open mindedness that gave them a different perspective about things in general. Alejandra knew she had assimilated many of those beliefs, which she did not express openly, although she thought about them all the time.

After lunch and a long walk through the lively Ramblas neighborhood, they stopped in front of Teatro El Liceo, a white classical-style building with arched entrances and windows. A clock placed at the top of the impressive facade showed it was almost four in the afternoon. Her eyes gazed below to the large posters taped on the windows. As she walked toward them, she noticed a modern illustration, and then she read:

El Sombrero de Tres Picos (The Three-Cornered Hat)
Music by Manuel de Falla
Costumes designed by Pablo Picasso
Performance this Friday at 8:00 p.m.

"What is it?" she asked her mother, who was only a few feet away.

"I believe it's a flamenco ballet based on *Danza del Molinero*, a novel by Pedro Antonio de Alarcón," Lidia said.

"It was premiered last year in London," Edward added.

"And how do you know that?" Lidia asked.

"London *Times*," he said.

"Can we go to it?" Alejandra asked.

"If there are still tickets," Edward answered.

"But for now it's time to go back to the hotel," Lidia said as Edward seemed awfully tired while carrying his son in his arms.

In the evening before retiring to their rooms, Alejandra stayed behind in the hotel lobby and asked permission from the hotel clerk to play the piano, which was located in an alcove of a large salon. Fortunately it was busy and noisy enough so no one would mind. Still lingering in her ear was the atmospheric-like melody she composed in her mind at Sagrada Familia, and she played the first notes. The inspiration garnered by what she saw and felt at the unique church had not abandoned her; yet after playing only for a few minutes, she left the salon and took the elevator up to the third floor.

She quietly turned the key to open the door, thinking her little brother might be asleep, but he wasn't there. She took the pen laying on the nightstand and sat on the bed as she pulled out her musical journal from her embroidered purse. She leafed through it until she found a blank sheet of paper and wrote the title "God Lives." Beneath it she wrote the few notes of the melody, b, d, f#, and f, and then wrote, "It is amazing God lives in every soul." She asked herself when she might finish the musical composition and lyrics she had started, but she had no answer except some other place, some other time.

As promised, Lidia took her family to a very popular place in Barcelona known by her family. Located by the shores of the Mediterranean Sea, high on the mountain of Montjuic, was El Castillo de Monjuic, built in 1640. As they approached the stone castle, Lidia said, "My grandfather Ignacio told me once that as a young boy, he and his friends frequently hiked up the hill and pretended to be pirates, until one day they were caught and forbidden from ever returning."

"How disappointing for him," Alejandra said.

"It was, but before he left Spain, my grandfather and his friends, as adults, posed for a photograph outside the castle."

"And the photograph?"

"Your grandmother Delia keeps it with her most valued possessions, as it is the only photograph she has of her father."

When they reached the castle, the views of the expansive sea were breathtaking as the blue-green waters shimmered while sunlight hit the forceful waves that crashed against the rocks. She stood by the stone fence, breathing in the humid, salty smell in the air when an older man standing by his tri-pod camera offered to photograph her. Lidia asked the man to take a picture of the whole family. The young man smiled and said, "Con mucho gusto," (Happy to do so).

With the Mediterranean Sea as background, they posed for their own family portrait. Alejandra asked if he could take other shots of the surrounding area, in particular the ocean scenery, but the photographer insisted on taking one of her, and she reluctantly agreed. After several more shots, the photographer promised to bring the photos the next day to their hotel. "Muchas gracias," (Thank you very much) Lidia said to him. Later, they learned from a guard dressed in military attire that the castle was closed for the afternoon, and therefore they would not be able to see inside.

"Well, at least we'll have photographs of the exterior," Edward said with his usual humor, taking his wife's hand and kissing it.

"I guess I'll have to tell you the rest of my grandfather's memories of this place over dinner," Lidia said, resigned.

They took a cab to Els Quatre Gats, also known as Four Cats Café, and once inside, a young man, maybe nineteen years old, took the family to a table near the dance floor, leaving the menus on top of the old wooden table. The menu's cover, designed by Picasso, was different in style; they called it cubism, Lidia noted. The menu itself offered traditional Catalán cuisine. Ten minutes later, the waiter took their order. Lidia ordered *escalivada*, a grilled vegetable medley including aubergine with onions and red peppers. Edward ordered *escabeche*, a traditional fish (trout) dish and *espinacs al la Catalana*, spinach with pine nuts and raisins. Alejandra ordered *truita*, tortilla *española* made with potatoes, and for Eddy the same. The server brought them *Pa amb tomaquet*, toasted rustic bread with a tomato spread.

"*Disculpe* (excuse me), do you know anything about your menu's cover?" Lidia asked the waiter.

"No," the waiter replied.

While they waited for their supper, the café began to fill up with tourists, and a troupe of flamenco dancers stepped onto the raised wooden floor.

"Flamenco, a blend of folk music, dancers, singers, and acoustic guitarists," Lidia said to Alejandra.

"I don't suppose you know its origins, too," Edward said humorously.

Lidia smiled. "Of course. Flamenco originated in Andalusia, southern

Spain, the music of Gypsies, Moors, and its own Spanish blend. My grandfather told me when I was child," Lidia said, when three ladies began to play their castanets as they danced in polka-dot ruffled dresses in hues of red, green, and black. Their special high-heeled dance shoes punctuated the high-pitched voice of the band's woman singer and the gypsy-like melody played by the guitarist.

Edward George, now two years old, stood up from his chair and joined the dancers who graciously allowed him to stay for a minute, until Lidia brought him back to the table with the promise of a *churro* (a sweet Spanish pastry). After performing a variety of traditional songs for nearly thirty-five minutes, the young guitarist, with dark brown eyes and a moustache, asked permission to sit with them.

"Sí con gusto," (Yes, with pleasure) Edward replied as he spoke Spanish with his American accent.

The charming musician, Salvador, invited the Stanford family to a solo performance at one of the museums, where they had an exhibition of works by Pablo Picasso.

"Surely," Lidia said. "Do you know him?"

Salvador smiled and said, "No, but my father did, before he became famous. Picasso's first exhibition was here at the Four Cats Café back in 1900. I'm very fond of his early works, particularly his Blue period when he lived in Barcelona from 1901 to 1905."

"Blue period?" Alejandra questioned.

"It is said that after he returned from Paris, Picasso's closest friend committed suicide from heartbreak. Picasso became depressed, and at the time he was also rather poor," Salvador added.

"So I suppose it was with this emotion that he painted these works. I'd love to see them," Lidia added.

"And I look forward to hearing you play," Alejandra said.

"It has been interesting meeting you. We'll see you tomorrow," Edward said as he gave the young musician a handshake.

"Hasta Mañana" (until tomorrow), Salvador said.

When they returned to the hotel lobby it was almost nine o'clock in the evening, and Alejandra asked to stay in the lobby.

"What do you have in mind?" Edward asked her, as if he didn't know.

"I'd like to play for a little while," she said with a "please . . . " smile.

"You two stay, I'll take Edward to bed," Lidia said.

Alejandra kissed her brother and mother, as Edward picked up his son. "Now you listen to your mother and get to bed. We'll be up soon," he said to his son.

He picked up a magazine from a nearby table. "All right, my dear, you go on. I can see and hear you from this comfortable chair," Edward said.

"Thank you, Papá," she said excitedly and almost ran to the piano after the clerk recognized her and waved.

Feeling happy, almost ecstatic, and inspired by the music she had just heard, Alejandra began to play. The images of the Mediterranean Sea from the morning tour and the flamenco dancers at the café merged together in one image in her mind. To her, the dancers seemed like peacocks moving about the floor, dancing a *siguiriya* dance with their castanets, colorful and proud.

Her fingers moved slowly at first, improvising, until the piece began to take shape; then the melody and tempo of the composition soon reached a crescendo, and the lively rhythm, full of energy, marked the pace, as if the notes played against the castanets. She played her new composition several times to memorize it, until she noticed several people had gathered around her who began clapping their hands. She continued for a few more minutes, but felt slightly embarrassed and then stopped playing. A young man yelled out "More, more." She smiled and graciously said, "Muchas gracias." Moments later, she got up and met her father who was in the lobby.

"Very, very nice, Ale, was that something new?"

"Yes."

"Do you have a name for it?"

"'Castanets,'" Alejandra said as her father proudly embraced his daughter and together they walked toward the elevator.

The Museum housed in the Gothic Quarter, was an old brick building with a fantastical exterior of gargoyles and carvings of stone flower designs. Its weathered stone and pointed arches seemed like a place out of the dark Middle Ages, she thought as she and her family approached the building. Waiting for them in the entrance was the tour guide, Dolores Del Prado, a corpulent woman of maybe forty or more years who spoke very good English, but with a heavy accent.

"Good afternoon and welcome," she said.

"Buenas tardes," (good afternoon) they all replied.

"Is there any place you'd like to start?" she asked.

"Wherever you would like," Lidia replied.

Dolores took them first to the east side of the building to see a historical exhibit of the larger community of Catalunya, of which Barcelona is the capital. The exhibit depicted Catalunya's history, from an ancient Greek colony to the present modern city. After almost fifty minutes of listening to historical facts and seeing artifacts from several periods of the various centuries, Edward politely suggested they move on to the Picasso exhibit. The tour guide did not take his suggestion graciously, and in a bad-mannered way replied, "Sir, this is perhaps the most important exhibit of the two!"

"Yes, pardon me, my urgency is not because I don't find the exhibit interesting, but we have time limitations," he said.

Dolores realized she had been mistaken in her assumptions, and responded more pleasantly, "Pardon me, I sometimes lose myself in history, and I forget history is not everyone's 'cup of tea,' as you Americans say."

Alejandra smiled at her remark, for she could relate to Dolores very well, when she too lost herself in history, to the consternation and sometimes even ridicule of her friends. They followed the tour guide through a dark corridor with a damp and musty smell. She felt a shiver, and putting on her peach-colored sweater, imagined what it must have been like to live there, in the cold and dungeon-like castle. A most strange sensation, as if something awful was about to happen, spread to her bones. She suddenly remembered a story her friend Olga had told her about one castle in particular she had visited while she still lived in Germany. And as she thought of the wretched legend, an unexplainable and dreadful feeling intensified.

Then she heard Dolores say, "Picasso's works are a mix of realism and modern styles which are in contrast to his traditional works and his later, cutting-edge style of Cubism. And as you will see, we are fortunate to have works of his Blue and Rose periods. These paintings depict highly emotional and, perhaps, even unfortunate-looking subjects, which apparently he seemed to relate to at the time," Dolores said as they entered the smaller set of galleries. "The ethereal and haunting images of his Blue period depict men, women, and children with melancholy," Dolores added.

For Alejandra, *The Old Guitarist*, created in 1903, was a powerful image contrasting with the sounds of the lively guitar and music played by Salvador, who was sitting at the center of the room as if he himself was part of the exhibit. He smiled at her and continued playing. She walked about the crowded room, and found her favorite piece of the collection, *Desamparados* (Forsaken). The image of a veiled woman and her child with a haunting expression of sadness and hopelessness reminded her, in an odd way, of John Whitman and his mother, who had become homeless after her husband died in the war. She had become quite fond of the little boy, whom she saw every Saturday for almost a year at the settlement house back in St. Paul. While they were thousands of miles away, it seemed to her as though John and his mother were inside the painting.

After immersing herself in memories of the Whitmans, Alejandra returned to the present moment when she came upon a set of other paintings in the next gallery from the Blue to the Rose period. Picasso's self-portrait as a harlequin brightly illustrated his attire in shades of pink, red, and blue. The emotion expressed on his and the other faces in the painting had transformed from sad to, if not happy, serious. The 1905 painting about a Paris cabaret was *At the Lapin Agile.*

"Mother, what do you think Picasso was feeling when he painted himself?"

"Different people may have their own interpretations, but I think he was on the very fine line between sadness and hoping for contentment, as if forcing his colors to change the mood," Lidia replied. "That is why I love to paint portraits."

"What do you mean?" Alejandra asked.

"I seek to paint faces with an expression; the eyes have to reveal an emotion," Lidia replied. "Composers express their emotions through their melodies, rhythms, arrangements, and tempo, while we painters express emotions with lights and darks, colors, lines, contours, it's always a challenge," Lidia added.

"A good painting must move you in some way," Dolores added.

"And move we must. We have a long trip ahead of us," Edward said humorously.

"Thank you so much, Dolores, you were a wonderful guide," Lidia said as they all bid their farewell to her and Salvador.

Later that evening, the Stanford family traveled aboard the continental train to the city of Venice, Italy.

TRACK FOUR

17 Adagio in G Minor

Back in Minneapolis, Steven and Olga attended a high school graduation celebration at the home of Phillip Barnes. After an evening of much gaiety and forbidden drinking, Chase asked Olga to dance. She knew him to be a great dancer, and accepted the invitation with her usual flirtatious manner. Chase, who was smitten by her provocative dress, said, “Olga, you look appetizing, whoops, I mean appropriate.” Then he let out a small burp. She laughed at this insinuation.

After dancing with him most of the night, she saw Steven, who was looking out from the corner of the room, quite displeased with her lack of decorum. His usual happy disposition was replaced by a sullen face, almost angry as his brow furrowed when she approached him.

“Steven, forgive me, I didn’t realize how fast the time had passed,” Olga said.

“You’ve been dancing with Chase almost exclusively. Perhaps you like him better,” Steven said.

“Well, no, but you should not be upset, I was only having a little fun,” she said.

“A little!” he said. “You practically let him kiss you.”

“No, but you kissed Desirée, did you forget?” Olga reminded him.

“I didn’t forget, but that was a long time ago,” Steven added.

“Well, this was only a dance,” Olga said disdainfully.

“You can continue dancing all night with him, if you like.”

Olga became terribly upset with his remark. “Then I shall,” she said, and left the room to go outside and smoke a cigarette. Chase followed her to the patio and asked her, "Do you want to go home?"

"Yes, I would! There is no point in staying here any longer," she said while grabbing her purse angrily, throwing the cigarette to the floor and stamping it out with her shoe. Then she went back inside, walked to Steven, and defiantly said, "I'm leaving with Chase."

"What!" Steven remarked angrily.

"I'm leaving, I said!" she repeated forcefully.

"So be it," Steven said.

The following morning Olga refused to leave her room. She felt disgusted and utterly depressed. When she came home in the middle of the night, she showered feverishly, and then locked herself in the bedroom. After hearing several knocks on her door, Olga replied, "Please leave me alone! I want to stay in my room today."

She lay in her bed crying, reliving every moment that had taken place the night before in Chase Sullivan's car. She had been very foolish to leave with him in such a state, as he was heavily intoxicated, but she never considered he would rape her. She was desperate. In a brief moment of darkness, Olga contemplated suicide like the legendary story of Rembrandt's Lucretia, which she heard when she was younger. But, even in her darkest moment, she knew that drastic measure was not the answer. Amid her anger, shame, and self-pity, she loved life too much to end it by her own hand.

There had to be another way out of her misfortune and misery, she thought, as she played out all the various scenarios in her mind. If she told the truth, she would for sure lose Steven, whom she did love. She would be disgraced if she became pregnant, for Chase would never agree to marry her. As a second day went by and she refused to leave her room except for personal necessities, her parents became increasingly alarmed. They threatened to knock down the door. With all the inner strength she possessed, she came out as if nothing had happened. With swollen eyes and a red nose, she partly opened her bedroom door.

"Oh mother, I'm better now. It was one of those days of the month, a little bit more painful than usual," Olga said, containing her tears and her despair.

"Steven was here to see you yesterday. Did you have an argument with him?" Ana, her mother, asked.

"No, everything is fine, really," Olga said.

"Your father and I are going to Sunday service and we'll be having lunch at the church, then we're going to buy groceries. Would you like to come?" Ana asked.

"I don't feel well enough to go out, but you and father go," Olga said with convincing reassurance.

"Your brother won't be back until late tonight. Please call us at the church if you need anything," Ana said.

"Yes," she replied.

When they left, Olga returned to her bedroom and pulled out a bag from under her bed containing her soiled clothes. She took them outside to the trash bin, opened it, and placed them at the very bottom. She returned to the wash room and bathed again, scrubbing herself so hard that her skin almost bled. Still consumed by sadness, she slowly dressed, wishing her brother Franz was there to counsel her. He was the sensitive one of the two, the poet, and the one who understood her best. They had never kept secrets from each other.

She went to his room and sat on his old shabby wool-covered chair, as if being among his things would give her the comfort she needed most at that lamentable moment. There on Franz's desk, she noticed his most cherished things—his poetry books, his writings, and a few of his favorite recordings. She got up and browsed through them, remembering how she always made fun of him when he played his music—"sentimental music," she had said.

Olga took one of the recordings that read *Baroque Melodies*, and played it on the phonograph next to his desk. As soon as the melody began to emerge, she understood for the first time in her life how music could ease a broken heart. Tomaso Albinoni's Adagio in G Minor was the most soothing yet sorrowful music she had ever heard.

She began to weep again intensely, for the pain and anger she felt were consuming her. She felt her agony was being washed away by the tender notes of the piece, even if momentarily. She lay down with a pillow in her arms, on her brother's bed, listening to the low and high dramatic movements of the composition, as the music was helping her to mourn. She cried incessantly until there were no more tears to shed.

Maybe forty minutes later she heard a knock on the door, and stopped the phonograph with a quick gesture. She rushed to the bathroom and combed her long wet hair. For a moment she paused, fearing it could be Chase. But it wouldn't be him—he's a coward, she thought. She opened the door to Steven.

"Olga, are you all right? I've been worried about you since you left Phillip's home so suddenly," he said as he noticed her red eyelids.

"I'm perfectly fine. Sorry I left that way," she said.

"No, it's I who must apologize for my behavior. You know I love you," Steven said as he kissed her on the lips. Olga held him tightly, and in that tormented moment realized what she had to do. She began to sob once more.

"Why are you crying?" Steven asked.

"Because I thought I had lost you. I want to be with you," Olga said as she kissed him with mixed emotions of pain, anger, and lust. They were alone, how timely, she thought. This would be her only chance to seduce him. She asked him to sit down on the brown sofa, brought out two crystal glasses and placed them on the table, and from her father's cabinet, she took out a bottle of vodka that was hidden in a drawer. Then she filled their glasses to the top. Steven was a little shocked by her blatant insinuations.

"We are going to be alone all morning," Olga said as she lifted her skirt up to her thighs, and placed his hand on her leg. Steven attempted to hold her back, but in the end he succumbed to her, for he too could not resist his own lust and her seductive ways.

A week later, Steven and Richard left for New York, and then took the ocean liner across the Atlantic into Southampton, England. After nine days of travel, they were in the city of London.

One Aldwych hotel was located in Covent Garden. A distinctive Edwardian building, the hotel was within walking distance of all the city's attractions, including some of its most historical sites: St. Paul's Cathedral, Buckingham Palace, and Trafalgar Square. Richard, however, was interested in seeing a polo match firsthand, so he and Steven wasted no time the following day to do just that. After consuming a hearty English breakfast in the small, dark restaurant with some of Richard's favorites—porridge, kippers, sausage, eggs, and two cups of strong coffee—the friends attended a polo match south of West London, close to the River Thames. As they walked to the site of the match, Richard turned to Steven with his usual commanding voice.

"Polo's history is quite interesting," he said. Steven looked at him as if saying, what's the matter with you!

"You're a historian now?" Steven asked jokingly.

"Your cousin has influenced me," Richard said, laughing.

"All right, then, tell me in one paragraph or less," Steven said.

"That might be hard, for one could read a lengthy book on the subject, but I'll try my best. Polo originated in Persia, and it goes as far back as the fifth century B.C. It spread to the Indian subcontinent and China, from where it derives its name *pulu*, a Tibetan word meaning ball. The British made it popular in the 1830s starting in Manipur, India, and here we are," Richard said.

"Not bad," Steven said. "Are we betting?"

"I'll bet on the home team," Richard said.

"The odds are not good," Steven said.

"Since when do I care about odds?" Richard replied boastfully.

"Ten pounds it is," Steven said as he shook his friend's hand.

Steven and Richard sat on the bleachers facing the 300-by-160-yard playing field. Two teams of four mounted players began the exciting task of scoring goals against each other with long-handled mallets, as they chased the small ball in seven minute intervals called *chukkas*. When the third period ended, Richard, Steven, and the rest of the spectators gathered for a unique tradition called divot stamping, replacing the mounds of earth torn up by the horses.

"Personally, I think this is more fun than the match itself," Steven said.

"You're kidding," Richard said.

"Naturally," he said. "I would much rather mount one of those beauties," he said with a full laugh as he looked at all the attractive ladies around them.

"So clever," Richard said as they returned to the bleachers after ten minutes.

"Do you think Alejandra would like this sport?" Richard asked.

"Actually, yes, she loves horses," Steven said. "Why do you ask?"

"Wondering," he said.

"You never just wonder," Steven replied as he looked, bemused, at his friend.

Once the match resumed, for a brief moment one of the horses got too close for comfort. As there was no fence between the spectators and the match, the dirt spattered all over a lady's dress who was sitting in the front row.

"Goodness, I'm a mess!" she said, disgusted, as she got up and left.

Richard thought, I must be sure to sit in the back when I bring

Alejandra here someday. What I am thinking—she will soon marry someone else. I must be insane, he said to himself.

The match was won by the home team, for which Richard rejoiced as Steven handed him a small roll of pound sterling bills for his winning bet.

Toward the end of the week, Steven and Richard journeyed through the River Thames, from Hampton Court through the historic heart of London, until reaching Westminster Bridge at the western end. The two lads disembarked from the crowded boat. They walked by the famous Victorian tower called Big Ben, known for its large clock tower that chimes loudly every hour. As they continued from there, at six o'clock, they walked through busy Fleet Street with its fishy smell, food markets, and pubs. Looking around him, Steven said, "Let's stop at Temple Bar."

"Sure," Richard replied.

The smoky bar filled with locals was a welcome change from the touristy sites, Steven commented, as they searched for a place to sit down. Richard spotted two empty stools by the counter of the bar. Before he sat down he told the old and grumpy bartender, "A large London porter, please."

"Two for me," Steven added.

The bartender, who seemed rather brash, brought back the three mugs and placed them on the counter, spilling some of their contents.

"Thank you sir, and cheers," Steven said, turning to Richard with his beer mug in his hand.

"Cheers, my old friend, and where shall we go next, Wales or Venice?" Richard asked.

Steven could not believe his ears, and shook his head.

"Venice?" Steven questioned as he raised his eyebrows.

"Isn't your uncle Edward there with his family?" Richard said with a devious smile.

"Yes, they'll be there in a few days. You do remember that Alejandra is engaged!" Steven said.

"She is not married yet; perhaps I can change her mind," Richard said confidently.

"Quite presumptuous, but I'm not sure even *you* can do that at this stage. She and her fiancé seemed well suited to each other. And you have not always been much to her liking," Steven said with some humor.

"Don't be so hard on me. I think she tolerates me rather well these days," Richard replied.

"Tolerate is the key word," Steven said. "It would take a miracle, but Venice it is. Perhaps I should send them a telegram."

"No, let's wait. I have an idea," Richard said.

On the two-day trip aboard the Orient Express, Richard and Steven planned an elaborate scheme to surprise the Stanford family.

18 Sunset in Venice

Venice, Italy

When Steven and Richard arrived early in the afternoon at Hotel Des Bains, they quickly went to their room, changed clothes, and then left for the *lido* (beach). For the next two days, the young men frolicked under the sun, enjoying the beautiful beach while sampling every aperitif from Campari, to Negroni, to Prosecco. Steven, who could not drink alcohol openly back in the United States due to Prohibition laws, indulged in drinking a bit too much during the trip. Meanwhile, Richard was more preoccupied with his plans to—as he put it—"conquer Alejandra." With a Venice guidebook in one hand and a martini (which he ordered stirred, not shaken) in the other, Richard planned a week of activities that he hoped would appeal to the Stanford family. Prior to their arrival, he left an envelope at the reception desk of the Metropole Hotel in Venice proper, addressed to Mr. Edward Stanford.

Two days later, on Wednesday evening when Edward checked in at the hotel, the front desk manager handed him the sealed envelope. Both Lidia and Alejandra were standing next to him.

"What is it dear?" Lidia asked worriedly.

"I'm not sure, perhaps news from home," he said as he opened the envelope and pulled out an invitation that read:

> Honorable family Stanford:
> You are cordially invited to a Venetian Carnivale

Black Tie Masquerade Ball
Friday, July 16, 1920 at 7:00 p.m.
at the Hotel Des Bains.
A water taxi will be waiting for you at
6:30 p.m. in front of Piazza San Marco.

Sincerely, Luciano Giatti

"Is everything all right?' Lidia asked.

"Yes, it's an invitation for a Venetian carnival," he replied.

"Who is it from?" she asked.

"Luciano Giatti," Edward said as he approached the front desk clerk.

"Pardon me, do you know a Luciano Giatti?"

"Yes, he's the manager of Hotel Des Bains," he replied.

"I suppose there is no harm in going if you would both like to attend," he said.

"Oh, yes, yes, Father," his daughter said excitedly.

"Perhaps he wants our business," Lidia said.

"But I don't have a costume to wear, Mamá."

"Leave that to us," Lidia said as they all ascended the stairs to their hotel rooms on the second floor.

The next day, Edward and Lidia spent the morning walking about the shops surrounding San Marco Square, while Alejandra stayed with her brother. After going into several stores, they finally found a small boutique that sold vintage clothing in perfect condition. As she looked through the extensive selection, Lidia settled on a traditional Venetian Renaissance gown for her daughter. The richly detailed gown, with a low-cut neckline in a coppery-toned velvet cloth and Venetian lace around the waistline, was complemented by an intricate headband with pearls.

"This will be absolutely gorgeous on her," Lidia said to her husband.

For herself and Edward, she bought costumes in the fashion of Henry the Eighth's court in tones of black and beige.

When Friday arrived, the Stanford family walked to Piazza San Marco dressed in their costumes and boarded a small boat from the public dock. As the vessel left the shore, the sun illuminated a row of ancient buildings and palaces on the water's edge. For Alejandra, Venice's Grand Canal was the most enchanting place she had ever visited. She thought of Franz, and how much he would enjoy the fabulous views. When they approached the Hotel Des Bains, she was startled by a singing trio dressed in Renaissance attire that was waiting for them at the beach, singing the music of Giovanni Gabrieli a capella. They waited as the group of four singers finished their song while admiring the beautiful Italian-style landscape, surrounded by Greek- and Roman-style sculptures and tall cypress trees.

"Molto grazie, (thank you very much)," Edward said to the group as he tipped them and then walked with his family toward the terrace of the hotel.

From an almost-hidden garden behind a row of hedges, Richard was secretly looking at Alejandra. She looked absolutely stunning; graceful, svelte, and yet curvaceous, he thought, and more sensual than he had ever seen her before. With her gorgeous costume, and from afar, there was a regality to her that he observed for the first time, not that she would ever admit to possessing that quality. For in her manners and attitude, she was down to earth with everyone she met. He then realized it was perhaps this duality in her personality and appearance that most captivated him.

"It's time for us to greet them," Steven said to him.

"No, let's wait until dinner," Richard added nervously.

"Are you concerned she may be upset when she sees you?" Steven asked.

"Yes, I'm afraid to spoil her time in Venice," Richard said.

The Stanford family entered the grand salon decorated in Art Deco style, which was filled with people dressed in an array of exotic costumes from every period since the fifteenth century. In the center of the salon, a large group of musicians and singers were performing Monteverdi's five-voice composition "Hear, Now, the Waves Murmur," an Italian madrigal, which is a form of poetry and music. It was like being transported into another era, thought Alejandra. She walked toward the stage and stood there in complete admiration as the singers skillfully moderated their voices. Whether loud or soft, they were always exquisitely in perfect pitch, through every melodic turn.

"What a gift it would be to sing like that," she said to her mother, who was standing next to her.

"Yes, my dear, we all have gifts, and that's the beauty of humanity," Lidia said pensively.

Enamored with the music, Alejandra's eyes stayed fixed on the musicians, but if she would have turned slightly to the right she might have spotted a masked man dressed in Tudor fashion, staring at her intensely from across the room. The tall man lifted his mask for a few seconds. It was the face of Richard, and his gaze was that of someone passionately in love. If only it could be he whom she was about to marry in a few months, he thought.

He donned his mask again, walked toward Alejandra, and sat on a Victorian arm chair upholstered in toffee-colored velvet, just a few feet away from her. He enjoyed the anonymity the mask gave him. He wanted to hold her hands, embrace her, kiss her on her soft pink lips, and then caress her long neck with his mouth, for he desired to taste every inch of her. He had never seen her dressed in a low-cut neckline, and it exposed part of her bosom, accentuated her cleavage and her luminous skin. She turned her face toward the masked man, but her eyes quickly glanced away again to her parents, who had walked away to get something to drink and were waving at her to join them. Completely unaware of the identity of the mysterious man in the mask, she passed him and lost herself in the crowd, leaving behind a most luscious and alluring scent. Richard inhaled her smell, as if he was craving all of her.

Moments later a masked Steven approached Richard and whispered in his ear.

"They will be serving dinner soon."

"Let's wait a few more minutes," Richard said.

"Wait for what?" Steven said, annoyed.

"Until they sit down. They might leave if she sees me."

"Rich! That's utterly ridiculous. I've never seen you like this. My uncle and aunt, nor Alejandra, for that matter, would do that. Don't give yourself so much importance," Steven said, exasperated.

"You're right, she clutters my reason with her femininity and sensuality," Richard replied.

"And your words, too," Steven said jokingly.

Moments later, when the Stanford family sat at a table in the elegant dining room decorated in Belle Époque style in tones of gold, brown, and lime green, the table quickly filled except for two seats that remained empty for almost twenty minutes.

Edward and Lidia greeted the other two couples who sat at the table. Both couples, in their sixties, were English and very proper.

"Good evening to you," the two ladies said as they quickly took their cloth napkins and carefully placed them on their laps. One of them noticed a tiny speck of dirt on the tablecloth and said, "How careless."

"It's but a tiny stain," her husband said, and began to converse with the Stanford family about their stay in Venice. Alejandra noticed the grand hall was completely crowded with maybe two hundred people, but the musical ensemble caught her eye as they prepared to play in front of a large dance floor. Two masked men approached the table and sat in the empty chairs; the one next to her said, "I hope you're enjoying the evening."

"Excuse me," Edward said, stunned by the familiar voice.

"Is that you, Steven?"

"Yes, uncle, forgive us, we wanted to surprise you," Steven said apologetically, as he pulled down his mask.

They all laughed.

"And your accomplice—is it who we think it is?" Lidia said, still laughing.

"Guilty, good evening," Richard said, as he too pulled down his mask.

"Goodness gracious! What are you two doing here?" Alejandra asked almost in shock as she thought about Franz.

"Are you disappointed to see us here?" Richard asked.

"No, nothing can disappoint me here, it's Venice of a thousand years," she said smilingly, though in fact, she was concerned.

"You certainly like to make an entrance. I suppose it was you who sent us the invitation," Edward said, nodding.

"Yes, I hope you don't mind, Mr. Stanford. We were in London, and thought we couldn't possibly skip Venice when we were but a short train ride away," Richard said respectfully.

"A short train ride?" Alejandra said.

"Compared to across the Atlantic, I would say yes," he replied.

"How long have you two fellows been here in Venice?" Lidia asked.

"Since Wednesday," Steven said, but Richard was doing most of the talking.

"You must tell us about your travels to Paris and Barcelona."

"It was marvelous," Edward said as he raised his champagne glass. "And here is to Venice, once the pinnacle of wealth and influence," he said.

"It was also the crossroad for traders and travelers," Richard said with pride at his newly acquired knowledge.

"What did you and Steven see and do in London?" Alejandra asked.

"Polo matches, horse racing, and a little touring here and there. Seeing a distant cousin was perhaps the highlight," Richard said.

"Distant cousin?" she asked.

"Yes, we still have extended family there. It was delightful to meet a relative who shared an interesting anecdote about my great-grandparents," he said.

"What kind of anecdote?"

"I'll tell you only if you promise not to laugh," Richard said.

"I can't promise that, for the story might indeed be funny. Maybe you can share it with us some other time. I don't want to pry," she said pleasantly.

"Ale, perhaps you and your family can join us tomorrow for the Redentore Festival," he said.

"Redentore, as in the church?" she asked.

"Yes, it's an ancient Venetian tradition since the sixteenth century to commemorate the end of the horrendous plague that killed a third of the Venetians. The celebration is held at the Church of the Redeemer every year on the third Saturday of July, and all of Venice comes together at the Redentore," Richard said.

"Poor Richard has become a historian. I think he wants to impress you, cousin," Steven said.

"And what is so poor about that? It explains and connects things, it's endearing," Alejandra replied.

Richard was pleased to hear her come to his defense.

"Yes, we were planning on attending the celebration," Edward said.

The waiter began to pass fancy plates filled with Venetian cuisine, including *fegato alla veneziana* (liver and onions), crabs and oysters, sauteed cauliflowes, and steaming polenta.

"I hope you are all hungry, this is quite a feast," Edward said.

"Steven is always hungry," Alejandra said in good humor.

"And you, Ale, with the love you have for desserts, I don't know how you stay so slim and fit," Steven replied, laughing.

The other two couples at the table listened in amusement until the eldest looking gentleman said, "You young people have all the energy in the world, so enjoy, enjoy everything you can."

"Sir, I completely agree," Lidia added.

The man smiled, but his wife said, "Before you know it, you'll be an old goat like him."

Everyone laughed, as they never expected the very proper lady to say such a thing about her husband.

"Then let's dance before the night ends," Steven said to Alejandra as Shostakovich's "Second Waltz" started to play. The two cousins walked to the dance floor, but Richard could not contain himself as he watched her dance, and halfway through the piece he cut in next to them.

"May I please finish this dance with you?" Richard said.

Steven shrugged his shoulders and said, "It's only for two more minutes, Ale."

She cautiously agreed to dance with Richard. He put one of his hands around her waist and held her hand with the other as he breathed in her sweet scent deeply. He noticed a large cameo ring on her finger.

"What a lovely ring," he said.

"Thank you, it was my grandmother's," she replied, feeling his sweaty palms and his heart pumping fast, as he held her close to him. She looked in his eyes, filled with desire and intensity, which made her nervous, and her cheeks became red. As she danced with him, she felt a tinge of guilt and thought about Franz. A few moments later, when she was about to pull away as she felt his body on hers, the waltz ended to her great relief, and they returned to the table.

For the Redentore celebration, Edward rented a decorated boat for the special event, as he, his family, and the newcomers accompanied hundreds of Venetians in the Grand Canal for the evening's sunset, and later, to watch spectacular fireworks at midnight. The city of Venice witnessed an extravaganza of lights unrivaled by anything she had ever seen. It was as Lord Byron had once said, "As from the stroke of an enchanter's wand/ The revel of the earth, the masque of Italy!" She remembered the words from a poem Franz had read and given her before she had left Minnesota.

The celebration continued Sunday morning with a religious ceremony and procession, as most of the faithful crossed into the Giudecca canal until reaching the Redentore church. In the afternoon the residents and visitors of Venice watched a gondola regatta. While Edward and his family stepped into a larger boat to watch from a distance, Steven and Richard participated in the race; yet after making their best effort, they came in last place. Richard humorously stood up in the gondola pretending to be a *cantante* (singer) gondolier, and tipped it over, landing himself and Steven in the cold water.

"Come on, Rich, let's turn this boat up," Steven said, annoyed by his friend's silliness.

"No, I want to swim to Alejandra," Richard said playfully.

"You're crazy, you can't do that," Steven replied.

"Of course I can," Richard said.

Steven rested his arms on the upside-down gondola as he shook his head in disapproval and saw his friend swim across the lagoon toward the Stanfords' gondola yelling, "Save me, save me," ridiculously but amusingly. Edward and Lidia were not amused, but Alejandra smiled, extended her hand, and helped him inside the gondola, dripping water on her dress.

"Richard, you are bold, but it's good to see you didn't hurt yourself with your foolish antics," Edward admonished.

"We need to get Steven before he catches a severe cold."

Richard realized he had crossed a line, and vowed to himself to act more properly in the future. "Yes, pardon me," he said.

"No harm done," Edward replied.

By now Edward and Lidia had realized Richard was deeply in love with their daughter. They felt some sympathy for the fellow who was making every attempt to win her favors, including making a complete fool of himself, and only hoped she would not be hurt in any way by this unfolding romantic drama.

Overextended from two previous days of touring, the Stanford family stayed in the hotel for some needed rest. But the following day they attended a musical concert at Chiesa Santa Maria della Pieta to hear the music of Venetian-born composer Antonio Vivaldi. A string quartet and harpsichordist performed some of his best-known compositions. She found Concerto no. 8 in A Minor a favorite, a melancholy melody played in faster tempo, which, to her, was always a most interesting combination.

After another day of an extensive walk about the meandering, narrow, and quaint streets of Venice, St. Mark's Church, the Rialto Market, and Palacio Doge, Edward, Lidia, and their young son retired to their room late in the evening. Alejandra, who needed her usual dose of piano playing, stayed behind in the Victorian-decorated salon of the hotel. As she played some of her favorite pieces on an old grand piano with yellowish keys that still had a beautiful sound in perfect tune, a friendly waiter approached her.

"Miss, can I bring you something to drink?" he asked.

"Yes, hot chocolate, thank you very much, and what's your name?" she asked.

"Ludovico," he said.

"Lovely to meet you," she said and extended her hand to his.

When he returned, he placed a silver tray on the top of the aged piano.

A porcelain pot, cup, teaspoon, and a plate with pistachio-filled pastries seemed the perfect ending to a most bewitching day through the ancient streets and canals of Venice, she thought.

Ludovico leaned toward the piano.

"You know miss, if you would have lived here in Venice in the seventeenth century, you might have been one of Vivaldi's students," Ludovico said.

"What do you mean?" she asked.

"The great Vivaldi lived here in this very hotel for over thirty years. It wasn't a hotel then, it was a chapter house of La Pieta Church. Vivaldi was the music teacher at several of the all-girls schools and orphanages," Ludovico said.

"You're well informed," she said. "Yes, it would have been a privilege to be taught by such a gifted and prolific composer," she added graciously.

"Do you know any Vivaldi pieces you can play?" he asked.

"No, I must admit, not by heart, but perhaps before we leave, I can find some of his scores written for piano and play them for you," Alejandra said.

"Excuse me miss, another customer just came in," he said.

Alejandra thought about what Ludovico told her, and the thousands of stories that must be hidden in the walls and crannies of the hotel, the streets, and the city.

On the last day of their trip, and after one day of not seeing Alejandra, Steven and Richard stopped by the Metropole Hotel, and found the Stanford family having dinner at the hotel's restaurant.

"Please join us," Edward said.

"Thank you, uncle, but we had supper an hour ago. We want to invite Ale for a walk about Venice," Steven said as he looked toward her.

"Would you like to go with them?" Edward asked her.

"No, Papá, I'm not sure, I feel a little tired," she said.

"Oh, dear cousin, please come with us for a short walk. I've been with Rich for almost three long weeks, and it's getting tiresome with only the two of us," Steven said.

She was highly aware of her situation, as someone about to be married. It was very important for her to have impeccable decorum at all times.

"Steven, you put me in a difficult spot," she said.

"Ale, it's only a walk with me and this old friend of mine. We want to show you great works of art by Titian and Tintoretto, Venetian's own

Renaissance painters, at a church I think you will appreciate," Steven said.

"It is tempting," she said.

"We insist," Richard said.

She paused for a few moments, considering what was being said.

"I suppose there is no harm in going to a church with you," she said hesitantly. "What could possibly go wrong with that?"

"Nothing! We will be back soon, aunt and uncle," Steven said.

The three friends walked out of the hotel.

"Ale, we may walk, which would take a little longer, or we may take a gondola across the Grand Canal to La Salute," Steven said.

"La Salute?" she questioned.

"Another church in honor of the Virgin Mary of Good Health, for delivering Venice from the plague," Richard said.

"You have taken history quite seriously," she said in jest.

"If that is what it takes to impress you," he said.

"It would take much more than that, but I do appreciate it," she replied with a smile. "Let's go on the gondola."

After they crossed the Grand Canal, the water taxi parked in front of the steps of Santa Maria Della Salute. Richard quickly disembarked and helped her step out from the vessel. Together they ascended ten steps up to the only church in Venice designed in baroque-style architecture. Built in the seventeenth century, its facade with exuberant arches, volutes, and more than 125 statues, sat gloriously on the Grand Canal. She stood quietly in front of the church for a few moments as she admired its gorgeous architecture, then she walked inside.

As she entered the church, she noticed a simplicity in its interior décor, in tones of white, gray, and blue, which made the colorful paintings more outstanding. She looked up to the ceiling, covered in illustrations of David, Goliath, Abraham, and Isaac. Then she continued toward the sacristy and saw the paintings of Titian, and the painting *Marriage at Cana* by Tintoretto, which showed a very different interpretation from the one she had seen at the Louvre two weeks before. She turned her eyes to the baroque high altar, looking at the Byzantine sculpture of the *Madonna and Child* created in the twelfth century, and softly whispered in awe to herself, "Oh, what a magnificent and sacred place to be married."

Richard, who was close behind her, heard and approached Alejandra, stopping next to her as he almost touched her hand.

"Alejandra, imagine yourself here dressed in your wedding gown, and I dressed in my tuxedo next to you," he said.

Incredulous as to what he had just implied, she remained silent. His words pierced through her being with a mix of pain and delight, and she turned to him.

"Richard! You are a most daring man. You flatter me so, but please say no more," she said, slightly amused at his forwardness as she took a deep breath and gracefully walked away.

His words stayed with her as they left the church. Minutes later, the two gentlemen and the lady stepped back into the gondola. With a magnificent sunset behind La Salute, they rode across the Grand Canal to Piazza San Marco, and no one said a word during the short ride. Upon returning to her hotel, Alejandra thanked them and excused herself.

In a meditative and inspired state, she retired to her cozy room and walked toward the window from where she could see the sunset, still softly illuminating the Venice sky. She sat down on a desk facing the window and began to write a string of lyrics:

In ancient Venice sunsets glow,
Above Salute and Saint Mark
A city so mysterious, a city so romantic
A thousand years have passed and still capture the heart of poets
and of you. . .

She woke up the next morning to the sound of church bells from across the Grand Canal. As if her spirit had taken over once again, she got dressed and walked down to the Victorian-decorated salon next to the lobby of the hotel. Still lit by a Murano chandelier, the room was inviting, and she began to play as if her fingers had a will of their own. She closed her eyes, surrendered to the creative energy within her, and let a new musical composition emerge, called *Sunset in Venice*.

The next morning, the Stanfords took the Orient Express back to England to return to the United States.

TRACK FIVE

Sonata in C Major

Aboard the *R.M.S. Mauritania*, a wistful Alejandra lay on a wooden lounge chair on the upper deck of the ocean liner as the sun was rising in the east. She felt a strong breeze on her face, slightly cold, and she covered her chest with a woolen blanket as the gentle sway of the ship rocked her.

With her eyes closed, she thought about the unforgettable memories of the last month. Each place they had visited had its own sound, smell, and images that she could still see in her mind like a running film with a beginning, but no end. Something deep inside her had awakened that she could not explain in words. Her thoughts turned to her upcoming audition at the Institute of Musical Art in New York, but she was suddenly startled by the voice of a young woman who sat a few feet away from her.

"Jacob, let me rest for a few minutes. We've been awake since six."

A curly haired boy, maybe seven years old, walked toward Alejandra.

"Hi, I'm Jacob and that's my sister Hannah Mendes."

"Hi, I'm Alejandra Stanford."

"Where are you from?" he asked.

"Minnesota."

"Where is Minne . . . what?" the young boy asked.

"It's in the Midwest. We're having breakfast, would you like to join us? I'd love some company my own age," Hannah said in a friendly voice.

"Sure," Alejandra replied.

Hannah's long, dark-brown, wavy hair moved wildly with the breeze, and framed her beautiful face with large eyes, a narrow nose, and wide lips.

"This humidity is terrible for my hair," she said as she took an orange-colored ribbon from her purse and wrapped it around her expanding hair.

"I think it's better to have a full head of hair than none at all," Alejandra said as the two girls burst into laughter.

"Wait till you see my father," Hannah said.

"Why?" Alejandra asked.

"'Cause he has been bald since I can remember," she answered jokingly. "And sometimes he says he is going to cut off my curls and placed them on top of his head, imagine that!"

Alejandra found the image humorous, as she pictured a bald man with long, hanging curls draping from his skull. Five minutes later, they were in the ship's restaurant, and the three new friends sat together at a table by a window. During breakfast the two girls related to each other very well; and Hannah was not only interesting, but very funny and entertaining as she shared her experiences in Austria, Germany, and Budapest.

After spending most of the day together, Alejandra was pleased to have made this new acquaintance, and for the next days they were inseparable, more like old friends, for they had found much in common with each other. They both loved music; Hannah played the cello, and even more astonishing and coincidental were her plans to attend the Institute of Musical Art in New York in the fall. Their parents, who also met, seemed to have connected with the same comfort and ease as their daughters—especially the mothers, who spent almost an hour talking about cooking and the latest cookbook *The Perry*, by the ladies of Perry, Kansas.

At the end of the voyage, the two families met for their farewell at the promenade deck when the ship approached the New York harbor. It was a sunny, clear day with a slight wind. As the Stanford family waited for the Mendes family, they stood by the railing, surrounded by dozens of other passengers who also came out to the deck. Edward pointed to a most famous landmark as they admired it from afar, and then from up close. The impressive Statue of Liberty stood gracefully at the water's edge, as if she was welcoming all newcomers and those returning home to America.

Alejandra turned to her father as he stared at the magnificent view, and waited for him to give a description of the grand sculpture in the foreground. She knew him too well, she thought, for just before he was about to give his usual architectural discourse, her father would pull on his moustache. Sure enough, seconds later, he did that and said, "The Statue of Liberty was a gift from the French people to the Americans on the occasion of the centennial of the American Declaration of Independence. The copper sculpture is one of the greatest works of art ever created by Frederic Bartholdi and Alexandre Eiffel," Edward said as he held his son in his arms, with his wife and daughter by his side.

Alejandra remembered the statue of the *Angel of Independence* back in Mexico, which was also on the occasion of their centennial Independence celebration. She felt proud and privileged to have roots in both countries—to have been born in America, and to have an American father and Mexican mother whose cultures had enriched her life. She wondered if that was how her own grandmother Clara, Franz, Olga, and all the people who come to America felt when they left their countries behind. She admired their courage, for she herself could not fathom leaving her homeland permanently, by her own choice.

When the two families disembarked from the ship, Alejandra and Hannah warmly embraced each other.

"I'll write you," Hannah said.

"I will too; besides, you must all come to my wedding," she said joyfully. "Goodbye, Mr. and Mrs. Mendes."

"It was a pleasure to meet you," Edward said as he extended a handshake to the couple.

"I'll have my daughter mail you that recipe," Mrs. Mendes said to Lidia.

"Thank you," Lidia replied, as she too said goodbye to their new friends.

Before returning to Minnesota, the Stanford family stayed in New York for two days at the Algonquin Hotel located between Fifth and Sixth avenues. After the bellboy took their bags and some of their luggage from the taxi, the family of four walked through the elegant vestibule of the hotel, decorated with architectural detail from dentil moldings on the ceiling to wooden square columns. The large reception area was filled with potted palm trees, and the plush-cushioned sofas were all occupied by other guests. Alejandra and her brother sat in a couple of rocking chairs as Edward checked in.

"Eddie, come sit on my lap," she said. "I have something for you."

The little boy dressed in short trousers and a striped blue and white sweater gladly went to his sister.

"Ale, what do you have?" he said with a big smile.

She pulled out a toy ship from her purse. He grabbed it from her hand, jumped off her lap, and began to run around her in circles. She smiled, for he was behaving exactly as she felt at the thought of visiting the Institute of Musical Art the next day. She had prepared for the audition rigorously back in Minnesota and whenever possible, she practiced on the piano while on the trip, including aboard the ship. She had chosen three pieces from the baroque, classical, and romantic periods. She had been waiting for this day to arrive for what seemed to her an eternity, and now, it was almost within her reach. She only hoped the chosen piece and her performance would be good enough for her to be accepted into the renowned musical institution. Then she heard her father's voice. "Our rooms are ready."

A few hours later, when they left the hotel to visit several important landmarks and walked down Forty-fourth Street, she noticed the streets filled with Model T Ford cars as if they were in a parade, and the hustle and bustle of life in the city was evident at every turn. As they made their way to Madison Avenue, Edward noticed a tobacco shop, but two stores down, she noticed the busy storefronts, in particular, a music store with a huge exterior poster of the *Ziegfeld Follies of 1919* that read *Mandy*. The image of the blond woman holding a mask was carnival-like, but Alejandra focused her attention on the name of the composer listed in small letters.

"Father, can I wait for you there?" she asked. Her father looked at the large exterior sign, and nodded affirmatively. She entered the small shop, and saw rows of stands containing sheet music, and more large posters on the walls showing dozens of stage productions dating back to 1907.

"May I help you, miss?" an older, robust gentleman asked.

"Thank you, do you have the music of Irving Berlin?" she asked.

"You're in the right place," the man said as he walked to the center of the store and pulled out the sheet music of "Watch Your Step" from the shelf.

"This music is from his first musical," the man said.

"What about the score for *Mandy*?" she asked.

"That was from last year, and we're sold out, but there's a better selection at our other store in Tin Pan Alley."

"That's a strange name," she remarked.

"You're not from here," he said.

"No," she replied.

"It's a stretch of blocks on west Twenty-eighth Street famous for music publishers, and it's where most pianists work. They say it sounds like housewives banging tin pans," he said.

She silently smiled at the comparison, as she imagined herself banging at the piano while Milly banged her tin pan in the kitchen back home. Maybe they could make a duet, she thought.

"Hopefully I'll be back here soon. I'll take this one," she said as she took out sixty cents from her leather wallet and gave it to the man.

"Thank you," the man said. He placed the sheet music in a paper bag as the shop's bell rang and the door opened.

"Father, wait till you hear what I've bought," she said.

"I can't wait," he said.

Twenty minutes later they approached St. Patrick's Cathedral. The soaring spires, maybe over three hundred feet in height, were impressive, and her father asked, "Now, Ale, you've seen enough cathedrals to last you for a lifetime. Any idea what style of architecture this might be?"

She raised her eyebrows, "Something Gothic?" she said with a doubtful expression.

"Pretty close, Gothic Revival," he said as they walked through the grand doors. The first thing that caught her attention besides the magnificent ribbed ceilings, arches, and the nave was a circular Tiffany cobalt-blue stained glass window in the far background. Blue was her favorite color, but seeing it in a stained glass window was lustrous and opulent. She recalled her mother telling her that Egyptians used lapis lazuli to depict the heavens. She realized then that going to cathedrals not only offered refuge, but aesthetic beauty, filled with magnificent works of art and architectural details. One could skip the whole sermon and still leave the cathedral inspired by the smell of incense, the paintings, sculptures, and the music accompanied by celestial choir voices. If this wasn't man's creation inspired by God, then what, she thought as she lit one of the candles inside a small copper container, amid dozens of them placed in wrought-iron holders.

At nine in the morning, a taxi cab was waiting outside the hotel to take her and Edward to the neighborhood of Morningside Heights. Once there, they found the Institute of Musical Art housed in a neoclassical building. Aside from its beautiful facade, Alejandra was more interested in seeing its interior, walking through the hallways, and perhaps hearing the music of future composers and conductors. When she entered through the wooden door, she felt a tingling in her stomach. A mixture of musical sounds welcomed her, sounds one might hear when members of an orchestra are in the process of tuning their instruments as they search for the perfect pitch.

The father and daughter were welcomed by the school's director, Mr. Samuel Applebaum, who immediately directed them to the audition room. The slightly thin, fifty-something gentleman with graying hair and deep brown eyes was polite but serious. Once she, her father, and the director entered a small music room, he pointed to the piano. She was nervous yet glad to play her chosen piece, finally, for the audition: Mozart's Sonata in C Major.

She slowly sat down in front of the piano, straightened her back, placed her fingers on the keyboard, and played the spirited piece until the end. When she finished playing, her heart was beating faster, and she waited for his response or request to play another piece. She knew his decision to admit her into the school was based on her performance, for he had already received her letter and application for admission. Mr. Applebaum pulled down slightly on his beard and said, "Your pedal technique needs some work, but welcome to the Institute of Musical Art."

Alejandra sighed in great relief and closed her eyes, trying to contain her emotion as she only let a couple of tears run down her face. She quickly wiped them away and said, "Oh! Thank you, thank you."

After they discussed the particulars of the music curriculum, expectations, and other matters, they toured the large facilities. The most interesting room was the brightly lit reception area on the second floor, where many of the students gathered together for group practice. She imagined herself sitting at the grand piano as she played with other students. The ability to perform with other musicians was something she had briefly tasted when she was in high school, but it had left her longing for more, as when someone is starving, she thought, but is only allowed to eat a tiny sliver of food. She hoped Franz would be as happy in New York as she would be. When they left the building, her father, who was holding a large informational package, turned to her and said, "Ale, I believe you'll find this place most exhilarating."

"Yes, father, I can't wait," she said.

Symphony No. 7

After being away for more than a month, Alejandra was thrilled to be back home. Edward brought her luggage upstairs and she began to unpack her clothes. She took out several small packages, which she placed on the window bench except for one she took to Milly, who was preparing dinner in the small kitchen.

As soon as Alejandra entered the pungently scented room, she noticed the housekeeper cutting vegetables and boiling lamb on the stove.

"Milly, this is for you," she said.

"Oh Miss Ale, thank you," Milly said as she washed her hands in the sink and then opened the box. She pulled out a hand-painted floral fan from Barcelona.

"I love it," she said. "Thank you."

She was quite fond of the ever-faithful cook and housekeeper, who had been with the family since 1907. And because she had never married, Lidia considered Milly part of the family.

"I know it can get pretty hot here sometimes," Alejandra said.

"Yes, very hot," she said. "Franz has come to look for you several times, many times."

"I'm afraid we stayed a little bit longer than planned," she said as she excused herself, and then walked out of the kitchen and into her father's library. She picked up the telephone and dialed Olga's number.

"Hello," a female voice answered on the other end of the phone.

"Good evening, Mrs. Wensing, is Olga there?" she asked.

"Ale, good to hear you've returned! Franz was very worried," she said.

"Let me get Olga for you."

"Thank you."

"Hello, Ale," she said.

"Good to talk to you. When can you come for a visit? I have so much to tell you," she said.

"We'll be there tomorrow afternoon," Olga said. "Franz is not here right now."

"I'll see you tomorrow then," Alejandra said.

That night she couldn't sleep, as she was excited to see Franz once again. But she dreaded telling him about the unexpected visitors for fear of his reaction.

The next day, to keep her mind off the meeting with Franz, she picked up the debut novel of Scott Fitzgerald, *This Side of Paradise*, and began to read it as she sat on the golden-toned upholstered divan in the drawing room. She opened the book to the first page and read: "Amory Blaine inherited from his mother every trait, except the stary inexpressible few, that made him worthwhile . . . " Suddenly this reminded her of a recent conversation regarding her family's traits. She recalled Lidia saying that Alejandra had inherited her mother's physical attributes and her open-minded attitude, and in personality she was more like her father—inquisitive and a perfectionist, except she didn't always possess his unrivaled fieriness. She was thinking about Franz, whom she would marry in only a few months, and his character traits when she heard his voice as the housekeeper greeted the Wensing twins. Moments later, they were in the drawing room.

"So glad to see you both," Alejandra said.

Franz tightly embraced her, as did his sister, but there was something different about Olga; her bubbly personality seemed subdued, Alejandra observed as she handed each of them a package. Olga opened hers first to find a handmade white laced *mantilla*.

"Ale, thank you," Olga said as she put the Spanish-style shawl around her shoulders with a touch of melancholy. Franz then opened his two gifts, the fedora hat and poster of the *Three Muses* Alejandra had bought for him in Paris.

"Thank you," he said. "We have so much planning to do, but first you must tell us about your trip."

Milly walked into the room and placed a tray on the table.

Alejandra served her friends a cup of spicy orange tea and a slice of a*pfelkuchen*, one of Franz's favorite pastries.

"Thank you, Ale," Franz said.

"Well, tell us!" Olga said.

"It was sensational, no words can quite capture the experience. Paris and Barcelona were absolutely gorgeous, the music, museums, and fashionable streets, each with its own charm. But Venice was as it has been for centuries, untouched by modern buildings; it was absolutely magical. I thought of you often, Franz. Someday, together, we must visit there," she said.

She wanted to tell him about Steven and Richard, but she couldn't do it, and decided to put it off till the next day.

"What about you, is there any exciting news?" she asked.

There was a tense silence, each one of them bearing their own secret, but no one was ready to divulge it. It was a matter of time before it was all revealed, each one thought. The openness between the three friends had disappeared, and while no one said it, they all felt it.

"Well, did you buy your wedding gown?" Olga asked.

"No, I'd like to wear my mother's."

"You'll be the most beautiful bride," Franz said, as he held her hands.

"I'm sure that's what all the grooms say," Olga said in a sarcastic tone.

"Yes, it's true," Alejandra added and patted her friend on the hand, as there was certain bitterness in Olga's voice that Alejandra could not explain.

"Oh! Franz, the best news to tell you is that I was accepted into the Institute, and my father looked at several apartments for us to consider. He is planning on speaking to you about it later. Isn't it exciting!" she said.

Franz and Olga looked at each other with concern, but said nothing.

"Have you applied yet to New York University?" Alejandra asked him.

Olga was about to speak when Franz interrupted her, speaking in German before turning to his fiancé.

"I didn't understand what you said, you spoke too fast," she said jovially.

"Oh! Something exciting I'm planning," Franz said. "You must be tired from your long trip abroad. I'll come tomorrow afternoon, and we can discuss our future plans."

Alejandra smiled at him in agreement and handed him a package. "Franz, this is for your mother," she said.

"Thank you. What is it?" he asked.

"It's also a mantilla, but in floral patterns," she said.

"We will see each other later in the week," Olga added as she and her brother left the room.

Alejandra was disappointed with herself for not telling Franz about the visitors in Venice. She promised herself she would do it the next day. Perhaps, sometimes, she strived to be perfect, as her mother had told her. She reminded herself, not only was it unrealistic to be so, but also perhaps even a weakness.

When the two siblings got into the car, and throughout their drive home, they kept their thoughts to themselves until Olga finally said, "When are you going to tell her the truth?"

"Don't you dare tell her! I will, when the appropriate time comes," he said with a stern voice.

At four o'clock in the afternoon of the following day, Franz found Alejandra setting the table in the dining room when he came from behind and placed his arms around her. She felt a slight shiver, and turned toward him.

"Hi, let's go into the drawing room. I have something to tell you, but promise me you won't get angry," she said somewhat submissively.

"No, tell me here," Franz said with a disconcerted look.

Still standing, she took a deep breath and slowly raised her eyes to his. "Though I didn't know it when we first went to Venice, Steven was there as well, and he came to visit."

Franz' face turned red with anger, but he contained himself.

"He was with Richard, wasn't he!" he said angrily. "I knew he'd find a way to be with you." He pounded on the table with his fist.

"Please don't be angry," she said in anguish.

He walked about the room in a disturbed manner, and then turned to her with a raised voice.

"I'm not upset with you, only with Steven and his odious friend," he said.

"Please calm down, there is no need for it. Steven is my dearest cousin, and he'll always be connected to us. As for Richard, it doesn't really matter. You and I will be married in December," she said in a soothing voice.

His eyes narrowed, and he told himself, "In a few months I will take you away from here, and it will be the end of both of them and their schemes." Then he turned to her. "Yes, Ale, you're right. Let's instead focus on our wedding." He held her in his arms, reassuring himself she would be his very soon.

Steven returned from Europe, tired and worried about his last meeting with Olga. He decided to wait until the following morning to see her, for it would be best if he had the chance to have a good night's sleep. On her part, Olga was counting the days till his return, as before long everyone would notice her condition. On the next day in the early afternoon, she was in her bedroom when she heard Steven's familiar voice as the housekeeper led him to the parlor. Franz, who was also in the parlor, was the first person to greet Steven.

"Hello, good to see you. Is Olga here?" he asked.

"Yes, let me get her for you," Franz said rudely, and left abruptly.

A minute later, Olga appeared. "Steven, you're back," she said.

"Yesterday," he said. "How have you been?"

"We need to talk in private, let me get my purse."

"I'll wait for you in the car," Steven said worriedly, cracking his knuckles as he often did when he was nervous about something.

He walked outside and, looking at the cloudy sky, decided that going to the park was not a good idea. He then waited by his car, leaning back on the window. Moments later he saw her approach him.

"It looks like it might rain," he said.

"Who cares? Let's go anyway," she said in a demanding voice.

"Where to?" he asked.

"Calhoun," she replied.

For the next ten minutes no one said a word. Then Olga said, "So, I hear you and Richard went to Venice."

"Yes, we made quite the entrance," he said.

"Really, was it your idea?" she asked.

"No," he replied and remained silent until they arrived at their destination. For the next fifteen minutes no one said a word, until the car came to a complete stop.

"Here we are," he said as he clasped his hands.

"Let's take our chances—I don't want to sit here," she said.

The young couple got out of the vehicle and walked slowly toward the lake. They stopped in front of a large willow tree. Olga, who was holding a blanket underneath her arm, unfolded it and placed it on the grassy ground next to Steven's umbrella. Steven lay on it as if he didn't have a care in the world, trying to hide the fact that he did. He put his arms behind his neck and waited for her to say something.

"How was London?" she asked.

"It was lots of fun."

"What made you go to Venice?"

"It was a last-minute decision," Steven said casually.

"Franz didn't like that you were there," she said. "He was furious when he found out about it."

"Why, it's my family," Steven said.

"It's not that. He's convinced Richard is in love with Ale, too," she said.

"Well, he shouldn't worry about it. Franz is the one who is marrying her. But let us talk about what you want to tell me," he said.

"I don't know how to say it," Olga said.

"Just say it," Steven said impatiently.

"I'm pregnant," she said.

Steven sat up. "So soon?" he questioned. He was afraid that might be the case.

"Yes, so soon, it takes but one time," Olga responded sharply.

"Forgive me," he said.

"That's it," she said.

"I suppose we should get married then?" he said with a sigh.

"You suppose!" she said loudly.

"I mean let's get married," Steven said as he changed his position and embraced her. "I do love you," he said assuredly.

Olga felt a heavy load had been lifted from her, and her worries vanished almost instantly. She would pray and hope that the child would indeed be Steven's. If not, however, that would be her secret to bear.

"I'm glad to hear you love me," she said with some sarcasm. "When shall we marry?"

"As soon as it can be arranged. I don't want our child to suffer in any way for our lusty behavior," Steven said jokingly as he placed his hand around her waist. "I will speak with your parents tonight."

By the next day, the news had traveled quickly among the family, and Franz was livid. That evening, he went to see his fiancée. Once Milly let him in, he found Alejandra in the parlor. He told her Steven had dishonored his sister, and that his parents were disgusted. Their wedding would take place on Saturday, August 14. She was embarrassed by her cousin's actions, but not all that surprised, as she now had an explanation for Olga's behavior the last time they were together. Franz continued to denounce Steven's character until she stopped him.

"Not to excuse his behavior, but I know Steven very well, and he would never force himself on anyone," she said with a firm voice. "Olga could have said no."

"Perhaps, but it was still dishonorable," Franz said.

"Yes, it's true. Although, you must look on the bright side, they do love each other," she added.

When the wedding day arrived two weeks later, a small number of people gathered at the Lutheran church in Minneapolis. In her white wedding gown, Olga walked down the aisle with her father. Her head was covered with the white lace mantilla she had received two weeks earlier. Her face beamed with happiness. Standing at the altar was Steven, and next to him, Richard, his best man, while next to Olga was her maid of honor, Alejandra, holding a bouquet of yellow roses. Franz, who was sitting in the front pew, couldn't help seeing the irony of the unexpected scene before him. Not only would Steven be part of his family, but Richard and Alejandra were standing there before him by the altar together, if only for a brief moment. He reminded himself Olga was happy, which appeased his tormented spirit. This was his sister's wedding day, and soon she would have a child. And deep in his heart, he knew Steven would be a good husband to her.

Several months later in late October, Alejandra and Franz's wedding plans were almost complete. With a guest list of three hundred people, the ideal place for the wedding ceremony would be St. Mary's Cathedral on Hennepin Avenue in Minneapolis, followed by a reception at the Nicollet Island Pavilion. The menu had been tasted and approved, the flowers had been selected, and the wedding invitations would be sent out in two weeks.

On Saturday, October 30, six weeks before the wedding, Olga hosted a bridal luncheon for her future sister-in-law at her new Tudor-style home. After lunch, several dozen or more young ladies sat in the drawing room to begin a traditional game that required the future bride to step out for a few minutes. When the bride-to-be walked back into the drawing room, she overheard Olga say, "Franz has delightful plans for her."

"What are they?" asked one of the guests.

"You mustn't say a word; they'll live in London," Olga said.

Alejandra almost fainted, as she felt dizzy for a moment. This must be one of Olga's silly jokes, she thought at first, but a most frightening feeling soon overcame her. When she sat on the olive green overstuffed chair, Olga asked her, "Are you all right? You are pale as a ghost."

"Yes, I'm fine," she said, but she wasn't. She wanted to ask Olga exactly what she meant. However, it would be inappropriate to do so in front of all her friends, she thought. For the rest of the afternoon, she smiled politely and was appreciative of every gift she opened, but her mind was elsewhere. What should have been a happy day was filled with doubt. Lidia noticed her daughter wasn't herself either. "Ale, can I get you something?" she asked.

"No mother, thank you, I don't feel so well," she said.

When all the guests left and Lidia went to the kitchen, Alejandra finally confronted Olga. "What did you mean that Franz and I will live in London?"

Olga's face became serious, "I'm sorry, you'll have to speak with my brother," she said, completely flustered. "My lips are sealed." Then she placed her hand on her mouth.

She didn't deny it, so it must be true, thought Alejandra. She felt such anguish, actually anger, but she knew it wasn't Olga's fault. In fact, Alejandra was glad for her friend's indiscretion. She kissed Olga goodbye, and thanked her for the luncheon. Then she went to the kitchen, and said to her mother, "I have something very important to do, can we please leave now?"

Lidia dried her wet hands with a towel. "Sure, what's wrong?"

"I'll tell you in the car."

Before leaving the apartment, Olga asked, "Ale, aren't you going to take your presents?"

"No, not now," she replied, leaving in haste with her mother.

When she got home, she went to her father's library, picked up the telephone, and called Franz. It was the first time she had ever done so. Moments later, she heard him say, "Hello."

"Franz, we need to speak immediately," she said angrily.

He was startled by her tone of voice. "What's the matter, Ale?" he asked.

"You'll know when you get here," she said.

"I'll be there in thirty minutes," he said apprehensively.

Alejandra was pacing back and forth while waiting for Franz in the drawing room, when he walked in. He tried to embrace her, but she stepped away from him.

"Please tell me what plans you have for us after our wedding," she asked.

Franz closed his eyes and placed his hand on his forehead. He knew Olga must have blathered his secret.

"Ale, please, let's sit down and I will explain everything."

"No, I don't want to sit down," she said.

"Please, I promise it will all make sense," he said pleadingly.

She reluctantly sat down by him on the divan, but her demeanor was still aloof, and her usual serene countenance was replaced by a serious and suspicious one.

"I wanted to surprise you! I was accepted into Oxford, and my uncle is going to have a job for me on the weekends, working at his musical antique shop in London. You will be able to continue with your music studies there. And by next year Oxford will also accept women into the university. Or perhaps you might even study at the renowned Royal Academy of Music. Your dream to study at a conservatory, what can be better than that? There are still lots of details to work out. But imagine how wonderful it would be to travel all over Europe. It's perfect," Franz said.

Alejandra was speechless for almost a minute; she felt her world had come apart.

"Franz, it's not perfect. Yes it sounds wonderful to you, but that is not what we agreed. And I don't like the fact that you didn't even tell me. And furthermore, you were planning on telling me after the wedding!" she said, still upset.

"I know that, as your future husband, I have to decide what is best for us," he said.

"No! Absolutely not! You cannot decide for me. We need to discuss it together. It's as though you completely ignored all my wishes," she said vehemently.

"What don't you like about my plans?" Franz asked.

"For one, I don't want to live abroad because I was apart from my father for many years. And I never want to be away from my family," she added.

"If we went to New York, you'd be far away," he replied.

"Yes, but New York is in the same country; we can visit each other often, and it would not be permanent," she said.

"If you love me, you would want to be with me wherever," Franz said possessively.

"Of course I love you, Franz, but it's not that," she said.

"Then what is it?" Franz asked.

"I don't like you planning everything for me."

"I won't in the future. I give you my word," he said.

Alejandra wanted to believe him, but she didn't.

"I don't understand, why did you agree to marry me? Was it so you would have someone to go with you to New York?" he said.

His words pierced through her like a sharp blade. "What?" she said, astonished by his insinuation.

"Again, if you love me, and your musical training is of utmost importance, you can have both by going to London. How is it that my plan does not satisfy you?" he said, exasperated.

"Franz, I need time to think it through; you changed everything without considering me, and it doesn't feel right," she said tearfully. "You must leave now. I'd like to be alone."

"Ale, I love you so much, we will be happy there," Franz said as he tried to kiss her hands, but she pulled away.

"Please leave," she said again, in a slightly raised voice.

"As you wish," he said, demoralized, and walked out of the room.

The rest of the day and the following day, she stayed in her room, barely eating and crying constantly. She was crushed with disappointment, and played over and over in her mind everything he told her. Franz's plan to live in London seemed reasonable on the face of it, she thought. She questioned whether she was being capricious, for after all, he also had his own aspirations. But the thought of him deciding for her and being away from her family, her country, and all that was familiar left her with such a dreadful feeling, she could not bear it.

Perhaps he was right—in her confusion, and with mixed emotions, she had agreed to marry him so they could both go to New York. But no, it couldn't have been that, either. Here was the opportunity of a lifetime—to study perhaps in one of the oldest music conservatories established in all of Europe. She wiped the tears from her eyes and got up from her bed. He was right—they could travel to Germany, Austria, France, Italy, and visit the places where Beethoven and Mozart had composed and performed. She felt a sudden excitement, but only briefly, for then she thought of her family. For the next few days, Franz went to see her, but she refused any visitors. Finally one day her mother knocked on her door. "Ale, may I come in?" she said.

"Yes mother, of course."

"You have been stowing away in this room for many days and nights. What happened?" Lidia asked as she sat on the window bench.

She recounted the story to her mother.

"I see. It seems you have a lot to consider. I do need to remind you the invitations will be sent out next week, and a decision on your part is of the essence," her mother said.

"I don't know what to do," she said as she started to cry again. "It's an agonizing decision."

"There is only one thing you need to know whole heartedly, and this will be your answer," Lidia said.

"What's that, mother?"

"Do you love him?" Lidia asked, as she pulled out a handkerchief from beneath her sleeve and gave it to her daughter.

When Franz came by again the next day, Alejandra was ready to see him. She was standing in front of the bay window in the drawing room, looking at the bare branches on the trees. A light snow, under a cloudy sky, was sprinkling the brownish grounds when she heard his voice in the room.

"Ale, darling, please forgive me if I have in any way caused you sorrow," Franz said as she turned to him.

He walked toward her and lovingly kissed her on the forehead.

She gently took his hands and said, "Franz, I've been thinking about everything you said. You were right, perhaps I agreed to marry you for the wrong reasons."

Franz's face became pale, and he felt heartbroken. If he had arrived anticipating a positive outcome, his hopeful feelings soon dissipated when he heard those disheartening words.

"You can't mean that," he said.

"Please forgive me, I cannot go with you to London."

"Then I shall stay here with you, and we'll maintain our original plan to go to New York," he said.

"No, that is not where you want to be," she said.

"I don't care anymore, if it means not having you by my side. I want to be with you wherever, wherever! Please, Ale, don't you know how much I have loved you?" Franz said desperately.

She tenderly caressed his face with her fingers, and then kissed him on the cheek.

"Yes, I know you do, but you always wanted to go there. And perhaps with time, I'll be ready to go with you wherever," she said softly.

"Are you saying we're not getting married?" Franz asked her, most discouraged.

"Yes, I can't hold on to you, if I cannot commit to you," she said as she took off her engagement ring and placed it gently on the palm of his hand.

"You must reconsider," Franz said as he embraced her, not wanting to ever let her go. "Ale, I will wait for you; I will return for you whenever you want me to."

At the moment Franz left, she walked into her father's library, but he wasn't there. She felt a profound sadness, for not only was she not going to get married and be with Franz, but studying in New York was out of the question. Her dreams for professional musical training were just that—a dream. She too felt great emptiness, for by her own choice, she had lost what, at the moment, was most important to her. But that was nothing compared to what Franz might be feeling, she said to herself. For a fleeting second she almost ran after him to tell him she had changed her mind—that she loved him. However, she knew she had made the right decision, even if it hurt deeply inside of her, as if someone had taken her heart and squeezed the blood out of it.

For the next several weeks, she spent most days reading and thinking about Franz. Not even playing the piano gave her comfort, for she had lost her purpose. Then on Sunday afternoon, in late November, Steven visited her as she was in the process of lighting the fireplace.

"Ale, let me help you," she heard her cousin say.

"Steven, what a lovely surprise," she said and then hugged him. "What brings you here?"

"I miss you. Sorry to hear you broke off the engagement."

"Yes, me too," she said.

"Are you having second thoughts?" he asked.

"Sometimes," she said.

"What about your music?"

"I don't know, I had my heart set on going to New York."

"Why don't you?" Steven asked.

"My father won't allow it," she said.

"You should ask him again, I don't think he has ever said no to you," Steven said humorously.

Alejandra's somber face brightened at the thought of it.

"You think he'll let me?" she asked.

"Maybe," he said. "You can at least ask. Since when do you give up so easily? What happened to the girl who started her own band, and went against a senior in high school?" She laughed at her cousin's words.

"I wasn't thinking then," she said laughingly.

"I don't think so," he said.

"Well, perhaps I will ask him again. How is Olga?" she asked.

"Getting bigger, and bigger, and very upset you broke her brother's heart," Steven said.

"I didn't mean to," she said as she looked down with remorse. "I do love him, but I couldn't bring myself to go with him."

"I know, don't feel sad. Franz left for London two days ago, he said he couldn't stay here any longer," Steven said.

"You're sure not making it easier," she said.

"No, I mean he'll at least find London a distraction," he said.

"I hope so," she said. "I care for him deeply."

"Well, I best go now, or I'll never hear the end of it," Steven said as he kissed his cousin on the cheek and left the room.

She waited impatiently for the next hour until her father came home that evening. During dinner she was quiet and her plate was almost full.

"Aren't you hungry?" her father asked her.

"No," she replied. "Father, I'd still like to go to New York," she said with a hopeful smile.

"Ale, yes I'm sure you would. However, it would not be proper for a young lady like yourself to live there in a house with complete strangers," he said.

"Oh, please, the Mendes family would be close by," she said.

"Absolutely not," he said.

"What about anything is possible, isn't that what you have always told me?" she said in a confrontational voice that even surprised her father.

"I've consented to you going to the university here. Most young ladies do not get that opportunity, much less across the country," he said.

"Yes, father and I'm very grateful; but if I'm going to take my musical studies seriously, I should be where there is the best academic training," she said.

"What are you going to do with all that musical training? You already play exceptionally well," he said. "Are you still dreaming of being a conductor?"

"Yes, a musical director, perhaps, like Anna Schoen-René."

"Ale, are you serious!" he said. "She studied in Europe, and probably spent years in training. Conductors are all men! And as much as I think anything is possible, this proposition is quite implausible."

Lidia, who was sitting next to Edward, couldn't believe her husband was so set against it, and neither could her daughter.

Perhaps he was right and her aspirations were impossible, Alejandra thought.

"I can try," she said with a pleading voice.

"I don't see how. End of discussion," Edward said as he took his napkin, threw it on the table, and walked away from the dining room.

"Ale, do not get discouraged, have faith, something will come along if it's meant to be," Lidia said as she patted her daughter on her arm.

Alejandra felt disillusioned and embarrassed for believing in her lofty dreams. Why did her father fill her head with ideas that everything was possible? Were they all empty words that he didn't believe, she asked herself? She went upstairs into her bedroom and sat on her desk. She pulled out her worn out musical notebook, as if searching for a hopeful sign that her aspirations were not insane. She recalled her father's hurtful words echoing in her ear.

How wonderful it would be if she could talk to Anna Schoen-René, she thought, and then she came across the name of Clara Wieck Schumann, a piano virtuoso born in 1819. She was able to travel all over Europe performing her own music at a very young age, and her father had been supportive of her musical career; yet against her father's wishes, she married Robert Schumann before she was twenty-one years old. Perhaps fathers are not always right. Could she go against her own father's wishes? It was strange to turn to someone who had died decades ago, but Clara Schumann's time was no different than her time. It was probably even a more conservative age. She probably felt the same despair as I am feeling now, Alejandra thought, as she put the journal away.

On Friday, December 17, 1920, Edward and Lidia, hoping to cheer up their daughter on her eighteenth birthday, took her to the Symphony

Orchestra's Friday concert. Because it was a last-minute decision, the seats were not particularly the best, as they were on the left side of the hall, far in the back. However, that didn't matter to her, for as she read the biography of the piano soloist, Katharine Goodson, it only made her question her recent decision even more. Performing on stage was a virtuoso pianist who had entered the Royal Academy in London at the age of twelve.

As the guest pianist and the orchestra performed Beethoven's Symphony no. 7 in A Major, 2nd Movement, Alejandra began to cry slowly, almost in tempo with the solemn but divine melody that intensified with every note. She felt as if the notes were piercing through her heart and swirling around her spirit, ta, ra, ra, ra . . . . The music was expressing the strong emotions she was feeling. She thought of Franz, to whom she would have been married on this day. She might have the chance to study in London and she had declined it. She was perhaps even too old to be a concert pianist, and of course being a conductor was now pure fantasy.

All these questions ran through her mind, mixing with the musical notes that played loudly in the hall. Perhaps this was a sign she should be with Franz. She covered her face and swallowed her tears. She felt more confused than ever; maybe she had been wrong to call off the wedding. Her mother whispered in her ear. "Are you all right?" She nodded yes, as she tried to compose herself. For the remainder of the evening, she tried her best to put on a good face, but inside she was filled with doubt and profound emotion, if not regret.

When she returned home that night, she thanked her parents and somberly went upstairs to her bedroom, where she let her feelings go as Beethoven's music lingered in her ear, like a bittersweet echo in the distance. She threw herself on the bed and cried until she finally fell asleep on her wet pillow.

Before Edward retired for the night, after the concert, he went to his library, and Lidia followed a few moments later. As he lit a cigar on his desk, she sat across from him.

"Darling, I need to ask you something that's been bothering me for some time," she said.

Edward turned to his wife, and said, "I think I know."

"Do you remember when Ale was a year old? You had such high hopes for her, and she's grown up hearing you say there's no limits to what mankind can accomplish."

"I do! And I meant every word." he replied. "But the years you were both away affected me more than I ever admitted to myself," he said regretfully.

At that moment, Lidia understood his ambivalence and refusal to consider their daughter's ambitions. She got up from her chair, walked toward him, and leaned on the desk.

"Yes, it affected all three of us, and I'm truly sorry for that. We must let her live her life, and you know she's wise well beyond her years," Lidia said as she placed her hand on top of his.

Edward put out his cigar in the ashtray, and took a deep breath.

"I'm tired, let's go upstairs," he said, as he softly caressed his wife's chin. "But I will consider our discussion."

On December 19, Alejandra received a letter from her friend Hannah Mendes. It had taken over a week to get to its destination.

> Dear Ale, I hope you receive this letter before your birthday, and have a happy one. I have some news that perhaps will cheer you up, but first let me say I was very sorry to hear that you ended your engagement with Franz. I know how much you were looking forward to your wedding. Perhaps, in a few months, you will be ready to marry him, and this will be but a small cloudy memory in your sunny sky.
>
> We are looking forward to celebrating Hanukkah, as you must be for celebrating Christmas. I'm saddened to hear we may not be able to start our musical studies together as we had planned. Considering everything, my family and I have a terrific proposal for you, that I hope you and your parents will accept. If you still wish to study here in New York, we would like it very much if you lived with us for the school semester until you become acquainted with this city. For my part, what better experience than to have a dear friend live and study with me. Please let us know of your decision, as soon as possible.
>
> Most fondly, Hannah

She could not believe her lucky stars. This was indeed a marvelous turn of events, for under these circumstances, how could her father refuse? She put away the letter, as she thought about the best time to talk to him.

It was early in the afternoon when she went to his library, but he wasn't there. Instead she went to look for her mother who was in the kitchen preparing dinner, as it was Milly's day off. She told her the amazing news and soon afterwards, she heard her father's steps in the dining room. She ran to see him, and found him in the drawing room. He quietly sat on his favorite leather wing chair and rested his head backwards. When he saw her walk into the room he said, "Ale, play something for me. I need to hear you play."

"Why?" she asked.

"I've felt quite unsettled since the last time we spoke. Who am I to take away your dreams?" he said as she sat next to him on the divan.

"Ale, I don't like to see you so sullen. What happened at the concert? You were crying!" he said.

"I was moved by Beethoven's music," she said.

"Was that all?" he said.

"Also confused," she replied.

"But today you seem to be in a better mood, and you're not angry with me anymore, I see," he said with a smile.

"Yes, I've been sad, I do miss Franz. But today I received a very hopeful letter," she said.

"You heard from Franz?" Edward asked.

"Yes, father, he has written me several letters since he left for London, but this one is not from him," she said. She paused for a moment before she could tell him what she'd been thinking in the last two days.

"I almost made the biggest mistake of my life, and now I see it. Franz is a good man; yet I was so wrong, for if I loved him the way he loves me, I would have married him. And it would not have mattered where we went."

"I suspect you love him as a friend, but not as a man," Edward said in a philosophical tone that surprised even him. "Your mother and I were pleased with your decision, if I may say so."

"Well, father, then you will also be happy to know that Hannah and her family have invited me to live with them while I study at the Institute. Oh please, Father, you must say yes now!" she said enthusiastically.

"I see why you're so happy," he said. "Did you plan this?"

"No, but I hoped for a miracle, and it was Hannah's idea," she said.

"It couldn't hurt for you to study there for a semester to start. I cannot say yes right now, but I'll make a decision after I speak with Mr. and Mrs.

Mendes," he said.

"Thank you, Father," she said, and hugged him.

A week later, on Christmas day, she found an envelope on the mantle of the fireplace with her name. She noticed all the Christmas cards next to it, including one from Franz which she read again, and felt a hole in her heart; for as her father said, she did love him, but as a very dear friend. She then opened the sealed envelope, and to her utmost delight, she discovered a pair of train tickets to New York. She then read the note:

> Dear Ale, we will depart from St. Paul on Monday, January 3. You will begin a new phase in your life. Make the best of it!
>
> Love, your mother and father

21 LIEBESTRAUM

NEW YORK CITY, 1921

The Mendes family lived on the Upper West Side of Manhattan. Built by the up-and-coming architect Rosario Candela, the apartment house, perched on a high corner, had fantastic views of the thriving city. When the Stanfords walked into the entrance gallery, they saw only a preview to the exquisite craftsmanship throughout the spacious rooms. With high ceilings and a southern exposure, the grand-scale living room was decorated with European antiques. A cello and violin stood against a window wall as though they were twin brothers, taking in the afternoon sun. In the center of the room, a Persian rug with geometric shapes in tones of burgundy, ochre, and brown lay below a heavy wooden cocktail table. Three medium-size upholstered sofas in hues of olive green and brown faced the limestone fireplace. Alejandra stared above it, and noticed the vintage Belgian tapestry, similar to one she had seen at the Institute of Arts back in Minneapolis.

"That is my mother's favorite tapestry. It illustrates the story of the Jewish Queen Esther," Hannah said. She continued to look around the room and noticed a painting of musicians.

"Ah! That is a Delacroix original, titled *Jewish Musicians in Morocco*," David Mendes said proudly as he asked Edward to sit down while the two young ladies went to their bedroom. Amelia brought in a tray with a pot of coffee and petite sandwiches.

"Thank you very much, Amelia," Edward said.

"My pleasure," Amelia said as she sat down to join them.

"Lidia and I are profoundly grateful for your kindness and hospitality toward our daughter," Edward said.

"It's wonderful for all of us to have Ale here. She will be an exciting addition to our family; and for Hannah, having someone who can practice Spanish with her will be an added bonus," Amelia said.

After further pleasantries, Edward informed David he was catching the late train back to Minnesota, but he and his wife would make several trips to New York later in the semester. Later, when Edward said goodbye to his daughter, she had a moment of apprehension as she remembered the last time they were separated back in Mexico.

"Thank you, Father! I'll write you every week."

Edward, on his part, could see her tearful eyes, and replied, "We will see you soon, I promise. Enjoy your stay here, and don't worry about anything."

"Yes, give my love to mother and Eddy," she said, as they kissed goodbye.

As night fell, the two girls retired to their bedroom, and Hannah turned off the lights and said, "Buenas noches, Ale."

"Good Night, Hannah, and thank you again for having me stay with you. I'm so grateful," Alejandra said from her twin bed, as she lay pensively looking through the window at the warm color of the full moon, which softly illuminated the small chamber. This was the first time she was sharing a bedroom with someone else, and she liked the feeling of sisterhood. A flood of emotions, excitement, homesickness, and nervousness overcame her, as she stayed awake wondering what was it going to be like living there for the next five months. What would school be like? When would she see her family again? Then she thought about Franz, as his image appeared in her mind; she hoped he was happy, as his memory made her smile.

She woke up the next morning to the smell of freshly brewed coffee. A few minutes later, she heard a knock on the door. Hannah opened it and helped her mother with the tray, which she placed on their dresser.

"It's six thirty, we want to leave here in an hour," Amelia said as she left the room.

"Thank you Mrs. Mendes," Alejandra said as she poured coffee into the flower-patterned porcelain cups and exchanged a brief laugh with her friend who had just come out of the shower wearing a forest-green bathrobe. The cinnamon-spiced coffee tasted delicious. Perhaps their mothers did exchange recipes after all, she thought, and momentarily opened the window to gauge the outside temperature. It felt quite cold, enough to wear a sweater and a heavy coat, but maybe not as freezing as Minnesota, said her friend as she left the room.

At exactly thirty minutes past seven o'clock, David drove the girls to school. The streets and sidewalks of Manhattan were busy with cars and merchants who were opening their shops just before eight in the morning. It dawned on Alejandra that in New York, the energy, and even the smells, seemed different than back home. A new decade was underway; the beginning of the 1920s brought a new attitude, carefree and optimistic.

Moments later, David parked their vehicle in front of the building, and the two girls got out, then waved goodbye as they approached the Institute of Musical Art. Once inside, they were directed to separate areas of study. As Hannah was walking away, she bumped into a young man.

"Pardon me," he said. She turned to her friend, shrugged her shoulders and walked away. The young man turned to Alejandra, who was still in close proximity.

"What's your friend's name?" he asked.

"Hannah Mendes," she replied.

"And yours," he asked.

"Alejandra Stanford," she said.

"Perhaps you can introduce me to your friend later during lunch," he said with great interest.

"Surely," she said as she too walked away.

As she waited in a large reception hall for a teacher to call her name, she read through her class schedule: composition, pianoforte, orchestral instruments, and more. She then looked around, and noticed several dozen students chattering with one another whose enthusiasm seemed to match her own. Ten minutes later, she heard a male voice say, "Alejandra Stanford, room number five."

She walked down a long hallway and knocked on the door.

"Come in," a male voice said.

Waiting in the music room was her new pianoforte professor, who was sitting next to an upright piano. He was perhaps in his early forties, and quite attractive for his age, she thought, but had a high-pitched voice, almost female, which nearly made her laugh. With a French accent he said, "Good morning, Miss Stanford, my name is Marcel Le Fleur."

"Lovely to meet you, Professor Le Fleur," she said as she closed the door behind her.

For the next hour he discussed the syllabus and expectations, and performed for her on the piano. She realized he would be very strict and demanding, and there was no chance of her choosing her own material; yet, she felt he would be an excellent teacher.

At noon the bell rang, and the two friends met once again in the dining room hall. With their trays on hand, they looked for an open spot at one of the tables when they heard someone yell.

"Over here," a male student said to them from across the room.

"That's the boy you bumped into this morning," Alejandra said to Hannah. "He wants to meet you."

They joined him moments later and placed their trays on the wooden table.

"Ladies, welcome," he said.

"You never told me your name, so I can't introduce you to my friend Hannah Mendes," Alejandra said pleasantly.

"My name is Benjamin Alderman," he said as he bowed his head to both of them. "Miss Mendes, pleasure to meet you."

"Is this your first year?" Alejandra asked.

"Goodness, no, this is my third," he said.

"What instrument do you play?"

"Violin," he said. "And the two of you?"

"Cello," Hannah said.

"Piano," Alejandra said.

"Well, all we need is to find another violinist, and we can form our own quartet," Benjamin said.

Alejandra felt a familiar excitement at those words, except she hoped it wouldn't be some kind of a tease as it was in high school. Benjamin seemed much nicer than Randall, and he couldn't possibly be as cruel, she thought as she smiled at her new classmate.

"Are you ladies local?" he asked.

"I am, but Ale is from Minnesota," Hannah said.

"The Godforsaken frozen tundra!" he said with a boisterous laugh.

"Maybe a little, but it's beautiful with thousands of lakes, one of the largest rivers, and amazing museums, not to mention being home to one of the best symphony orchestras in the country," she replied proudly.

"You sound like an advertisement," he said humorously.

"Yes, I suppose, but we Minnesotans are quite proud of the North Star State. Don't say any more unless you've been there," she said, laughing, too. "Minnesota comes from a word meaning sky-tinted water, named by the Dakota natives."

"Wow!" he said.

"My mother studied everything about the state when she moved there from Mexico, which she later shared with me," she added. "Need I also mention that Minnesota is home to the most generous philanthropy movements."

"All right, all right!" Benjamin said. "I see you feel passionate about it. But if it's a competition you want, I can top it," he said.

"Top what?" Hannah asked.

"Less than two years ago, a very wealthy textile merchant by the name of Juilliard bequeathed ten million dollars for the advancement of music. And rumors say our school may become the Juilliard School or something along those lines," he said giddily.

"Remarkable," Alejandra said.

"Perhaps some day I'll visit, what was it called?"

"Sky-tinted water," she said.

"And see its wonders for myself," Benjamin replied with respectful amusement.

"I believe it's time for all of us to return to our classes," Hannah said commandingly.

"You both barely touched your food," he said.

"We had a full breakfast this morning," Hannah replied.

"Next time I see you both, I'll have the fourth member of our quartet," he said boastfully.

"We look forward to it," Alejandra said as she drank the last of her glass of water.

The Mendes and their new guest attended services at their synagogue on the following Saturday. Alejandra was thrilled to have the opportunity to experience and learn more about Judaism and the history of the family's congregation. Shearit Israel, also known as the Spanish and Portuguese Synagogue, was the first Jewish congregation established in the United States and North America. The first Jewish immigrants came from Brazil and settled in New York, then called New Amsterdam, in 1655.

"As the oldest congregation in America, it was also called 'the birthplace of three of the most significant Jewish religious organizations,'" Hannah whispered before the services started.

After perhaps two hours of a religious service, the family met others in the congregation for lunch. Alejandra was still curious about the founders, and asked her friend, "Were they your ancestors?"

"Maybe. We've traced back our family tree to about 1700, but some records stop at that date," Hannah said.

A little before two o'clock, Mr. Mendes came to their table. "Are you ladies ready to go?" David asked the two girls as he brought them their coats.

"Almost, Papa, I want to introduce Ale to some friends," Hannah said.

"Hurry, I have something to do this afternoon at the shop. Ten minutes more," he said.

On the way home, the Mendes family and their guest stopped by the family's store, Mendes & Sons Ltd. David Mendes was a gold and silversmith, a trade that had been passed down to him from his father. It was a family tradition going back at least to colonial times. The small shop located in upper Manhattan didn't seem as luxurious from the exterior as it did inside, she noted. The store was filled with display cases and shelves containing intricate, handcrafted sets of tea and coffee pieces, mugs, bowls, and flatware, made in sterling silver, brass, and nickel, and fine jewelry made in gold. As she admired all the displays, Alejandra's eyes turned to a wooden box with silver-plated brackets lying on a marble counter against the south wall of the store.

"Mr. Mendes, what is this?" she asked, as she gently passed the tip of her fingers through the unique item.

"Ah! That's my own personal treasure. It's a Victorian tantalus," he said cheerfully, taking out a key from his coat pocket and unlocking the box. It held several compartments revealing crystal glasses and decanters, and a hidden drawer that contained a cribbage board and two decks of cards.

"Quite practical," he said. "Particularly when I'm working late into the night."

"What an interesting design. I love boxes; you never know what you're going to find. It's a little bit like my piano, I never know what's going to come out once I sit down to play," Alejandra said blithely.

"Then you must treasure it. What a special gift," he said to her.

While Mr. Mendes went to the factory in the rear part of the store, Hannah pointed out some of her favorite jewelry pieces in one of the locked cases. Soon after, Mr. Mendes came back holding a large cardboard box.

"A special delivery for one of my preferred customers," he said as he took it out of the store and placed it in the trunk of his car.

"Next time my parents visit us, we should bring them here; my mother would love some of the tea sets," she said as they left the store.

As tradition would dictate, the next day, the Mendes family and Alejandra went to the Lower East Side of Manhattan, where many of the tenement houses were home to newly arrived Jewish immigrants. Italian Americans also resided there, as well as in Brooklyn. Upon arrival, the family was welcomed by two dark-haired men who helped them unload heavy food containers from the trunk of the Mendes' vehicle. Amelia had spent most of the weekend cooking a variety of dishes that she shared with Jewish families. While everything was being unloaded, Amelia noted that there was a lot of poverty in this area, and that life for new immigrants was harsh, so anything one could do to mitigate their difficulties was a most worthy endeavor. They went inside the decaying building, and the three ladies put on their aprons and set up tables in a large dining hall.

Soon, the Jewish families living in the nearby houses would gather in the dining room to eat supper. What a terrific monthly tradition, thought Alejandra, as she remembered the large meal gatherings at her grandparents' hacienda in Mexico. Hannah poured out the delicious food onto worn, white ceramic plates and placed them on the serving counter. As each person picked up their plates, they said, "Ich dank aych zeyer," (Thank you very much).

"Hannah, please teach me how to pronounce it," Alejandra requested.

"I'll teach you Yiddish, and you teach me Spanish," Hannah said pleasantly.

"That sounds good," she replied.

After a very rewarding evening, the Mendes family returned home, and as Alejandra looked up into the dark sky from the motor car, it was an awesome sight. With its lit skyscrapers, New York was indeed the city of lights, and she looked forward to her friend's family traditions.

During her second week of school at end of the day, she found herself eager to learn if Benjamin had in fact found the fourth member of the quartet. As she and Hannah waited in the library to meet him, she couldn't concentrate on her reading. Finally, she saw Benjamin approach.

"Here you are, I've been looking all day for the two of you," he said as he pulled out several folders from his brown leather portfolio.

"Ladies, here are copies of the scores," Benjamin said bossily.

"Scores?" Hannah asked.

"Yes, we have a quartet; we can begin practicing tomorrow," he added.

"Practicing for what?" Alejandra asked.

"Our debut concert," he said.

"What!" Hannah exclaimed.

"Yes, I thought we could put on a ten- to fifteen-minute performance here in the lobby, on Valentine's Day," Benjamin said authoritatively, as he remained standing.

"And don't we also get to pick the music?" Alejandra asked.

"Next time," Benjamin said.

"I guess that's fair," she replied. "What will we be playing?"

"It's in your folders. Ah! Here he is, our fourth member," Benjamin said as a young man with glasses and disheveled hair introduced himself.

"Hello, I'm Raphael Cardozo," he said with the broadest of smiles.

"And you play which instrument?" Hannah asked.

"Viola," Raphael replied.

"Now that we are all here together, when is the best day for everyone to stay after school to practice?" Benjamin asked.

"Tuesday," Raphael said.

"Wednesday," Hannah and Alejandra said in unison.

"What about Fridays?" Benjamin asked. They all nodded yes.

"Friday it is. I have to leave now, but see you then at 3:00 p.m. sharp!" Benjamin said, as he gave the last folder to the fourth member of their quartet and walked away.

"You must excuse me as well. My father is waiting outside," he said to the two girls, and took the folder from the table.

"What do you think, Ale? Isn't he charming with those round spectacles?" Hannah asked with her usual humor.

"Sure," her friend replied. "I too must practice on the piano for at least an hour. Mr. Le Fleur is very strict and likes my hands positioned just right."

"See you later," Hannah responded as her friend took her belongings and walked out of the library.

Alejandra let herself into one of the empty piano rooms, placed her bag on top of the upright piano, and sat down on the bench. She took the folder Benjamin had just given her, placed it on the piano ledge and looked through the scores. She couldn't believe what she saw. Her eyes focused on the composer's first name when she saw it; even from afar he haunts me, she thought amusingly. It was the music of Franz Liszt. The first piece was "Hungarian Rhapsody no. 2," the second piece "Liebestraum no. 3," and the third "La Regatta Veneziana" by Rossini.

She felt a rush of unexplainable emotion, reminiscing recent memories of Venice, the regatta, and La Salute. Richard permeated every image and recollection of that unforgettable experience. She could not avoid it, even if she wanted to; but she put the memories aside as someone might place an intricately carved box in another room. She began to play a little of each piece of music, and realized she would have to practice intensively every day in time for the quartet's debut performance.

For the rest of the month, the four musicians met twice and sometimes three times a week to practice. It seemed as though every waking hour she was listening to Franz Liszt's music, if not in practice, in her mind and in her dreams. She knew all eyes would be on the newly formed musical group, which they appropriately named Regatta Quartet, regatta meaning to compete. Benjamin thought it was witty and symbolic, since they all had to race to practice the pieces.

Alejandra's obsession with history led her to discover that the Institute of Musical Art had two hundred first and early editions of Liszt's works with personal notes written on the manuscripts by his own hand. The first time she had ever heard the music of Franz Liszt was back in Minnesota when she attended a concert of the Minneapolis Symphony Orchestra and they performed "Hungarian Rhapsody." She remembered reading that Liszt had been inspired by the melancholic and romantic melodies of the nomadic gypsies who found a home in Hungary. While in her new school, she researched everything she could about the Hungarian composer, who was known for his "brilliance and sheer aura," and who made a great effort to bring attention to other composers of the time. During one of the rehearsals with her fellow musicians in late January, she could not help raving about the composer and his life.

"Franz Liszt was the first to invent the solo recital which he called soliloquies. And to add to his mystical legend, it is written he was once 'kissed by the lips of the immortal Beethoven,'" she said.

"He was a handsome man; wouldn't you have liked to kiss him, too?" Benjamin said laughingly to Alejandra.

"Oh! Benjamin, always so funny," she replied, as all the musicians were laughing whole heartedly.

"Are you falling in love with Franz?" Hannah said, now teasing her too with a double meaning.

"Oh yes, indeed, with Franz the composer," she said, laughing.

"His music is certainly very romantic," Hannah added.

"Well, we better practice much more if we are going to give any resemblance of justice to his music," Raphael said as he took his viola in hand.

"On the count of four let's begin with 'Hungarian Rhapsody,'" Benjamin said as he counted and signaled to start.

When they finished at around five o'clock in the evening, Benjamin suggested they all go to the newest speakeasy.

"Isn't that illegal?" Alejandra asked.

"No, everyone goes, it's not illegal. Drinking alcohol is illegal," he said with assurance.

"My father would ground me for life if he found out," Hannah said.

"He doesn't have to know, just tell him you'll be staying late for practice at my house," Benjamin replied.

"And lie?" Hannah replied. "What do you think, Ale?" Alejandra sat there quietly, not sure what to say.

"Oh come on, girls, I promise nothing bad is going to happen," he said insistently.

"Where is it?" Alejandra asked.

"A block south of Tin Pan Alley," he said.

Alejandra remembered that was the place where all the pianists gathered to play and write new music, so it couldn't be that dangerous, she thought. But she was also intrigued by the thought of going, if only to hear and see the famous, legendary musical avenue.

"Sure, why not," she said.

"Well, fine, I certainly don't want to be the spoiler," Hannah added.

Twenty minutes later, the group of friends embarked on their adventure. Benjamin parked the car on Twenty-eighth Street, and they all walked through the heart of Tin Pan Alley. Just as the storekeeper had told her the year before, there was music everywhere—coming from every publishing shop on the block, even at that late hour. For the only way to get the popular music out to the public was for the musicians to play the newest songs continually, on the piano.

"Let's stop here for a minute," Alejandra said, entering a poorly lit venue as the music within caught her ear. The virtuoso pianist was accompanied by a baritone and alto saxophone. The three-piece ensemble accompanied a blues singer named Gertrude "Ma" Rainey who was known as the Mother of the Blues according to one of the musicians. She had been with the group Rabbit Foot Minstrels, but now performed with the Vaudeville Singers. On that day she was rehearsing for an upcoming concert, and her powerful voice and amazing phrasing were mesmerizing as she sang several songs. After fifteen minutes there, Benjamin said,

"Come on, Ale, time to go."

"Can't we stay a bit longer?" she said.

"No," he said, as she waved goodbye to the musicians.

The four friends walked toward the dubious speakeasy, called Sam's Corner Pub, until they noticed a large crowd gathering outside. Some of the patrons were already drunk, so both girls hesitated momentarily, as a happy old fellow, a little tipsy and dressed in rags, began to play "New York Blues" on his accordion. Alejandra tipped the musician when she heard Benjamin say once more, "Come on, let's go in."

She wondered about the musician, who apparently still lived for his music even if he didn't make much of a living. When they entered the smoky, crowded bar, the two straight-laced girls looked at each other, as many of the bar patrons were drunk, loud, and rambunctious. Raphael, who was rather shy but always courteous, managed to find a small table in the back of the room, while Benjamin went to the counter and ordered four glasses of whisky. Back at the table, Hannah worriedly said, "Ale, if my father finds out, it will be my undoing."

"Mine, too," Alejandra said. "Then maybe we better go."

Alejandra had always been proper to a fault, but when it came to music she forgot any concerns she may have had; and just then, the host announced the band as musicians stepped onto the stage.

"Well, we can't really leave without the boys at this hour," Hannah said as Benjamin returned with the glasses. "Let's have this one drink and go."

"Fine," Alejandra agreed.

Benjamin complained that since prohibition the price of drinks had gone up substantially from 15 cents to 75 cents a drink.

"Okay girls, you drink like this," Benjamin said as he took one swift shot, consuming it all at once. Raphael did the same.

"Now you too, girls," Benjamin insisted.

Hannah drank half and stopped, while Alejandra barely tasted the drink. "It tastes horrible," she said as she wrinkled her nose, disliking both the smell and taste.

"If you drink it all, you'll forget the harsh-bitter taste in a few minutes," Benjamin said, laughing.

"Just a little more," she said. She plugged her nose to block the powerful smell of alcohol, but still didn't finish it.

For the next hour the four friends stayed in the sonorous and smoky saloon. The band, with a large wind instrument section, played mostly blues and Dixieland music. Raphael, whose family was of Brazilian descent, shared some interesting stories of one the country's most popular musical style, the samba.

"Originally a rhythm from Africa, it has become the symbol of carnival dances," he said. "And this summer, my parents are finally taking me to Rio de Janeiro."

"Oh, how fun, I'd love to learn how to play it. Will you teach me?" Alejandra asked him.

"Sure, anytime you want. But now I think Benjamin will need some assistance," he said, as his friend almost fell from his chair.

Benjamin had gotten so drunk that when it was time to leave, Raphael drove them home; he was sleeping and snoring in the back seat of the car within five minutes. When they arrived at almost nine o'clock at night, Mr. and Mrs. Mendes were waiting for Hannah and Alejandra at the entrance of the building. Raphael apologized profoundly for bringing the girls in such condition, as they were tipsy themselves. With Amelia and David by their side, the two young women giggled all the way up the elevator. And once in the house, Hannah's parents took them to their room and took off their shoes and coats as they both sank onto the beds. Amelia covered them with blankets, as she shook her head, with a slight smile.

"You are too permissive with them," David said forcefully to his wife.

"They can't always be perfect, it's not like you were," she said in their defense.

On Saturday, the next day, they woke up late in the morning with terrible hangovers.

"Ale, I feel like throwing up," Hannah told her friend.

"And I have a headache as if someone took a hammer and banged me with it," Alejandra added. "We should have said no."

"No, we're all to blame," Hannah said as they heard a knock on the door. It was Amelia.

"Your father is livid. He will not speak to you until you think about what you did, and Benjamin comes here and explains what happened. And you must apologize for lying to us," she said to her daughter.

"Yes, mother, I'm sorry. We were curious about those places," she said.

"Mrs. Mendes, I'm so sorry, too," Alejandra added.

"You are both young and adventurous; just don't let it happen again. A place like that can be very dangerous for young ladies," Amelia said softly.

Hannah called Benjamin and explained the situation, and in the afternoon he showed up at her house. For the next ten minutes, from her room, she heard her father raise his voice several times; but in the end he accepted Benjamin's heartfelt apology and reassurance it would never happen again. Both Hannah and Alejandra also apologized to Mr. Mendes, who grounded them for the next two weeks. Not only would they have their regular chores, but every day after school, they were required to clean and prepare meals in the tenement houses in lower Manhattan.

After weeks of intensive musical practice and volunteer work, the two friends were exhausted when they arrived home for dinner the night before the concert. The smell of cooking was in the air, and Amelia served some of her delicious Sephardic cuisine including lentil soup, salad, stuffed vegetables, roast lamb, and almond pudding, Hannah's favorite. Throughout the meal, they both sat quietly at the dining table, but ate everything on their plates.

"Girls, don't look so sullen, today is the last day of your punishment," Amelia said pleasantly.

The girls smiled at each other.

"Are you girls ready for your debut?" Amelia added as she poured each of them a glass of milk.

"Ready as we'll ever be," Hannah replied.

"I'm rather nervous," Alejandra said.

"I'm sure you'll all play strikingly," David said. "Tonight you are both dismissed from cleaning the kitchen. You need a good night of sleep."

"Thank you," they said, sighing with relief.

The alarm clock's obnoxious sound woke the two friends at six in the morning on February 14. Alejandra slowly got up from bed and walked to the washroom. With the anticipation of the concert, she had only slept for five hours. She noticed as she looked in the mirror that her eyes were puffy and had dark circles around them. She turned on the water faucet and splashed her face with cold water. Twenty minutes later, after showering, she was drying her arms and hands and noticed the mirror was all steamed up. Oddly, she was reminded of the year before; there would be no flowers on her door step. But despite her brief nostalgia for days gone by, she felt excited about the day ahead of her. She had to perform her best, for herself and the other members of the quartet.

Dressed in a light blue bathrobe, she joined Hannah in the bedroom and sat at the edge of the bed as her friend poured her a cup of coffee. Alejandra, who usually liked to sip her coffee slowly, practically swallowed the strong, hot liquid and drank three cups. Soon enough, the effects of the caffeine perked up her energy; when they left the house, both girls were in high spirits.

Upon their arrival at the institute, the two musicians walked into the lobby area and observed it was all set up—rows of chairs lined up next to each other. There in the front of the makeshift stage was a Steinway grand piano, and half dozen chairs on the side of it. A tingling panic overcame her; breathe deeply, everything is fine, you have practiced relentlessly, Alejandra said to herself. She reminded herself of the words of the institution's director, who said all students were ambassadors of music and their school. And she felt fortunate and grateful to be a student in such a renowned musical institution. She turned her eyes to a large poster on an easel that read:

Valentine's Day Recital
February 14, 1921—7:00 p.m.

Performances by . . .
The Regatta Quartet: Benjamin Adelman, Raphael Cardozo, Hannah Mendes, and Alejandra Stanford.

The . . .

She read the names of a few dozen other performers, which diminished some of her anxiety. The school had several hundred students, though only eight ensembles were scheduled to perform that day for the two-hour program.

As she rehearsed her part one last time at the end of the school day, she thought, the day went by so slowly; it seemed the longest day of her life. When it was after six o'clock in the evening, she joined the rest of the women performers in the tiny dressing room, and changed her casual clothes into an elegant velvet rose-colored dress with a V neck and long sleeves. It was exciting being with all the music students as they prepared themselves to appear on the makeshift stage. She softly brushed her hair, parting it on the left as she often did, and placed a small decorative silk rose behind one ear. She took a soft pink-colored lipstick and was carefully painting the outline of her lips when she heard a knock on the door. She looked for someone closer to the door to open it, but everyone was too busy to even hear the knock, so she got up and opened it herself.

"Surprise," a female voice said.

"Mother, Father!" Alejandra exclaimed with joy.

"We couldn't miss the recital," said Edward as he embraced his daughter.

"We're so thrilled to be here," Lidia said as she kissed her daughter on the cheek. "You look beautiful."

"Thank you, this is wonderful. I've missed you both so much. How is little Edward?" she asked.

"Fifteen minutes before the show starts," one of the students announced.

"He's fine, we'll talk more later," Edward said, as he and Lidia said goodbye and walked back to the lobby area to take their seats next to the Mendes family.

Fifteen minutes later the concert began, and one by one, each of the ensembles performed until almost to the end of the program when the master of ceremonies presented the Regatta Quartet—the second to the last group. The four musicians took their seats and Benjamin signaled them to start. The incredibly romantic and passionate melody of "Liebestraum" was hypnotic; it was Alejandra's favorite Liszt piece, she thought, as she surrendered to the music and her fingers played every note to its satisfying end.

The group then performed Liszt's "Hungarian Rhapsody," and Benjamin played his part with such deep feeling it was as if he was declaring his love for Hannah. Momentarily, he looked at her when she played a most exquisite solo on her cello. What a tremendous experience to be able to perform with other musicians. It was so much more fulfilling than playing alone, Alejandra thought as they performed "Regatta Veneziana," and Raphael played the viola. With its rich tone, it was a perfect complement to the other instruments.

The Regatta Quartet, like the other ensembles, had performed magnificently, at least according to the effusive applause. Then the last group, a string quartet, performed "Amor Brujo" (Bewitching Love) by Manuel de Falla, a composition so beautiful and enchanting, it was an ideal ending for the concert.

When all the musicians came together for the last time in front of the stage, they bowed their heads in unison as a loud and enthusiastic public stood up and continued applauding profusely. Alejandra turned to her parents and caught a glimpse of her mother tearing up. She blew her a kiss and then walked with the rest of the students back to the dressing room, but they could still hear the sustaining applause.

Hannah was ahead of the group and as she approached the door, she raised her voice in surprise.

"Look, look, there's a silver box on the floor."

She felt a bit dizzy, as though her being was flooded with emotion. "Ale, it has your name on it!" Hannah said.

Alejandra took the box from the floor and placed it against her chest, as if she was holding something most precious. From the corner of her eye, she saw him standing by the window several feet away. She slowly walked toward him, as he met her midway.

"It's been you all this time," she said, unable to contain her emotions as tears finally came down from her eyes. She was able to express for the first time a buried, romantic feeling within her. She had felt it since she danced with him at the Venice Carnivale, seven months before. Richard opened the box for her, and took out the white rose.

"The white rose represents the innocence I see in you; the red rose represents the love I feel for you; and your eyes, filled with beauty and wonder, started it all," he said as he tenderly wiped the tears on her face with the tip of his fingers.

She held the two roses as he contemplated her alluring eyes and lips. She too felt a strong desire to be kissed by him, but it wasn't the place for them to express such passionate feelings. They stared at each other for a few seconds until Hannah, who had been observing from afar, approached them.

"And who is this?" she asked.

"This is Richard Morrison," Alejandra said as her parents also walked into the expansive seating area filled with musical instruments. "And this is Hannah Mendes."

"Lovely to meet you," Richard said.

"Good evening, Richard. Another impressive entrance," Edward said humorously.

"Pleasure to see you again, Mr. and Mrs. Stanford," he said.

"Let's not keep the Mendes family waiting; we're all going out for a late dinner," Edward added.

Later that evening, she stayed with her parents at the hotel. As Lidia helped her daughter unpack her clothes from a small carrying bag, she couldn't help seeing a splendor in her daughter's eyes and her radiant facial expression.

"Did you ever imagine it was Richard who sent you the roses on all those Valentine's Days?" Lidia asked.

"No, Mamá, I always thought it was Franz," she responded, smiling, but did not expand on the topic. "Mother, I'm so happy you and father will be here for a few days. Tomorrow I was given permission to take the day off from school," she added.

"What shall you like to do, my dear?" Lidia asked.

"Richard is going to be here for one more day, and you'll never guess where he has invited us to go," she said playfully.

"With so many beautiful places to visit, it might take a while," her mother replied.

"The Metropolitan Museum of Art," Alejandra said, laughing.

Richard was waiting for the Stanford family in the lobby. Dressed quite formally in a brown suit and a hat, he seemed more like a businessman than the pre-medical student that he was. He frequently looked at his pocket watch, and every minute that passed, his eyes turned to the elevator. He wanted to make a good impression on Edward and Lidia. He was well aware that his previous silly escapades were allowable as Steven's friend, but now more formality was required. At fifteen minutes past eleven, Alejandra, who was wearing a fitted white suit with a melon-colored wrap folded on her arm, stood out in the distance as she stepped out from the elevator. Her face had a glow and freshness, like a flower that had just bloomed. When she and her parents met Richard, he said, "Good morning, Mr. and Mrs. Stanford, Alejandra."

"Good morning to you," they all replied.

"There's a taxi waiting for us, shall we?" Richard motioned with his hands, pointing to the hotel's exit door.

The Metropolitan Museum of Art was located on the east side of Central Park. As they walked up the dozen or more steps, the building's facade in Beaux-Arts style displayed an arcade of tall fluted columns. The size of the museum spanned several streets. The great entrance hall, with its arched vaulted ceilings and balconies, seemed more like a cathedral interior to Alejandra, who remarked, "It's gorgeous."

With less than two hours to see the various collections, Lidia expressed her desire to see the portraitures.

"If we get separated from each other, let us meet in this hall at 1:00 p.m. for lunch," Lidia said as she put her arm around Edward's and proceeded to the designated gallery. Alejandra and Richard walked behind them, and for a short moment neither said a word until he interrupted the silence.

"I wanted to see you since last November, but I didn't think it would be appropriate. How are you, Ale?" Richard asked.

"I'm actually very well. The time here in New York has been fascinating, and the music training exceeds all my expectations," she said.

"And Franz?" Richard asked.

"As you may know, we're no longer engaged. He's a lovely person; but perhaps I wasn't ready to be married or leave my family. It was a difficult decision to make, even agonizing, yet I believe it was the correct one," she replied softly.

"Well if you're happy, then I'm even more so with this welcome development," Richard said, with a pleased expression on his face. She smiled too, but said nothing more. Soon afterwards, they realized they had lost all trace of her parents.

"Where shall we go?" she asked.

"The concierge at the hotel told me the museum has several Rembrandt paintings in its permanent collection," he said.

"They would most likely be in the European galleries." She looked at the museum's map and continued walking.

"I hope you didn't find it forward for me to come so soon to see you."

"Richard, I've known you for maybe four or five years, I can't recall.

By now I'm quite familiar with your audaciously bold personality," she said playfully as he brushed his hand against hers when they both reached up to push the button on the elevator. "And thank you kindly for the beautiful roses. They arrived at the most opportune times of my life. I still can't believe it was you!"

Moments later, the elevator opened on the second floor. "Here we are," she said.

As they walked through the gallery slowly, they saw mostly paintings by French, Spanish, and Italian painters. They stopped at each one and explained their observations, until they came across a Rembrandt painting titled *Man with a Magnifying Glass.*

"Now that is truly impressive. His expression is intense and his facial attributes so precise, one could almost touch the creases on his skin; no photograph could capture it quite like this," Richard said in admiration.

"You seem as though you are looking at a portrait for the first time."

"Not the first time, but I'm seeing it with a new perspective," he said as he stared into her eyes. She smiled.

"Yes, he was indeed known for his ability to capture a person's emotions by the use of light and dark contrasts," she said.

There were at least four or more paintings by the famous Dutch master that they looked at in great detail, and Alejandra liked his self-portrait best.

"It's always fascinating to see how an artist sees and paints himself. There is seriousness, even sadness in his eyes," she said poignantly as she stared at the painting. "You know, Rembrandt loved to paint family portraits, and often relied on family members to be his models; it's deplorable to think he died in poverty," she added.

"Considering they now sell for millions." he said.

"Have you been reading a lot on the subject?" she asked.

"A little, you may say," he said as he peeked to see the time on his pocket watch, for he was concerned about meeting her parents on time.

"Goodness, it's ten minutes past one o'clock, we'll be late," he said.

"I'm sure they'll understand," she said as they both rushed down the steps to the main floor.

When they met her parents, Edward said jokingly, "Did you get lost?"

"No, Papá, we lost track of time," she replied.

"Let's eat, there's a very good Italian restaurant across the street from the museum," Edward said.

On their return to the hotel later that afternoon, the two couples walked through Central Park, the first park to be landscaped in the United States. Known for its sprawling land between several avenues, Central Park was the highlight of the city, set against tall buildings and populous streets.

"I've never heard so many different languages spoken in one place," Alejandra commented.

"This is indeed the gateway to America, and even from the time I studied here, the city has changed and grown dramatically," Edward said.

In the evening, Lidia suggested they take a horse-drawn carriage back to the hotel. Edward signaled a man who was smoking on the corner of Fifth Avenue. The young, red-haired man brought his carriage curbside and everyone climbed aboard. The weather was cold, but the moon and the stars brightly illuminated the skies, and the smell of wood burning in the air was appealing, thought Richard as he looked at Alejandra. The tranquility of the evening was interrupted when she suddenly asked with apprehension, "What time is it?"

"It's almost ten minutes past six o'clock," Edward replied.

"Oh, thank goodness, I almost forgot we're supposed to meet Hannah and the rest of our quartet in twenty minutes," she said.

"We'll take you to the Mendes' residence, but we shall not stay," Edward said to his daughter.

"Perhaps I should stay there tonight," she suggested. "If that is all right with you, Papá."

"Yes, that would be fine," Edward said.

"I'd like to join you and your friends, with your parents' permission," Richard said, as he looked at them and waited for their response.

"I guess that would be all right," Edward said.

"We shall not see you tomorrow, Richard. Have a lovely trip back home," Lidia said.

"Thank you," Richard said as they reached the Mendes' apartment building and the coach stopped at the curb. He helped her get down from the carriage, and she waved to her parents.

"Ale, we shall be here tomorrow morning to take you to breakfast," her mother said.

"Good night to you," she said.

When the couple arrived at her friend's apartment on the seventh floor, Hannah, Benjamin, and Raphael were already there in the parlor. They cordially greeted one another, as Alejandra introduced Richard to her friends.

"You all performed splendidly last night," Benjamin said loudly. "There's a place I'd like to take all of you."

"Not another speakeasy," Alejandra said with a laugh.

"No, I promise you," Benjamin said.

"You went to a speakeasy?" Richard asked in amusement.

"Yes, it's a long story," she replied as she rolled her eyes humorously.

"So where are we going this time?" Hannah asked.

"It's a surprise, and only your parents know. But bundle up in comfortable warm clothes," he said coyly.

Minutes later, Benjamin opened the automobile's door for Hannah, who sat in the front seat while the other three friends sat, a bit cramped, in the back. They drove for about twenty minutes until they reached their destination. Hannah laughed and asked, "How did you know?"

"Know what?" Raphael asked.

"That I love ice skating," Hannah said, smiling.

Alejandra sighed, and with a worried look on her face, said, "I'm not a very good skater, in fact not at all."

"I'll teach you," Richard quickly replied.

After the five young friends put on the skates that Benjamin rented, Richard helped Alejandra onto the rink. Hannah entered it like a swan gliding on a lake, and was followed by Benjamin and Raphael.

"Please let's go slow because the last time I remember skating, I was five years old," Alejandra said as she momentarily paused.

"And?" he questioned.

"I fell on the icy floor, and my cousin Anne was there," she said as she recalled her childhood memories.

"Steven's little sister?" Richard asked.

"Yes, she stayed with me until two little boys helped us get up," she said.

Richard started laughing so hard, he almost lost his balance.

"And why is that so funny?" she asked, puzzled.

"Because that was me!" Richard said with a beaming smile.

"Oh! You were the mean boy who told me to learn to skate or stay home next time, little girl. I still remember your words to this day, like an old bad dream," she said now, laughing, too. "Since I haven't learned to skate very well, I should go home," she added coquettishly as she pulled her hand away from his.

"No, no, you're doing just fine," he said as he reached out to hold her hand, but then they both lost their balance and fell on the frozen pond while they continued to laugh wholeheartedly.

"Do you two need help?" Benjamin yelled, sarcastically but warmly.

"No, we're fine, in fact very fine," Richard yelled back, as they got up and continued skating.

"So, I suppose you can now say you've known me since you were a child," he said confidently.

"It's no wonder I didn't like you," she said laughing as they turned around in the skating rink.

"Maybe you'll feel differently now," Richard said as he squeezed her hand.

"We shall see!" Alejandra replied with her flirtatious, teasing smile.

Hungarian Dance No. 5

Richard Morrison had completed his third year of college at the University of Minnesota. He had found science courses to be not only stimulating and interesting, but also a defining factor in his intended profession. The time had come to make a decision regarding his future plans. His family had great hopes he would follow in his father's footsteps; but while business was exceedingly prosperous and bursting out everywhere in the Twin Cities of Minneapolis and St. Paul, it was not his calling.

In late May he announced to his mother he would continue his studies in the field of medicine, and he had taken a job as a research assistant at the university's research department. But his thoughts were also preoccupied with a certain lady, whom at last he was free to court openly. While for at least two years he had been in love with her, there were times he doubted if she would ever feel the same. Since last February, though, she had given him a glimmer of hope. Her eyes spoke of affection, if not love.

Disastrously, Richard's mother, who for years had been planning secretly to have him marry one of her friend's daughters—in fact any of them—had a formal dinner party at the Morrison mansion. During the evening's festivities, it became clear to Vivian Morrison that not only did her son show no interest in any of the available women attending, he practically ignored them and excused himself often throughout the night, though he was polite and courteous. When everyone had finally left, to Richard's great relief, he retired to the library. Moments, later, a disappointed Mrs. Morrison came into the room and sat in the leather sofa across from his desk.

"Richard, you seemed awfully absent tonight," she said.

"Forgive me mother, I wasn't much in the mood for socializing."

"Don't think I don't know why," she said.

"You do?" he asked.

"Yes, it's Alejandra who's on your mind," she said.

"She will be returning in two weeks, and I'd like to plan something special," he said.

"Are you upset with me for trying to have you meet other young ladies?" she asked.

"No, mother, you've been trying for years. But since we are being honest with one another, it's time you stop!" he said, with a firm voice.

His mother was not entirely surprised by his bluntness; yet she had some concerns. "She is certainly a very lovely young woman and comes from an excellent family, but the same can be said of many other ladies. Do I need to remind you she has ignored you for a long time? Is that why you like her so?"

Richard laughed a little. "No mother! That might have piqued my interest in the beginning, but not now."

"Then what is it?"

"There is more to her than a pretty face. She has the ability to see the world with a different perspective, and while we share many values, she doesn't feel tied to rigid ideas about things even if they are established norms. And she's not afraid to speak her mind. But perhaps what I like best about her character is her caring nature. And when I deem she feels the same way about me, I will ask her to marry me," he said.

"Oh son, you're not so bad yourself; and I had no idea how strongly you felt about her," his mother said resignedly, as she stood up from the sofa, walked toward him, and gently tapped his shoulder.

"Let's hope she agrees with you," she said with uncertainty in her voice.

New York, May 1921

Meanwhile, far from home, Alejandra found that Richard was ever present in her thoughts. Since his departure last February, he had written her several letters, and his words expressed seriousness about their relationship. At the same time, she felt profoundly guilty for having romantic feelings about him, as if she was somehow still betraying Franz, though they had ended their relationship six months before. With her parents hundreds of miles away, she turned to a priest for counsel. On a Saturday afternoon, she went to confession at St. Patrick's Cathedral. To her dismay, the sacred place was almost empty, but the quietness was comforting. She walked up to the confessional booth, and sat on the wooden armchair inside a small cove behind a burgundy-toned curtain, waiting to hear the priest. She waited for almost ten minutes before she heard him speak.

"What brings you here, my child?"

Alejandra expressed her concerns. The voice of what seemed to be an older man said, "Feelings of love or affection are nothing to feel guilty about, but acting on them before marriage is a sin."

She had not ever contemplated acting on her feelings in the way the priest insinuated. It bothered her so much she considered leaving the confession booth for a moment, but instead said, "Father, forgive me, that's not what I meant."

"Well, then, you must know that love is the most pure expression of the soul, and so long as you are always honest with yourself and others, you should have no concern," the priest said.

After a few seconds of thoughtful silence, she said, "Thank you most kindly for your guidance, Father." She listened to his words of absolution and made the sign of the cross.

As she left the church, for the first time she felt free to reciprocate Richard's feelings. And while she rarely went to confession, she was glad the priest helped her deal, so wisely, with her senseless guilt.

Days before her return to Minneapolis, Edward and Lidia met their daughter in New York to witness the bar mitzvah ceremony celebrating the religious maturity of Hannah's cousin Ishmael before his thirteenth birthday. As everyone gathered for the morning service at the historic synagogue, the young man eloquently read verses in Hebrew from the ancient *Torah* (Jewish Law). Ishmael's parents described their son in near-poetic words, praising his life and his preparation, which had been rigorous in the last months. Later, he and the rabbi walked about the aisles around the congregation as they held the ancient Torah.

Alejandra was thankful to be with the Mendes family to share such a blessed Jewish tradition. As the service ended, she felt sad to leave that familiar and welcoming place of worship, for while Jewish rituals and beliefs may have been different from her Christian upbringing, the core values of faith and love were all the same. In that moment, she felt fortunate to have experienced another faith in such a close, personal manner.

The next morning, the Stanford family said their last farewell to the Mendes family. While sitting in the sunny parlor, Amelia brought her a gift. Alejandra carefully tore the paper, revealing a sterling-silver *tzedakah* box with engraved letters reading A. Stanford.

"A box used traditionally for donations," Amelia said.

"Thank you so much for all your generosity. I'll never forget it. Living here with you and studying at the Institute have been some of the best experiences of my life," she said to Amelia and the rest of the family, and then hugged each one of them. Lidia then offered a gift to Hannah. She unwrapped the large package and to her absolute delight, she discovered an oil on canvas portrait of herself when she was thirteen years of age.

"It's stunning!" Hannah remarked. "But how . . . "

"Your mother gave me a photograph of you last February," Lidia said.

David looked at the portrait and was equally impressed.

"Have you considered selling your work?" he asked. "It's marvelous."

"No," Lidia replied.

"Well, if you do, I'd love to display it in the store," he added. "I have very wealthy patrons who would love your paintings."

"Thank you, that's very kind of you to offer," Lidia said.

"Hope you will visit us in Minneapolis," Edward said.

"We will," David said. "I'd like to see all of Lidia's portraitures."

Lidia hugged Amelia. "We are so appreciative for your hospitality toward our daughter. I hope someday we can return the favor," she added.

"Remember, my dear, we would love to have you stay with us for the next school year," Amelia said.

"I'll miss you all," Alejandra said as she and her parents walked out of the apartment house.

As they boarded the train back to Minnesota that afternoon, Alejandra sat quietly in the cabin. She was deep in her own thoughts when the train's loud whistling sound startled her as it began to move forward. She took out her musical journal, and reviewed some of the latest entries, but not even that could keep her from thinking about the young man who had captured her attention. Would he be waiting for her at the station in St. Paul?

The next day, when the train came to a complete stop at the platform, Alejandra felt butterflies in her stomach. She took out a small mirror from her purse, retouched her lips with red lipstick, brushed her hair, and pinched her cheeks to add color. "I don't know why I'm so nervous. I've known Richard for so long, but it feels as if I'm meeting him for the first time," she said to her mother who was sitting next to her.

"Perhaps your feelings have changed for him," Lidia said.

"Oh, Mom, you indulge me too much," she replied.

Edward smiled as he heard his wife and daughter in such good spirits. He looked at his daughter, and in one of those rare moments parents encounter from time to time, he realized that Alejandra might soon leave the nest.

"He's only a boy, crazy about you," he said to his daughter.

She smiled while putting on her feathered cloche, and waited for most of the people to leave the train. Before leaving the cabin she turned toward the window, but didn't see him anywhere.

When she and her parents stepped onto the sidewalk, she noticed it was a warm, sunny June day. She looked in every direction, but still saw no sign of Richard. Instead a young, well-dressed man carrying a case walked up to her.

"Miss, please excuse me for a moment, I have something for you," he said as he opened his violin case, took out his instrument, and began playing a Gypsy-sounding melody that Alejandra did not recognize. She remembered another violinist playing at Piazza San Marco in Venice when she, Richard, and Steven returned from visiting La Salute. When the musician finished playing the piece, she said, "Thank you sir, that was very, very beautiful."

Just then, Richard approached her. "Welcome home, Ale," he said as he bowed his head to her and her parents.

Edward nodded and smiled while Lidia looked at their daughter, whose eyes sparkled with the look of love.

"Richard, you do enjoy making an entrance," she said as he took her small carrying bag, and together they left the depot.

By the end of the summer their relationship took on a more mature tone, for in between long walks around the lakes, visits to museums, dinner parties, and formal rendezvous, they conversed intimately on many topics. It had taken them years to come to that comfortable stage of a relationship where they could express their thoughts freely without prejudice, awkwardness, or pretention. Besides the intense physical attraction they felt for one another, they had also become very good friends.

Toward the middle of August, they attended the last summer concert of the season at Lake Harriet. It was early in the evening before sunset, and she waited from him to bring her an ice cream cone. Moments later, he approached her, and the young couple sat in the last row of the outdoor venue.

"Here's one strawberry ice cream for the lady," he said.

"Thank you," she replied as she daintily licked the refreshing sweet treat. While they waited for the orchestra to begin playing, he turned to her and asked her something he had not done up to this point.

"Is it true you want to be a conductor?" he asked.

She looked at him with an inquisitive smile, wondering where the question was going.

"Yes," she replied. "Why do you ask?"

"I was trying to picture you up there with all those men. It's a mostly male-dominated profession," he said.

"Well, so is everything else," she said.

"That's true. What is it about being a conductor that you like?" he said.

She thought about her answer, and she too pictured herself in the conductor's place and smiled.

"If I had to say one thing, or maybe two, it would be the ability to choose and interpret the music of musical geniuses," she replied.

"Whose music would you choose?" he asked.

"Ah! That's the beauty. I'd have several seasons to choose to my heart's content," she said. "One would have to learn perfectly the timbre of each instrument of the orchestra, their relationship with each other and with the composition, and of course the musicians must be of very high caliber. And, equally as important, you must consider the public's taste and preferences."

"I thought you might say, tell them all what to do," he said and began to laugh.

"Very funny." She nodded her head and laughed, too. Suddenly she realized that perhaps being a conductor was indeed a far reach, but she wasn't ready to give up on a dream she had been holding onto for so long. It's not like she would be the first woman to do so. And she also felt she was beginning to rely more on his opinion, for she trusted him, even if she wasn't ready to admit it to him.

"When you become a conductor, I'm going to sit in the front row to watch your every gesture," he said mischievously.

"And if you don't behave I'll take the baton and gently tap you on your shoulder," she said with a laugh.

"Gently?" he asked.

"No! Perhaps more like a very angry schoolmaster," she said, as they both continued to laugh.

With rain forecasted for the afternoon one day in late August, Alejandra took her umbrella from the closet and waited for him to pick her up. She and Richard had made plans to visit her cousin Steven and meet his newborn, although she feared the encounter with Olga, for she wasn't sure what to expect from her. The last time they had seen each other was the previous year.

Upon arrival at the Johnson's residence, Richard knocked on the door. A stern-looking man opened it and said, "Come in, wait in the parlor." As soon as they spotted Olga, it was clear she was still not the same as she used to be. Something dramatic was different about her and Alejandra sensed it, but didn't know exactly what it was; perhaps she was still angry with her friend for not marrying Franz. Throughout the brief visit, Olga was cool and distant toward both Alejandra and Richard, to the consternation of Steven who could only discreetly overcome his wife's lack of manners. With his usual charm and ease, he picked up his son from the small bassinet and gave the baby to his cousin. She held the little baby in her arms, and gently touched each of his tiny fingers.

"Olga, he's precious, he looks like you with his golden locks and your smile," she said pleasantly.

"Yes, that's a good thing!" Olga said coldly.

Alejandra placed the baby back in his crib, sat on a floral upholstered chair, and handed Olga a package.

"What is it?" she asked.

"For the baby," Alejandra replied.

"Open it, Steven!" Olga commanded her husband, who thanked his cousin and unwrapped the gift.

"How are your family and Franz?" Alejandra asked softly.

"You care?" Olga responded harshly.

"Of course I do, we were all such good friends for many years, and I wish him the best always," Alejandra said as she looked Olga straight in the face, hoping to connect with her.

"He is enjoying London, I'm sure," Steven said before his wife replied. "Can we offer you something to drink?"

"Sure," Richard replied while Olga left the room.

Steven opened the box and took out the gift. It was a blue knitted blanket.

"Ale, it's beautiful," he said. "Did you make it?"

"Believe it or not, I did," she said with a quiet smile.

"I never knew you could knit," Steven said as he spread the blanket across the baby's tiny body.

"Our grandma Clara taught me; she once told me if I didn't know how to cook, I should at least know how to knit," Alejandra replied with a smile.

Their butler brought in a tray and placed it on the table, and Steven poured everyone a cup of coffee.

"So what are you working on these days?" Richard asked Steven.

"Business is booming, electricity has become a necessity, and most homes, if not wired for it, want it now," he said.

A long silence between them followed, until Richard said, "I'm afraid we have another commitment we must attend."

"Well, congratulations again," she added as she patted Steven's hand.

"You know, I still want you and Richard to be our son's godparents. Just give her time," Steven said to Alejandra.

"We'd love to," his cousin said to him and kissed him on the cheek.

Richard stood up from the cracked brown leather chair where he was sitting as Olga returned to the room.

"Thank you for the delicious coffee cake," he said.

"You have an adorable son," Alejandra said as she and Richard walked toward the door. "Good to see you again, Olga, my best regards to your family."

"Thank you," Olga said in a slightly softer tone of voice.

When they left the house it was pouring, so Richard opened the umbrella and together they walked out of the house and into his automobile. While in the car, she remained quiet as they drove back to her house.

"Ale, are you all right?" Richard asked her.

"Perhaps I should have come by myself," she said.

"I don't think it would have made much of a difference. She never did like me; but I must agree with you, Olga is not as she once was," he said as he gently squeezed her hand.

"She was my dearest friend," she said.

"Ale, don't be sad, I've some interesting news to tell you."

"About?" she asked.

"The field of science," he said as he changed the subject altogether. "One of the professors at the research lab said researchers in Canada have found a potential breakthrough in the treatment of diabetes," he added.

"Diabetes?" she questioned.

"It's a debilitating illness that can cause many problems including blindness," he replied. "And my sister Vivian has suffered from it since she was a teenager."

"I wasn't aware of that," she said. "What are the symptoms?"

"It affects the ability to produce insulin, a hormone that controls the amount of sugar in our blood," he said.

"And what's the breakthrough?" she asked.

"Researchers extracted insulin from dogs that cured other dogs with diabetes, so they hope the same results can be applied to humans," he said enthusiastically.

"You must be excited to start your studies in a few weeks," she said.

"Yes, but I'm not thrilled. Summer is almost over and you'll be going back to New York," he said.

"I will not be going back there this semester," she said.

Richard smiled. "Ah! Very good news. And your music training?"

"It's very important to me, and I do plan to resume my studies next year. However, my family and I are going to Mexico to my aunt Carolina's wedding in October. We really want to be there for her after everything she has been through," she said.

"When do you leave?" he asked.

"Next week," she replied.

"Why did you not mention it before?" he asked with some distress.

"I decided two days ago. And the other exciting news is that Hannah accepted my invitation to join us. Her parents thought it would be a wonderful opportunity for her to become fluent in the Spanish language and experience another culture. They'll meet us in Kansas City," she said.

"When will you be back?" he asked.

"End of October."

"Well, I suppose it will be for only two months," he said as he tenderly caressed her hands. "I shall miss you terribly, you know."

Richard met the Stanford family at the train depot twenty minutes before their departure. For the last week, he had been extremely concerned about Alejandra leaving the country, for he remembered that the last time she went to Mexico she was gone for several years. He comforted himself with the knowledge that she had assured him she would come back in two months. Before she boarded the train, Richard embraced her, and then gave her a small package, saying, "I'll miss you, Ale, and will be waiting for your return anxiously. Happy reading."

"Thank you, I'll see you in two months, I promise!" she said as she stepped onto the train, after he gave her a loving embrace. She waved to him through the window from her seat, feeling a knot in her throat as he waved back. As soon as she could no longer see him, she unwrapped the small package. It was a book titled *Marie Curie, Recipient of the Nobel Prize in Science*. She turned to the first page and found a sealed envelope that she quickly opened.

> Dearest Ale:
>
> I am not a man of poetic words, or even many words, yet three words are certain, and they are edged in my heart.
>
> I love you. I have waited for so long just to say them, to see and be near you. I will be waiting for us to be together again very soon. Hoping you feel the same, Richard
>
> One more note, the violinist at the train station when you arrived from New York played Brahms' "Hungarian Dance no. 5 in G Minor."

Symphony No. 5

Mexico City, September 1921

It had been six years since the Stanfords' last visit to the Merino residence. It was located in a neighborhood known for its large colonial haciendas, monasteries, and historical buildings, dating back to the time of the conquistadores, and was once a recreational retreat for Spanish dukes, emperors, and kings. Now the locality was one of the preferred residential areas by Mexican families of reasonable means, ambassadors, well-to-do businessmen, artists, and travelers. As the Stanfords approached the stately Mexican-colonial home in San Angelín, they found it surrounded by a large fence with vines that spread throughout the walls, as they had many years before. The sun beautifully bathed the stucco exterior of the structure, leaving whimsical shadows on its facade like painted images.

A friendly man opened the wrought-iron gate to let the vehicle inside, until it stopped in front of a large courtyard. Calixto and Delia Merino were eagerly waiting for their daughter and her family to arrive, so when they heard the sound of the car doors opening, Delia said cheerfully, "Ya llegaron, ya llegaron" (They've arrived). It was wonderful to be back in Mexico, Alejandra thought as she and the rest of the family stepped into the house. It wasn't the smell of burned sugar that welcomed her this time. Instead she smelled the odor of baked bread, as it was almost time for the main supper at 2:00 p.m. Her grandparents immediately hugged her.

"Abuelitos, this is Hannah Mendes," she said, smiling.

"Bienvenida a México" (Welcome to Mexico), Delia said as she embraced Hannah, while Calixto gave her a hearty handshake.

"Gracias, I'm happy to be here with all of you," Hannah said.

Edward and Lidia greeted her parents, and before the girls walked away, Delia said to them, "We will be serving *la comida* (supper) in half an hour." Then she turned to the housekeeper. "Teresa, please show the young ladies to their bedroom."

They followed Teresa across a patio landscaped with a variety of azaleas, jasmine, and pink bougainvillea flowers. Leaving the fragrant smell behind, they entered their peach-colored bedroom with Mexican red tile floors, a collection of Mexican and South-American textile wall hangings, and linen bedspreads embroidered in floral patterns of peach, pink, and white. The two twin beds were separated by an antique dresser carved with a mother-of-pearl inlay. Hannah noticed a large desk by the window, where she placed her purse.

"Hannah, we've so much to see in a week, and then we'll go to Cuernavaca."

"I can't believe we're here together," Hannah said as they threw themselves on their beds as if they were two little girls. They changed clothes, and began to unpack and hang their clothes in a large wood and metal armoire. Then, as Hannah washed her face in the copper wash basin, she heard bells ringing.

"What is that?" She asked.

Alejandra laughed. "It means lunch is ready. With the courtyard in between the bedrooms and living areas, it is too far for anyone to hear. So my grandmother uses bells."

"Great, I'm starving," Hannah replied.

Moments later, they walked across the courtyard and into the main part of the house as they passed the grand salon, and Hannah noticed her cello next to a piano. Alejandra was heading in that direction when Hannah said, "Come, Ale, we can play later."

The dining room with its large window facing the street was brightly illuminated with a bronze crystal chandelier, and several sconces adorned the surrounding walls. The sound of a small parrot named Rico made for lively conversation as Teresa began to serve the authentic Mexican food on pottery dishes. The cobalt blue decanter and glassware, made by Mexican artisans, stood out beautifully against the white embroidered linen tablecloth and the floral arrangement containing azaleas.

The colorful and elegant décor was inviting and warm, thought Hannah. She noticed a collection of pottery figurines and a most interesting sculpture on the console table. "What is that?" she asked Alejandra.

"Chalchiuhtlicue," she replied.

"I'm not even going to try to pronounce it, what does it mean?" Hannah asked.

"She of the Jade Skirt, and the image represented the Aztec goddess of fertility and water," Alejandra said. "It's over a thousand years old."

"And the color in here is fabulous," Hannah added.

"It is said that the Mexican color palette is a result of the keen observation by the natives of this land of their natural environment. They were inspired by the plurality of colors—the purplish mountains at sunset, the reds and pinks of the volcanoes, the greens of the lush forests, the turquoise seascapes, and the amber deserts," Doña Delia said.

Hannah then turned her eyes to a portrait above the carved wooden buffet. "Mrs. Stanford, did you do that, too?" Hannah asked.

"Yes, that came from a photograph of my mother when she was twenty years old," Lidia replied.

"Personally, I think that was your best," Don Calixto said.

"Oh my goodness, Ale, the resemblance between you and your grandmother is remarkable," Hannah commented.

"You do me favors," Alejandra said graciously.

Later, after discussing all the latest news on Carolina's wedding, Calixto tapped his wine glass with a tea spoon.

"I have a phenomenal announcement to make," he said.

Everyone looked at each other, waiting to hear the rest.

"Continue, father," Lidia said, knowing well that particular expression on his face as he widened his eyes and licked his lips.

"Ale and Hannah, how would you two ladies like to continue with your musical training while you are visiting here?" Calixto said.

They both smiled with a perplexed look.

"How can we?" Alejandra asked.

"As life would have it, your old piano teacher Luis Orozco is now one of the professors of the Conservatorio Nacional de Música (National Conservatory of Music)."

"Luis is a professor there now?" she questioned.

"Yes, when he left Cuernavaca, he dedicated himself for several years to the study of musical composition and orchestration, and he teaches those subjects now in addition to piano studies," Calixto said.

"We're only going to be here for two months," Lidia said.

"Yes, but perhaps you may want to reconsider staying for the semester instead, and leave after the New Year," Calixto added.

"I must admit, it's a wonderful opportunity for the girls, if Hannah's parents would accept," Edward said optimistically.

Lidia could not believe her ears. Why would Edward be so willing to let her daughter stay all of the sudden?

"Edward, your job?" Lidia asked.

"What's two more months in a life span," he replied.

"Thank you," Lidia said to her husband most gratefully.

"And you ladies, what do you think?" Edward asked.

"I'd love it, absolutely love it," Hannah said, exceedingly enthusiastic.

"Abuelito, what could be better," Alejandra said as she thought of furthering her studies in music composition; but strangely, she thought of Richard, and worse yet, not seeing him for more than four months, especially after she had promised she would be back in two months.

"Ale, you're so quiet," Lidia said.

"Pardon me, I was thinking of all the possibilities, but yes, yes, of course!" she said as she swiftly drank her glass of freshly squeezed limeade.

"Well, we must contact Hannah's parents immediately," Edward said.

"It is settled, I'll make the necessary arrangements. You can stay here during the week, while our two young musicians attend the conservatory, and spend weekends in Cuernavaca," Calixto said.

As the girls retired to their bedroom, Alejandra lay there pensively as she listened to the sound of the water dropping down the garden fountain. It was a soothing rhythm, yet her thoughts about the day ahead prevented her from sleeping. Tomorrow, Alejandra would see Luis Orozco, and she recalled the first time she met him. What did he look like now? He must be married and with a few children, she thought smiling, while looking at Hannah who fell sound asleep, almost immediately, after her head touched the pillow.

The next morning while Edward was driving, Don Calixto pointed out some important landmarks built in the seventeenth and eighteenth centuries. The National Conservatory of Music was located in the area known as *Barrio Universitario* on the northeast side of the zócalo in

Mexico City. However, Alejandra was not listening. Instead, she was thinking about her former piano teacher, the quiet man who diligently came twice a week to the hacienda to teach her how to play some of the most beautiful music composed for piano. A flood of grateful emotions and memories overcame her, for she never imagined she would ever see him again, much less be taught by him. She recalled how she felt when he abruptly ended the lessons, and admitted to herself she had developed a crush on him when she was entering puberty.

"Here we are," Edward said as he stopped the car and parked in front of an imposing ancient colonial building. He then opened the door for the young ladies. They walked toward the main entrance and stepped into a large hallway, and just then she saw him from afar, walking toward them. Luis Orozco had barely changed and was as handsome as ever, but what she felt was brotherly love and nothing more.

"Alejandra, you are a lady now," Luis said as he affectionately embraced her.

"Luis, this is my friend Hannah Mendes from New York," she said courteously.

"Mucho gusto," (pleasure to meet you) Luis said. "Don Calixto and Edward, good morning."

"Luis, wonderful to see you again," Calixto said.

"You haven't changed a bit," Edward added.

"Come, let us take a look at the facilities, and then we can sit down to discuss your musical studies," Luis said as he escorted the visitors through all three floors. The building, while several centuries old, was in great condition. At the center there was a courtyard with limestone floors, stone arches, and pillars. This was the place used for concerts and other performances. At the end of the tour they stopped in his office, a large room with a small window facing the patio. The visitors sat around his desk as Luis pulled out a course catalogue from one of the drawers. The two young ladies, who were sitting next to each other, browsed through it together as Alejandra translated from Spanish to English and read out loud.

"Pianoforte, voice, strings, orchestral instruments, harmony, composition, art history, music history, aesthetics . . . "

"Aesthetics?" Hannah asked.

"A branch of philosophy having to do with the essence and perception of beauty and ugliness, and the psychology of art, you could say," Luis replied.

"That sounds intriguing," Alejandra said as she continued to read out loud. "Anatomy, languages, and dramatic art."

"Goodness, an incredible selection," Hannah added.

"The academic curriculum is modeled after that of the Paris conservatory," Luis said. "And also the German conservatory, some may say."

"How long has the Conservatory of Music in Mexico been in existence?" Edward asked.

"Since July 1, 1866; it was through the Philharmonic Society and its members that the National Conservatory of Music was established. The conservatory became so popular after its inception, that two years later it had over eight hundred students. You might want to read the words later, spoken by the priest Agustín Caballero during the inauguration. They are incredibly inspirational," Luis added.

"I suppose one must give credit to former President Porfirio Díaz for investing in the arts and sciences," Don Calixto said.

"Indeed!" Luis said.

"What do you feel might be the most appropriate courses for me to take, since I'm not quite fluent in Spanish?" Hannah asked.

"Which of these subjects interests you most?" Luis asked.

"Certainly string instruments, Spanish, and perhaps even dramatic art. That is something I've always been curious about," Hannah said.

"That would be fine," Luis added. "And you, Ale?"

"My two loves—music and art history, oh yes, and musical composition, orchestral instruments, and . . . " she said without finishing.

"I see you are as eager to learn now as you were when you were a little girl. Perhaps you can start with four courses for this semester," Luis said.

"At what level of study will they be?" Edward asked.

"There is a distinction between aficionados, new students, scholars, and those who reach the highest level or who deserve a professional title. Alejandra and Hannah would start at the first level, although we would take into consideration the studies they fulfilled at the Institute of Musical Art," Luis said.

"When can they start?" Edward asked.

"I need you to fill out several forms, but they can begin tomorrow at 9:00 in the morning," Luis said.

"That's excellent," Edward said. "We are very thankful for all your efforts, Luis."

"It's my pleasure. I believe the young ladies will find the conservatory a most inspiring place to be," Luis said.

"Until tomorrow, Professor Luis," Alejandra and Hannah said.

As they left the conservatory, Don Calixto turned to his granddaughter's friend.

"We have much to do this afternoon, but first there is a place I'd like to show you, Hannah."

"Yes, Mr. Merino, what is it?" she asked.

"You shall see very soon," he said.

They drove through several neighborhoods in Mexico City until they stopped at a house located in a neighborhood called Colonia Polanco. "This is the house of the Fasja family, and it is where many Sephardic Jews come together as a congregation. They are planning on building their first synagogue next year. I want you to meet them, and we can bring you here anytime you like," Don Calixto said.

"Is there a large Jewish community here in Mexico?" Hannah asked.

"Yes, many came in the sixteenth century, and more recently in the nineteenth century from Eastern Europe, Turkey, Lebanon, and Greece. And we also have a large population of Arab Mexicans who came from Syria, Iraq, and also Lebanon."

"How interesting," Hannah said.

"Very pluralistic society, indeed," Edward added.

At the request of Hannah, who was greatly interested in seeing some of Mexico's most important historic sites, the Stanford family stayed in the city for the weekend in late September. With the Revolution over, there was much to do and see in the area. On Saturday, very early in the morning, they visited the enormous archeological site of Teotihuacán (Place of the Gods) with its large-scale pyramids of the sun and the moon dating back to 200 BCE. Don Calixto told Hannah that at its peak, perhaps in 450 CE, the city had up to 250,000 inhabitants, making it one of the largest cities in the world at that time. In the afternoon, they visited Chapultepec Park, and later, Chapultepec Castle, which had become a presidential residence. In the past it had been a military academy, the imperial residence of Maximilian I of Mexico, and an observatory.

Perched on a hill more than 7,000 feet above sea level and surrounded by a forest, the view of the city was breathtaking, remarked Hannah when they reached the top of the castle. With limited access to the historic site, they toured a few rooms open to the public that were decorated with Louis VI furniture. Don Calixto mentioned that at one point, during Benito Juárez's reign, it had been suggested the style of furniture be changed, but Juárez said it should remain exactly the same because it was part of the Mexican history. Calixto also gave Hannah a brief history of Mexico, from ancient times to Mexican Independence, the Treaty of Guadalupe, and the Revolution.

When they left the castle and stood in the courtyard facing the city, he added, "Since 1920, José Vasconcelos of the Ministry of Education envisioned Mexico's heritage as one where traditions from all the peoples of Mexico—Natives, Asians, Africans, Arabs, and Europeans—integrate. And the rich and diverse cultures of our people, reaching back more than two thousand years, make our country a wealth of traditions and cultural heritage worth learning, respecting, and celebrating."

"I see you haven't lost your passion for Mexican culture, Father," Lidia said in good humor.

Don Calixto smiled. "It's our legacy," he said.

The next day, as they did on many Sundays, the Merino and Stanford families and their guest went to Alameda Park, a public gathering place for all the social classes in Mexico City next to the unfinished Palacio de Bellas Artes (Fine Arts Palace) between Hidalgo and Juárez Avenues.

Surrounded by Greco-Roman inspired fountains and poplar and alamo trees, the park was once an Aztec marketplace, but its current form was created in 1592, explained Don Calixto. Alejandra and Hannah walked about and noticed two statues. One was a monument honoring former Mexican President Benito Juárez as he held a book representing the Constitution of 1857; his most famous quote was carved on the base of the grand sculpture.

"Ale, please read it to me," Hannah said.

"Entre los individuos, como entre las naciones, el respeto al derecho ajeno es la paz."

"What does it mean?" she asked.

"Among individuals, as among nations, respect for the rights of others is peace," Alejandra said, reading Juárez's quote.

"Wonderful quote and so true," Hannah said admiringly. "It should be carved in everyone's forehead," she added in her usual humorous way, as she swiped her index finger across her forehead.

Alejandra laughed, too, and walked to the other monument, which was on the other side of the plaza.

"And this one, as you can see, is in honor of Beethoven, commemorating the centennial of his ninth symphony, and donated by the German community living in Mexico."

They then joined the rest of the family on benches surrounding a kiosk where an ensemble of musicians played classical waltzes and popular music. Hannah noticed dozens of young women dressed in fashionable gowns walking around the kiosk.

"What's going on?" Hannah asked.

"It's a tradition called *verbenas* where young men give roses to the ladies," her friend replied as she turned her eyes to the florists selling roses. There was a huge contrast between the social classes, not only because of the differences in their clothing or even their demeanor, but rather what their lives might be, Alejandra thought. She didn't quite understand it as a child living in the seclusion of the hacienda. But she realized in that brief moment what her abuelito had told her numerous times when she was a child—the economic differences between classes were too great.

She looked at one young girl in particular, maybe fourteen years old, who was holding a large basket filled with flowers. Her hair was disheveled, and her dress appeared to be washed out, but her face, tan and sunburned due to daily sun exposure, had a smile as she seemed to be enjoying the music performed by the orchestra. It was in some small measure something she could enjoy every Sunday, and Alejandra silently shared that moment with her. In that pensive mood, she smelled the yellow rose in her hand and returned her attention to the musicians playing in the kiosk.

On the morning of October seventh, the Stanford family and Hannah departed for Cuernavaca, Mexico, to attend the wedding of Carolina Merino and Anthony Solberg. The weather was similar to how it had been when she traveled at the age of seven. Much had happened in her life, in Carolina's life, in all their lives, she thought, as they drove through curves on treacherous roads. She couldn't help but feel some fear, and it seemed to her that something wonderful was always accompanied by something horrendous. In her own silent thoughts, she hoped that Carolina's happiness would last for a lifetime. Then she thought of Richard, and how she needed to tell him that she wouldn't be back to Minnesota until January of 1922. She missed him more than she would ever care to admit.

"Hija (daughter), you're awfully quiet back there," her mother remarked.

"Oh Mamá, I was thinking about the first time we went to Cuernavaca, so many happy and sad memories," she said in a reflective tone.

"Yes, but tomorrow it will be a blessed occasion for your aunt and all of us," Lidia said.

"Hannah, you too are quiet today," Lidia said.

"I was looking at the stunning landscape, and thinking about how my parents would like it here," Hannah said.

"Well, maybe we can invite them to visit us," Lidia suggested.

"Yes, indeed, I'll write to them," Edward said.

"Father, what's to become of the hacienda in the future?" Alejandra asked.

"It looks like after many years of negotiations, your grandfather will be allowed to buy back the hacienda," Lidia said.

"The sugar mill, too?" Alejandra asked.

"No, that was gone a long time ago. In fact, the whole sugar cane production industry collapsed at the beginning of the Revolution," he added.

"I think my father is rather relieved to know the land is owned by greater numbers of Mexican people," Lidia added.

When they finally reached the hacienda an hour later it already felt like a celebration, for it was filled with dozens of workers who were busy preparing for the occasion. As they got out of the car, clusters of flowers were spread out everywhere in large containers, and tables were stacked together next to piles of table linens.

"Ale, this is more beautiful than any of your descriptions," Hannah said.

"Thank you. Let's walk about the grounds," she told her friend as the two wrapped their arms around each other and left. "The first place I want to show you is the *salón de música*."

A few seconds later, Carolina welcomed her sister and brother-in-law.

"So glad you're here now. Anthony and his family are in the dining room," she said.

"We're so happy for you," Lidia said as she hugged her sister, and they walked together through the flower-filled pathway. Anthony met them half way. "Good to see you," he said.

Moments later, they joined the rest of Anthony's family and introduced one another. For the next thirty minutes, they talked mostly about their trip and other pleasantries.

"How is your Spanish?" Edward asked Anthony.

"Muy bueno," he said laughingly.

"Muy bien," (very good) Carolina corrected.

"But with a teacher as a future wife, I'm sure it will be perfect," he replied.

"So now that you are a resident here, what have you found most surprising?" Lidia asked.

"Its lush forests, friendly people, and large immigrant population."

"No doubt, who can refuse its mild climate year round," Edward added. "I hear you and Carolina started your own furniture business."

"Yes, we will be exporting fine hand-crafted Mexican- and Spanish-style furniture to the United States," Anthony said.

"We even have a name for it," Carolina said proudly.

"Sol & Berg Fine Furniture."

"We can be your first customers," Lidia said.

"Edward has a lot of contacts, too."

"Thank you," Carolina said.

The following evening, the families came together in the hacienda's chapel and watched Carolina, dressed in a simple white dress and a mantilla cover, walk through the arched, candlelit tunnel, filled with floor candelabras and white flowers. The candlelight illuminated her joyous face. So much was going through her mind, and life had given her a second chance at love. As she approached the altar, Anthony looked at her lovingly; then she held his arm and together, they knelt before the priest. Carolina Merino married Anthony Solberg in a ceremony spoken in both Spanish and English.

When Carolina and Anthony came out of the chapel under a clear night sky, mariachis began to play and sing traditional ballads of love and new beginnings, using melodies inspired by Mexican waltzes. After a sumptuous dinner that lasted two hours, the musical highlight of the wedding occurred when Alejandra, Hannah, and two violinists played "Quartet in E Minor" by Mexican composer Julian Carrillo.

For the next two months, the two friends thrived at the music conservatory. They both had the opportunity to perform frequently as a duet in various concerts. Alejandra discovered the music of Mexican composers—Julian Carrillo, Felipe Villanueva, Manuel M. Ponce, and Miguel Lerdo de Tejada and his Orquesta Típica, which brought Mexican music to Carnegie Hall in 1917. She also discovered the music of Carlos Curti, with his own orchestra that toured the United States, including the Cotton Exposition in New Orleans in 1884. In music history class, Alejandra's favorite readings went as far back as the Greeks who believed that music possessed *ethos*, the power to influence a listener's emotions and behavior.

Inspired by this idea, she attended one of the last concerts of the season in November to hear the music of Manuel M. Ponce, who exclusively performed his own compositions, including "Tres Preludios," "Tiempo de Schottisch," and "Melody of Gavota." He had the power to influence anyone who heard him play, which may have been why he was termed the father of the Mexican Music Nationalist movement. As a professor of the conservatory, director of the symphonic orchestra, and concert pianist, he had also performed in 1916 in New York at the renowned Aeolian Hall. His music and his movement was yet another musical awakening of great resonance for Alejandra.

In December, the National Conservatory of Music sponsored a concert performed by the National Symphonic Orchestra of Mexico under the direction of its exceptional Mexican conductor, Julian Carrillo. He was also a virtuoso violinist, composer, and the creator of the thirteen sound theory, which enabled musicians to go beyond the twelve notes that constitute an octave in conventional western music. He had been conductor of the American Symphony Orchestra in New York earlier in his career, and this was the second year he was directing a Beethoven festival in Mexico City at the university's concert venue. His symphonic orchestra was internationally recognized as superior in performance excellence to those in other countries, according to many established performers including Polish-American pianist Leopold Godowsky. The Stanford and Merino families, guests, and hundreds of people therefore looked forward to attending the gala concert with great anticipation, and when they did, it was a fascinating experience.

The instant Carrillo stepped on the podium and his orchestra began to perform the first notes of Ludwig van Beethoven's Symphony no. 5, in C Minor, Alejandra became completely hypnotized by the majestic music reverberating magnificently in the hall. This was the first time she had ever heard this symphony played in its entire glory. It was the most fantastic, powerful, and sublime music. Beethoven's fifth symphony was an infinite sound bearing down on every soul who listened to it, as if the composer was speaking through his music from the vastness of the universe. How can words describe such music, she thought to herself as she attempted to do so in her mind. Her mother, Lidia, had for years raved about this symphony in particular, which was her favorite of all of his symphonies. She then finally understood her mother's obsession with Beethoven's music.

If in her recent past she had begun to doubt her convictions and dreams about being a conductor, in that momentous occasion while she listened to every note and its divine musical motif, she felt the music overwhelm her spirit. Alejandra knew she could not nor would ever give up her aspirations to be a conductor, no matter how impossible it seemed, no matter what anyone said, and no matter how long it took her to accomplish it. To her, being a conductor was more than the idea of getting up on the podium or directing scores of musicians. It was about connecting musically with the composer, and understanding his profound emotions and genius through his or her music. She then read in the concert's program notes a description of Beethoven's fifth symphony, according to composer Hector Berlioz:

> The Fifth Symphony mirrors Beethoven's innermost thoughts, his hidden grief, his pent-up anger, his reveries full of misery, his nocturnal visions, his moments of bliss. . .

It was the most spectacular concert she had ever attended, and as she turned to her mother, who was in tears, Alejandra realized it was a preliminary celebration for her parents' twentieth wedding anniversary.

We Have Been Waiting

It was December 16 when the families left for Cuernavaca to celebrate Christmas. Once at the hacienda, Hannah and Alejandra spent the following day wrapping gifts, helping with decorations, and playing music together in the evenings. On Alejandra's nineteenth birthday, she found she wasn't much in the mood for celebrating. After a casual family gathering, she retired quietly to the salón de música. She had recently taken to composing on sheet music, a new skill she had acquired at the conservatory. It was an intensive task that distracted her from thinking about Richard. She realized she loved him, and for the first time, she knew what romantic love felt like. It was divinely sublime with a taste of sweetness, a tinge of pain, and a lightning flash of pure, passionate emotion. How was she going to reconcile the love she felt for Richard and her equally strong love for music?

She felt as though she was being pulled apart by incredibly powerful opposing forces, splitting her being in two. Even though Richard was thousands of miles away, she felt his love from wherever he was. She began to play the piano, and inspired by the happy feeling she found when thinking of him and his words, she began to compose a lively melody with an upbeat rhythm. Two hours had passed when she realized it was almost ten in the evening; then she put words to music:

> We have been waiting, waiting, waiting long for us to go together to our favorite place. We have been waiting, waiting, waiting love for us to be together under moonlit skies ...

At one of the loveliest Christmas Eve dinners she could remember with all her family, Alejandra joined Hannah in a duet of traditional Christmas and Hanukkah music. During their performance, she realized they had become more than friends, as they had a spiritual bond, a kinship and trust between them. Not only did they share the pleasure of playing music together, but they talked to each other as if they were sisters.

Late that night, with a dimmed light on in the room, they lay on their beds and Hannah turned to her friend.

"Ale, these four months have been amazing, and in a few days, I'll be returning to New York. Have you thought about what you will do?" she asked.

"I don't know. First I thought I'd return to New York with you, but now that we have studied at the Mexican conservatory, I think for me, staying here with my family would be more acceptable to my father," Alejandra replied.

"And Richard?" Hannah asked.

She sighed. "I can't stop thinking about him either, I love him so much, but he's so far away, and my plans are to continue with my musical studies," she said. "I feel terrible, for I had promised to return in two months."

"Have you written to him?" her friend asked.

"Yes. I explained the situation, so I may not see him for a very long time," Alejandra replied. "And you and Benjamin?"

"Maybe," Hannah said.

"He certainly seems wild about you," Alejandra said.

"And my parents actually like him, even after the whole debacle with the speakeasy," Hannah said as both girls laughed.

"Well, you're lucky because you both share such a love for music that it will never conflict with your aspirations," Alejandra said.

"That's true, although sometimes we argue about how to interpret the music," she said with a laugh.

"Well, only time will tell. Good night," Alejandra said as she turned off the lights.

For the next two hours she lay there, unable to fall asleep as she sometimes suffered from insomnia, particularly when something was on her mind. That night she wondered if Richard had received her letter telling him of her plans to stay in Mexico until she completed her musical training. She didn't like things unresolved.

It was probably midnight or even later when she got up from her bed and put a white knitted shawl over her shoulders. She quietly took her sandals and put them on her feet. She took the oil lantern that hung next to the bedroom door, carefully opened the door, and walked across the courtyard. The full moon and stars were the only other source of illumination that guided her path. She walked through the arched stone tunnel toward the chapel. From afar, she noticed the ever-present lit candle on the statue of Saint Anthony that hung on the far wall. The light shone brightly at the end of the tunnel like a star in a moonless sky.

As she reached the chapel, an overwhelming feeling of love and serenity spread to her soul. The stillness calmed her worries and only the sound of crickets crept in. She knelt on the front pew to pray, but noticed a small box wrapped in red paper on the altar. She stood up and took a few steps toward the altar to move the small box to its rightful place, next to the grand Christmas tree which had no decorations, noticing how beautiful it was in its simplicity.

Then she heard steps in the chapel that startled and frightened her. She felt her heart rise, and looked behind her. At the back of the chapel, he was standing and staring at her. The young girl before him evoked a most desirable combination of innocence and sensuality. Her auburn curls cascaded down to her partly bare shoulders, and her semi-transparent nightgown perfectly outlined her firm body, her breasts, and her nipples, he thought. She looked as if she was posing for one of those painters she had frequently discussed and admired in their conversations.

Instinctively, she pulled her woolen shawl over her chest. But it was too late, for he had already lost his will in her beauty, and was overwhelmed with love and desire. His desirous eyes pierced into hers as he slowly approached her. She felt her blood rush through her body as she smelled his masculine scent when he reached her and gently pulled her hair back with his two hands. He then kissed her passionately on her plump and rosy lips. She embraced him, and kissed him back with her whole being as she had never done before.

"Ale, I love you, for longer than you know. I've been waiting for you since we danced together on your fifteenth birthday. Please, marry me!" Richard said as he reached for the box and opened it, and taking a diamond ring from the small jewelry box, he placed it on her slender finger.

Without any hesitation or doubt and with complete happiness, Alejandra said, "Yes!" She tenderly caressed his lips with her fingers.

The young couple stood there staring at each other for a moment, as if they were making a silent commitment to one another before the five-hundred-year-old altar.

"I shall speak with your parents at first light. I had hoped to arrive last night and speak to them, but delays in my travel plans brought me here an hour ago. A man let me in and said I could wait in the chapel till morning," Richard said. "And where shall we get married?"

"In our favorite place," she said smiling. "And I too have a gift for you, a love song."

"And the title?" he asked.

"'We Have Been Waiting,'" she replied, smiling.

After an hour-long conversation with Richard the following morning, Edward consented to the wedding, on one condition: Alejandra and Richard must wait at least one year for their nuptials.

TRACK SIX

PART THREE

25 Enchanting Lover

Venice, February 14, 1923

Santa Maria Della Salute was elegantly decorated with dozens of lit candles and white roses. When the church bells rang at three o'clock in the afternoon, the bride, dressed in an ivory-colored lace and pearl fitted wedding gown, walked down the aisle with her father. In her hand she held a bouquet of six white roses with one red rose in the middle. Standing handsomely and happily was the groom, wearing a black tuxedo, and by his side was his best man, Steven. And once the bride reached the altar, before he took her by the hand, she gave Hannah and Olga, her maids of honor, her bouquet.

After being apart for a year, Richard and Alejandra's wedding day was the most anticipated and sacrosanct occasion of their lives. In a church filled with dozens of white roses, the paintings of Titian and Tintoretto, and the music of Schubert's "Ave Maria," performed by a string quartet, they exchanged their vows before God, their families, and closest friends. As they heard the words spoken by the priest, "Do you promise to love, honor, cherish, and protect, forsaking all others . . . ," natural sunlight peered through the church's window, highlighting their blissful faces.

"I do," they each replied, placing the rings on each other's fingers and repeating the words, "With this ring, I do thee wed . . . "

At the end of the ceremony, the priest pronounced them husband and wife. Richard lifted Alejandra's veil and kissed her soft, moist lips.

The couple walked down the aisle seeing the smiling faces of their loved ones, and from a distance, Tintoretto's painting of the *Wedding at Cana*—a reminder of Richard's prophetic words about this very moment more than two years before.

Floating on the water outside the ancient church was a baroque-decorated gondola. The jubilant couple stepped inside the fragrant vessel covered in red rose petals and crossed the Venice Grand Canal toward Palazzo Grassi.

Among the twenty guests who gathered for the celebration, the bride and groom dined, and later danced, in an intimate salon to the music of Wilbye's "So Light is Love," Johann Sebastian Bach's "Badinerie from Suite no. 2," and Mozart's "Andante." When the sun set on the horizon, the newlyweds vanished to their private quarters on the top floor of the one-hundred-fifty-year-old building. The next day they departed for their honeymoon to Italy's Amalfi coast.

From Sorrento to Positano through a narrow and meandering road with cliffs and magnificent views of the coastline, they were driven to a small villa called Casa Antica. Upon their arrival, Richard carried Alejandra over the threshold of an open honey-colored wooden door. The living room with white-on-white décor furniture, flower and lemon topiaries on the terrazzo marble fireplace, and water-scene mural paintings was dazzling, but it was the smell of lemon in the air that captured the essence of the place, as if all the objects themselves had been marinated for decades in that bittersweet fruit.

When the newlyweds stepped onto the expansive terrace, the house attendant Flavio was placing two glasses and a pitcher filled with limonata on the tablecloth-covered wrought-iron table adorned with a flower centerpiece surrounded by lemons. Nestled in the hills of the town of Positano, the villa's private balcony looked onto the ancient *Torre Saracena* (Tower Saracena), and the sun brightly bathed the crystal blue waters of the Mediterranean Sea.

"Shall we, my dear?" Richard said as he pulled out a chair for his new wife. "For our stay here, I've planned a variety of activities that I hope will be to your liking," he added.

"I'm sure they will be," she replied.

They stayed there for another forty minutes while sampling a selection of olives, cheeses, breads, and fruits. Flavio, who had been preparing the food platters in the kitchen, stepped outside onto the balcony.

"Mr. Morrison, the piano is here. Where do you want it?"

She looked at her husband with amazement.

"What! You rented a piano?" she asked him.

"Naturally, music for you is like the air you breathe; I'm certain you'll find inspiration by the sea in the three weeks we'll be here," he said.

She quickly went inside to the villa's parlor and spotted an empty corner by the window.

"Please, there," she said as she pointed to a spot facing the terrace. The two gentlemen, waiting outside the door, then carried the upright piano to the designated area. "Molto grazie!" she said.

"You're welcome," one man said as he left Casa Antica.

"Mr. Morrison, would you like me to return this evening to prepare your dinner?" the attendant asked.

"Not tonight, we will probably go out. Thank you, Flavio," Richard said as he lustily gazed at his alluring bride, who was standing most desirably by the terrace's railing.

For the next two weeks, the happy couple visited all the historic places in Positano, Sorrento, and Capri, but mostly they stayed in their villa.

By the end of the second week, Richard left early in the morning while Alejandra was still sleeping to make plans for the remaining week. He and his English-speaking guide drove to the Archaeological Museum of Naples, for earlier in the week, he had discovered unexpectedly that a secret museum existed inside the larger art institution, where only men were allowed to enter. Knowing how much his wife loved art history, he wanted to have all the answers for her before their visit later in the week, even though she herself would not be allowed to go inside the censored gallery.

As he entered the site, what he found was considered shocking; although perhaps not so much for him, as a medical student familiar with anatomy and seeing naked bodies. The forbidden museum contained an immense quantity of erotic artworks, from frescoes, to statues, to talismans, to mosaics. Considered pornographic and salacious in nature, it had been sealed from public viewing. According to the rules, only those with "respected morals and maturity" were allowed to see the objects discovered in the ancient city of Pompeii.

After spending the morning in the museum, early in the afternoon he and his driver left Naples. Most unfortunately, on the treacherous winding road to Positano, a flat tire caused the car to veer onto a rocky hillside and it crashed.

When Alejandra woke up in the villa and Richard was missing, she felt his absence as strongly as if he had been gone for days. She then saw a note on the nightstand.

> My sweet Ale, I will return in the afternoon.
> Love, Richard.

As the day went by with no sign of Richard, the minutes and the hours seemed endless. Toward the evening, she went onto the balcony, and from there she could see fishermen along the shoreline carrying large baskets filled with fish. She heard a knock on the door, and excitedly ran to it.

"Signora (Madam), I have dinner for you," Flavio said.

"Thank you, please leave it on the table. My husband isn't here yet," she said.

"Would you like me to stay with you until he comes?" he asked.

"Very kind of you, but I'm sure he'll be back soon," she said.

"Ciao (Goodbye), and please call if you need anything," he said.

She looked at the food, but even the scent of fresh fish cooked in spices and pasta could not stimulate her appetite. She poured herself a glass of red wine from the hand-painted decanter on the small dining room table, took a book from her large purse called *Music at a Medici Wedding*, and went onto the terrace. She placed the book on the empty chair, walked toward the rusty railing, and rested her elbows on it, which felt a little rough. She admired the terraced houses as they sloped steeply down onto the beach. Far into the background, the jagged rocks made of white limestone with outcrops of plants and flowers seemed like a perfect visual metaphor for how she felt at that moment, disturbed by her husband's absence but filled with love. She decided to read to keep her mind occupied, sat on the chair and opened her book.

> Renaissance court music-making, at its most spectacular, took place at state weddings, and nowhere more lavishly than in Medici Florence.

She went on to read that the celebrations culminated with a dramatic spectacle called Intermedio, perhaps, in fact, a precursor to opera. But she could not concentrate, as the skies were getting darker and there was no sign of Richard. She returned to the parlor, placed the food in a small ice box, and then decided to take a bath to distract her from worrying about his whereabouts. She turned on the old vintage radio in the bedroom as she undressed and wrapped a towel around herself while the mosaic tub filled with warm water. Five minutes later she immersed herself in it, reached out for a jar from the corner of the bathtub, and then rubbed the lilac-scented oil onto her skin. The melodic piece playing on the radio was one she did not recognize, but it had a soothing orchestration that included mandolins and a harp.

After maybe thirty minutes, she stepped out of the tiled bathtub and dressed in her silk lavender-colored nightgown but left her hair up in a bun. She took the lilac body lotion and spread it over her arms, legs, and neck. A cold breeze swept through the room. She closed the window, and then wrapped a silk shawl around her shoulders. As she returned to the parlor, she took the wine glass from the table, drank all its contents, and then went to the balcony. The skies were completely dark, and not even the soft moonlight, stars, or ocean waters could give her consolation. She felt a few sprinkles on her face, and her thoughts went from worry, to anguish, to anger, to full-fledged passion. She ached to caress him and see him as her thoughts and feelings tormented her.

It was almost ten o'clock. Feeling alone and literally a prisoner of the night, she went inside and closed the French doors. She sat in front of the piano and began to play the keyboard, hoping the music would quell her desperation, when a strong gush of wind violently opened the doors. She felt Richard was casting his haunting spells from a far, as she had felt many times during their engagement when they were separated for eleven months. But his secrets, even if they turned into the most pleasant surprises, were starting to concern her in a profound way.

She stepped, once again, onto the balcony and felt a strong wind on her face, which lifted her gown above her knees. Hearing the tempestuous sea as waves crashed against the rocks, she wanted to stay on the balcony under the starry, gusty night, as if that was the only way to feel her husband. But the lightning skies frightened her, or perhaps it was the thought that something awful must have happened to him. She came back inside the small cottage and briskly shut the French doors, this time locking them. In her anguish, she began to play once more on the piano, expressing what she felt in her heart.

After two hours of improvising, a new composition began to emerge with a tango rhythm. She played the new music many more times until it was completed. As she always did when she sat down to play, she lost track of time and realized suddenly that it was midnight. She took her musical journal, which was laying on top of the piano, and looked for a blank piece of paper. Words were swirling in her head like the wind outside her window, and she began to write:

> Enchanting lover, you cast your spells from afar and in a moment I feel you there with me. You have me prisoner, you haunt my existence, soy prisionera de tus encantos soy (I'm prisoner of your charms). . .

It must have been almost one in the morning when she finally went to bed. In the early hours but in the black color of night, perhaps just before dawn, she felt Richard lay beside her on the bed. He softly caressed her neck and back as he whispered, "My sweet love, sorry for being gone so long. I'll tell you everything in the morning."

She placed her index finger on his lips as she breathed a sigh of relief. "Promise me, no more secrets," she said tearfully and kissed him.

The next morning when she woke up he was still sleeping. With several bruises on his body and a few scratches on his face, she carefully covered him with a blanket, thankful he was unharmed and back with her. Quietly, she got out of bed, showered, and dressed. She then went into the kitchen to prepare coffee, and from the window she noticed the sea was calm. As she was slicing up some apples, oranges, and melon, he came from behind, completely naked.

"Did you miss me?" he said with his usual openness and humor that made her laugh.

"You have no idea!" she said as he took a slice of the apple and ate it. "What happened to you?"

"It's a long story. We had a car accident coming back from Naples. I was taken to the hospital, and was unconscious for several hours."

"I knew something bad must have happened, but don't ever, ever leave me again!" she said. "It was the most terrifying night of my life." She tenderly rubbed his back with her hands.

"Oh, Ale, I want you!" he said as he took her back to the bedroom.

They stayed in the villa, enjoying each other's company and

conversation until the third day, when she was ready to see the famous city of Pompeii.

After a hearty breakfast, they drove to the city of Naples first. Richard, who had read the entire tourist pamphlet, explained, "Pompeii was buried under twelve feet of ashes for almost eighteen centuries after the volcanic explosion of Mount Vesuvius in 79 A.D. A more detailed account of the event and its treasures are here," he added as he gave her the published guide of the Naples Museum before entering it.

"And the forbidden museum?" she asked.

"Well, I'll give you more details tonight!" he said with a titillating laugh.

The chauffer smiled, for he had been to the secret museum with Richard a few days earlier, but said nothing. To himself, however, he said, Oh! What a sight to behold—new love.

Several hours later, they left the museum and headed to the historic archeological site of Pompeii. On their arrival, she was glad to have changed from sandals to her short boots, for the ground was dusty and covered in ashes. It was like walking through a city of ghosts. The streets were filled with dilapidated buildings, structures that must have been a remarkable contrast to the city that had once been so prosperous and glorious. Yet it was still enchanting and mysterious, even if there was an air of decay, she thought as they walked through the city's labyrinthine streets. In some of the remaining roofless villas, they saw faded, painted frescos on the walls. She imagined their full splendor, with the fountains in the courtyards and all the exotic objects she had just seen in the Naples Museum. As they continued on their walk, stepping into one of the remaining buildings, she noticed a fresco, the painting of a Lar, a Roman ancestral deity that was honored and worshiped in household shrines called Lalariums.

"Lars were common representations of guardians of family life," she said. "I'm thinking about what you saw in the secret museum, and admiring the Roman culture."

"Why do you say that?" he asked.

"Thank goodness for art. It depicts everything, the divine, dreams, realities, emotions, people, life, and even humanity's most natural expressions. I think it's wonderful the artists of Roman times were allowed to express themselves so freely. Imagine what their villas looked like. On one side they had frescoes illustrating youthful-looking deities with buckets and drinking horns, and on the other—" she said. But before she could finish her sentence, Richard interrupted, "Frescoes of naked human bodies engaged in carnal pleasures," he said, laughing.

"My darling, if anyone else heard you speak this way, they might consider it heresy," she said jokingly. "Although, didn't Michelangelo paint the most beautiful nudes in the Vatican's very own Sistine Chapel, commissioned by no other than Pope Julius II?" Alejandra stated.

"Yes, indeed," he said.

"And what about his truly, almost holy, sculptures of the human male body—and that is but one small example, which up to now I've only read about," she said.

"I've always wondered how in the world he was allowed to do that," Richard remarked.

"It is written that Michelangelo said the human body was an expression of the divine," Alejandra replied. "But, some people may say there's a difference between nude and erotic."

"Fortunately, one is the extension of the other," Richard said with a devious smile, as he placed his hand on her waist and they turned the corner through another meandering street in the ancient city.

"Yet, I cannot help but feel sadness for what was an incomprehensible act of nature. At least the world has a visual record of how these artistic people lived," she said.

Toward evening they returned to Casa Antica, and after a sumptuous dinner prepared by Flavio on the last evening of their stay in Positano, she sat down to play on the piano for the last time. In that *ensueño* (daydream), she looked through the window at her husband, who was reading one of his favorite mystery novels, and then her eyes turned to the shimmering blue waters. Her fingers started to move slowly over the keyboard. She composed "Amalfi," her farewell serenade to the city by the sea, a bewitching place to be savored for a lifetime.

The next morning the Morrisons left for the city of London.

TRACKS SEVEN AND EIGHT

Moonlight Sonata

Richard was delighted to arrive with his new wife at Brown's Hotel in the heart of London. He reserved one of the suites on the upper floor. It was cold and late at night, so when they entered the lavishly decorated Edwardian suite, he picked up Alejandra outside the hotel room and carried her through the passageway and directly onto the poster canopy bed. She chuckled and said, "Wait, let me take my coat off."

As he had ordered, the wood-burning fireplace had been lit and emitted a warm glow of light. Yet nothing could be as captivating as his wife taking off her coat and showing perfectly the curves of her body, which he now could see to his utmost pleasure. Moments later, the bellboy came into the room and left the luggage. Richard gave him a tip, and the instant the door was shut, he got comfortable, undressed, and suggested his wife do the same. But she was modest, and could only discreetly laugh at her husband's openness and brazen attitude. She noticed by her nightstand a vase filled with two roses, and then stood up next to her husband. Very slowly, he began to undress her, until all her clothes were on the floor. He gazed upon her arousing breasts, and caressed them delicately as if he was a Greek artist shaping his own perfect Venus de Milo. He whispered, "Ale, I'm so in love with you!" In that rapture, he ravenously lifted her from the waist toward him, as she too succumbed to their mutual desires.

It was light in the room when they woke up the next morning, and the clock above the fireplace showed it was almost nine o'clock. He ordered coffee, which was promptly delivered ten minutes later. He poured them both a cup and placed hers next to the nightstand. Richard, whose heritage was of English descent, was thrilled to show Alejandra the sights and sounds of his great-grandparents' birthplace.

"Where are you taking me today?" she asked as she put on her woolen emerald-green suit.

"Where would you like to go?" he asked.

"You know what I like, so for this time I'll leave it all up to you," she said with a coy smile.

"Where to start?" he asked rhetorically.

"At the beginning," she said.

"Well, since 79 A.D. is still fresh in your mind, the Romans founded London twenty-nine years earlier in approximately 50 A.D., and they inhabited this land until about 407 A.D. Since then, the city went from Roman London to Saxon London, and then much later to Tudor London. By the eleventh century, Edward the Confessor had Westminster Palace and Westminster Abbey built, and this is where we will start. Perhaps you already know some of this from your father," said Richard.

"You've become quite the chronicler, and yes, my father has told me many tales about his great, great, grandparents, who were born somewhere in Wales—but I must admit I don't know as much as I'd like. So I shall be your student for the week," she said, smiling.

"I will enjoy that if you promise to obey my every command," Richard replied with a laugh, placing his hand on her right leg as she put on her nylons.

It was one of those cloudy days in London when the couple left late in the morning to visit Westminster Abbey. With umbrella in hand, she walked arm in arm with her husband as the rain began to pour down. They arrived at the thirteenth-century church, constructed in Gothic style with soaring pointed arches, rose windows, and flying buttresses. When they entered the lavish interior with ribbed vaulting, the highest Gothic vault in all England, Alejandra made the sign of the cross on her forehead. She then sat in the back pew to admire the church's interior architectural details and stained glass windows. She closed her eyes, placed her hands together, and thanked the creator of all things, as she sometimes referred to God in her private thoughts. Richard sat and waited for her to finish her prayers, and then said, "Are you to pray in every church?"

"Perhaps," she answered in a whispery voice.

They sat in complete silence for a few minutes until Richard turned and said, "I find it interesting that the father of evolution would end up buried in this religious place, of all places. I wonder what he might have said, if he could speak now."

"Who can know what the great Charles Darwin might have said," she replied. "But whatever anyone believes, his brilliant mind and transcendent discoveries came from a genius that no one can deny nor explain," she added.

"Well, he's in good company, buried next to another great scientist, Sir Isaac Newton," Richard whispered to her. "And all the monarchs of England," he added.

"How many of them have been coronated here?" she asked.

"All of them, perhaps with the exception of one or two, I believe," he said, as the boys' choir at the Abbey began to rehearse Gregorian chants.

"Please, let's wait for a few more minutes. I love this music," she said. Richard smiled, for since he'd known her, there wasn't anything that would put his wife in better spirits than music. He held her hand and made plans for the afternoon in his mind.

When they came out of Westminster Abbey it was pouring, and thunderous lightning muted the sound of the church bells as they rang at two o'clock in the afternoon.

"My dear, we shall have to skip our afternoon tour, and go straight to the hotel room," he said with a sinister smile.

"Oh! Richard," she said, amused.

"We are on our honeymoon, my dear!" he said as he embraced his wife and signaled a nearby taxi to stop.

As the rain continued through the evening and into the next day, the lucky newlyweds stayed in the suite of their hotel.

It was almost ten in the morning when they woke up. She drew the curtains, and while it had momentarily stopped raining, there was still a grayish sky. Dressed in her silken cherry red nightgown, she turned to her husband and said, "So long as we are going to be here all morning, I was thinking about the anecdote you never told me about your great-grandparents."

"You remembered?" he questioned.

"Certainly, how could I forget the masked man who sat at my table during the Venetian Carnivale?" she said, laughing. "I didn't want to be indiscreet at the time, but I've been curious ever since."

"Let's have breakfast, first," he said. "What would you like?"

"Orange juice and fresh fruit will be enough for me," she requested as he picked up the phone and placed the order. When he hung up the phone he adjusted his pillows until he was comfortable. He placed his hand on the bed and signaled her to join him. As soon as she sat beside him, he bent over and kissed her on her bare shoulder and then began his story.

"Apparently one day my great-grandmother, who was a devout Roman Catholic, almost as devoted as Queen Mary I of England, was on the way to church to attend mass at seven in the morning when a drunken fellow, returning from a late outing, bumped into her and made her fall. He spent the next six months writing her apology letters and requesting to see her, but my great-grandmother refused to see him."

"What were their names?" Alejandra asked.

"Jillian and Wallace," he replied. "So, then, the poor lad, who had fallen in love with her, decided to go to early mass whenever he knew she would be there, which was twice a week. After another six to eight months, Jillian finally agreed to see him only if he promised to always go to church with her," Richard said. "And for the rest of their lives he did, which by the way also cured his alcoholism," he added with a laugh.

"I see where you get your perseverance," she said.

"The things that men do for love!" he said.

"Had you not heard the story before from your parents?" she asked.

"No, my mother is too proud and highbrow to admit to such a weakness in her grandfather's character," Richard said.

"I'm not sure it was a weakness but rather a strength," she added. "It couldn't have been easy to rid himself of such an affliction, unless he had a strong will to do so."

"Never thought of it that way," he said.

"But on another topic, I do hope your mother won't mind us living with her," Alejandra said.

"No, she was the one who insisted, at least until I'm done with medical school," he said as the hotel's waiter knocked on their door with their breakfast.

A few hours later, after another long nap, the newlyweds were awakened at ten minutes past four o'clock when they heard three knocks on the door.

"It's room service," Alejandra suggested.

Richard quickly put on a robe and opened the door, yet saw no one there. Twenty minutes passed when they heard another knock, and again nobody was there. Richard picked up the phone and complained.

"Sir, can you please check our corridor? We are in room 409, and twice someone has knocked on our door. Thank you," he said to the front desk clerk.

"Perhaps it's a ghost," Alejandra said jokingly. "The concierge told me yesterday their popular ghost tour starts from this hotel."

"Ghosts! No such thing, it's rubbish as they say here," he said vehemently.

"You know that while I lived in Mexico, I heard dozens and dozens of ghost stories. Like here, many people believe in them. It must have something to do with ancient cities and legends," she said. "Who can know for sure?"

However, when a third knock on the door was heard, Richard, annoyed by the interruption, got up from bed quickly, not even dressing himself, and opened the room's door.

"Pardon me sir, I did knock on the door. Would you like our complimentary tea service?" a very embarrassed girl in her late teens said as she briefly saw him naked before he moved behind the door.

"Pardon me, miss, it's that this was the third time someone knocked on our door, and I thought it was some kid fooling around. Please excuse me," he said from behind the door. His wife threw him his robe and he put it on. Alejandra gingerly smiled at the humorous scene, and reached out for her robe from a nearby chair.

"Please come in," he said.

"Good afternoon, madam," the girl said as she curtsied, and then brought in a cart with a tea set, cucumber finger sandwiches, and French pastries.

"Thank you, miss," Richard said as he gave her a handsome tip.

"You're welcome, sir," she said and let herself out.

Richard brought a cup of tea to his wife. "Would you like something to eat, too?"

"No thank you, darling, just tea," she said.

"There's an envelope here, addressed to us," he said as he ripped it open and began to read it out loud.

March 10, 1923
Dear Ale and Richard:

Let me give you my congratulations for your recent wedding.

Forgive my intrusion into your blissful time together, but I thought it would be rude of me not to invite you for dinner while you are visiting London. After all, we are practically extended family, and I would most appreciate hosting you for at least one evening. I have taken the liberty of making reservations for tomorrow at 7:00 p.m. at the Restaurant Queen Victoria. If you do not come, I will understand; although I promise you will not regret our meeting.

Sincerely, Franz Wensing

Alejandra placed her hands over her face in utter disbelief. "Oh darling, do not bother yourself with this. It's probably a prank," she said.

"But, by who?" he said. "Don't worry, even if it's true."

She sighed with much relief and walked toward her husband. "You're not angry?"

"Why should I be? Even if it is Franz, I wouldn't mind seeing the poor fellow," he said in jest.

"I don't want to go, really," she said.

"Oh, why not? Sooner or later we shall see him again. It's true he is practically family—the brother of your cousin's wife," Richard said in a lighthearted tone.

"Show some compassion," she said.

"Forgive me. Then let's go for that reason, so we may make peace with one another," he said.

"Well, in that case, yes," she said.

He picked her up, kissed her, and then playfully put her on their bed for an afternoon interlude.

Franz Wensing was fifteen minutes early at the restaurant the following evening. He asked for a private table in a secluded area of the opulently decorated but dark Victorian venue. When he saw his former fiancé walk in with Richard, he thought she still had the graceful, discreet demeanor he remembered; yet she was more seductive than ever because she had the confidence of a fulfilled woman. Dressed in a sleeveless fuchsia silk-velvet dress with an embroidered hem border in tones of gold, she looked stunning, Franz thought. She had her arm wrapped around her husband, and Richard looked proud with his head tilted upward, as if he was saying "She is mine." Franz noticed it, but stayed calm, even though inside, he was filled with jealousy; for in his mind, he should have been the one Alejandra married.

He had been out with several girls, but no one compared to her. As they reached the table, he said, "Wonderful to see you both, congratulations again. You are a very lucky man, Richard!"

"Yes, indeed," he replied.

"Franz, it's good to see you again. Olga tells us you are very happy here in London," she said.

"Can't complain," he replied. "Please sit down." Then he pulled out a chair for Alejandra. "I'm delighted you accepted my invitation," he said.

"Sure, why not? We are old acquaintances," Richard added.

Franz poured champagne into three crystal goblets and then turned to the couple. "Let us drink to your new life together," he said graciously.

"Here, here," Richard said.

"And may you find everything you want," she added, noticing the fedora hat she had once given him hanging from the coat rack next to the table.

After an hour of small talk and eating a succulent dinner, Franz lit a cigarette, let a few puffs out, and said, "Ale, perhaps you may recall that I work at a musical antique shop, owned by my uncle."

"Yes, I do," she said.

"I'd like you and Richard to accept a wedding gift from me," he said.

"You don't need to do that," she said.

"But I want to!" he said with insistence.

"What is it, Franz?" Richard asked.

"Is a signed copy of a partiture written by the hand of a famous composer, which I purchased from my uncle at a family rate," he said. It was one of his most valuable possessions."

"Franz, even though it's a copy, it may still be worth thousands of pounds sterling," Richard remarked. "And why would you want to give it to us?"

"For many reasons," Franz said.

"What reasons?' Richard asked.

"For one, Alejandra loves music; two, you are the godparents of my only nephew little Steven; and three, it's my way of saying I wish you both a happy life together," Franz said.

Alejandra, who was at times sentimental, felt a knot in her throat. She turned to her husband and waited for his response.

"Franz, that is most generous of you and your uncle. We will accept it as a sign, to you, that Ale and I wish the best for you," Richard said as he held his wife's hand tightly under the table.

"Great! You may then come tomorrow evening when the shop closes at six. My uncle would like to meet you both," Franz said as he handed them a business card with the address and name of the shop, Wensing Musical Antiques.

"And the composer?" she asked in haste.

"It is a gift, after all, and you'll soon find out," Franz said with a mysterious smile.

It was almost one o'clock in the afternoon of the following day when Alejandra and Richard left their hotel and stepped into a cab. He handed the taxi driver the address of their destination.

"Are you going to tell me where we're going?" she asked.

"We're going to see one of the greatest museums of the world, founded by the collections of a physician and scientist, Sir Hans Sloane," he said.

"I see why you are so interested. A physician's brain child?" she said. "What museum is it?"

"The British Museum," he replied.

The Greek revival–style architecture with its magnificent columns was inspired by ancient Greek archeological sites, which were rediscovered in the 1750s. With a quadrangle-shaped floor plan, the museum's four wings housed collections from all over the world.

"It's two o'clock. What would you like to see?" Richard asked his wife.

"The Medieval European collection, the Middle Eastern, and the Asian collections, but perhaps with the little time we have, we should start with London in 1753, and see how this city, the river, Covent Garden, St. James's Mayfair, and Westminster might have looked liked then," she replied as she read from the museum's guide book.

After two hours, they had only finished touring half of what she wanted to see. However, she was glad to have seen the complete Medieval European collection, which turned out to be one of the best with its enormous assortment of tapestries and religious altar pieces.

"Sweetie, we best be on our way. It's almost thirty minutes past five," Richard said as he gently pulled her away from the gallery.

When they came out of the museum it was drizzling. They quickly stepped into a taxi cab, drove past Hyde Park, and turned into Piccadilly Street. The musical antique store was inside a quaint red brick building. Richard paid the driver, and she took her umbrella and walked across the street toward the establishment. He opened the door for his wife and together they went inside.

Her first impression was marvelous. It was like being in a time warp, with several centuries all clustered in one spacious room that was beautifully illuminated with Tiffany lighting. There were harpsichords, Stradivarius violins, harps, cellos, French horns, bagpipes, oboes, clarinets, accordions, zithers, Egyptian flutes, a Chinese erhu, gongs, rattles, bells—anything and everything. The musical instruments were on one side of the room, and on the other, sculptures of figures holding musical instruments. In the middle, she saw a large area containing hundreds of scores, but instead of perusing them, she went to see the only harpsichord in the store. She looked at the tag, which read "1778, once the property of Buckingham Palace."

Alejandra, who could never resist playing a keyboard, played a few random notes on the ancient instrument, a precursor to the pianoforte with its own unique sound. It was like transporting herself back to the eighteenth century. What would it have been like living then, she wondered, when she heard a familiar voice.

"Ale, I see you've found your special niche," said Franz.

"Oh yes, wherever there is a piano or anything with a keyboard, expect her to play it," Richard said jokingly.

"Franz, nice to see you again," she said and met him halfway.

He kissed one of her hands. "My uncle will be here soon. He was called away unexpectedly," Franz added.

Richard greeted him warmly.

"This is the most fascinating shop I've ever seen, and I could spend days rummaging through everything," she said joyously.

"Yes, I knew you would love it," Franz said, with regret in his voice. "I want to show you something," he continued. There, on a shelf above his desk was a lyre. He picked it up and said, "Greek legend says 'Orpheus was given the gift of music since the beginning of time. He played so divinely he could charm everything from the trees, to the mountains, to wild animals with his music.'"

"And who do you plan to charm?" Richard replied.

Alejandra turned to her husband and gave him a disapproving look, as she made a slight pout.

"You know, he has a wicked sense of humor," she said.

"I take no offense," Franz said.

"What kind of sheet music do you have?" she asked.

"Everything from old manuscripts to more modern music, including the newest musical fad, jazz," Franz said.

"I'm not sure it's a fad, I think it's here to stay," she added.

"We have a score of the American composer George Gershwin, Swannee," he said.

"What about music from women composers?" she asked.

"Like who?" Franz asked.

"Hildegard von Bingen, Clara Schumann, Fanny Mendelssohn, to name a few," she replied.

"I've heard of the last two, but who is Hildegard von Bingen?" Franz asked.

"She lived in the eleventh century, a theologian and a mystic," she replied. "Perhaps the first woman composer recorded in history."

"I think we might have something by Clara Schumann," he said as he looked through the sheet music in the racks. "Piano Trio in G Minor, opus 17," he said as he pulled out the score and read it out loud.

"I'll take it," she said. "It's unfortunate there isn't more published music by women composers."

"Ale, why don't you pick as many as you would like," Richard said.

"And your dreams of being a concert pianist or a conductor?" Franz asked.

The question was unexpected, she thought. "I still have them, not so much a concert pianist, but a conductor, perhaps someday," she said, letting out a slight laugh. "For now, I'm satisfied to play and write music whenever, wherever I find inspiration."

"Well you're only twenty years old, there's a life ahead of you," Franz said.

"What about you and your poetry?" she asked Franz.

"It turns out I'm not a very good poet," he said, laughing at himself. "These days I do mostly acting."

"I always thought you were an outstanding actor. Do you have a play coming up? We'd love to see you," she said.

"Not for another three weeks," he said.

"What is it about? She asked.

"It's rather lecherous actually, based on Rubenesque-style paintings," he said.

"What role do you play?" she asked.

"An art dealer who is obsessed with one of Rubens' models," he said.

"How interesting. I'd love to have seen it," she said.

"Me, too!" Richard said with a laugh.

At that moment his uncle walked into the shop. He was a robust man with a broad smile and cleft chin. In fact, she thought Franz looked more like his uncle than his father.

"Lovely to meet you. I've heard so much about you, and this must be your new husband," Mr. Wensing said to Alejandra as he took off his Bavarian alpine hat.

"A pleasure to meet you," Richard said, and extended his hand.

By then Alejandra was holding a pile of sheet music on her arm.

"I see you've found something to your liking?" Mr. Wensing added.

"Everything here in your shop is to my liking," she replied.

"Everything?" Richard asked playfully.

"You know what I mean," she said to him.

"I think that if she were to stay a bit longer she would want to buy the whole store," he said.

A minute or so later, Franz left to get the gift.

"How is Olga?" Mr. Wensing asked.

"She's wonderful, pregnant again," Alejandra said as Franz came into the room.

"Here it is," he said as he handed her a wrapped package.

"Richard, you open it," she requested.

"Why don't we both," he said, as she placed all the music manuscripts on a nearby table, and then returned to help unwrap the package. As soon as she could see the front cover of the partiture, she could not believe her eyes. She saw the name of the composer, then the title of the piece, and began to cry softly.

"Excuse me, thank you so much Franz, and Mr. Wensing," Alejandra said as she very gently took the signed manuscript from the box.

"Will you play for us Ale?" Franz said. She looked at her husband.

"Certainly, Franz, I'd love to," she said as she walked to the harpsichord and placed the sheet music on the ledge of the ancient instrument.

She slowly sat on the antique bench, wondering who might have been the last person before her to play this gorgeous instrument, weathered but unspoiled. Then she turned to the first page of the sheet music and began to play her own favorite composition by Ludwig Van Beethoven, "Moonlight Sonata." At that moment a flood of memories overcame her as she remembered the first time she read the title when she was only a child. She then played the music. Richard looked at his wife with adoring love, but he also noticed the way Franz looked at her from across the room, and it was clear he was still in love with her. When she finished playing, Franz said, "You still have the gentle touch."

She smiled. "Thank you."

"Yes, she does," Richard said as he took his wife by the hand. "Well, we probably should go. Thank you again, Franz, for your most generous gift. Not only do we greatly appreciate it, but my mother-in-law will probably faint when she touches it," Richard said. They all laughed.

"There is an amazing exhibit on the violin at the Royal Academy of Music," Franz said as Richard paid him for the sheet music.

"Yes, it's on my list," Richard replied as he patted Franz on the back.

"Mr. Wensing and Franz, we're so grateful for your generous wedding gift, and we hope someday you'll visit us in Minnesota," she said, shaking hands with Franz and his uncle. "And best wishes for your career in theater."

The Morrisons then walked out the door with two large bags filled with music scores.

The smell of wet shrubbery was in the air, and there was a mystical fog with the moon hovering over the skies like a spotlight at the center of a stage. Upon their arrival at the hotel, Alejandra suggested they spend some time in the English garden. "What a night," she said as she once again took a deep breath of the fresh smell of fallen rain.

When they arrived at the perfectly sculpted garden with its tall post lamps, they walked to a bench that was wet from the rain. Richard took out his handkerchief and dried the bench as best he could. They placed their packages on the ground and sat next to each other. She felt a few drops of water from a tree above them on her cheek.

"Oh! London is mysterious yet lively," she said.

With a very serious expression, Richard turned to her. "You don't regret having married me instead of him?"

She sat up straight. "Richard, what a thing to say!" she exclaimed, rather shocked. "Where did that come from?"

"Your life would be so different if you married Franz. You would be living here, maybe even studying at the Royal Academy, and your dream to be a conductor would more likely be fulfilled here," he said with certain angst.

"It's not like you to say something like this, but no! If I love London it's because I'm here with you," she said as she turned to him and tenderly caressed his face. "I love you!"

"And your music as a profession?" he insisted.

"True, I didn't complete my musical training, but the music will always be there. It's like my mother once told me—when you find a love like ours, nothing else matters. This is the path I have chosen, to be with you. And if in the future there is opportunity for both in some way, I'll embrace it with open arms," she added with such intensity that he felt overtaken by her sincerity and love. He took her hand and kissed it lovingly.

"Shall we go to the room now?" he asked with his usual seductive smile.

"Yes, as you wish," she said.

With only two days left, the Morrisons visited the Tower of London, preeminent in English history and the site where the crown jewels are stored, but also known as one of the most haunted places in England. And in the afternoon, Richard took his wife to a polo match, as he had envisioned eighteen months before. On the last day, they visited Windsor Castle, the largest occupied castle in the world. With its magnificent grounds and breathtaking architecture, the tour included the Crimson Room, Queen Mary's doll house, and other rooms open to the public that housed some of the most gorgeous furniture and antiques dating back centuries. Lastly, they visited the chapel. As she stood there admiring the enormous stained glass window, Alejandra realized it was an idyllic ending to the most romantic honeymoon she could ever have imagined.

That evening, when they returned to their hotel, she was exhausted from walking all day. She put on her blue sapphire nightgown, and sitting on a small vanity bench in front of a mirror, she lit a white candle in its silver-plated candlestick. As she rubbed lotion on her face, Richard came from behind her and placed a gold chain with two conjoined oval pendants—one a diamond, and the other a ruby—around her neck. He then kissed her neck, then her shoulder, and then turned off the lights . . .

27 Eroica

The Morrison newlyweds arrived in Minneapolis late in the afternoon on March 22, 1923, at their Mediterranean-style mansion. It was the home of Richard's mother Vivian, who had insisted her son and his wife live there while he completed his medical training. Alejandra was uncertain about the proposition, but agreed with Richard's persuasive reasoning. Fortunately the house was large, and the couple took the bedroom in the west wing of the stately mansion. As she began to unpack, the bedroom with its expansive windows facing west had an amazing sunset that reflected the waters of Lake of the Isles; yet not even that beautiful image could keep her from feeling like a stranger in the house.

When Richard returned to work two days later, she found herself wondering about her new life. As she took out more of her belongings from the hall closet, she realized there really wasn't much room for them in the bedroom. She decided to leave most of them in boxes, except for a pile of sheet music and her metronome that she brought downstairs into the parlor, placing it on top of the grand piano.

She walked about the large house, decorated in Arts and Crafts style, and her every footstep made a cracking sound as she stepped on the wide wooden plank boards in the hallway. The silence felt threatening, and with Richard being gone long hours, she could not imagine herself being there without much to do. Surely she would play the piano while he was gone, but she needed something more substantial—a job related to music whereby she could advance her professional aspirations. She proceeded to the sunny porch and sat down on the wicker bench. The newspaper had been left on the small side table, and she began to browse through the ads when Lena, the cook and housekeeper, interrupted.

"Madam, what would you like me to prepare for dinner?" she asked.

Alejandra thought about Richard's favorite, and said, "Pot roast with a side of mashed potatoes."

"Yes, madam."

She realized she better start looking for recipes to use when her mother-in-law was gone, but the last time she had tried to learn how to cook she had left in total disgust when Milly prepared stew. The cook had taken a calf's head, removed its brains, and then boiled the head until the bones dropped out while adding butter, pepper, and salt to improve the taste. After that experience, Alejandra lost her appetite and what little interest she had in cooking. For the moment, she decided it was better to resume her search for a job in the newspaper ads, though she did not find any prospects of interest to her.

The next day when her husband was working late, she accompanied her mother-in-law to a benefit concert on March 25 at the Minneapolis Auditorium. While still a bit tired from the trip, she was eager to attend the musical event, which would benefit German children. This would be the first time that a performance would be broadcast on radio. Aside from the technological advances, she was impressed to learn that the evening's performers included virtuoso violinist Henri Berbrugghen and pianist Bruno Walter. To her great surprise, the former would also be guest conductor for the final concert of the twentieth season of the Minneapolis Symphony Orchestra. For many years she had carefully observed the gestures of the orchestra's longtime conductor, but now she would have the opportunity to see someone else at the helm. How different would the orchestra sound? What music would he choose?

On April 15, Alejandra and Richard attended the final concert of the season. The evening's performance included *Spanish Caprice* by Rimsky Korsakov, *1812 Overture* by Tchaikovsky, and other selections, but what caught her attention as she read the program notes was that five guest conductors had been introduced in the last season as the permanent conductor, Mr. Oberhoffer, had resigned from his position. With so many changes, she thought perhaps there might be job opportunities—a long shot, but worth exploring. In the end, from among the five guest conductors, who included Albert Coates, Bruno Walter, Walter Damrosch, Ossip Gabrilowitsch, and Henri Verbrugghen, the latter was chosen to be the permanent conductor of the Minneapolis Symphony Orchestra.

As good fortune would have it, two weeks later, Alejandra took a part-time position as assistant to the librarian at the symphony orchestra. There, she thought, she would have intimate knowledge of every reference and source of information on the symphonic repertoire, not to mention knowledge of the workings of an orchestra. Most importantly, she would be as close as she might ever get to the musical life of a symphony orchestra conductor, a look from the inside out.

The opportunity she had been waiting for was finally a reality. The experience of hearing the new conductor's interpretative style and his musical choices would be a learning experience beyond anything she could have imagined or even hoped for, she thought when she arrived home that afternoon.

She was anxious to tell her husband the good news, although it would be several hours before he came home. She checked on dinner, then waited in the parlor while she continued to read her mother's latest gift, the popular home cook book *The Perry*. Below the title, there was a quote that her mother had repeated many times, "The way to a man's heart is through his stomach." She wondered how true these words might be, although she had decided to follow the book's advice and try her best to fulfill those duties that might indeed please her husband. That night she was trying on a new recipe, and she would put to the test all the highly recommended recipes.

When it was almost seven o'clock in the evening, she went to the dining room to light candles inside their hammered copper candleholders, and then Richard came in.

"Hello, darling. How was your day?" she asked.

"Long," he replied as he sat on the armchair.

"How was your day, Ale?" he asked.

"Wonderful, more than wonderful," she said. "Dinner is ready, and I've so much to tell you." She placed her hands around his neck and gave him a soothing massage; he took one of her hands and kissed it.

"Where's mother?" he asked.

"She had a meeting," she replied as Lena brought out the dinner plates. They sat across from each other, and she began to serve food onto his plate from the serving dishes.

"What is all this?" he asked her with a big smile.

"Baked fish with chili, salmon croquettes, and asparagus salad," she replied.

"Looks delicious," he said.

"I hope you like it," she said. "Anything new in medicine?"

"Always, but I'd rather hear about your news," he said.

"I have a job," she said.

He looked at her in disbelief. "Doing what?"

She recounted her news, but Richard was speechless and wondered how she had managed to keep her plans a secret. He never thought she would actually pursue a career related to music, other than perhaps perform in recitals. It was becoming clear she had no intention of giving up her musical ambitions.

"Ale, congratulations," he said, rather indifferent.

"Do you not like it?" she asked.

"Well, I suppose it will keep you busy while I'm gone," he said.

"Yes, but don't you think it's a terrific opportunity?" she said with an unusual exuberance, as if trying to convince her husband.

"Maybe," he said. "What will you do when you get pregnant?"

"It's only part-time, I think I could manage," she said.

"Pardon me, I'm sure you will," he said as he noticed her bewildered expression at his lack of enthusiasm.

"Yes, I'm looking forward to it," she said.

"Of course," he said as he gently patted her hand.

For the next twenty minutes, they talked about local news, but he seemed to be someplace else. For his part, Richard was not thrilled about his wife's employment, particularly in his societal position, where it was unheard of and perhaps even frowned on for a woman to have a job. But he knew she was determined; he would have to let things play out, at least for a while. When he finished eating, he turned to her affectionately.

"Let's continue our conversation over a cup of coffee in the drawing room," he said as he got up from the table.

"Yes, I'll be there soon," she replied. "We made hickory nut cake for dessert."

She felt he had not taken her seriously. Perhaps he had a long day, she thought, and let it go.

Alejandra's position as assistant to Mr. Chandler Manning, who was himself an extraordinary musician, was not only stimulating, but highly rewarding. With the entire repertoire chosen for the 1923-24 season, the most exciting part of her work was organizing and maintaining musical scores, making requests for music acquisitions, and participating in the librarian's recommendations for future concerts. That year the symphonic repertoire included the music of sixty-three composers, including Beethoven's nine symphonies.

As she looked through each of the scores, she was reminded that each had its own story. Looking at the orchestral score of the *Eroica* and Symphony no. 5, she noticed a dedication on both scores' front covers to Prince J.F.M. Lobkowitz. Who was this prince, and why did the magnificent Beethoven dedicate such glorious symphonies to him, she wondered. Later, she would discover the prince was from Czechoslovakia and had been Beethoven's benefactor. Alejandra's heart was filled with joy and gratitude to be working at the symphony's library where she could discover and research all the stories behind the composers' music.

The symphony's new season would include sixteen Friday evening concerts, twenty-three Sunday afternoon popular concerts, and four young people's concerts. A few days before the opening concert of the season in October, she listened to the rehearsal from the last row of the auditorium's theater. The orchestra's thirty violins, eleven violas, ten violoncellos, eight basses, three flutes, and dozens of other instruments came together to create a magical symphonic sound—but something more extraordinary caught her attention that morning. Among the eighty-five men, one woman sat in the violin section. She was Miss Jenny Cullen, a member of Mr. Verbrugghen's former string quartet. With that discovery, her admiration for the new conductor became more personal. It was a transcendent moment in her mind because it meant that a small window had opened for professional women musicians in Minnesota. And to Alejandra, it was a quiet victory for them.

On the opening night of the twenty-first season on Friday, October 19, she attended the concert with both her husband and mother-in-law. The Minneapolis Symphony Orchestra under its new conductor Henri Verbrugghen performed Beethoven's *Eroica* funeral march in memory of four men. Three of them—Edmund Phelps, William Harris, and D. Draper Dayton—had founded the Minneapolis Symphony Orchestra twenty-one years before, and a fourth, Oliver Wyman, was a supporter of the orchestra.

Later on in the orchestra's performance, she focused her attention on the conductor's hand and arm gestures, which went from swiftly sliding his long baton to graceful wrist motions through the various movements of the symphony.

As she observed the Brussels-born conductor, Alejandra realized her admiration for him had grown since the first time she saw him at the benefit concert in spring. He was more than a person on a podium directing an orchestra. He was a man who had studied the works of Beethoven for twenty years. He was also an arranger, and he had successfully directed the music conservatory in Australia. He loved horses and chamber music. Once, she even had a glimpse of his antique musical collection. On the few occasions he happened to be in the room with the orchestra, he smelled of French tobacco like her grandfather George. Above all, however, Mr. Verbrugghen seemed to be a man of great musical talent, compassion, and sensibility.

28 Clair De Lune

With great anticipation and jubilation, the Morrisons found out in late October that they were expecting a child. For the next weeks, the elated parents-to-be made plans for their announcement to the rest of the family, and decorated the empty room next to their bedroom. When their families gathered before dinner for Thanksgiving, Alejandra turned to the guests and said playfully, "There is something we would like to show you upstairs."

Her parents in particular were rather intrigued by the mysterious nature of the request. Soon after, to their great surprise, they entered their future grandchild's room. Painted in lavender colors with a musical-themed border in blue and yellow, silk-organza sheer curtains, and painted white furniture. The nursery was airy, bright, and beautiful.

"Ale and Richard, congratulations!" Lidia exclaimed cheerfully. She hugged her daughter, as did the rest of the family.

Several minutes later, Mrs. Morrison came into the room and stated dinner was being served, and everyone left except for Alejandra, who stayed behind.

Feeling flooded with emotion, she realized she had never felt as fulfilled and happy as she did at that moment, except perhaps for her wedding day. She looked around the room with hopefulness, and noticed a lonely white stuffed teddy bear in the almost vacant built-in bookcase. She picked it up and placed the toy in the baby's crib. Then she sat in the rocking chair next to the window and blessed the infant growing within her. As she thought of several boys' and girls' names, Richard walked into the room and said, "Ale, we're waiting for you!"

In another twist of fate after Christmas, the promise of a new life vanished in an instant when Alejandra woke up one morning and found herself drenched in blood. Terrified, she yelled out for her husband, but he wasn't there. Lena came to her aid, and realizing immediate medical attention was needed, she rushed downstairs to find Mrs. Morrison, who then called for an ambulance. The medical technicians sat with her in the ambulance until they reached the hospital. Yet it was too late to save Alejandra's child.

Shortly after, Richard came into the dark hospital room and found one of the most horrific scenes he had ever witnessed. His wife was shaking and sobbing uncontrollably. As soon as she saw him, she embraced him as he tenderly caressed her head.

"I'm so sorry, I lost our child."

"It's not your fault, these things happen," he said to her in anguish. Her eyes were so red and watery she had blurred vision, and couldn't see his sad and disappointed expression.

"Stay with me," she pleaded.

"Of course, but sleep now, my sweet. You need to rest."

She continued whimpering, almost like an infant. "It was a boy, it was a boy!"

"I promise you, we will have another child," he added.

For the following weeks, she was withdrawn and inconsolable. She had lost interest in everything, and she took a leave of absence from work. Most days she stayed in her bedroom, refusing to leave except to eat, and sometimes didn't even do that. She had suffered other losses before, but nothing compared to what she felt after losing her unborn child. She felt a profound guilt, thinking frequently that perhaps it was her active work schedule that caused the miscarriage. She was, in fact, impenetrable, as though she had shut herself from everyone.

Richard had started his second semester of medical school, and there were days he came home so tired from his studies and his job that seeing her in such a state left him morally exhausted. He not only felt the loss of their child, but also her loss as they had stopped communicating in every way. He couldn't cope with it, and finally turned to his mother-in-law.

In late January of 1924, Lidia came to see her daughter, knocking on her bedroom door. "Ale, it's your mother, I'd like to speak with you," she said as Alejandra opened the door, looking unkempt and desolate. Lidia had never seen her daughter in such a miserable state. She opened the heavy drapes to let some light come into the room. And with a look of consternation, she said, "Ale, I don't like to see you like this. Come sit with me by the window."

Alejandra covered her eyes from the bright sunlight until her eyes adjusted to it, then sat on the armchair next to the bed while her mother sat on the window bench.

"You must deal with this and be strong," Lidia told her.

"Mother, you don't know how this feels. Maybe it was all the hectic time at work for the last few months."

"Nonsense, this happens more often than you think, and I know first-hand," Lidia added.

She turned to her mother in disbelief. "What do you mean?"

Lidia stood up from the bench and looked through the window. She herself had never discussed with anyone what she was about to reveal to her daughter. There were a few moments of silence. Alejandra noticed some hesitation, and did not push for an answer, but Lidia then walked towards her daughter and sat on the edge of the bed.

"Why do you suppose you were an only child for a long time? I had several miscarriages, and the last one was before we went to Mexico back in 1910," Lidia said softly.

Alejandra realized something she had always asked herself.

"Is that why we stayed so long there?" she asked.

"Yes and no, that was part of it. First, of course, it was the ill health of your grandmother. Then it was the Revolution, but later there was a certain comfort in knowing that if I wasn't with your father, I couldn't get pregnant. And I could not bear losing another child; I had five miscarriages," Lidia said with emotion as tears ran down her face. She felt relieved to have shared her past sorrow with her daughter.

"Did father know that was the reason we stayed in Mexico for so long?"

"I think so, although we never talked about it, for it must have been terribly difficult for him to be without his family for that period of time," Lidia said. "I never wanted to know what he did in those four years I was absent."

Alejandra looked at her mother, who rarely showed her emotions publicly. "Oh mother, I'm so sorry," she said, feeling her own misfortune was small compared to what her mother had endured through so many years. She wiped her tears and embraced her mother.

"I do remember hearing you cry often when I was a child," she added. "And how did you deal with it?"

"I had you, your father, we have no choice, but to go on," she said. "Will you try?"

"Yes, I promise. Perhaps I've been selfish and have not considered Richard's own feelings in all this," she said as her mother kissed her on her forehead, adding, "He needs you," before leaving the bedroom.

Alejandra then went to the bedroom closet, took out a large padded storage box, and placed it on the bed. She began to browse through the papers and photographs, mostly mementos from living in Mexico. She wanted to see her mother's face when they first arrived there in 1910. She found the photograph taken at the baptism of her little cousin Sol. There in black and white, her mother's face revealed a profound sadness; yet she never showed it in her interactions with me, Alejandra thought. She took that photo, and placed it on her nightstand. She saw other similar photos, and then she saw en envelope that read, *Inauguration Speech of the National Conservatory of Music in Mexico in the year 1867* by the priest Agustín Caballero.

She opened it and as if by some providence from above, the uplifting words said:

> No one has imagined the heavens adorned with paintings, statues, or portals no matter how beautiful and magnificent they may be, but all artists paint the heavens with the sweet, harmonious choirs of angels who intone hymns of praise to the Almighty. Music is one of those arts that cannot produce wrong to anyone, yet it provides delight of a most pure and innocent nature. What can be more gratifying to a man's heart than to have provided sweet entertainment to his fellow men, letting them forget for a few hours the sad hardships of life!

Alejandra took the inspirational speech of the priest to heart; it was cathartic. How strange that amidst her profound sorrow, words that were spoken more than fifty years before could touch her so deeply and give her comfort. Once again, the meaning and purpose of music brought her back to living life.

When Richard came home that evening, he opened the front door and his heart swelled with emotion as he heard his wife playing piano in the drawing room. He placed his suitcase and books on a wooden console table in the entryway, nearly upending the flower-filled vase nearby. He quietly walked toward the room, trying not to intrude as he stood beside the door.

After a long day working at the research laboratory and preparing rigorously for a looming examination, Richard truly savored the sweet, melancholic, and romantic notes of Claude Debussy's composition "Clair de Lune" on the piano. It was the first time, in fact, he had heard Alejandra play on his family's piano, although she had played before when he was at work. He laughed to himself, remembering how he had invited her to his home when they were both adolescents. And here she was, now his wife, he thought, as he walked over to the piano bench and sat down. He was glad she had emerged from her somber mood, and decided not to bring up the painful subject, for fear she might start to cry again. Instead, he resumed his old habit of joking.

"I see you finally accepted my invitation to play on the family's piano; it only took you seven years," Richard said, laughing.

She laughed. "Better seven years late than never," she said as he kissed her with his usual sensuous intensity; then he asked, "What's for dinner? I'm starving."

On a sunny afternoon, Alejandra was in the large parlor room, decorated, like the rest of the house, in Arts and Crafts style, an English innovation of the late 1800s. As she admired her mother-in-law's taste and decorative style, she noticed above the fireplace a new landscape watercolor on paper by Winslow Homer titled *An October Day.* The painting, in tones of blue, gold, and green, and almost impressionistic in style, was both striking and haunting. From her seat she glanced at the living room furniture designed by Gustav Stickley, and an Oriental rug in tones of green and turquoise. A poppy vase in cucumber green adorned the side table. The interior decor was certainly beautiful, but what was most remarkable for Alejandra was that for the first time since her arrival there, she felt at home. When she finally resumed her reading, moments later, she heard her husband walk into the room.

"Ale, we're taking a vacation," he said.

"When?" she asked.

"The week of February 11," he said.

"Goodness, I hope I can extend my time off from work. It's two weeks away," she said. "A little sudden. What do you have planned?"

"Something special, but I'm sure your boss will understand."

"Yes, he has been very understanding. I will contact him immediately," she said. "He did write me a note a week ago, telling me to take as much time as needed."

"Well, if he says yes, I'm taking you to New York for our first wedding anniversary," Richard said.

Her facial expression was jovial, but inquisitive. "I must call Hannah right away," she said.

"She already knows," he said. "I thought you might like to be there for her engagement party and other things."

"Her engagement party?" she asked.

"Yes, they decided to have it on the fourteenth. And she called you a few weeks ago to see if by chance we could be there, but at the time I said no because of what happened."

"She probably didn't want to tell me when she wrote me," she said. "I'm so happy for her, I'll call her anyway. And what are the other things?"

"You'll have to wait and see," he said.

"We said no more secrets," she said, smiling.

"Small surprises are suitable; you can't take that away from me!" he replied as he sat next to her and patted her hand gently.

29 Rhapsody in Blue

On a very frigid and overcast day, the ninth of February, the Morrisons arrived in New York. As they entered the Algonquin Hotel, they found it a familiar and memorable sight, but not more pleasing than seeing Hannah and her fiancé Benjamin in the hotel lobby.

"Hannah, Benjamin, so good to see you both," Alejandra said joyfully. "Congratulations."

"Good to see you again," Richard said to both of them. "Let me check in, I'll return in a few moments."

"Ale, I have so much to tell you, but I'm so pleased you are feeling better," Hannah said to her friend as she gave her a hug. "So sorry about the baby."

"Yes, it is still very painful," Alejandra said sadly. "But let's not talk about that. I want to hear about you. When is the happy day?"

"Not until the summer of next year," Hannah replied. "Benjamin wants to save enough money to buy us a house."

"You know I like everything perfect," he said.

"Yes, we do!" the two friends replied smiling, as they both remembered his strict discipline and perfectionism while they were students at the Institute of Musical Art.

"Well at least you won't have to be apart as Richard and I were after our engagement," Alejandra replied.

"I still can't believe your father made you wait that long," Hannah added.

"He wanted me to be completely sure," Alejandra said, laughing.

At that moment Richard returned, and hearing the comment, he added with a smirk, "Ha! I think it was you who wanted to study for another year in Mexico."

"Perhaps, but it was definitely at my father's insistence, and I missed you terribly," she said.

"Well, you know the writer Miss Stickland's famous quote—absence makes the heart grow fonder," Hannah added, with a laugh.

"Indeed," Richard said.

"And how is your family?" Alejandra asked.

"They're all in good health and very pleased, you'll see them at the festivities," Hannah said.

"Let's freshen up first," Alejandra said. "We have early dinner reservations at the Oak Room," Hannah said.

"We'll be down in fifteen minutes," Richard said.

An hour later, the couples were finishing their dinner when the waiter brought them four cups of espresso coffee and peppermint iceberg puffs for dessert. Hannah reached into her purse and pulled out an envelope which she gave to Alejandra.

"An early present from your husband," Hannah said.

She looked at Richard with questioning eyes, and then proceeded to open the white envelope. She pulled out four tickets and read the top one:

> *An Experiment in Modern Music*
> Directed and produced by Paul Whiteman.
> Tuesday, February 12, 1924.
> Aeolian Hall, 7:00 p.m.

Alejandra turned to her husband and whispered, "Thank you, but who is Paul Whiteman?"

"He's a bandleader who loves jazz, and hopes 'to bring it the respectability it deserves in the formal concert venue.' Actually, he has a classically trained arranger who arranges popular tunes for his forty-piece orchestra," Benjamin said.

"You'll never guess who will be one of the performers," Hannah said.

"No idea, but this time, I want to be surprised," Alejandra replied as she looked at her husband.

"The music will be a mystery, too," Hannah added.

"I have a feeling it will be groundbreaking," Benjamin said.

"We can hardly wait," Alejandra said.

Two nights later, the couples went to the Aeolian Hall, located in midtown Manhattan on West Forty-second Street. When they walked into the packed eleven-hundred-seat concert venue, Alejandra thought about the performers and the music she was about to hear as they sat in the seventh row of the ornately decorated hall. She imagined the face of the Mexican composer and music conservatory professor Manuel Ponce, as he might have appeared on stage, when he performed in this very place several years earlier in 1916. And as she wandered off to another time, as she frequently did, Mr. Whiteman was introduced to the audience. After a welcoming round of applause, he began by giving a complete history of jazz from its earliest beginnings. Then the performers played the first number, "Lively Stable Blues," then "So this is Venice," and so on . . . .

Next came the penultimate piece that everyone had been waiting for. The virtuoso pianist and composer George Gershwin, the son of a Russian-Jewish immigrant, stepped on stage and sat in front of the grand piano. The audience applauded and eagerly waited for him to play the first note. As predicted, he performed the world premiere of his new composition *Rhapsody in Blue*, a magnificent blend of jazz and classical elements orchestrated by Ferde Grofé.

"This was perhaps the defining moment in what came to be known as the Jazz Age and its formal acceptance into the mainstream." But to Alejandra, even more satisfying was the fact that as a lover of music, she would never have to choose between classical or popular music to be a conductor; for she realized any popular music could be arranged for a symphonic orchestra. It had been another eye-opening event in the world of music, and in her musical development. Once again, as before, she conceived a plan in her mind—but first she would celebrate the reason for coming to New York in the first place with her husband and friends.

The morning of Valentine's Day, she woke up as she felt a soft, almost velvety caress on her face. It was Richard, who had taken a red rose and gently brushed the petals around her eyes, cheeks, and mouth, continuing down to her chest and navel. With her eyes barely open, she smiled.

"Happy anniversary," he said.

She took the rose from his hand. "You are a very naughty boy," she said as she placed the red rose in the flower vase on the nightstand, next to the white rose. "Happy anniversary to you."

"What would you like to do this morning?" he asked.

"Anything you like," she said.

"Anything?" he said, with a penetrating gaze into her eyes.

"Almost anything, only for today!" she said, laughing.

Upon arrival at their apartment house, later that evening, the Morrisons were welcomed by the Mendes family. As they greeted each other in the vestibule, Alejandra gave Mrs. Mendes a white flowering plant.

"Please, let us go into the drawing room," Amelia said. Nothing in the décor had changed except for the portrait of Hannah which hung on the wall by the window, above her cello. Just then Benjamin arrived with his violin case.

"We can't very well have an engagement party without music," he said, as he lovingly looked at Hannah who seemed as happy as ever. Benjamin then greeted everyone else.

The two friends sat next to each other on the plush velvet-covered sofa.

"Well, I think before everyone else arrives, this is as good a time as any to give you both your engagement present," Alejandra said as she pulled out a wrapped white package from Richard's briefcase and gave it to their friends.

"Benjamin, sit with us, there is room here," Hannah said as she began to open the package. Benjamin read the sheet music titles out loud: String Quartet in E flat Major by Fanny Mendelssohn, and then String Quartet no. 3 by Maddalena Lombardini Sirmen.

"Thank you, Ale and Richard, what a wonderful gift. And congratulations to you, too, on your anniversary," Hannah said.

"Who is Maddalena Lombardini Sirmen?" Benjamin asked in a playful manner.

"She was a woman composer, but also a virtuoso violinist who entered one of the many Venetian orphanages in the eighteenth century at age seven. She was, in fact, the only woman to attend one of the Venetian conservatories. It was said that a 'violin in her hands was played as gracefully as Orpheus played his lyre,' although she later became an opera singer," Alejandra said.

"Wow, you remember all that," Benjamin asked.

She smiled.

"Don't even get started, Benjamin!" Hannah told him as she remembered their shared spirit of competition, which was often fun while they were all students.

"Well, then, we must play both of these pieces tonight," Benjamin said.

Hannah took the sheet music and placed it on the table, just as Richard's briefcase fell over, spilling out a medical journal.

"Here, let me put this someplace else," he said.

"How is medicine?" Benjamin asked.

"Always interesting and challenging," he replied.

"Our bedroom floor is saturated with medical books," Alejandra said laughingly. "Sometimes he stays up reading until one in the morning."

"Can you sleep?" Hannah asked.

"Oh, yes, there's a small seating area next to the bedroom," Alejandra said. "Besides, I'm also a late sleeper."

"Yes, I remember that!" Hannah replied and smiled at her friend.

After their closest friends and family had arrived, approximately thirty guests in all, the group sat down for a scrumptious five-course meal that lasted nearly ninety minutes. Then Benjamin made a toast and announced his engagement to Hannah Mendes.

"And to continue with our celebration, we, the Regatta String Quartet, would like to perform a selection of works for strings, starting with compositions by two women composers," he said.

The other two musicians were Raphael Cardozo on viola and Simon Grusco on second violin. As they played the second piece, Alejandra noticed how illustriously Hannah was playing the cello. No one in that room could know how Maddalena Lombardini Sirmen's hands on the violin could have sounded, but Hannah played her cello gracefully and divinely, as never before.

When the Morrisons returned to the hotel before midnight and walked toward the elevator, Alejandra asked, "Tomorrow is our last day here. Any plans?"

"We can't very well skip a play on Broadway," he said.

"Which play?" she asked.

"*The Assumption of Hannele* by German playwright Gerhard Hauptmann," he said. It's the opening night at the Cort Theater."

"Do you know what the play is about?" she asked.

"It's about an abused child as she lies dying and dreams about her entrance into heaven," he said. "It was the only one I could find opening tomorrow. Is it too dramatic?" Richard asked.

"A little, perhaps, but a reality for some," she said with a contemplative expression. "I'd like to see it anyway."

Moments later, he reached for the room's key in his pocket and opened the door. The lights were off, yet with the draperies opened, under the soft moonlight of the night they kissed goodnight.

The Three-Cornered Hat

It was the month of June in 1924, when Vivian Morrison, Richard's mother, was busy in her library, making plans for her latest social event of the season. Since her husband's death and her daughter's marriage, she had dedicated herself to fundraising for charitable causes, particularly those related to children's welfare, medical care, and the Elliot Memorial Hospital. She was very well known in the Twin Cities, so it was no revelation when she decided to enlist her new daughter-in-law to help with her endeavors.

On Friday, after returning from work, Alejandra went into the parlor for her afternoon piano practice. Mrs. Morrison came into the room. Alejandra heard her footsteps and immediately turned to her.

"Mrs. Morrison, how are you feeling?" she asked pleasantly.

"Much better, thank you. It's allergy season," Mrs. Morrison said as she sneezed and took a handkerchief from her sleeve. "They are worse every year," she continued, pausing momentarily to sit down across from her daughter-in-law. "I have a proposition for you."

"Yes?" Alejandra questioned.

"Well, as you know, I'm quite involved with several charity organizations, and we have several fundraisers throughout the year. And I thought that perhaps we might put your piano abilities to good use. How would you like to perform at some of these functions?"

"Do you think people would like to hear me play?" she asked.

"Most certainly. I've listened to you play for over a year, and you are indeed very good. All you would need is to choose a repertoire for each performance," Mrs. Morrison said.

Alejandra paused for a few seconds. "It makes me a little nervous," she said.

"Why? You've performed publicly before," Mrs. Morrison declared.

"Yes, but always with other musicians and never alone in public, other than at home with friends," she said. "It's funny, as a teenager I wanted to be a concert pianist, although I gave up on that idea a long time ago," she added. "I have tremendous admiration for concert pianists, for it requires extraordinary dedication to the craft, to the audience, and lots of travel. And I couldn't very well leave my husband behind," Alejandra said with a touch of humor.

"Well, then this would be ideal. I think you would be marvelous," Mrs. Morrison insisted.

"Thank you for your confidence in me, then, yes," she said optimistically. "Perhaps for the concert, I can play a mix of classical and popular pieces," she suggested. "What do you think, Mrs. Morrison?"

"It's a lovely idea. Then it's settled. You prepare a musical program lasting about fifty minutes to an hour, and I shall take care of the rest," Vivian Morrison said as she left the room.

As she thought about the musical program, she immediately thought about the plan she had conceived back in New York—to bring classical music to a more popular realm. Alejandra realized what a privilege it was to have learned and listened to various musical genres. Each style offered a different color, landscape, texture, and emotion. What a task it would be to settle on only a dozen musical compositions, choosing from hundreds of them. She was living through the 1920s, and the Jazz Age. It was a good place to start, and perhaps, little by little, she could showcase the music of forgotten or unknown composers. After many days of pondering her selections for the concert, she chose the music of Juventino Rosas, Ernesto Lecuona, Scott Joplin, George Gershwin, Franz Liszt, and Ludwig Van Beethoven.

In September, everything was in place, and when she organized a birthday celebration for Richard's twenty-fifth birthday, Mrs. Morrison took the opportunity to distribute the invitations for the upcoming fundraiser. Richard was the first to read the program out loud while they had cocktails in the drawing room:

You are cordially invited to a Harvest Luncheon
An afternoon of jazz, waltzes, and sonatas
At the Schubert Theater to benefit programs of
The Hennepin County Medical Society Auxiliary
Established in 1910

Saturday, October 18, 1924, 11:00 a.m.

Piano performance by Mrs. Alejandra Morrison
R.S.V.P.—Miss Margaret Adams—Telephone: 2-8620

It was the typical fall day in Minnesota. Dressed in her robe and feathery sleepers, she drank a glass of water from her nightstand and then walked down the steps and outside into the small garden in the backyard. With the temperatures in the fifties it was snippy. She took a deep breath and smelled the scent of fall, a mix of firewood, apple crisp, and eucalyptus. The kaleidoscope of earthy tones on the trees and the sunrise was another reminder of what a lovely day it would be, even if she felt a bit apprehensive.

"Good morning, Ale, come join me," Mrs. Morrison said.

"Yes, good morning to you," Alejandra said as she went back indoors and sat next to her mother-in-law in the sunroom.

Minutes later, Lena brought them a tray of pastries, which she placed on the wooden table. The faithful middle-aged housekeeper was always smiling and pleasant, but spoke little English.

"Thank you, Lena," Mrs. Morrison said. She smiled.

The smell of baked apples made Alejandra hungry. Her mother-in-law, who was reading the newspaper, turned to her. "How do you feel?"

"Excited and nervous," she replied.

"You'll do wonderfully," Mrs. Morrison said.

"I want to express my appreciation for considering me for this event; I know how much work you've put into it," she said as she broke off a piece of pastry from her plate.

"You're welcome, my dear," Mrs. Morrison said.

"What is the organization hoping to do with the funds it raises?" Alejandra asked.

"Measles is very prevalent among children these days, so the society is hoping to provide for a greater number of immunizations," Vivian said.

"Is it a devastating illness?" Alejandra asked.

"With good care it can be cured, although I've heard some reports that 'in foundling hospitals, as many as fifty percent of patients may die,'" Mrs. Morrison replied.

"Oh! My goodness," she said.

Watching Mrs. Morrison drink her coffee, Alejandra quietly admired her mother-in-law as elegant, but not particularly warm. With her perfectly coiffed hair, manicured nails, and impeccable wardrobe, she was a woman of great style and class, even if at times she seemed distant. Alejandra never imagined she and Mrs. Morrison would find something in common, much less enjoy each other's company. Yet, since they began to work together, her perception of Mrs. Morrison had changed. Music had the ability to break down barriers.

Later that day, almost two hundred people attended the fundraiser, which raised nearly one thousand dollars for the medical society. Mrs. Morrison was thrilled for the resounding success of her efforts and her daughter-in-law's enthusiastic performance. As the remaining family gathered in the reception hall, Richard turned to her.

"You see, my dear, you have put your musical talent to good use, and I especially loved your performance of Lecuona's 'Malagueña,'" Richard said smiling.

"Thank you, it's one of my favorites," she said.

"Now you can quit your job," Richard added.

"Quit my job, I wouldn't think of it!" she said.

"Congratulations, hija (daughter), you'll now be quite busy, for Mrs. Morrison already has several events planned for next year," Lidia said.

"I hope in the future you'll include some of your own music. You shouldn't be shy about it," Edward said.

"Yes, I suggested that, too," Richard said. "But then she doesn't always take my advice," he added laughingly.

"I do, darling, but not now," she said as her cousin Steven and Olga, whom she had not seen in a while, stood next to her.

"I've missed you. Next time choose a song for me to sing," he whispered. She smiled and replied, "I'd love it."

Alejandra felt much personal gratification to have contributed, even if in a small way, to the event, and for the opportunity to perform and share the music of cherished composers. But what she found the most rewarding was using her skills in the service of others.

Excited to return to work with the symphony orchestra, she left early on the following Monday morning. As she was proofreading the program notes for upcoming concerts, she discovered that on November 28, the symphony would perform the music of a Spanish composer. At the end of the day, she purchased concert tickets for all her family. When she left her office that day, she drove to her parents' house.

Edward was diligently working in his library when she knocked on his door. "Papá, may I come in?" she asked as she realized how much she missed him and being there—even missing the smell of his cigar, which pervaded the room.

"Ale, what a lovely surprise," he exclaimed as she kissed him on the cheek. He quickly rolled up the sketch he was working on and placed it on the side of the architect's table.

"What are you drawing this time?" she asked.

"Just another project," he said. "What brings you here?"

"Can't a daughter visit her family?" she said with a smile.

"Sure, but you've been so preoccupied with all your activities, we don't get to see you as often."

"I know. I have something for you, mother, and Eddy," she said as she took the three concert tickets from her purse.

"Tickets?" he asked.

"You'll never guess what music the symphony orchestra will be performing," she said with a mischievous smile.

"Don't I get a hint?" he asked.

"Something we didn't get to see and hear in Barcelona."

He paused for a few moments, trying to remember. "I can't recall anyone," he said as he squinted his eyes.

"I bet mother would remember," Alejandra said as her mother walked into the library.

"Ale has concert tickets for us. Do you know what music we didn't get to hear in Barcelona?" he asked.

Lidia kissed her daughter. "Yes, of course, *El Sombrero de Tres Picos* (The Three- Cornered Hat)," she replied, laughing.

"Oh yes, by Manuel de Falla," Edward added. "When is it?"

"On November 28 in the orchestra's new venue, the Lyceum Theater, completely remodeled," Alejandra replied.

"That's over a month away," he said.

"Yes, I was very excited about it after reading the program notes,"

Alejandra commented.

"Now if they could someday play the music of Ponce or Rosas, that would be lovely," Lidia said.

"That is one of the reasons I want to be a musical director, so I can choose music of unknown composers around the world."

"Well, you're starting to do that already," Edward said.

"That's true," she replied. "By the way, Richard and I are taking you all to dinner at Table D'Hôte next Saturday," she added.

"And tonight, would you like to stay for dinner?" Lidia asked her daughter.

"I'd love to, but Richard and I have plans for the evening with his colleagues," she said. "I'll stay for tea."

"Great," her mother said as she left for the kitchen.

"In the meantime, I want to see Eddy," Alejandra said.

"He's upstairs reading," Edward said.

"Reading?"

"Yes, ever since he discovered Jules Verne's science-fiction novels, he can't get enough," Edward said.

"Like father, like son," Alejandra said playfully and left the room.

A month later, the Morrisons and Stanfords met at the new musical theater. Decorated elegantly and with improved acoustics, the music had a richer and crisper sound as the orchestra performed the music of Manuel de Falla. His lively melody with an Andalusian flavor was a welcome change from the traditional music often performed. The orchestra's new conductor had ventured into other musical styles, and the public seemed to appreciate it.

Toward the end of the performance Alejandra browsed through the program notes, which included advertisements she did not see when she proofread the program notes. The headline, "The Juilliard Musical Foundation—School of Music" caught her eye. And when she saw the names of the school's faculty below the headline, her heart almost stopped beating when she read the name Anna E. Schoen-René. Here she was, possibly the first woman conductor in the United States, a musical pioneer in Minnesota who had returned from Europe—and she was now back in the United States, teaching at Juilliard. Alejandra had known about her since she was a child. She had dreamed about meeting her for years, as if she was some lost relative.

Though she was not aware of it before, Schoen-René had become Alejandra's inspiration, her role model, and her secret advocate. How many times had she envisioned herself talking to the legendary musical pioneer? She would write to her, and perhaps even meet her while in New York for Hannah's wedding. Alejandra was so happy, she could have gotten up from her seat to dance as she listened to the orchestra perform the last movement of Manuel de Falla's *The Three-Cornered Hat.*

Almost six months had gone by when the Morrisons traveled to New York to attend the wedding of Hannah Mendes and Benjamin Adelman. Two days before, Alejandra's long-standing dream to meet Anna Eugenie Schoen-René in person was finally realized. They met at the new Juilliard Graduate School, which later merged with, her former school, the Institute of Musical Art. As she and her husband approached the Vanderbilt Guest House at 49 East Fifty-second Street, they entered the grand mansion and were directed to wait in a large drawing room. Richard told her he would return for her in an hour.

With great anticipation, she sat nervously on a large brown velveteen sofa, across from an ornate fireplace with a large mirror above it. To her right there were two sets of large windows, and in the corner a grand piano. In a few moments, she would finally see the woman who had unknowingly allowed her to keep her dream of being a conductor alive. When the door opened, she turned her eyes to the person entering, but it was a young, corpulent man perhaps her own age, who sat on another sofa across from her.

"Good afternoon, are you a student here?" he asked.

"No, only visiting," she said. "And you?"

"Yes," he said. "I hope to join the Metropolitan Opera someday."

"I see, voice is your instrument," she said. "And your teacher here?"

"Schoen-René," he said. "She too was a singer who studied under the great Pauline Garcia-Viardot."

"I've never been at the opera house in New York, perhaps I can visit while we're here," she said.

"I think they are on break now, but they will resume their long-standing performance of Verde's *Aida* in the fall," the young man said as Anna Schoen-René walked into the room.

Containing her excitement, she stood up and walked toward the woman, who could only be described as someone with a large presence.

Miss Schoen-René's round face and big brown eyes were welcoming, although her facial expression was strong and determined.

"You must be Alejandra," she said as she shook her hand. "I see you met one of my pupils."

"Pleasure to meet you, Miss Schoen-René. Thank you so much for seeing me," she said pleasantly.

"How could I refuse such a warm and personal letter, knowing that your mother was listening to my concert just before you were born," she said with a smile. "Let's go upstairs into my private office."

"Miss Schoen-René, I was just leaving," the young man said.

"Then I suppose we can stay here. The piano may come in handy," she said with her strong German accent as she sat next to Alejandra. "Congratulations. From your looks, you are with child," she added.

"Yes, most fortunately!"

"How many months?" she asked. "And is this your first?"

"Yes, and I'm four months pregnant," Alejandra replied.

"Well, you might have to postpone any career plans," Miss Schoen-René said with authority, though in a friendly manner.

"Somewhat, although playing and composing would not interfere in any way," Alejandra said. "But, with great sadness, I did resign from my position with the orchestra."

"Understandable. That must have been quite an experience," Miss Schoen-René said. "I'm pleased to know how successful the symphony orchestra is, and now with a new conductor. It's very well known throughout the country, I suppose thanks to their excellence and touring efforts."

"And radio broadcasts and recordings, which they actually made last year here in New York," Alejandra added. "Weren't you a pioneer in the beginning?"

"In some ways, you could say that," Miss Schoen-René replied. "With obstacles, I might add."

"Obstacles?" Alejandra questioned.

"My dear, there are always obstacles, and I've had my share. Yet having firm goals, a mentor, and teacher who supported me went a long way."

"Was your teacher Pauline Garcia-Viardot?" Alejandra asked.

"Yes, for eighteen years. She was the daughter of the internationally known Spanish tenor Manuel Vicente Del Pópolo Rodriguez Garcia," Miss Schoen-René said.

"Yes, one of your pupils at the University of Minnesota told me about this many years ago," Alejandra replied.

"And who was that?" the professor asked.

"Johann Hausberg," she said.

"Oh! He was always so loyal to me."

"But please go on," Alejandra said.

"Where were we?" Miss Schoen-René asked.

"The Spanish tenor."

"Manuel Vicente Garcia was the first to bring Italian opera to New York in 1825. His voice was so grand that Rossini wrote the part of Almaviva in *The Barber of Seville* for him."

"Yes, yes, my grandfather in Mexico has a sketch of him made by my great-grandmother, when she saw him while touring in Mexico in that same period. And your teacher, Pauline Garcia?" Alejandra asked.

"She was the most graceful, kind, and intelligent woman. She spoke eight languages and was considered the best opera singer in Europe by such luminaries as Wagner, Chopin, Verdi, Tchaikovsky, Schumann, and Debussy, to name a few. She was friends with all of them, and through her I was able to meet some of the best performers of the time. She was also an excellent pianist who performed alongside Franz Liszt, who was her teacher," Miss Schoen-René said. "Pauline was a gift to the world, and an inspiration to me, and someday, I should like to write a book and dedicate it to her," she continued with emotion in her voice.

"You must have been quite fond of her," Alejandra said. "Please tell me more about you and your career in Minnesota."

"Let's start at the beginning. My father died when I was only ten years old, and soon after, I entered the music conservatory in Berlin. Later in my career, Pauline became my teacher and I studied with the best voice instructors throughout Europe, including Pauline's brother Manuel Garcia who taught at the Royal Academy in London. The Garcia family was considered one of the most talented musical families in Europe, and I later became the Garcia's representative as a teacher of the singing style, bel canto.

Initially, I came to New York to sing opera in the late 1880s, but my poor health forced me to relocate to Minnesota with my sister, who taught German at the university. Despite that setback, 'I had two very ambitious goals. The first was to advance music in Minnesota and in the Midwest. And the only way to accomplish it was for my students to learn the difference between good and bad music.' For that reason, I brought some of the best living artists of the day who were accompanied musically by the choral union at the university. And my students participated in that process. I think that goal was accomplished," she said. "Would you like some water?"

"Yes thank you," Alejandra said.

Miss Schoen-René poured two glasses of water from the water pitcher on the side table, and gave a glass to her guest. She drank the water slowly, and then asked, "And your second goal?"

"'To create a symphony orchestra in the Northwest, and I almost did. It was to be named the Northwestern Symphony Orchestra and would have served both Minneapolis and St. Paul. Several patrons assured a backing of thirty-thousand dollars for the purpose of engaging a conductor and musicians.' However, upon my return from traveling abroad, another wealthy patron provided almost twice as much money for a different symphonic orchestra. Despite my struggles, 'I was fortunate to have loyal supporters, including William Haskell, owner of the *Minneapolis Journal*. He was so kind in arranging meetings for me with distinguished individuals from Minneapolis—Frank Peavey, John and Charles Pillsbury, and others. I had sworn not to leave Minneapolis until those two goals were accomplished,' and they were, so I left in 1909," she said.

"Any regrets?" Alejandra asked.

"You are very direct," Anna Schoen-René said. "But no! Regrets come only from not doing your best for something you believe in," she continued. "I'm satisfied, for perhaps I left a lasting musical legacy. My resolution of elevating music to its highest standards in the Midwest has been achieved."

"And your life as a conductor?"

"It was short lived, although it wasn't something I personally pursued. My original ambition was to be an opera singer, as I've said before, but life takes you in different directions, and for me it was teaching," Miss Schoen-René said.

"Your words mean so much to me, and I'm profoundly grateful to you for sharing all these inspirational stories of your life," Alejandra said.

"You must remember, my dear, that the titles are not as important as the music itself. And reaching for your dreams is always worth your time and energy in the service of music excellence, if this is, of course, what makes you happy. Never give up." The professor added, "Before you go, play something for me."

Alejandra smiled and said, "With pleasure. I'd like to play a piece titled 'Sevilla' (Seville) by Isaac Albéniz, since you were so fond of the Garcia family."

When she finished playing the piano, Anna was taken with emotion and walked over to Alejandra, giving her a warm embrace. "Call on me whenever you like," she said. "And best wishes on the birth of your child and your friend's wedding."

"Yes, thank you," Alejandra replied. "And again, it was wonderful to have finally met you in person."

Before Hannah's wedding, she, her family, and friends gathered at her home for a special ceremony called the mikveh ritual. In a small room lit with candles stood a large bathtub. Surrounded by women, Hannah immersed herself seven times in the warm, fragrant water to achieve ritual purity in preparation for her nuptials the following day. All the women sang Hebrew songs and praises, and their blessings poured over her as rose petals might be thrown in the air. While watching the ceremony, Alejandra gently rubbed her abdomen with her hand, as she also prayed for the life inside her. She heard the sweet voices of the women singing, and looked in admiration at her joyful friend and her beautiful Jewish tradition. At that moment she decided that if she were to have a girl, she would name her daughter Lidia Hannah Morrison.

The following day on June 6, 1925, Hannah walked down the aisle alone until she was met by her parents, Amelia and David. They took her by the arms and then presented her to Benjamin, who was proudly waiting at the altar in his tuxedo, wearing his *kippah* (skullcap). A young child sang in Hebrew as the Rabbi stepped in front of the altar and began to read from the Torah. As he performed the wedding ceremony, the bride, groom, and their parents faced the congregation. When the ceremony neared its ending, the Regatta Quartet performed the couple's favorite Jewish musical composition, "K'shoshana Ben Hachochim."

God Lives

Minneapolis, November 1926

She heard her infant daughter crying in the next room. Lidia Hannah had been born the previous year, and in a few weeks she would be a year old. Yet, before Alejandra was fully awake, Richard walked into their bedroom at six minutes past five o'clock, at dawn.

"Ale, your father has been taken to the hospital," he said with great concern.

With her eyes still half closed at first, she thought she was dreaming until she felt a soft kick in her midsection, as she was expecting her second child. At that moment she opened her eyes and saw Richard dressing frantically, and she realized that his words were indeed real. She felt great apprehension, but the child inside her required her to be calm. She took a deep breath, and with difficulty, lifted herself from the bed.

"Richard, I need to go to Liddy's room first," she said, somewhat confused. "Is my father all right?"

"I don't know, your mother just called from Eitel Hospital and said he was taken there by an ambulance. I'm going now! Don't worry about Liddy, Lena is feeding her already," he said.

"Wait, then, let me get dressed, I want to go with you," she said worriedly, as she quickly changed her clothes.

Thirty minutes later, they arrived at the hospital's waiting room and found Lidia sobbing profusely.

"Mother, Mother, what happened?"

"Oh! Ale, your father is dead!" Lidia said, shaking.

"Mamá, it can't be," she replied as she too started to cry, in a state of shock. "How?"

"Heart attack, when he arrived at the hospital he was already gone; there was nothing they could do," Lidia said, as her daughter embraced her.

"Mother, I'm so sorry, so sorry," Alejandra said, devastated, as she took her mother in her arms and continued to cry and console her. She couldn't believe it. Her father was too young.

"Please come sit here, you shouldn't be up for too long," Richard said as he held his wife and brought her to a chair.

"I'll be back soon," he added.

Lidia's eyes were red, and in an almost-confused capacity she said, "What am I going to do without him, Ale? How could this happen? He was only fifty years old."

"Mother, you've always told me to have faith," she said as she placed her hand on her abdomen, as if trying to contain her own grief for the sake of the life within her. Ten minutes later, Richard returned and placed his arm around his wife.

"Do you know what caused it?" she asked.

"Some type of genetic coronary disease," he said sadly, holding her hand.

"I want to see him, I want to see him!" Lidia exclaimed.

Alejandra also wanted very much to see her loving father, but she was afraid of her own reaction. Her doctor had warned her to rest and avoid any extraneous physical or emotional stress. She considered all these factors as she continued to cry, now intensely, and decided not to go with her mother.

"Ale, I think you need to stay here. I'll take your mother to see him for the last time," Richard said, cautiously.

"Yes," she said, mortified.

Moments later, when Lidia walked into the cold and dark hospital room and saw Edward lying lifeless on a metal bed, she felt as though someone had stabbed her in the heart. It was irrefutable! Before she saw him, she had hoped in the most inner part of her being that it was all a mistake. She held his hand, looking at his closed eyes. She then kissed him on his lips, still warm, and whispered to him, crying, "Please forgive me for leaving you all those years. It was never my intention. And now I'll be without you forever." She clung to him, as if she herself could die and be with him, but despite all her suffering, she saw the image of their young son, Edward George. He had just lost his father, she thought. She said goodbye to her beloved dead husband, whom she caressed most adoringly and tenderly, kissed once again, and blessed.

Richard helped his mother-in-law get up from the chair, and together they walked slowly as she turned her body several times, wanting to return to her husband once more. The nurse took the sheet and covered him up completely. When Lidia and Richard returned to the waiting room, they found Alejandra with a serene expression. She had stopped crying, and seemed to have momentarily compartmentalized her agony into a part of her being.

"Richard, darling, I'd like us to move in with my mother until our child is born," she said decisively. He was familiar with her calmness and determination, and knew it was something she needed to do; perhaps to give consolation to her mother, perhaps to be in some way near to everything her father had touched, or both. He remained silent for a few moments and embraced her.

"Yes, my dear, if that's your wish."

Lidia couldn't say a word, but held her daughter's hand. It was as if she completely understood all the reasons and was comforted by her decision.

When they arrived back at the Morrisons' residence, Alejandra went to her baby girl's room, finding Liddy sleeping peacefully in her crib. Lena, who was by the crib, stood up as soon as she walked into the room.

"We must pack all her things, please, for we will be staying at my parents' home for the next several weeks," she said.

"Yes, madam, I will have everything ready in a few hours," Lena replied.

"Thank you," Alejandra said.

That night, the Morrison family took two of the guest rooms on the second floor of the Stanford residence. After everyone had fallen asleep, Alejandra lay on her old bed as she stared at the ceiling, thinking about everything that had happened. She wished she could diminish her mother's sorrow and burden. It was rather curious to be back at her parents' home, except she would never see her father again. She heard her daughter's faint whimper down the hall, and quickly went to the bedroom, hoping no one else would wake up.

She picked up her daughter, who was now giggling as if she was talking to someone, though of course she was not. Her diapers were wet, and she changed them. Alejandra then sat on an old rocking chair and placed Liddy on her lap with some difficulty, being already seven months pregnant. She began to nurse the baby and spoke to her in a quiet voice.

"Liddy, you were lucky to have known your grandpa."

Very quietly, Alejandra sang a lullaby until her daughter slowly closed her eyes and fell asleep again. With the baby on her chest, she stayed with her for another half an hour until Richard, who had awakened, came into the room, took the girl, and placed her carefully in Eddy's worn-out crib.

When Alejandra woke up the next morning, Richard had already left to pick up the rest of their belongings from his mother's house. It was barely seven in the morning, so she put on her robe and went downstairs into her father's library. The room felt cold and empty as she gently passed her fingers over every object, as if touching her father. She took the framed photograph with an image of him and the family to her lips, and kissed it; then walked to her father's architect's table and noticed a sketch of a house's exterior elevation. She then glanced above the table to Hiawatha's portrait.

Next, her eyes turned to Edward's Chinese brush pot containing a dozen or so architectural drawings. Above his favorite chair he had a Chinese landscape finger-painting from the Ming Dynasty. It was his love of nature that had always attracted him to Asian artwork, she recalled. Alejandra took a few steps toward the bookshelves that contained all his architectural books, and said to him, "I'll remember everything you've taught me, and the love you gave me." She was praying for her father in silence when she heard a voice in the room.

"Ale, Ale, where's Father?" her brother asked. She thought of whether she should tell him, or wait to have their mother tell him.

"Let us go and find our mother," she said to Edward George as she hugged him.

Later that morning, with a heavy heart, Alejandra made all the funeral arrangements.

On December 3, 1926, the service took place at the Basilica of St. Mary in Minneapolis. Almost three hundred people gathered for the ceremony conducted by their long-time friend Father O'Gara, who gave a most touching homily. Moments later, George Stanford walked toward the podium to give the eulogy.

"We are here today to celebrate the life of Edward Stanford, the son, father, grandfather, brother, friend, and husband whose optimistic, enthusiastic, and above all loving nature was always inspirational to everyone who knew him. From the moment he was born, with his kind nature and charisma, we knew he had been a blessing to Clara and I. Only few can imagine the profound pain in losing a child; but I turn and pray to our God almighty to keep Edward in His care, with my wife by his side.

I rejoice in the knowledge that during my son's life, he brought much love and happiness to his family, friends, and colleagues."

George, who always had a commanding and controlled demeanor, broke out in tears as he added, "May his memory be alive in your thoughts, and may his thirst for life be a guide in your own lives. And may his profound love for his family carry them for the rest of their lives."

Lidia and her children once again started to sob, as the soothing sound of the choir voices merged with their cries. But to Lidia, having her parents and sister there was most comforting.

Later that afternoon all of Edward's family and friends attended a luncheon at the Stanfords' home. After the meal, Doña Delia, who had a special bond with her son-in-law, played a musical tribute on the piano to him that included one of his treasured compositions, Nocturne op. 9 no. 2 by Frédéric Chopin.

The Merino and Solberg families stayed with Lidia and her children through the end of the year. Yet to them and everyone else, Edward's passing had been an immense loss, and his absence was deeply felt. That holiday season, the Stanford residence was devoid of all the usual Christmas celebrations. However, on the twenty-fifth of December when her family sat down for dinner, Lidia summoned her inner strength, and reminded everyone that while one precious life had been lost, a new one would be born in a little over a month.

Early on January 28, 1927, at ten minutes before six in the morning, Alejandra was taken to Eitel Hospital after she woke up with labor pains. Once they arrived at the medical facility, the doctor determined it would take many hours before she gave birth, for her water had not yet broken. She was placed in a double room with another woman who had given birth to a boy at dawn. The woman lay asleep next to her infant son. Alejandra tried to be as quiet as possible while her husband left to speak to the physician. As she lay there silently, the newborn baby woke up and moaned softly. His mother, who must have been in a deep sleep and exhausted, did not wake up. The infant continued to whimper, and no one arrived to help. She carefully got up from the bed and approached the baby, who was in a bassinet. Gently, she touched him on his forehead until he stopped crying. He wrapped his little hand around her index finger, when his mother woke up.

"How long has he been awake?" the woman asked.

"Oh, maybe ten minutes or so," Alejandra replied.

"Looks like you're ready to pop," the friendly lady said as she drank a glass of water. "Is he or she your first?" she asked.

"My second."

The lady was about to pick up her baby, but then asked, "Would you like to hold him?"

"Yes, I would. He's adorable with those blue eyes and that little nose," Alejandra said, as she carefully picked up the tiny baby wrapped in swaddling clothes. "What's his name?" she asked.

"William George," the woman said. "My first-born."

Alejandra remained quiet as she softly caressed him on his cheek. Unknown to her, by coincidence, this little baby she was holding in her arms would someday follow in the footsteps of her own grandfather as head of Peavey Company, and be known for his great compassion and generosity.

"And what is your name?" Alejandra asked the cheerful woman.

"Florence Stocks."

"Lovely to meet you both."

"And your names?" Florence asked.

"Alejandra Morrison. If we have a boy his name will be Richard Edward, and if we have a girl her name will be Delia Rose." Alejandra then very gently kissed the baby on his head and gave him to his mother.

"Thank you. You'll see in no time we shall have two babies side by side, sharing the same birthday," Florence said as she started to feed her hungry son.

After a difficult birth, and at 11:20 p.m., the Morrisons' first son was born. When Alejandra woke up the next day, her room was filled with flowers, and her newborn was next to her sound asleep. Richard, who was sitting on a wing chair looking at her, said, "I thought you would never wake up."

"Well, it seems he likes to delay his entrances like his father, and left me drained," she said, smiling. At that moment, all her family came into the room and congratulated the happy couple. Later, she introduced them to Florence and her son William.

For the remainder of the week, the two mothers talked about their lives and their hopes, as if they were old friends. When they said goodbye to each other, Alejandra wondered if she would ever see this lovely, lighthearted, and wise woman again, hoping she would. Florence was just the kind of person you wanted to be with, and her great sense of humor was contagious.

"Until we meet again," Florence said, with a big smile, as she, her son and husband left the hospital room.

The Morrisons came home with their newborn. After an informal gathering, Lidia, who was still in profound mourning, announced she would be going to Mexico with her parents in three weeks, and planned to stay there until fall.

In late February, with a saddened heart, Alejandra saw her mother, brother, and grandparents leave, as they departed for Mexico very early in the morning. Her eyes filled with tears, as she felt as if suddenly two of her anchors were gone; but now her own family was her base. She stared through the window until she lost sight of Lidia's vehicle in the distance. There was a formidable silence, almost unbearable, she thought. With Richard and the two children still sleeping, she went to the drawing room and closed the double doors.

She sat in front of the piano, and realized she had not played music for over four weeks. She reminisced about all the times her father had walked into the room to listen to her. She felt as though his spirit was still there, lingering like an echo in the distance. She could see his image in her mind, as real as if he was sitting on the gold velveteen divan, reading the most recent news on technological advances but listening to her at the same time. He never tired of her constant practice, as his library was next to the drawing room. Sometimes he would just pass by to pay her a compliment and say, "Ale, that sounds beautiful, don't stop, play it again for me . . . "

Her father's words of love, encouragement, and wisdom rang in her mind like a sweet melody murmuring continuously during a sacred procession. The death of her father and the birth of her son happening within a span of two months brought the duality of life into focus.

Alejandra was reminded of a melody she had started many years before, in fact, while she and her parents visited la Sagrada Familia church in Barcelona. She had never been able to finish it then, but that morning, guided by her father's love and the miracle of her newborn's life, she was able to complete the composition. As she had done many times before, note by note, phrase by phrase, she composed "God Lives."

Then she took a pencil, and wrote lyrics for the song:

God of souls, sublime, light guides since before times,
Feathers waiting to fall,
And in our lifetime, souls live as flesh and blood,
It is amazing God lives in every soul . . .

A very distant scream from her newborn brought Alejandra back from the deep trance-like state she was in while composing. She went upstairs to attend to her son. Once in the bedroom, she picked him up from the wicker bassinet. Richard Edward's face was the spitting image of his father, but his eyes where those of his grandfather Edward, she thought, observing every inch of her baby boy as she breast fed him.

She thought about her father's optimism and philosophy—that life should be without limits, where everything was possible and every achievement attainable. But even at the young age of twenty-five years, Alejandra had learned, perhaps the hard way, that this was not always the case. There were always sudden personal, national, even catastrophic events that disrupted the harmony of existence. But to her father, what was most important was to maintain a thirst for life, and to go forward no matter what obstacles crossed one's path. This was perhaps the greatest lesson she had learned from him, and one she hoped to impart on her own children. Twenty minutes later, she placed her sleeping son on her bed, and then lay down next to him and fell asleep. A short while later, she felt her husband's warm body beside her, when he put his arms around her and the baby and whispered, "I love you."

With spring in the air, Richard came home with the mail in his hand. After going through it, he noticed the monthly bulletin from the museum. He opened it, and was quite taken aback by its front cover. He searched for his wife in the house, but through the dining room window, he noticed she was planting flowers in the garden. He went outside to join her.

"Ale, Ale, I think you might want to go to the museum this month."

"I know it's been a little while since we've been there, but why that smile?" she asked.

"It's an exhibition your father would have loved."

Alejandra, quite puzzled, put the flowers aside, and wiping her hands on her apron, took the bulletin from Richard's hand. It was as though her father was greeting her from his grave. The cover read, "Exhibition of Architectural Etchings." She sat on a wrought-iron bench nearby and read the bulletin's contents. The exhibition included dozens and dozens of architectural etchings by Charles Meryon and David Cameron.

"Oh, gracious, I'd love to go, but first we have to finish planting these flowers; this is what my father did every year at this time," she said as she started to cry softly. "Oh! Richard, I miss him so deeply."

"Yes, we all do," he said as he knelt beside her, pulled up his sleeves, and helped her finish planting a bed of hearty perennial plants.

The Morrisons visited the Minneapolis Institute of Arts the next day. The etchings by Charles Meryon were from buildings all over the world. Meryon had once said, "Buildings have souls," and Alejandra realized in those three words that her father felt the same way, and that was the reason he loved architecture. Her favorite drawings were those of the Pont Neuf (New Bridge) and a view of Notre Dame in Paris. She recalled her visit to Paris after she had graduated from high school. As her father had once pointed out, great works of art were sold for little money by artists, and Charles Meryon's sketch of Notre Dame was sold for just a few francs—but after his death, the sketch sold for thousands. When they finished walking through the gallery, Alejandra thanked Richard for bringing her there.

"I wouldn't miss it," he said.

"It's most gratifying to see you've acquired a taste for art," she said jokingly.

"How could I not?" he replied with a smile.

Several weeks later, on May 21, 1927, she was about to take her two children for a walk around Lake of the Isles and was waiting for her husband to return from visiting his mother. Milly helped her bring out two strollers, and as they both stepped out onto the sidewalk Richard came home. He greeted his wife and children, and turned to the nanny.

"Thank you, Milly, I'll take it from here," he said as he pushed one of the strollers forward. Together, the family of four started their walk.

"Do you know we'll be able to fly soon?" he said. Alejandra looked perplexed, and for a moment said nothing, but then remarked, "Fly?"

"Another Minnesotan has made news," he said.

"What news?" she asked.

"Charles Lindbergh just landed in Paris, completing the first solo flight across the Atlantic," Richard said with excitement.

Once again, she immediately thought of her father, and how he had always told her that a day would come when people could fly. It seemed such a foreign concept, she thought.

"If my father was only here to witness it," she said somberly.

Richard attempted to brighten up the conversation and said, "Next time we travel abroad, instead of taking an ocean liner, we'll take an airplane," he said spiritedly.

"That would be marvelous, but for today, let's take our walk around the lake," she replied as she pulled the knitted afghan up to her son's neck in the stroller.

TRACK NINE

32 Magical Night

Richard was awakened abruptly by the sound of a thunderstorm a little before six in the morning. It was the day of his graduation from medical school. He reached out to his wife, but she wasn't there. Concerned, he quickly got out of bed, put on his plaid woolen robe, and walked toward the window, noticing the overcast sky. After he went to the washroom, he went into his children's room, to see they were still sleeping. He covered his daughter with the colorful quilt, which had fallen on the floor. He walked down the steps and went to the kitchen, but his wife wasn't there, either. He then heard a door closing and met her in the hall.

"What are you doing up so early?" he asked her.

"Good morning, Doctor," she said as soon as she saw him.

"Not yet," he said.

"I couldn't sleep with the storm. I sure hope it's going to clear up for the ceremony," she said. "There's coffee out on the porch. Let me bring you the newspaper."

Richard went outside to the covered porch and poured himself a cup of the hot beverage as he waited for his wife to return. He thought about how to tell her the secret he'd been keeping since they were married. Soon she would know the truth about his frequent absences on the weekends, particularly in the last year. Just then she came back with their baby son in her arms.

"Rich, darling, your daddy is going to become a doctor today," she said as she placed her son on his father's lap. "I'll return in a moment," she said once again.

Richard stayed with his son, holding his tiny hand and lovingly caressing his hairless head. He noticed that the rain had subsided and the sun was breaking through the clouds.

Moments later she came back with a package. "Congratulations," she said, and took the baby from him.

Richard smiled at her and slowly opened the medium-size package. "A stethoscope, thank you, darling," he said.

"It's the first of its kind with a combination bell and diaphragm chest piece," she said.

"Yes, it's been a big deal among the medical students," he said.

"Now you can check our lungs and blood pressure," she said in a humorous tone. "But not my heartbeat."

"Why not?" he asked.

"You don't need an aid for that," she replied as her son began to get fussy, and she left once again to feed him.

Richard stayed there thinking about what she said, and he wondered if she knew he had been lying to her. He decided to not reveal his secret just yet, and instead went upstairs to shower and get dressed.

Later in the morning he went downstairs to eat breakfast. She seemed a little anxious. "Scrambled eggs, ok?" she asked as she placed the food platters on the dining room table. He served himself a plate of fresh fruit and drank a small glass of orange juice.

"Yes," he replied.

"How do you feel?" she asked.

"Glad to be done," he said. "But, you know that during residency I'll be gone more than usual, sometimes overnight."

"Yes, I'm not looking forward to it," she said. "With two children, I'll keep busy. Besides, it's only temporary."

"Well, I need to leave soon to pick up mother," he said.

While she seemed a little distant, he fixed his tie before he left the dining room.

"Are you all right?" he asked before leaving.

"Oh, yes, I want everything to be perfect for your graduation dinner tonight," she said.

Wearing the latest flapper fashion, a chiffon mint-colored dress and fancy hat, she stepped into their automobile, greeted Vivian Morrison, and then looked at her husband, who seemed a bit serious compared to his usual bold and confident self. Perhaps he is nervous, but he is not the type to ever feel that way, she thought. When they arrived at the landscaped grounds outside the medical school building on Sixth Street and Ninth Avenue in Minneapolis, they were met by George Stanford, Steven, and his wife Olga.

"Thank you all for coming," Richard said as he greeted each one of them. Even Olga had seemed to have softened her attitude towards him. "Steven wouldn't have missed it for the world," she said.

"Shall we? The event is about to start," Richard said.

Once everyone had entered the hall and taken their seats, the dean of the school, Dr. Elias Potter, stepped on the podium and began by congratulating the class of 1927. He had been influential in developing a medical school, which ranked as one of the finest in the country. The school's diverse program consisted of several departments, including histology, embryology, gross anatomy, neurology, physiology, surgery, and at least a dozen more areas of medicine. In his commencement speech, Dr. Potter recognized one of the founding fathers of the school.

"Medical education in Minnesota today represents the realization, at least in part, of the dream of a small group of medical pioneers of the Northwest. The leader of this group was Dr. Perry H. Millard. We should dedicate ourselves to the furtherance of the high ideals that we hold for medicine and medical education."

When it was time for Richard to step up to the stage to receive his diploma, Alejandra couldn't help but notice how handsome her husband was. Not only did the striped suit made him look distinguished, the confidence with which he carried himself was most appealing. She thought about how he said he would have to stay some nights in the hospital, and didn't like it one bit. Fortunately, she wasn't the jealous type and trusted him completely, although she did feel a little disconcerted when he told her about his new schedule.

After the ceremony, the school organized a casual reception in the lobby. Mrs. Morrison hugged her son. "Congratulations, I'm very proud of you. And if your father were here, he would revel in your accomplishments," she said.

"Thank you, mother," Richard replied as the rest of his friends also congratulated him.

"So what's next?" Steven asked him.

"Residency."

"In what," George asked.

"Surgery," he replied. "But tomorrow, Ale, I, and the kids are taking some needed time off."

"Where to?" Steven asked.

"We're finally going back to the Lake Minnetonka district," he said as he held his wife's hand.

"Can you believe it!" she said.

Richard was not one to delve into sentimentality, but that day it was clear he was a very happy man. He openly expressed his affection as he thanked each of his friends and family for attending his graduation ceremony.

The next day, the Morrison family left for a holiday trip west of the Twin Cities. They had not returned to Lake Minnetonka since the summer of 1919 and it seemed a world away, Alejandra thought as they drove for over an hour on the winding road around the vast lake.

The road to Wayzata and then on to the township of Orono was very different, much more populated, but it was still as beautiful as she remembered it, with its wetlands, forests, and quaint lakeshores. When they reached a road entrance with two-hundred-year-old oak and maple trees, Richard turned the car onto an unpaved narrow road, which they followed for about a quarter of a mile. When the car came to a complete stop, she placed her two hands together and stared in complete admiration. She immediately recognized the façade of the structure; it was the exterior elevation she had seen sketched on her father's architect's table last November. The small, Mediterranean-style villa, with dozens of apple and crab trees surrounding it, was gorgeous. She remained in the car, speechless and filled with emotion.

"This is our home! Your father designed it and bought the land for us many years ago, and I've been saving money for its construction until I could afford it. Last year he started building it and our plan was to bring you here in the spring, once the baby was born," he said.

She envisioned the trees in full bloom with their tiny purply flowers in spring.

"This is the secret I've been keeping from you," Richard said with a knot in his throat.

She burst into tears and embraced him, as she felt extremely happy and also felt much gratitude toward her father.

"It's unbelievable," she said. "Beyond anything I could have imagined."

"You're not mad at me for not telling you all these years?" he said.

"Well, no, if this is how my father wanted it, how can I be angry?"

"Come, you'll like the interior even better," he said enthusiastically, now that he could finally enjoy their new house with her.

"One question—is this where you have been coming on the weekends?" she asked.

"Yes," he said.

"I was starting to get a little suspicious about your weekly departures. But next time, for sure no more secrets," she added, most relieved.

The white stucco house displayed two twelve-foot columns at the entrance, with a mahogany eight-panel door. As they entered their new home, she noticed the high ceilings and wood floors. However, the most scenic part of the property was located directly across from the entrance—a pair of glass doors with a magnificent view of Crystal Bay. Inside the house there was a dining room on one side, and on the other a seating room with a large stone fireplace. She walked through the hall carrying her son toward the French doors. She opened them, stepped onto the rectangular screened porch, and sat on one of two amber-toned wicker rocking chairs.

"Look at the lake," she said to her son as she held him up on his legs facing the view. "Your grandpa built this house."

Richard followed his wife as he held Liddy, and they sat on the other chair.

"You're everything, and so much more to me, and this house, on this land, will always be my favorite place," she said as she held out her left hand to his right hand.

"I thought Venice was," he said.

"Not anymore," she replied.

They both sat silently for a few more minutes, admiring the spectacular landscape until the newborn boy began to cry.

"You best show me where the bedrooms are," she said as she stood up from the chair. On her way inside, she had noticed the house was sparsely furnished, but a piano was not missing. Placed in front of a large window in an alcove by the seating area, she recognized the piano from her grandparents' home.

"Your grandfather insisted on giving it to us," Richard said. As she approached the steps, Alejandra saw one more piece of furniture close to the fireplace that brought up a stream of memories, as she remembered her father playing chess every Sunday with her when she was a young girl. With the baby, who had stopped crying, in her arms, she went to the small chess table, picked up the knight piece, and remembered her father saying, "Ale, if you can ride through life as good as you move your knights on the board, you'll be just fine." She smiled.

"I still can't believe how you all kept this secret for so long."

"It was how your father carefully planned it," he said as they proceeded to the steps and ascended them. Moments later, they entered the almost-empty master bedroom, with only a bed, a dresser, and two nightstands. With its French doors leading onto a balcony, as far as she was concerned, it was all she needed. She placed the baby on the bed to change his diapers.

"You'll need to do your own decorating, and together we can select the rest of the furniture, except in the dining room," he said with a curious smile.

"The dining room?"

"Your aunt Carolina and Anthony will send us a dining table in their next shipment," he said.

"Made by Anthony?" she asked.

"Apparently," he said.

"So for now, there is a small table in the kitchen," he said.

The next morning, while, Richard was cleaning his twenty-six-foot Dart-Crusader boat, she sat on the sandy beach with the children. She recalled the afternoon on the lake years ago at Hotel Otero, when she told her father she wanted to return to this lake every summer. Now thanks to him, her children would grow up in this splendid family retreat.

For the next two weeks, she felt as if she was on her honeymoon again, except with two children that left her and her husband utterly exhausted. Fortunately, once the children fell asleep, nothing could wake them up. Toward the end of the weekend, she was a little tired, but not tired enough to go to sleep right away. Instead she went downstairs to join her husband, who was reading one of his medical books on the porch. She sat beside him and contemplated the velvety sky with its stars and the moon as it softly illuminated the calm waters of the lake. She wished she could stay in that magical place with her husband and family. Yet, her feelings were a mixture of happy and sad.

With a strong impulse to play her musical instrument, she went insidc thc housc but left the French doors open. She sat on the bench, and then pressed the pedal that mutes the sound and played a few notes as a warm breeze swept through the room. Inspired by the warm evening, the subtle wind, and the lake, she composed "Magical Night." Then she took her pencil and began to write words:

> Look around, it's a magical night, luring you to unknown places you've never seen.
> Feel the air, it's contagiously light, lifting you until dawn, letting your passions free.
> And see the sparkles again and hear the flute of the wind, it's a magical night . . .

TRACK TEN

Remembrance

It had been almost nine months since Lidia's husband had passed away. She'd been in Cuernavaca, Mexico, since February. When she returned to Minneapolis and opened the door to her house in mid August 1927, she felt a certain comfort in her home's familiar walls, but everything was embedded with Edward's memory. She placed her luggage in the parlor, as her son Eddy, now 10 years old, ran up to his bedroom. The house was quiet, for her daughter and her family were away at their lake home.

She walked across the hall and into Edward's library. She sat at his desk and pictured him standing in front of his drawing table. Everything was exactly as he had left it; even a pen laying across a letter he'd started, addressed to his sister Margaret. The date on the letter was November 27, 1926, the day before he suffered the fatal heart attack. While the library was visually the same, it lacked his smell, it lacked the sounds of his steps, and it lacked his presence.

The empty feeling brought on by his absence made Lidia begin to cry once more; it felt as if she was suffocating. She had dreaded this moment—facing herself alone in the house without Edward. She got up and opened all the windows, and let the air flow through the room. She saw her daughter's house sketched on the architect's table, and then touched it with her fingers—his fingerprints must be on it, she thought. Then she lovingly caressed his chair and his framed photographs.

She had been in mourning for almost a year, and as she looked around the room, she pondered whether she should leave it intact. She asked herself, what would Edward want her to do? And the answer was right there in front of her as she looked at the portrait she had painted of him, hanging above his desk as though he was speaking to her from that unknown place called death. In Mexico, that word was not feared; it was celebrated in a mystical sense. After a person's passing, his or her life was honored on the Day of the Dead. Lidia thought of the murals of Diego Rivera she had recently seen in the universities and governmental buildings in Cuernavaca and Mexico City, depicting Mexican history. Among the murals she saw while in Mexico were those titled *Day of the Dead, The Distribution of Lands, The Creation*, and many more.

Diego Rivera had returned to Mexico in the early 1920s during the Mexican Renaissance, after studying in Italy and living in Europe for many years. Along with Jose Clemente Orozco and David Alfaro Siqueiros, he had started a mural movement that would spread across Mexico and the United States like wild fire. Orozco painted destruction as rebirth, and Rivera painted reality with a sense of compassion.

Rivera's massive frescoes inspired Lidia so tremendously that she too resolved to create her own reality and an *ofrenda* (offering) for her husband, perhaps for the day of the dead on the second of November. Upon further consideration, however, she decided to present her ofrenda on the anniversary of Edward's death. And in a strange way, the tribute to her husband she had suddenly conceived gave new life and purpose to her saddened spirit, and to her husband's memory.

In the past, she had painted small murals directly onto the wall surface. Now, she would attempt to paint a fresco using the centuries-old technique of applying painting in pigment mixed with water and egg yolk to fresh plaster spread over the wall. It would be an enormous task, but it was what she required to deal with her abysmal heartbreak.

For the next four months, she worked from dawn until dusk, with the help of her son and daughter who also created their own ofrendas to their father. On the day of the dead, November 2, the invitations were sent out to family and close friends, written in Eddy's shapely handwriting:

You are cordially invited to a celebration to commemorate the
life of Edward G. Stanford on the first anniversary of his death.
November 28, 1927, 7:00 p.m.
Stanford Residence-Minneapolis, Minnesota.

The morning of the twenty-eighth began quite hectically, with Lidia making the final preparations to honor her husband's memory. As Milly served breakfast before eight in the morning, Eddy came down for the morning meal and sat in the dining room. Lidia poured a cup of milk for her son as Milly brought in a platter of poached eggs, ham, and fresh fruits. The young boy filled his plate with an assortment of sliced apples, bananas, and plums while Lidia took a piece of warm bread, spread butter and raspberry jam on it, and placed it on his plate. He turned to his mother, saying, "Mommy, can I bring my friend Stewart tonight?"

"Of course, anyone you like," she said.

"I want him to see my father's portrait," he said in a quiet voice. "So he'll know what he looked like."

"Oh, Eddy, all he has to do is look at your handsome face; you look exactly the way your father did when he was your age," Lidia said with a smile as Richard came into the room.

"Mrs. Stanford, I'll try to get out of work early tonight. Is there anything you'd like me to bring or do?" he asked.

"Oh yes, can you please pick up Grandpa George? He was a bit under the weather yesterday," Lidia replied.

"Yes, I can do it at the same time I get my mother," he said. "By the way, the room looks outstanding!"

"Yes, I'm very pleased," she said.

"I can drop Eddy off at school on my way to work, if you'd like," Richard said.

"Thank you, Richard!" Lidia said.

Eddy kissed his mother, and left with Richard. Moments later, Alejandra came down for breakfast.

"I have maybe a few minutes before the children wake up," she said. "How do you feel, mother?"

"Tired, but looking forward to this evening," she said. "And delighted that the Mendes family will be here."

"Yes, especially since they couldn't come to Father's funeral. You know, Father would love what you are doing."

Lidia looked out the window and said, "I wish I'd done it before when he was alive."

"Mother, remember today is a celebration of his life," Alejandra told her.

"Yes, every day I'm reminded of his absence and the wonderful things he did in his life. Yet, somehow all this work has been beneficial to my state of mind, and now, I feel a sense of acceptance and peace."

Alejandra stared at her mother's beautiful face, filled with love and serenity.

"Mother, there is a place I'd like us to visit with the Mendes family while they are here," she said.

"And where would that be?" Lidia asked, surprised by the seriousness in her daughter's voice.

"Last May twenty-first when you were in Mexico, a new museum opened, the Walker Art Gallery. I've been waiting to go there, but did not want to go without you. I still remember when you and Father took me to Mr. Walker's art galleries as a child," she said with melancholy.

"Oh, Ale, what wonderful news. I shall love to go there!" Lidia said when her granddaughter came into the room and sat on her mother's lap.

"Good morning, Liddy, are you hungry?" her mother asked her.

The little girl nodded yes, and Alejandra gave her a small plate filled with fruit.

Loud screams were heard from the upstairs bedroom.

"You go on, I'll stay with Liddy," Lidia said to her daughter.

Sometime shortly after half past six in the evening, guests began to arrive at the Stanford residence. Milly passed around a tray of beverages, as Lidia and Alejandra greeted all their friends and family as they came into the room. When David, Amelia, Hannah, and Benjamin arrived, it was almost surreal, thought Alejandra as they affectionately hugged and kissed each other. After all these years, the Mendes and Adelman families were finally in Minneapolis.

At 7:15 p.m., when approximately eighty people had arrived for the occasion, Lidia announced, "Thank you all for coming here today to commemorate the life of Edward Stanford. Please join me in my husband's former library room, now officially christened as the Stanford-Merino Art Gallery, in his memory. My husband Edward had always wanted me to show my portraitures publicly, and today I show them to you, along with his own architectural sketches. And as of this date, we begin a yearly tradition of an art exhibition for those we wish to honor," she said as she proceeded to the new gallery. She opened the door, and the guests walked in behind her in complete reverence. They stood in the large room, astounded by the display of exquisite artwork and the room's decor.

The former library had been completely renovated. With a room eighteen by twenty feet in diameter and a ceiling fourteen feet high, the library was spacious and gorgeously decorated. The walls were painted in a lustrous pearled wash almost like plaster, and the wood floors had been resurfaced in a darker stain. A large wrought-iron chandelier hung from the middle of the ceiling, and the room was heavily lit with sconces and candles that brightly illuminated the art gallery.

The windows had been changed to French doors with direct access to the backyard, and a path led to Edward's English garden and then to the street. The glass doors' draperies were made of a gold satin fabric, and two tall bookcases stood at each corner of the wall, filled with architectural, art, music, and literature books. On one wall hung all of Lidia's portraiture paintings. At the center of the wall was Edward's portrait, surrounded by all the historical figures Lidia had painted since she was fourteen years old.

Beside Edward's portrait were the portraits of Benito Juárez, Juventino Rosas, Amadeus Mozart, Ludwig Van Beethoven, Francisco Goya, Diego Rivera, El Greco, Sor Juana Inéz de la Cruz, and also the familial faces of Clara, Anne, and Sol. On the other side of the room were Edward's framed architectural drawings, and at the center of that wall were the elevation drawings of dozens of houses Edward had built over the years.

On the fourth wall, opposite the French doors, there was a fresco. The mural covered the upper two thirds of the wall. At the center of the composition was a familial portrait of Edward, Lidia, Alejandra, and Eddy sitting together on a wooden park bench. Behind them were several trees, with their branches and leaves drooping over the family as if they were under a natural umbrella.

Above the horizon line, there was an expansive blue sky, with the sun on one side, and moon on the other. On Lidia's side, she had painted images of Mexican workers farming and harvesting the land; on Edward's side, there were images of American workers building at a construction site. Edward was holding a metal cross, while Lidia was holding a painter's brush. Alejandra was holding sheet music and young Edward was holding a book. On the corner of that wall, Eddy placed his ofrenda to his father, a potted deep purple flowering plant. Below the mural, there was a carved wooden settee, an antique nineteenth-century American sofa with horsehair upholstery designed in Grecian style with moldings, scrolls, and lion paws. This was Edward's favorite piece of furniture, and had been in his family for nearly fifty years.

It was eerie, but extraordinary, thought George Stanford, as did the rest of the viewing public, who enthusiastically congratulated Lidia for her astonishing work. George hugged Lidia in a rare display of public emotion and affection.

"This mural, this gallery is absolutely stunning," Mrs. Morrison added. "I've never seen anything like it."

"He would be so proud of you," George remarked.

Mrs. Morrison, who always had fundraising in mind, added, "Lidia, do you plan on selling any of your work? You must, my dear!"

"I'm not sure," she replied.

David, who for years had a profound interest in seeing Lidia's portraits, seemed to be the most enthusiastic about her work, and was extremely impressed.

"Yes, I wish she would. These paintings would sell like hotcakes in New York," he added.

"Lidia, you must tell me how you came to do these paintings, particularly those of Mozart and Beethoven." David asked.

"Well, when I was on the grand tour, I went to several museums in Europe and saw paintings of composers and painters, and I sketched the images, to be transferred later to a canvas. The first one, while it is not a copy, resembles a posthumous oil painting of Mozart by Barbara Kraft. Beethoven's images come from two paintings, one by W.J. Mahler, and the other by J. Stieler," she said.

"What I love about your work is your own unique style, a blend of baroque and Renaissance," David said.

"Thank you, and there is a third painting of Beethoven," Lidia said, as David and the others looked around the room, but didn't see an image of him. She walked to the right side of the wall, and showed them a painting of Beethoven's hands, saying it was based on a sketch by J. Danhauser.

"Why had you never mentioned it?" Alejandra asked her mother.

"It was my own little secret," Lidia said, smiling.

"Lidia, you must sell them," David said.

"Perhaps someday," she said. "Although I could never part with some of these paintings. They have too much sentimental value."

"You could sell and donate the proceeds to worthy causes of your own choice," Mrs. Morrison insisted.

She paused, but then replied, "Well, I shall give it some thought. But first, please enjoy the exhibition. There are refreshments and hors d'oeuvres in the dining room," she said as she invited the guests to join her at their leisure.

Later that evening, when the clock chimed nine, Lidia invited the guests to return to the drawing room for a short recital in memory of Edward. Lidia thanked everyone once more for attending the event. She then presented Alejandra, Hannah, and Benjamin before they performed Serenade for Piano and String Quartet op. 3, no. 5 by Joseph Haydn, followed by "Intermezzo" by Manuel Ponce. The last piece that was performed was her daughter's musical ofrenda to honor her father, titled "Remembrance."

TRACK ELEVEN

Carnival of Life

It was the evening of Tuesday, October 29, 1929, when Alejandra read to her children a fairy tale story called "Once on a Time" by A.A. Milne. The previous two years had been characterized by a happy home life, with the usual hastiness and commotion of a family. Richard had settled into his medical practice, and Alejandra concentrated on raising Liddy and Rich, while performing in various fundraisers around the city several times a year. But as she had often seen in her life, there were always turning points. This day was one of them, as her husband came home in a very agitated state to tell her his family had lost a large portion of their fortune in the collapse of the stock market. He handed over a newspaper with the headline "Wall Street Lays an Egg." As she read the unprecedented news in shock, she remained silent as Richard sank into the sofa, devastated. He leaned his head backward and closed his eyes. In all her life she had never seen him in such despair and hopelessness.

"Children, please go upstairs and put on your pajamas," she said.

"Oh! Mami," they replied.

"Now, please go on!"

Once they were alone, she turned to her husband. "I understand how you must feel. It's a terrible thing, but we are going to be all right," she said as she placed her hand on his.

"My mother's shares are worthless! One tiny sliver of hope is that her house is completely paid for. I'm very, very worried for her future," he said in anguish now, in a loud voice. Rarely did he raise his voice in anger. "And your mother, do you know much about her finances?" he asked.

"I don't know. She is fairly conservative in her expenditures, and her house is paid off, too. Perhaps, it has more of an effect on my grandfather," she replied.

"Let's hope that's the case for your mother," he said.

"For us, we don't have too much in our name, except for the lake house; and fortunately you have a good job at the hospital. We will manage," Alejandra added as she attempted to console him.

"There will be hard days ahead! We'll have to postpone buying a home here in Minneapolis. We're going to need to move back with my mother, so I can help her with the expenses. It's a very large house that requires a lot of maintenance. Prepare yourself for it," he said.

"We are like gypsies, from one place to another, but if that is what we need to do, we shall; for with our third child on the way, we must be hopeful," she added.

"Yes," he replied in a calmer tone of voice.

As the months went by, after the stock market crash and the subsequent Great Depression, the Morrison family experienced some economic hardship. They learned to live as frugally as possible. At one point, Richard considered selling his mother's mansion, but Vivian pleaded with him to keep it, even if it meant cutting other expenses such lavish dinners, trips, art collecting, and decorating. Many newspaper articles described the financial collapse as a result of wealth and excess of the 1920s.

To Alejandra, the crisis became real when she learned her own mother, who had been reluctant to sell her paintings, was now doing so at reduced prices to subsidize her income to support herself and her son. How ironic it seemed that Lidia was like many of the artists Alejandra had heard about, selling their work for little money just to keep afloat. She offered her mother Beethoven's signed manuscript, but Lidia, while incredibly grateful, declined the offer. She told her daughter that so long as the sale of her paintings was keeping her economically solvent, Alejandra should hold on to the manuscript, for it was worth more to her and the family than any money it could provide.

In mid April, Lidia hosted her spring art exhibition at the Stanford-Merino gallery. Alejandra and Richard attended, and as she looked at her mother's new collection of portraiture paintings, she noticed her style had changed, from baroque to mannerism. The faces and figures were elongated and the colors were brighter, but with uncanny detail. She wished she could buy them all, but Richard had told her she could only pick one piece per season. With much difficulty, she chose a portrait of a young girl dressed in rags holding a bouquet of orchids, which reminded her of the flower girl she saw in Mexico many years before, selling flowers in Alameda Park.

Many of the portraits had a common theme, a realism connected to the current times. With stories of increased crime in the cities, she was worried for her mother's safety with dozens of strangers coming in and out of the gallery. It was fortunate that at least the place had its own separate entrance to her mother's home. Sales were not particularly good. Many visitors came to look, only a few of the customers were buying paintings, as they were considered luxury goods. Lidia also began to paint custom portraits, something she had never done before, and she finally took Mr. Mendes' offer to sell and display her work at his shop. According to the latest accounts, she was selling more paintings in New York than in Minnesota.

After a long day at the gallery and toward evening, Alejandra, who had been helping her mother wrap the few sold paintings, sat down on the settee below the mural. Fatigued from standing up and in her ninth month of pregnancy, she knew she was due any moment, but wanted to help her mother. Lidia began to wrap several paintings to ship out to New York. Among those was Alejandra's favorite, the portrait of Sor Juana Inéz de la Cruz.

She never thought of herself as having great attachment to material things, yet she felt emotional at the thought of parting with the painting she had seen every day of her life as a child, as if the portrait was that of a family member. Curiously, she remembered when her father had asked if she wanted to be a nun like Sor Juana. She realized that at some unconscious level, she had tried to be like the nun, or at least the image she represented in the painting, perfectly poised, graceful, devoted, and educated. She knew not even a nun could have been perfect. She smiled, and feeling the child within her, was grateful and extremely happy she didn't become a nun.

"Oh, Mother, Sor Juana's painting? No, not that one. She was the imaginary sister I never had," she said, and though her tone was playful, she was quite serious. "I shall buy it from you!"

Lidia noticed her daughter's attachment to the painting.

"Ale, you don't need to buy it from me. I never knew how you felt about it. Please accept it as a gift for your newborn," Lidia said, as she looked at her daughter's big belly.

"Even if it's a boy, I'm not sure what Richard would say about it," Alejandra replied, now with laughter. As she struggled to get herself up, she suddenly felt a contraction.

"Wait here, I'll get Richard," Lidia said.

As she waited for her husband, Alejandra's labor pains subsided and she looked around the room, admiring her mother's work. Lidia was truly an exceptional artist, yet it had never been her ambition to be a professional painter. Now, by yet another turn of fate, she would probably become a very well-known portraiture painter in the years to come. Cheered by this notion, she greeted her husband as he came into the room, and together they left for the hospital.

After a rather speedy and almost painless delivery sometime during the night, she gave birth to their third child, whom she and her husband named Delia Rose Morrison. She was born on April 15, 1930.

In July, the family of five and Lena the housekeeper left for a month-long retreat to their lake home in Orono, as they had done every summer. Every weekend, Richard commuted between the two cities. Their house was modest in size and furnishings compared to their parents' homes, but it was their own, and Alejandra enjoyed the simplicity of life on the lake immensely. They appropriately christened their house *Casa Del Lago* (House on the Lake), although most visitors remarked it was more like a house of music, for she had decorated it with a musical theme.

Among the art objects were several of her mother's portraits, including one of Alejandra sitting by the piano, which she hung on the parlor wall above a carved wooden sofa table. The signed Beethoven and Rosas partitures, as well as other favorite musical scores, were framed and placed on the walls surrounding the piano. In fact, looking for old musical manuscripts had become a hobby for Alejandra, and she had recently acquired a letter from Frédéric Chopin where he talked about Pauline Garcia Viardot and her kindness for singing his mazurkas.

Above the fireplace there was a family portrait, and on the mantle she proudly displayed her tzedakah box and a collection of miniature musical instruments. The living room furniture, a large sofa and chairs upholstered in velvet burgundy reds and sage greens, surrounded a carved coffee table stacked with musical and medical books.

After the family had settled, they ate dinner at the wooden dining room table, handcrafted by Sol & Berg Fine Furniture. Afterward, the family gathered around the piano. Alejandra pulled out sheet music from her mother's old chest while Liddy took her violin out from its case. As they started to play music together, Rich, who was now five years old and who had acquired his mother's liking and talent for the piano, insisted on playing along. The impromptu concert became a playful intermezzo for the family. Richard, who sat on the sofa, looked on with amusement as his wife attempted to teach their son a few notes from the melody, while Liddy complained loudly that he was spoiling the concert.

"Liddy, someday it might be your brother who accompanies you, and not me," Alejandra said, as she let her son play the first notes of Mozart's Sonata for Piano and Violin in F Major.

As August approached, she found herself less and less willing to return to Minneapolis. She had found her lake home an idyllic place for her family, and an escape from the daily solemn news of the economic depression. And while she felt physically tired from the daily management of house matters and the care of the children, her spirits were high.

Then, late in the month, she suddenly fainted with no apparent reason. Richard abruptly cut the vacation short, and they returned to Minneapolis the next day. During the next five months, Alejandra began to feel melancholy. She attributed this to constant, harrowing images in the paper of long bread lines, homelessness, and tragic stories of suicide, which had become common in many cities, including Minneapolis. But in reality, she was also suffering from a yet unknown medical condition.

The situation worsened economically around her during the holidays. While many friends forgot their troubles temporarily through films like *The Blue Angel*, which were the newest forms of entertainment and all the rage, she could not. The economic downturn had affected some of her closest family members. To her dismay, some acquaintances became involved in unsavory businesses, and there were strong rumors that Steven had started a bootlegging operation originating in Canada and supplying liquor to the Minneapolis/St. Paul area.

Alejandra could not imagine that her dearest cousin, who once had been a choir boy with high morals, would now be involved in illegal affairs of such a dangerous nature; and this worried her terribly. For the moment, she did not want to know, and decided not to ask him if there was any truth to the rumors. At some point in the future, though, she resolved to find a way to talk to him, no matter how difficult it may be. However, it was no surprise when she and her husband received an invitation to one of Steven and Olga's lavish social gatherings to reign in the New Year. As she did not plan to attend, she put the invitation away and forgot about it.

Two days before the celebration, Richard suggested that they go to the party. While she was not much in the mood for a display of outrageous consumption, thinking instead about the poverty outside her walls, he insisted it would do her good to get out of the house, and she acquiesced to her husband.

AT THE RESIDENCE OF STEVEN AND OLGA JOHNSON

On December 30, while Olga made the last preparations for the pending New Year's ball, Steven came home late in the evening and found his wife already celebrating with a glass of scotch in her hand as she placed dozens of party favors on the dining room table.

"Olga, I have some terrible news to tell you," he said.

She was already a little drunk and replied, "You dooooo!"

"Come, let's sit for a moment in the parlor," Steven suggested as he held her arm and directed her to the green velvet sofa.

She plunged herself onto it, finished the contents of her glass, and turned to her husband.

"So, what's the bad news?"

"I just came from visiting Chase's family," he said.

Olga's attention became more focused. "And."

"First he was ruined financially, and yesterday he was taken into police custody after a woman claimed he had raped her," he added.

"How wonderful," Olga replied with a laugh, as she felt that justice had finally been served after all these years.

"Why in the world would you be so happy about the misfortune of Chase Sullivan, one of our oldest acquaintances?" he asked in confusion.

"Oops," she said. "Because that is what he is, a rapist."

"How do you know that?" he asked her. She closed her eyes and kept silent, but Steven continued to pressure her into answering him. Finally, she replied, "Because he raped me."

"Olga, you're drunk. How? When? It's crazy what you're saying."

"Yes, I may be drunk," she said as she burped, "but I know what I'm talking about. Do you remember the night we were at Philip's house after high school graduation, and I left with him that night? The bastard did that to me in the car," she said with a lot of anger, and poured herself another glass of scotch from the bottle that was lying on the table.

Steven could not believe the words coming out of his wife's mouth.

"How could you have kept this from me?" he said.

"If I'd told you, would you have married me?" she asked him.

He got up from the sofa, walked toward the liquor cabinet, and he too poured himself a glass of scotch. He drank it in one swift shot and then turned to her.

"Yes, I would have married you because I loved you then, and I love you now! And I would have confronted him, but now he got what was coming to him. Olga, you must know it wasn't your fault what he did to you!" Steven said in a firm and loving manner.

"I blamed myself, and I thought you would have blamed me," she said, starting to cry.

"No! It would have been wrong of me to blame you, for whatever your behavior, it didn't justify his horrendous assault," Steven said. "No woman should ever have to suffer such a violent act."

Olga continued to sob as she finally let all the emotions out that she'd been keeping inside. Steven embraced her with profound compassion, and then asked, "I want the truth, Olga. Our little Steven, am I his father?"

She looked down and then replied, "I don't know."

Steven thought about the child, and even with a doubt now cast on his paternity, he felt in his heart the boy was his son.

"It doesn't matter, for I love him just the same." he said.

"Then do you forgive me for not telling you?" Olga asked.

"Yes," he said in a resigned voice. "Let's never talk about this again, nor ever tell our son."

Olga, for the first time in years, felt great freedom and conciliation with herself and the world.

"I promise I'll make it up to you," she said.

"You already have with all the beautiful children we have," he said. "But please cut down on your drinking."

"I will!" she said.

On New Year's Eve day, dressed in current 1920s attire, the Morrisons drove to Steven and Olga's home to join their masquerade ball. The economic downturn seemed not to have affected them in the least, nor did it affect dozens of other people who arrived dressed in raccoon fur coats and expensive jewelry. If they were affected, they disguised it very well. As Richard and Alejandra entered her cousin's luxurious Tudor-style home, they found it was indeed a carnival of sorts, and perhaps more like an extravaganza, Richard commented.

With more than a hundred people attending the celebration, every conceivable costume was on display. It reminded Alejandra of a similar event back in Venice many years before, but in Venice it seemed a natural part of the place, the landscape, the history. In her cousin's home it was theatrical, if not farcical. Yet the energy and gaiety were contagious, if only temporary. As soon as Alejandra and her husband stepped into the drawing room, Steven, who was dressed as a gladiator, greeted them very affectionately.

"Ale, so good to see you. How are you feeling?" he asked her.

"Been better, thank you for asking. You look fabulous. Is Olga dressed as who I think she is?" Alejandra asked, smiling.

"Of course," he replied.

"Wow, the house looks amazing," Richard said.

"Olga decorated it. She's in the ballroom," Steven said as he patted Richard on his back. "Let me take your coats," Steven continued, as he handed the coats to one of his service staff. "Come, Ale, there are beverages in the next room."

Though there was loud laughter and drinking, the music was one of the night's saving graces, Alejandra thought when she entered the dance hall, richly decorated in gold and silver trimmings and dozens and dozens of balloons and serpentines draped over the banisters and hanging from the coffered ceiling. A live band played the music of Cole Porter and other jazz favorites, and even one of the performers was dressed as Louis Armstrong as he played "West End Blues" on trumpet. Olga, who was more flamboyant than usual and dressed as Cleopatra, was dancing and reveling in the moment. The band began to play a Charleston and she waved and yelled out, "Come, Ale, join me and my pals."

The dance floor became crowded, and the Morrisons danced with Olga, but after only one song, Alejandra left for the powder room.

"Steven, I'm worried about her," Richard said to his friend.

"Why?"

"I'm not sure, but she hasn't been herself lately."

"Maybe the times are taking a toll on her. You know she has certain sensitivities. She is concerned about her mother, too," Steven said.

"Perhaps it's only that," Richard replied as she returned.

"Ale, what can I get you?" Steven asked her.

"Water," she replied.

"Champagne for me," Richard said.

Moments later, Olga arrived on the scene and hugged her old friend. "Just like old times, ha!" she said as she grabbed another glass of champagne for herself and another for her friend.

"Here, drink with me," she said.

"I can't, I'm still nursing," Alejandra replied.

"A little won't hurt you. It didn't affect me one bit when I was nursing my fourth child," Olga said with a laugh.

"Richard doesn't think it's good for the baby," she said.

"Always so proper, aren't you," Olga said, laughing.

Alejandra wanted to respond, but was happy to see Olga merrier than she had been for years, so instead she complimented the lapiz lazuli necklace that her friend was wearing.

"I had Steven make me a replica of the one we saw at the museum," Olga said.

"That was a long time ago," Alejandra said.

"I told you then I wanted one. And how do you like my sphinx earrings?" Olga asked as she pulled her hair back.

"Olga, they're beautiful and suit your costume perfectly," Alejandra said as her husband took her by the hand.

"Come, darling, I want you to hear something you'll like."

There on the stage in the ballroom was a young female performer, perhaps in her late teens, singing in Spanish. Alejandra recognized the song titled "Imposible" by the famed Mexican composer Agustín Lara, known for his romantic lyrics and ballads.

"She has an exquisite voice," she remarked as she listened to the young woman and musicians.

Forty minutes later when the band finished playing the set, Richard invited the singer to join them for a drink. She was a brunette with shiny, long hair and big brown eyes. "Hi, my name is Marie Fuentes," she said.

"Lovely to meet you," Alejandra said. "I was listening to you sing, and your Spanish is perfect."

"Yes, my parents are Mexican," she replied. "We now live in West St. Paul."

"You must let us know where you are performing in town, so we may come to hear you sing," Alejandra said.

"I perform every Saturday at Manny's on Wabasha Avenue," Marie said.

"We'll be sure to visit," Richard replied as the young woman was called by one of the other musicians.

"Nice to meet you," she said.

"Yes, we'll see you soon," she replied.

Alejandra felt a yearning she could not explain. It had been years since the last time she talked openly about being a conductor, and while she had not given up deep in her heart, her aspirations had receded as she was content and happily married. She felt her dream slipping further and further from her grasp, although it would remain dormant and ready to awaken when the right time came along. Richard noticed her momentary quiet demeanor. "Ale, what's wrong?"

"Nothing, nothing, just daydreaming," she replied, smiling.

"About?"

"Orchestras, music, and the spark of life," she said now with laughter as the countdown for the New Year was yelled out by the noisy crowd, "Twenty, nineteen, eighteen . . . ten, nine, eight, seven . . . three, two . . ."

"Happy 1931, my sweet," Richard said. "May this be our best one yet."

"How can it get any better for us?" Alejandra said. "I love what we have, and I wouldn't change a thing."

It was one o'clock in the morning when they arrived home. In high spirits and inspired by the sights and sounds of the New Year's celebration, she went into the bedroom of her children, and saw they were sound asleep as she quietly and gently caressed each one of their cheeks. The littlest one was in the crib, and the other two children on twin beds. She went into her bedroom, took off her shoes and jewelry, and placed her necklace on top of the dresser, but kept her dress on while putting on her slippers, which were by the bed.

"Aren't you changing into something more comfortable?" her husband asked mischievously.

"Not yet, I promise I'll be back in less than ten minutes. There is something I need to write down before I forget," she said as she walked down the steps into the library and sat at her husband's desk. All the revelry of the night was still fresh in her mind, and she took the pencil and began to write a string of lyrics.

> There's a theater in the streets,
> Everyone is the cast, what role do you play?
> Some are leaders of the show, others follow just for show, and some have no choice.
> There's a theater in the streets,
> Everyone wears a mask, what mask do you wear . . . ?

Then she heard Richard open the door. His breath still smelled of liquor, but it was pleasant and sensual. He kissed her on her earlobe and caressed her bare arms, stroking them up and down seductively.

"Finish it later," he commanded, but sweetly. She looked into his imploring eyes, and knew she could not resist.

On New Year's Day in the afternoon, as the children played with Lena in the nursery and Richard was in his study, she went to her piano and composed the music for "Carnival of Life."

TRACK TWELVE

A Song In My Heart

By the summer of 1931, Richard became alarmed when his wife was not only often fatigued, but had lost considerable weight. Even more concerning was her difficulty breathing. He insisted that it was no longer pure exhaustion from caring for the children, and that something was wrong. He took Alejandra to see the family physician, who couldn't find any reason for her symptoms. They went to get a second opinion, and the doctor could not diagnose the illness, although he suspected something of a serious nature, and ordered a variety of laboratory tests.

All the while Richard assured her there was nothing to worry about, though he thought it could be anemia or even the much-dreaded illness of the time, tuberculosis. In September all the results were in, and it was clear it was neither. Furthermore, with no available brain scans or other helpful markers at the time, the only form of accurate diagnosis was through exploratory surgery; and in some cases, the prognosis was fatal.

After discussing it further with his colleagues who suspected probable malignancy of some type, Richard informed his wife of their discussions with profound heartbreak. He himself couldn't believe that a malignant cancer could be the case. He could only hope for the best, but he wasn't optimistic. Alejandra felt profound grief and impotency as he spoke. She was only 28 years old, too young for such a possible medical condition.

For two days, she withdrew to her bedroom. In her moments of solitude, she went from denial to pure terror as she cried in despair and powerlessness over the outcome. Even worse was the realization that she may not survive to see her children's next birthday. Yet in the midst of sorrow and much doubt, she consoled herself in her family and her faith.

On September 19, she emerged with such serenity that Richard couldn't comprehend what had caused the change. Yet he was familiar with her nature, knowing that in the most difficult times in her life she seemed to summon her stalwartness, and he admired that trait in her the most. When she came down for breakfast and joined him, she said with a subtle smile, "Good morning."

"Ale, good morning," he said as he pulled out the chair for her.

"How do you feel?"

"The same physically, but better here," she said with humor as she pointed to her heart.

He poured her a cup of hot chocolate.

"Ale, everything will be all right, you'll see," he said with a hopeful expression on his face. "But we must talk about the surgery."

"Later, please, later, I want to spend time with the children this morning. I only came to see you for a moment," she said, running her fingers through his hair as she often did. She then excused herself and walked upstairs into the children's bedroom. Two-year-old Delia Rose was playing in her crib, and Alejandra picked her up and kissed her tenderly on both cheeks.

"Mommy crying," the little girl said.

"Dely, I love you. You're going to grow up into a very lovely girl," she said tearfully as her daughter touched her tears with her tiny fingers. "Let's go find your brother and sister," Alejandra said as she picked up her daughter and walked down the steps.

Rich and Liddy were outside in the garden, playing ball with Lena.

"Mommy, Mommy," Rich said as he ran to hug his mother around her legs.

She sat down on the grassy ground, placed Delia Rose on her lap, and then hugged the boy as her other daughter sat beside her.

"Oh, I love you with all my heart," she said as Richard came outside to speak to them.

"How would you all like to go to the lake house tomorrow?"

"And your work?" she asked.

"I took a few days off. It will be good for us to go, would you like to?"

"Yes, yes, I'd love to," she said as the two older children jumped up and down and yelled out "Yeah, yeah."

The next day, it was late in the morning when she sat at her writing desk in the bedroom and wrote a letter to her grandparents in Mexico. But before she could finish it, her oldest daughter Liddy came into the room.

"We're ready to go, Mommy," she said as she quietly stood by her mother, as if she could understand what was happening.

"Oh, Liddy, so mature for your age," Alejandra told her.

She left with her daughter to go to the children's bedroom and pack a few more of their things. After a hearty breakfast, the Morrison family left for their lake home late in the morning.

As Richard drove their large six-passenger vehicle, his wife remained mostly silent, while the children caused a small commotion in the back seat as Lena refereed between the two oldest. Alejandra seemed absent from the present moment, and stared through the window, momentarily tuning out as she imagined her children's life without her. Perhaps she should write them letters and tell them as much as she could, but the thought of that caused her great pain, and she quickly scrapped the idea.

"Are you all right?" her husband said.

"Yes, sorry, I was looking at the autumn landscape," she replied.

"It's even more radiant here," he added.

"Yes, indeed," she said as they turned into their long driveway.

The large maple trees in front of the house had begun to change color to become golden yellow. The leaves shimmered with the sunlight. It was warmer than usual, for the temperature was in the high fifties. As soon as the car stopped in front of their house, the children got out and ran to play with the fallen leaves in the front garden.

"Let's change our clothes, 'cause we're going on a boat ride after lunch," Richard said in a loud voice, though inside he felt sad. He tried his best to hide his feelings, and Alejandra held his hand as they approached their house together. Once inside, the children followed their mother into the kitchen. She began to prepare lunch, while Lena took the youngest child upstairs to change her diaper.

"What would you like to eat?" she asked.

"Grilled cheese," both children replied.

Alejandra took the bread out from the cupboard, opened the ice box and took out cheddar cheese and ham from one of the shelves. She looked through the kitchen window and noticed a family of deer in the distance, but as she was going to point them out to the children she felt intense emotion, and the words could not come out. She wiped her tears before her children could see her and turned on the stove with a match. She placed the bread on the skillet, then took out orange juice from the ice box and poured each one of them a glass of the fruity liquid.

"Go and get your father, we will eat soon," she said to her son Rich, as she and her daughter set the table in the dining room. After lunch she put together a picnic basket and filled it with water canteens, apples, and sandwiches, and then placed it on the kitchen table. She went upstairs and found Lena feeding Delia Rose. "Let me finish doing that," she said to her. "Please take these sweaters to the children."

She picked up her daughter and sat with her on the rocking chair for a few minutes as Delia Rose finished her milk bottle. Dely looked like Alejandra the most; the child had the same color eyes, and even the shape of her mouth and nose were like Alejandra's own features. She started to cry softly, for she thought this might be one of the last times she would hold her little girl.

Then she heard steps. "Ale, are you ready?" Richard asked as he walked into the room and picked up his daughter.

"Give me five minutes, I'll be right down," she said as she tried to compose herself.

Minutes later, when she came down, the three children and Richard were already on the boat.

"Put on your life jackets," Alejandra said as Richard handed her Delia Rose, and she sat next to the two older children on the back bench. Richard navigated the boat at a slow pace. The soft wind, nature's caress, felt rejuvenating on her face, even if a bit cold, she thought.

How many times had she seen those crystal blue waters? How many times had she seen the fall colors? And how many more times would she be there with her family? She smiled at the sight of her children as their hair moved wildly to the rhythm of the wind. The afternoon sunlight shone on their faces, cementing in her mind their innocence, their pure fascination, their unmitigated happiness. She looked at Richard, whose earth-toned eyes stared into hers with such love that she mouthed "I love you." His oval face with masculine features made him look dignified but sensitive, and his body was still muscular. He was as handsome as ever, and through the years, she had grown to love him ever so deeply—for he was such a kind man, and with a humorous side that often made her laugh.

"Rich, come take the captain's wheel," he said to his son as the little boy sat on his lap. The two girls stayed by her. Lidia Hannah's features were a combination of both Alejandra and Richard, and she was the sensitive one who noticed everything. Little Richard was very much like his father physically and in character, bold, outgoing, and courageous. Alejandra thought about all this while she heard young Richard say "Weepy," as the boat lifted upward when large waves passed beneath it.

"Are we fishing, daddy?" he asked.

"Yes, as soon as we find a good spot to anchor the boat," Richard replied.

When he did, he threw the anchor down, pulled out two fishing rods from the back of the boat, attached a small plastic jig at the end of one of them, and gave it to Rich. Fifteen minutes later, to his amazement, Rich yelled, "I've caught a fish, I've caught a fish!"

Liddy quickly took the fish net and gave it to her father, as he helped his son reel in his catch. Richard then released the fish from the hook and let it fall on the net.

"Is that a walleye?" Rich asked.

"Yes," his father replied.

"We'll have a nice dinner," Alejandra said to her son.

"Mami, I'm thirsty," Liddy said.

"Me too," Rich said.

Alejandra pulled water canteens out from the family's picnic basket, and a few minutes later, Richard pulled in the anchor and let the boat drift to the natural flow of the lake. There was such contentment and love in that familial moment that Alejandra knew this would sustain her for whatever came next, or whatever time she had left with her family.

When they returned to their small house on the lake, Lena had prepared them a sumptuous dinner with grilled fish, potatoes a la gratin, baked green beans, orange rolls, and apple crisp, the children's favorite dessert. Rich handed her his catch of the day.

"This one I'll grill right now!" Lena said to the happy boy.

"I want to eat it," he said. "Yes, sir," she replied.

After dinner, Alejandra gave their children warm baths, dressed them in pajamas, and tucked them into bed. She began reading them a story from her old notebook, but the children soon fell asleep. When she went downstairs, she found her husband placing several wood logs on the fireplace. He then crunched some newspaper and lit a match to start the fire. She sat on the comfortable, deep sofa, and watched him move about the room as he brought in more logs and placed them on the side of the stone hearth. The clock above the mantle chimed at eight o'clock, but even that sound made her feel sullen; for she wondered how much time she had left. Richard turned to her, and noticed her sad expression.

"Ale, I love you," he said, and then he sat beside her as they both quietly watched the warm glow and hypnotic flickering of the fire. They remained silent for many more minutes, until she took several of her musical journals from the wooden cocktail table. She browsed through them one by one, looking at all the entries, ideas, musical notes, and feelings she had written, reminders of various times in her life. She then took an ink pen and began to write on a blank page:

With a song in my heart I felt each day and each night,
The sun and the moon appeared in the skies.

With a song in my heart I felt the rain on my face,
The wind on my hair and the gentle touches of sweet
endless love.

With a song in my heart I lived through the tears of my youth
and the years of romantic preludes, and discovered the stories of
century-old paintings by masters from across many lands.

With a song in my heart, I heard my children's sweet laughs and
my husband's sweet whispers of love.

With a song in my heart, I renewed my spirit each day and each
night, and lived all the while with its melodic embrace.

In that spirit of love and acceptance, she leaned over her husband's arm as he said, "Ale, don't be afraid."

"I'm not," she replied. "And the surgery?"

"In a little over three weeks," he said.

"Rich, if I don't make it, promise you will keep my love alive for them and their family's roots. I want them to know their family history, and I want them to always look forward, no matter how difficult circumstances may be in their lives," she said in a soft voice.

"Sh . . . sh . . . don't say anymore," he said, as he brought her left hand to his lips and tenderly kissed it.

Not a cry, whisper, or a sound was heard when she woke up the next day. She read the note he left on his pillow: "Ale, I took the kids into town, we'll be back soon."

She felt such loneliness and pain in her heart, as if someone had punctured it, and it was slowly bleeding out. She slowly got dressed, went downstairs, and walked to the dock. She sat on a wooden bench under the dock's canopy for a few moments, feeling the sun's warm rays on her face as she listened to the gentle lapping of the waves. She thought of her father, who had left a legacy of optimism and kindness. She wished he was there with her, now more than ever; she missed him. Then she returned to the house, sat on the old piano bench, and started to play the piano. She had written a poem for a new song the previous evening. She poured all her tenderness, love, and emotions onto the black and white keys, as if it might be the last time she played them. Note by note, she composed a new waltz. It would be, perhaps, her last composition, she thought as she penciled in the title, "A Song in my Heart."

When her family returned, the children were thrilled to be holding pumpkins, which they placed at the front door. A pile of fresh mulch was on the side of the house, and Richard began to spread it around the small garden she had started in the summer. As Alejandra watched him and the children do these simple things, she took pleasure in the thought that everyday living was a blessing, and that they would manage without her somehow, for Richard was a wonderful father.

That night, once the children had gone to sleep, she gathered all the art and musical notebooks she'd written since she was a child—a total of twenty-two—along with the scores of her musical compositions, and placed them neatly, in chronological order, on the carved wooden chest by the piano. Her husband, who was in the kitchen, came out with two cups of aromatic cinnamon-spiced tea.

"Ale, join me," he said as he placed the cups on top of the table.

She was kneeling by the chest, next to the piano.

"Darling, everything I've written is here," she said as she closed the heavy lid on the antique chest. "Please share them with our children, so they'll know our family's story, and mine."

Richard took a couple of steps forward, reached out, and helped her get up, as he did when they were children.

"Ale, it won't be necessary, for you'll tell them our story as they grow up," he said.

On Saturday, October 18, just before sunrise, she lay awake in her bed, and placed her two hands on her chest. Then she spoke in almost a whisper. "Did the doctors say anything more?" she asked him.

"No, but I'm hopeful that after the surgery we'll know what's wrong, and they will recommend an appropriate treatment," Richard said as he caressed her on her shoulder. "But how would you like to go out tonight?"

"Tonight?" she asked. "I'd rather stay here with you and the children."

"Ale, I think you'll want to come," he insisted.

"Where?" she asked.

"To a benefit event, please," he said.

"How can I ever resist that look?" she said to him as she felt the emotion behind his pleading eyes.

It was almost five o'clock when she went upstairs to her bedroom. She wasn't much in the mood to get dressed. In fact, she was feeling quite weak and had more difficulty than ever breathing, but she forced herself to get ready to be with her husband to please him. She went to her closet and chose a dress that she knew was Richard's favorite. She placed it at her feet and slowly pulled it up, as he came from behind and buttoned the violet blue silken gown with silver brocade around the collar. Alejandra then walked to her jewelry box on her dresser, and pulled out the diamond and ruby pendant-necklace that he had given her on their honeymoon.

She looked in the full-length mirror and noticed the dress was a little loose, and her face was pale. She put on some rouge and ruby red lipstick. Her hair, pulled back to one side, outlined her exquisite face. "As do your eyes of beauty and wonder," her husband said pleasantly. She smiled while he took her white coat and helped her put it on. "Thank you," she said as she gently patted his face.

"Shall we?" he said as they walked down the steps.

When they arrived at the Lyceum Theater, most people were already seated, and several hundred people were there. The lights were dimmed and the master of ceremonies stepped on the stage. Mr. Thomas Lundstrom thanked all of the audience members and dignitaries from the university and announced that the proceeds from the concert would benefit their medical research department. Then he introduced the musicians.

"It is my pleasure to introduce Luis Orozco, professor and virtuoso pianist from the Conservatory of Music in Mexico City, and the Regatta Quartet from New York—Benjamin Adelman, Hannah Mendes, Rafael Cardozo, and Vincent Myers. I'd also like to introduce Eugene Hempel on clarinet and flute, Ezequiel Vazquez on guitar, Samuel Johnson on bass, and Miss Jeanne Marie Fuentes on vocals," he said.

Her heart began to beat faster and faster as tears ran down her face. All of her family, including her grandparents and aunt from Mexico, were seated in a row behind her. This has to be a dream, perhaps I'm already in heaven, she thought, but when Luis made the signal to start and the string quartet played the first notes of "Vals del Sol," she had a revelation that had taken years to discover. The orchestra then played all her music, "Nostalgia Mexicana," "There with You," "Castanets…" They were playing her life; with every note, there was a moment, with every phrase there was a day, with every song there was a season. She whispered to her husband, "You've fulfilled my most buried wish." He looked puzzled by her comment.

"I thought it was to be a conductor," he said.

"No! It was the one thing most of the composers whose biographies I've read had in common," she said.

"And what was that?" he asked.

"To have one's music performed by fellow musicians," she said as she opened the palm of her hand and waited for her husband to hold it. She felt overwhelmed by love for him. This man, who had not impressed her much when she was younger, gave her more than she could ever have imagined as a grown woman. There was nothing, absolutely nothing she would ever change or want more than him and her family by her side. Before the orchestra played "A Song in my Heart," she placed her arm around her husband and whispered in his ear, "How in the world did you manage all this?"

He smiled and then replied, "The things that men do for love!"

As she listened to the last composition, she hoped that the public enjoyed the music she had written. When the program ended, the generous audience stood up and enthusiastically applauded. The musicians came together and held each other's hands, and then bowed their heads.

The most gratifying aspect of the night involved the people in her life. Each one had contributed in some way to her learning, her understanding of things, and her inspiration. And the love they had given her filled her heart with profound gratitude. At that point, the Morrisons youngest child was brought to them, as the couple held hands with their two older children. Together, they left the concert.

Waiting at her parents' house later that evening were all Alejandra's musician friends and family. She profusely thanked them for doing what they did, and for being there. Among those friends, to her utmost delight, were Steven, Olga, and Franz.

"Ale, congratulations," said Franz, as a beautiful blond and pleasant woman joined him.

"This is my wife, Emily," Franz said.

"Lovely to meet you. I'm so glad and very thankful you are all here," she said to Franz and his wife.

Then a seventeen-year-old boy gave Alejandra a bouquet of white daisies. "Miss Ale, these are for you," he said with a shy smile. "Do you remember me?"

She hugged the young boy. "Of course I remember you, John Whitman. How wonderful to see you all grown up, and thank you for the flowers," she said as she took one, and cutting off the stem, placed the daisy behind her left ear.

"You'll be happy to know I have a full-time job playing piano at a local pub," he said.

"That's marvelous," she said. "What kind of music?"

"Jazz standards," he replied.

It was probably one of the best surprises of the evening to see the former student she'd met at the settlement house in St. Paul more than ten years before.

"Well, then, if you'd like, you must play for us," she said.

"It would be my pleasure," he replied.

And for the rest of the evening, she had the joy of being with her family and friends, for perhaps the last time.

The Morrisons and their families attended mass at St. Mary's Cathedral in Minneapolis the next day. She remembered her father Edward once again, for it was here, only five years before, that services were held in his honor. As she thought about him, she felt his spirit was there with her. Somehow she found comfort in the belief that if she was to leave this world, her father would be there waiting for her.

At around six in the morning of the next day when she opened her eyes, Richard was already awake, looking as though he had never gone to sleep.

"My dear, how do you feel?" he asked her.

"I had the strangest dream," she said in a quiet voice as she put on her robe and sat with him at the edge of their bed.

"What was it about?" he asked.

"It seemed so real. I dreamed that my father was alive for a brief moment as he came to talk to me, in this very room. He told me I mustn't fear death, for he was in a place filled with love, and asked me if I wanted to go with him." She paused for a few seconds. "I wasn't afraid of what he said. I told him I had too many things to do in my life," Alejandra said meditatively.

Her words gave him hope, for maybe, just maybe, it really wasn't her time to go, and she might see her twenty-ninth birthday. She left for the children's room. Even though they were still sleeping, she kissed them goodbye. She walked down the stairs and Richard followed her onto the back porch.

"I want one last look at the autumn landscape," she said as she stared at the almost-naked trees. She walked toward the garden and purposefully stepped on the dead leaves as she heard their crunching sound, one she avoided when younger; but now she hoped she would hear it again next year.

"It's cold out here," he said.

"Yes, it's invigorating. Reminds me what it feels to be alive," she said serenely. "I'm filled with love and faith, and regardless of what happens, we've been very blessed."

"Ale, don't say that," he said.

"I must, 'cause you must know I've accepted, peacefully, whatever is before me, and so should you," she said.

An hour later, she and Richard left for the hospital. Late in the morning, before she was taken to the operation room, he held Alejandra's hand while she lay on the gurney and said, "Don't you dare leave me!"

TRACK THIRTEEN

AMALFI

The surgeons found an abnormal growth in her lungs which was blocking them, and which also explained her difficulty with breathing and weight loss. After a long operation the surgeons were able to remove the growth successfully. For Richard, the time he spent waiting for the pathology reports to return after the surgery became the two longest weeks of his life. Late on Friday afternoon of the second week he received the anxiously awaited report. Expecting the worst but hoping for the best, he opened the folder, and carefully read the medical results. He placed his wife's file on his briefcase, and quickly left the physician's office. Amid a gushing wind, he got into his car and drove home as fast as he could. The lights in his house were lit, and from the street he could see his wife, sitting at the piano.

Richard parked his car and rushed into the house. When he entered, he threw his raincoat on the leather sofa, and was quite surprised to hear Alejandra singing, which she rarely did. He practically ran to the drawing room and sat beside her. As she turned to him and looked into his eyes, her face was luminous. He touched her fingers to his lips and kissed them.

"Ale, I like hearing you sing," he said.

She had always been reserved about singing; but after being on the verge of dying, she found singing was the best medicine for her agonizing thoughts.

"Oh! If not now, when!" she said to him with a slight laugh.

He caressed her face. "A new song?" he asked.

"Yes and no. The music you probably recognized—I wrote it while we were in Amalfi—but the words were written this week, inspired by your love, my feelings, and the memories of being there," she said.

Richard looked at the page in front of her and read the words she had translated from Spanish to English, as the song was written in the former language.

> Amalfi, place in my heart, where you and I lived our love.
> The days and nights by the sea. How can I forget your kisses as I woke up . . .

After he finished reading all the lyrics, he said with a broad smile, "Well, if what you want is to live!"

"Yes!" she said, as she took a deep breath.

"And if you want to return to Amalfi, then we shall. The results came in today and you are now in perfect health!"

Alejandra placed her two hands together. Her eyes became watery, and she was filled with happiness at such magnificent news. She embraced him intensely.

"Thanks be to God! Your words are music to my ears," she said.

"Now, please sing it for me 'til the end," Richard requested.

"Amalfi lugar de mi corazón donde tu yo vivimos nuestro amor. Los pájaros cantaban bajo el sol, como olvidar tus besos al despertar. Quiero vivir, quiero vivir, siempre a tu lado, quiero cantar y descrubrir nuevas melodias . . . " Alejandra sang.

TRACK FOURTEEN

THE END

Notes from the Author

The first goal for this historical novel was to write an original fiction story around true events that occurred during the early twentieth century. Inspired by the history of music in my native hometown of Mexico City, my adopted homeland of Minnesota, and the role of a conductor, I began my research for this work several years ago. Since then, dozens of pioneers who were influential in the development of the arts in both countries came to the forefront. While it was not possible to include everyone, as this was first and foremost a novel, I referenced several public figures and institutions. For a list of sources and publications that were useful in writing this book, please see the selected bibliography. The references listed are by no means a complete record of all the works that were consulted, yet they provide the most relevant sources of information pertinent to the story.

A second objective was to compose a musical score to be included with the book. The audio CD *A Song in My Heart* brings to light pivotal moments in the main character's life. Alejandra Stanford's creative voice is expressed through the compositions. The music was specifically written for the novel, although some tracks are also found on my first album *Carnival of Life*. All the new music and new mixes for the musical score were recorded in 2010 and 2011. A list of all the music and lyrics included on the CD are in Appendix A, and a list of the musicians performing on the CD are listed in Appendix B.

The third goal was to set music to the entire novel, as the music itself was intrinsic to Alejandra's emotional and intellectual journey. Each chapter is titled with a musical composition chosen specifically for this purpose. If the reader would like to explore all the musical compositions and composers cited throughout the novel, a comprehensive list is on Appendix C. Most of the music can easily be found in other recordings or in the Internet.

A Song in My Heart is the first installment of a trilogy. God willing, my next book, Striking the Right Note, will begin in the year 1933 in the city of Berlin, Germany.

APPENDIX A

A *Song in My Heart* Audio CD

Music and Lyrics by Roma Calatayud-Stocks

1. Vals del Sol
2. Nostalgia Mexicana
3. There with You*
4. Castanets
5. Sunset in Venice*
6. We Have Been Waiting*
7. Enchanting Lover*
8. Amalfi
9. God Lives*
10. Magical Night*
11. Remembrance
12. Carnival of Life*
13. A Song in My Heart*
14. Amalfi*

**With Lyrics*

"There with You"

When I think of happy days
In the spring or summer days
Walking in the park, walking
Until sunset comes, la, la
When I see your handsome face
And you hold me in your arms
Dancing in the night, dancing
Near the water's edge, la, la

Chorus:

Since you came along
There's a mystery
Unexpectedly, I'm thinking of you
I see in your eyes, certain wondering
Suddenly I see, you want me there with you

"Sunset in Venice"

In ancient Venice sunsets glow
Above Salute and St. Marc
A city so mysterious, a city so romantic
A thousand years have passed and still
Captures the heart of poets and of you

What a pleasure walking by the Piazza,
The serenade of pigeons, and gondolas through bridges
In ancient Venice spirits live
Among the churches and canals

What a pleasure to see the lovers whisper,
Gothic and Moorish temples inspired by the Gods,
The Gods of sensual pleasures,
The art and sacred frescoes, my legendary love

What pleasure the Renaissance in Venice,
The journey through the ages,
The souls that have seen the glory of Venice

"We Have Been Waiting"

We have been waiting, we have been waiting, waiting, long
For us to go together, go together, to our favorite place
We have been waiting, we have been waiting, waiting, love
For us to be together, be together, under moonlit skies

And once we're there, only you and I, only you and I, belong
No one else matters, just us two
And from the deep ocean to the skies,
I'm yours forever darling, love
And you will always be my only love
Always be my only love

"Enchanting Lover"

Enchanting lover, you cast your spells from afar
And in a moment, I feel you there with me
Enchanting lover, why do you torment me?
I possess desires that chain me to you
You have me prisoner, you haunt my existence
Soy prisionera de tus encantos soy

Enchanting lover, what are these secrets you hide
Behind the masquerade
Who are you really?
Why do I only see you when you invoke my name?
You have me prisoner, you haunt my existence
Soy prisionera de tus encantos soy

Enchanting lover, you cast...
Give me the freedom to make my choices of you
No need to fear the truth
You have me prisoner, you haunt my existence
Soy prisionera de tus encantos, soy
(I'm prisoner of you charms)

"God Lives"

God of souls, sublime
Light guides since before times
Feathers waiting to fall
And in our lifetime
Souls live as flesh and blood

Feast of life, sublime
Music brings harmony
Drums, strings, bind souls through time
There's also sadness,
Despair and misery
When we fade in the dark,
Light, love, rises to heal

It is amazing God lives in every soul

"Magical Night"

Look around it's a magical night
Luring you to unknown places
You've never seen

Feel the air is contagiously light
Lifting you until dawn
Letting your passions free

And see the sparkles again
And hear the flute of the wind
Join the laughter you seek
It's a magical night

Let yourself be inspired tonight
By the velvet blue skies
And the stars of romance

"Carnival of Life"

There's a theater in the streets
Everyone is the cast, what role do you play?
Some are leaders of the show,
Others follow just for show,
And some have no choice

Some play righteous, and are sinners
Some are paupers, some play kings
Carnival of life, we play endlessly
En la vida, carnival of lies, es un carnaval de máscaras
En el carnaval de la vida

In the corner of the street
Someone's yelling dressed in rags
Listen to his plea
I don't want to play this role
Doesn't seem to fit at all
When I feel rich inside

There's a theater in the streets
Everyone wears a mask, what mask do you wear?
Some are happy, others sad
Some believe in their disguise, other just pretend
We play endlessly. . . .

"Amalfi"

Amalfi lugar de mi corazón
Donde tu y yo vivimos nuestro amor
Los pájaros cantaban bajo el sol
Como olvidar, tus besos, al despertar
La lluvia arrullaba al dormir,
Como olvidar caricias, sobre mi piel

Caminando voy, contigo amor, amor
Por la hermosa vida
Y soy muy féliz
Con tu amor por mi, la, la

Quiero vivir, quiero vivir
Siempre a tu lado
Quiero cantar, y descubrir
Nuevas melodias
Y regresar, una vez mas
Aquel ensueño

Los días y las noches junto al mar
Yo quiero sentir, de nuevo, esa emoción
Con mi amor, Amalfi, con mi amor

Amalfi place in my heart
Where you and I lived our love
The birds were singing under the sun
How to forget, your kisses, waking up
The rain's lullaby, while sleeping
How to forget, caresses on my skin

Walking together we go, love, love
Through a beautiful life
And I'm very happy
With your love for me, la, la

I want to live, I want to live
Always by your side
I want to sing and discover
New melodies
And to return, once more
To that daydream

The days and nights by the sea
I want to feel, again, that emotion
With my love, Amalfi, with my love

"A Song In My Heart"

With a song in my heart I felt each day and each night,
The sun and the moon appeared in the skies.
With a song in my heart I felt the rain on my face,
The wind on my hair and the gentle touches of sweet endless love.

With a song in my heart I lived through the tears of my youth
And the years of romantic preludes, and discovered the stories of
Century-old paintings by masters from across many lands.

With a song in my heart, I heard my children's sweet laughs
And my husband's sweet whispers of love.

With a song in my heart, I renewed my spirit each day and each night,
And lived all the while with its melodic embrace

APPENDIX B

A *Song in My Heart* Audio CD

Music and Lyrics by Roma Calatayud-Stocks

Arranged by Chan Poling

PERFORMANCES BY:

Roma Calatayud-Stocks: vocals; "Enchanting Lover," "Carnival of Life, " "Amalfi" String Arrangements; "Nostalgia Mexicana," "Amalfi"

Estaire Godinez: vocals; "God Lives," "Carnival of Life"

Molly Shields: vocals; "There with You," "We Have Been Waiting," "Magical Night," "Carnival of Life"

Chan Poling: piano; "Nostalgia Mexicana," "There With You," "Castanets," "Sunset in Venice," "We Have Been Waiting," "Enchanting Lover," "Amalfi," "God Lives," "Magical Night," "Remembrance," "A Song in My Heart" Guitar and String arrangements; "Castanets," "Amalfi," "Remembrance," "Carnival of Life," "A Song In My Heart"

Dean Magraw: acoustic guitar; "Magical Night," "Carnival of Life"

Gordy Johnson: bass guitar; "Enchanting Lover," "God Lives," "Magical Night," "Carnival of Life"

Dave Hanzel: percussion and drums; "Enchanting Lover, " "God Lives"

Russ Peterson: fluegel horn, flute; "God Lives," "Magical Night," "Carnival of Life"

Jim Price: violin; "Sunset in Venice," "We Have Been Waiting," "Enchanting Lover," "Amalfi," "God Lives

Mark Stillman: accordion; "Enchanting Lover"

Pancho Torres: piano; "Carnival of Life"

Nachito Herrera: piano; "Vals del Sol"

Aurora String Quartet: "Vals del Sol"
Julia Bartsch: violin
Theresa Elliott: violin
Diane Tremaine: cello
Annalee Wolf: viola

Matthew Zimmerman: drums; "Amalfi"
Production engineer; recorded and mixed at Wild Sound Recording Studio, Minneapolis, MN

Tom Herbers: production engineer; Creation, Minneapolis, MN

Jim Reynolds: production engineer; Minneapolis, MN

APPENDIX C

The following is a list of musical selections cited throughout the novel. **Highlighted compositions** *denote chapter titles in order of appearance.*

"**Ode to Minnesota**," Unknown

"America," Rev. Samuel F. Smith

"Symphony in B Minor," Franz Schubert

"Symphonic Poem," "*Les Preludes*," Franz Liszt

"La Traviata," Giuseppe Verdi

"Ecossaise in E Flat Major," Ludwig van Beethoven

"Alejandra," Enrique Mora

"Carmen," Juventino Rosas

"Festival Prelude," Richard Strauss

"Hymn to Liberty," Hugo Kaun

"Dance of Nymphs and Satyrs" (Cupid and Psyche OP. 3), Georg Schumann

"Silent Night," Franz Gruber, Josef Mohr

"New World Symphony," Antonin Dvorak

"Tannhauser," Richard Wagner

"Over the Waves," Sobre Las Olas, Juventino Rosas

"Don Juan's Serenade," Pyotr Il'yich Tchaikovsky

"In the Hall of the Mountain King," Peer Gynt, Edvard Grieg

"America the Beautiful," Samuel A. Ward, Katharine Lee Bates

"Kiss Me Again," V. Herbert

"Strellita," Manuel M. Ponce

"Lullaby," Johaness Brahms

"Maple Leaf Rag," Scott Joplin

"Pack Up Your Troubles in Your Old Kit Bag," George and Felix Powell

"The Blue Danube," Richard Strauss

"I'm Always Chasing Rainbows," Harry Carroll

"Liberty Bell," Halsey Mohr and Joe Goodwin

"Prelude in E Minor," Frédéric Chopin

"Georgie Rainbow," Leo Gordon

"St. Louis Blues," W. C. Handy

"Reverie," Claude Debussy

"Piano Concerto No. 1," Felix Mendelssohn

"One-Step," Dixieland Jazz Band

"Adagio in G Minor," Tomaso Albinoni

"Hear, Now, The Waves Murmur," Claudio Monteverdi

"Second Waltz," Dmitri Shostakovich

"Concerto Number 8 in A Minor," Antonio Vivaldi

"Sonata in C Major," Wolfgang Amadeus Mozart

"Symphony No. 7 in A Major, 2nd Movement," Ludwig van Beethoven

"Lieberstraum," Franz Liszt

"Hungarian Rhapsody No. 2," Franz Liszt

"La Regatta Veneziana," Gioachino Rossini.

"Amor Brujo," "Bewitching Love," Manuel de Falla

"Hungarian Dance No. 5 in G Minor," Johannes Brahms

"Symphony No. 5 in C Minor, Op. 67," Ludwig van Beethoven

"Quartet in E Minor," Julian Carrillo.

"Tres Preludios," Manuel M. Ponce

"Tiempo de Schottisch," Manuel M. Ponce

"Melody of Gavota," Manuel M. Ponce

"So Light is Love," John Wilbye

"Badinerie from Suite No. 2," John Sebastian Bach

"Andante," Wolfgang Amadeus Mozart

"Moonlight Sonata," Ludwig van Beethoven

"Eroica," Ludwig van Beethoven

"Spanish Caprice," Rimsky Korsakov

"1812 Overture," Pyotr Ilych Tchaikovsky

"Clair de Lune," Claude Debussy

"Rhapsody in Blue," George Gershwin

"Lively Stable Blues," Ray Lopez and Alcide Nunez

"So This is Venice," Harry Warren and Clarke Leslie

"String Quartet in E flat Major," Fanny Mendelssohn

"String Quartet No. 3," Maddalena Lombardini Sirmen

"El Sombrero de Tres Picos," "The Three-Cornered Hat," Manuel de Falla

"Malagueña," Ernesto Lecuona

"Sevilla" (Seville), Isaac Albéniz

"K'shoshana Ben Hachochim," Unknown

"Nocturne Op. 9 No. 2," Frédéric Chopin

"Serenade for Piano & String Quartet Op. 3, No. 5," Joseph Haydn

"Intermezzo," Manuel M. Ponce

"Sonata for Piano and Violin in F Major," Wolfgang Amadeus Mozart

"West End Blues," Joe Oliver

"Imposible," Agustín Lara

Selected Bibliography

Brenner, Helmut. *Juventino Rosas: His Life, His Work, His Time*. Michigan: Harmonie Park Press, 2000.

Bulletin of the Minneapolis Institute of Arts. Minneapolis: Historical Archives of the Minneapolis Institute of Arts Public Library, Minneapolis, 1915–1927.

Conservatorio Nacional de Música en México: Archivos, 1877–1922.

Cuarteto Latinoamericano. *Valses Mexicanos 1900*. Dorian Recordings, 2000, compact disc.

Forney, Kristine, Joseph Machlis. *The Enjoyment of Music*. New York: W.W. Norton, 2007.

Hoyt, Sandra L. ed. *Treasures from the Minneapolis Institute of Arts*. Minneapolis: Minneapolis Institute of Arts, 1998.

Hyslop, Sandra. *Minnesota Orchestra at One Hundred*. Minneapolis: Minnesota Orchestral Association, 2002.

King, Ross. *Michelangelo and the Pope's Ceiling*. New York: Penguin, 2003.

Larson, Paul. *Icy Pleasures*. St. Paul: Afton Historical Society Press, 1998.

Piper, David. *The Illustrated History of Art: Art through the Ages*. London: Chancelor Press, 2000.

Rivera, Diego, Gladys March. *My Art, My Life: Autobiography*. New York: Dover Publications, 1963.

Schmidt-Görg, Joseph, Hans Schmidt. *Beethoven Bicentennial Edition*. Hamburg: Beethoven-Archi, 1970.

Schoen-René, Anna Eugénie. *America's Musical Inheritance: Memories and Reminiscences*. New York: G.P. Putnam's Sons, 1941.

Schonberg, Harold C. *The Lives of the Great Composers*. New York: W. W. Norton, 1981.

Sherman, John K. *Music and Maestros: The Story of the Minneapolis Symphony Orchestra*. Minneapolis: University of Minnesota Press, 1952.

Smith, Bradley. *Mexico: A History in Art*. London: Phaidon Press, 1975.

Stokstad, Marilyn. *Art History*. Upper Saddle River: Pearson Education, 2009.

Streissguth, Tom. *The Roaring Twenties*. New York: Eyewitness History Series, 2001.

Tanner, Paul, David W. Megill, Maurice Gerow. *Jazz*. New York: McGraw-Hill, 2009.

Minneapolis Symphony Orchestra: Program Notes. St. Paul: Minnesota Historical Society, 1902–1924.

Weiss, Piero, Richard Taruskin. *Music in the Western World*. California: Clark Baxter, 2008.